Caste and Class in India

Caste and Class in India

Edited by

K.L. Sharma

Published on behalf of

Training for Development Scholarship Society, Pune

RAWAT PUBLICATIONS

Jaipur • New Delhi • Bangalore • Guwahati • Kolkata

ISBN 978-81-7033-205-3 (HB)
ISBN 978-81-7033-481-0 (PB)

Reprinted, 2023

Published by
Prem Rawat for **Rawat Publications**
Satyam Apts., Sector 3, Jawahar Nagar, Jaipur - 302 004 (India)
Phone: 0141 265 1748 / 7006 Fax: 0141 265 1748
E-mail : info@rawatbooks.com
Website: rawatbooks.com

New Delhi Office
4858/24, Ansari Road, Daryaganj, New Delhi 110 002
Phone: 011-23263290

Also at *Bangalore, Guwahati* and *Kolkata*

Typeset by Rawat Computers, Jaipur
Printed at Chaman Enterprises, New Delhi

Contents

Preface

The Training for Development Scholarship Society (TDSS), a voluntary organisation, conducted a national seminar on State—Specific Caste Class in India in December 1987. A large number of senior scholars participated in the intensively deliberated discussions in the seminar. More than thirty papers were presented. But we are able to include only twenty papers as other contributors either could not revise their papers due to some important commitments or published them elsewhere. The papers which we have included in the volume speak of the scope and magnitude of the seminar. The organisers of the seminar deserve our sincere gratitude for providing us this opportunity to deliberate upon the persisting problems related to the caste-class nexus. For allowing the publication of the volume, the TDSS deserves our genuine admiration as it would help not only the academia but also all those who are interested in the understanding of the vexed problem of caste and class interactions. Our thanks are to Messers Rawat Publications for seeking permission from the TDSS for publication of the volume. I am particularly grateful to TDSS for providing me the opportunity to edit the volume. I have taken a little more than the usual time in giving a shape to the volume due to various reasons beyond my control. My sincere thanks are due to the colleagues who consented inclusion of their articles in the volume. I also thank them for permitting me to carry out editorial changes in their papers. Finally, I am grateful to my colleague Dr. H.N. Singh of Jawaharlal Nehru University for providing me constructive help in editing the volume.

K.L. Sharma

List of Contributors

SEKHAR BANDYOPADHYAY, Centre for South and South-East Asian Studies, Calcutta University, Calcutta.

RANABIR SAMADDAR, 49, D.N. Chatterjee Road, Calcutta.

SRIJNAN HALDER, Department of Political Science, Uluberia College, Howrah.

SHAIBAL GUPTA, A.N. Sinha Institute of Social Studies, Patna.

BHAIRABI PRASAD SAHU, Reader, Department of History, University of Delhi, Delhi.

ANJAN GHOSH, Centre for Studies in Social Sciences, Calcutta.

GAIL OMVEDT, Kazegaon, District Sangli (Maharashtra).

IMTIAZ AHMAD, Jawaharlal Nehru University, New Delhi.

K.L. SHARMA, Centre for Study of Social Systems, Jawaharlal Nehru University, New Delhi.

GHANSHYAM SHAH, Centre for Social Studies, Surat.

SHARAD PATIL, Vadi-Bhokar Road, Dhule (Maharashtra).

RAJENDRA VORA, Department of Political Science & Public Administration, University of Poona, Pune.

SURENDRA JONDHALE, Department of Political Science, Shivaji University, Kolhapur.

S.P. PUNALEKAR, Centre for Social Studies, Surat.

GOPAL GURU, Department of Political Science, Shivaji University, Kolhapur.

A. NAGARAJA NAIDU, Government Degree College, Prodelature (A.P.).

A. SATYANARAYANA, Osmania University, Hyderabad.

RAJAN GURUKKAL, U.C. College, Alwaiya.

A.B. BARDHAN, Ajay Bhawan, Kotla Marg, New Delhi.

JAVEED ALAM, Department of Political Science, Himachal Pradesh University, Shimla.

Introduction: Some Reflections on Caste and Class in India

K.L. Sharma

Caste and class are viewed as the two most significant dimensions of social stratification. They are considered as closely interrelated, almost inseparable, basic processes of social life. It is one thing that caste is viewed as a sole model for analysing Indian society or class is used for analysing caste and power, but it is quite different in real life as caste and class are not only highly differentiated internally, complexities of their expression and articulation signify the vast ramifications of structured social inequality. Debate on caste and class has covered wide-ranging issues related to indicators of status, levels of equality and inequality, cultural and structural interaction, occupational mobility, etc. Conceptual schemes to analyse these issues highlight structural versus cultural, closed versus open, organic versus segmentary, interactional versus attributional and corporate versus individual dimensions regarding the nature of caste and class in India as systems of social stratification. A discussion on the main points of this debate may be warranted before a gist of the essays included in the volume is provided.

The notion of caste referring to it as a rigid, unchanging, archaic and oriental system though found functionally as inevitable and useful or as antithetical to the system based on class relations are deeply contradictory in terms. A rigid and unchanging system can only be dysfunctional. Caste has been considered dysfunctional uptil now, but it has also been looked upon as a dynamic institution. A dysfunctional system is not necessarily a static system. The caste-class divide was never as rigid as reported in various writings, and hence Indian society was also not as rigidly structured as depicted in several accounts of the caste system.

The 'ideal' and the 'actual' status was never the same. Inter-caste marriages produced 'mixed castes'. The study of Buddhist sources hints at 'status incongruities' in ancient India. The multi-dimensional nature of social reality comes out from Kosambi's emphasis on the study of 'production' rather than 'kinship' for understanding social formation in ancient India. Now the following questions emerge:

1. Is the notion of *homo hierarchicus* synonymous with India's caste system?
2. Have there been no elements of *homo equalis* in India's system of social stratification?

Contradictions within the caste system and influence of external forces of change on it rule out the possibility of it being *homo hierarchicus.* A long history of discontinuities, break downs, contradictions and changes in the caste system also negate its absolutist, unchanging and holistic nature. Both inequality and equality have been built into the ideology and practice of the caste system, and change has taken place in both as well as in the nexus between the two. Certain ideational and structural aspects of the caste system have persisted despite several setbacks suffered by the system because of the inbuilt balancing mechanisms in the system itself. Despite the priestly superiority of Brahmins over all other castes, the functionary lower castes enjoyed some 'ritual status', certainly not comparable in any way with that of Brahmins. The status and the protection accorded to them by the caste panchayats enabled them to protest against the injustices meted out by the upper caste patrons. Hence, a critical re-examination of caste as a system of ideas and rituals, and class as a system of relations between the rich and the poor may be desirable. The essays incorporated in this volume are largely addressed to this issue. Caste has acquired a new form, and it has also changed to a great extent as a system of social relations. What was considered as immutable and rigid has become quite a flexible part of the system, and what was thought to be an inevitable part of the system has withered away. The structural and ideological changes which were intended to bring about annihilation of the caste system have promoted it in many ways contrary to expectations, both explicit and implicit. Several unintended changes, both positive and negative, have occurred in the caste system having implications for changes in the class structure and power relations. The emergence of a new middle class disproportionate to the forces of production and the size of the upper and the lower classes has forged a new nexus between caste, class and power. The embourgeoisiement of the families of the principal agricul-

tural castes has given a new direction to the connection between caste, class and politics. The 'divide' between the upper and the 'backward castes' also adds a new dimension to the caste-class nexus.

Was caste ever a closed system? Can connubiality and commensality be considered as the only cardinal principles of inter-caste relations? Does caste as a 'superorganic' system encompass the economic and political relations? Most studies until the early 1960s responded to these questions in the affirmative, stressing upon the deterministic supremacy of the caste system and equating it with Indian social formation. The relgico-ritualistic order of the caste system was understood as a mechanism encompassing other 'orders', namely,economic and political. However, the caste system has never been uniformly rigid/flexible in different parts of India, and therefore, it has affected differently the other 'orders' of social life. There is a long history of anti-upper caste movements in India, a testimony not only of the structural and ideational changes, but also of the accretions, alterations and withdrawals in the caste system. Besides caste, the quality of agricultural land, infrastructure for cultivation, trade and commerce, invasions and migrations and power determined social status and mobility. Moreover, caste-rank is/was a *relative* phenomenon. For example, a *Kumhar* (potter) was a 'kamin' to a Brahmin/Kshatriya patron, but he was much less a 'kamin' to the intermediate castes, and not at all to the lower and 'untouchable' castes to whom he also rendered his specialised services of supplying earthen pots. Besides, being a functionary or a 'kamin', a *Kumhar* also belongs to a middle caste among the intermediate castes.

What can one say in defence of the caste system? Caste is not simply a system of inequality, a system consisting pre-eminently of 'ideas and values' determining the inequality. The notions of pure and impure are not just 'opposites', but as relative phenomena on a continuum they have signified the caste system more than other criteria in the past though their significance has rapidly declined paving way for a further increase of structural bases of status and power. 'Organic linkages' between different castes were characterised by division of labour and remunerative dividends with provisions for grievance redressals. The role played by values and norms cannot be underestimated in the organismic structure of relations, but the aim was not to simply uphold the value system at the cost of the interests of the people involved in the system. Besides this, the notion of pure and impure in real life has ramifications vis-a-vis caste hierarchy, and it has changed fast making 'pure' 'less pure', and 'less pure' or 'impure' a 'secular' phenomenon. Thus, caste has lost the traditional bases of its defence to a considerable extent. Then, what is caste? Or what is that remains of the caste system?

A shift from the emphasis on 'cultural' criteria has made the distinctions based on economic and political power the focal theme in the study of the caste system. Surfacing of incongruities between caste and other domains shows diminution of caste as an all encompassing system and the emergence of a new nexus with economy, polity, migration and religion as interlocking sub-systems. Since agrarian relations, economic transactions and service relations have changed, the caste system too has changed a lot setting in motion the process of 'role-reversal'. A couple of studies have highlighted the role of migration, education, occupation, power, style of life, ownership, control and use of land, inter-caste feuds, competition and bargaining for higher wages as the changing criteria of status-determination and the caste-class nexus. Agrarian reforms and the green revolution have affected caste, class and land relations by creating divides comprising various kinds of gainers and losers which also has implications for the emergence of a new power structure. The question is: How can 'caste' remain the same despite pauperisation, proletarianisation and downward social mobility among the upper castes, and embourgeoisiement and upward mobility among the middle and lower castes? Thus, neither 'caste' nor 'class' can serve as a model for analysing the emerging social reality, because caste is not the precise equivalent of class and class is not synonymous with caste. Castes are 'discrete', segmentary and flexible. Class relations can be analysed by juxtaposing them with caste, kinship, marriage and family. Thus, the 'shift' has not only weakened the commensal relations between different castes, caste as a system has transformed itself taking a new face and social space in Indian society.

Studies of the nexus between caste and class have highlighted the multifaceted nature of social stratification. The structural-historical perspective in particular is found relevant for analysing the historicity of the nexus. What is more important here is the fact that the studies of caste and class have moved away considerably from the hierarchical model of consensus, resilience and summation of roles and statuses. Processes of structural change simultaneously affecting various segments and families, both positively and adversely, have occurred particularly since independence. These studies have emphasised the emergence of 'caste free areas', downward social mobility and incompatibility of the pollution-purity principle with the entrenchment of the middle and lower castes in politics and modern jobs. The following questions have emerged time and again in regard to the studies of caste and class:

1. Whether changes in caste and class are 'transformational' or 'structural'?
2. Whether caste is 'closed' and class is 'open'?
3. Whether caste is 'organic' and class is 'segmentary'?
4. Whether caste is being replaced by class and political power or not?

Studies on caste and class cannot remain restricted to the analysis and interpretation of Sanskrit sources and archival materials. The problems created for the society by the systems of caste and class have to be dealt with both conceptually and substantively. The problems of exploitation, domination, poverty, alienation, distributive injustice, etc., could be understood by having a serious rethinking on the concepts of caste and class. The increased quest for equality among the weaker sections as well as the highly aspiring middle castes and classes too overrides the traditional bases of status and power.

Thus, let us state that caste and class are not polar opposites; caste and class are found in both rural and urban areas; caste is not simply confined to ritual ranking and class is not just a grouping of people based on common economic and occupational interests; both caste and class are corporate as well as individualistic entities; and the two have fixity as well as flexibility. Caste is not being replaced by class, and caste is still changing rapidly finding a place for itself in non-conventional and secular domains of social, political and economic life.

Caste is not today what it was before 1947; and it has also not become class or a replica of it. Based on the study of a village in Tamil Nadu, Harris observes that caste gives coherence and meaning to and structures actual social relations. Caste is both an actual structure of social relationships and an ideology. Caste structure does not rest upon unequal access to the means of production and the appropriation of surplus alone by a dominant caste. A dominant caste (or dominant families) must be a part of the dominant class. The two may be congruent phenomena, but not always necessarily. There are complimentary *unequal exchanges* between members of different castes, hence hierarchy and the exploitation of labour, the poor and the lower caste men.

The caste-class nexus has undergone a considerable change and yet there exists a close tie between caste and class. In Kerala, 'leader-landlord nexus' is reported as a new phenomenon, and a good number of the leaders (also landlords) belong to the Communist Party of India (Marxist) and hail from a high social stratum. Rural Assam too shows a highly stratified system with social and economic correspondences at different levels of society. No other state is apparently as divided as Bihar on the basis of caste. Since the 1970s, Bihar is viewed in terms of *forwards* or *twice-born, upper backwards, lower backwards* and *minorities, scheduled castes* and *scheduled tribes*. The question is: What is the basis of social stratification? What determines the nexus between different dimensions of social stratification? Certainly, in one way, caste has received a definite blow to its continuity in the traditional ideological form, but at the same time it has gained a new life in some non-traditional sectors of Indian polity and economy. It is this new form that goes against the very secular character of Indian society as envisaged in India's constitution and in subsequent policy pronouncements. However, some scholars believe that such an entrenchment of caste into polity and economy not only synthesises the old and the new, but also performs some very basic secular functions or at least adapts itself to the new forces of social change.

A couple of studies of peasant movements and peasant organisations in different parts of India have shown that wherever the lower castes have been numerically strong and also extremely poor, radical mobilisation has been far greater than in other areas where such a situation did not exist. At the same time, caste and other conservative forces have limited the scope of mobilisation in some parts. Mobilisation across caste lines is not quite clear even among the Communist-led movements. Even religious divides have been exploited by different sections of society for extricating the maximum possible economic and political advantages. The complexity of the caste system is seen in its functioning both as an ideology and as a praxis. Caste affects the people by constraining them to accept lower positions and conditions of work embedded with oppression and exploitation. On the other hand, caste also provided a ground in the past for various movements to emancipate the oppressed. Caste has created conditions of differential access to and control over resources. However, the role of caste has varied from region to region and from time to time. The lack of overlap between caste and class was reported earlier in various studies because the ideological moorings of the western scholars upheld superiority of class as a western phenomenon and denigrated caste though discretely as an archaic unchanging system. Caste and class have always been interrelated dimensions of the same social reality. The following observations may be noted:

1. A 'rich peasant class' has emerged. But this class has emerged mainly out of the ex-*rayots* who generally belonged to the upper stratum of the intermediate agricultural castes, and to the formerly landowning upper castes who have now taken up agriculture as self-cultivators. The green revolution has mainly benefited these sections of rural India.
2. A section of the upper castes has taken up white-collar employment as the basis of its livelihood. This has accorded it a high status, and has resulted in migration and mobility among them.
3. There has been an increase in the country-town nexus. Partly migration and mobility and partly the governmental strategies of development have led to this increased nexus between the two.
4. Politicization of caste identity, despite its weakening in social and ritual spheres, has occurred in the form of an easy means to seek political favours.
5. The scheduled castes and the scheduled tribes are still generally at the bottom of the socio-economic hierarchy barring a small minority of their political and administrative elite. Hence, they also show internal differentiation based mainly on economic and political criteria.
6. Urban-industrial social stratification is characterised by the capitalist-entrepreneurial, professional, white-collar and working classes to a large extent. All these classes are also highly differentiated internally.
7. Social mobility is complex and varied like social stratification in Indian society. Emergence of the elite from among the SCs and STs on the one hand and pauperisation of some upper caste families on the other are two contrary trends. It is also a fact that the upper castes have not maintained *status quo*, they have diversified their status-base, and at the same time also socially declined. The middle castes have improved their overall social position, while some families continue to remain backward even among the highly upwardly mobile castes. The SCs and STs, barring their 'elite', remain at the bottom of the social pyramid.

Since caste has been surfacing uninhibitedly in one form or other, the question which arises often is: What is so unique in the caste system that makes it persist in some form or the other? Though not so obvious, an answer to this question can be found in the continuously changing caste-class-power nexus and levels of social mobility. Thus, it is not that caste is used as a means of mobilisation for fulfilling certain interests by some castes and not others. Whichever caste aspires to use it for upward social mobility makes use of the 'caste idiom'. The castes which become economically and politically dominant also make use of caste for further upward social and cultural mobility. Therefore, caste is used not just for namesake, it is appropriated for economic and political goals in the first instance, and for socio-cultural mobility afterwards. It is opined that instead of 'caste and class', it would be appropriate to refer it as 'class and caste'.

However, there is no uniform pattern of the nexus between caste and class. Castes occupying leading positions in the competitive economy of the Punjab are also leading castes among Sikhs and Hindus. These dominant castes are in a position to mobilise their respective fellow men to defend their economic and political interests. On the contrary, the situation is quite different in Bihar where caste is used openly and unhesitatingly in a most virulent form to divide the society in real-life situations. Castes are presenting themselves as 'confederations' and *senas* (armies) against one another. The state is divided into *forwards, backwards, Harijans, adivasis* and *Muslims*. Caste-encounters, accompanied by fights, feuds, murders, etc., have been quite frequent. Thus, caste is becoming a political process in which class and power are inherently embedded. Since caste is a political process in the making, it can be thought of as a means of creating a contradictory situation in which conflicts and 'secularisation' could co-exist. But politics does not get 'secularised', therefore, caste itself gets 'secularised', but makes politics ethnic and sectarian.

The significance of major structural changes since independence is evident in the following patterns of mobility:

1. downward mobility and proletarianisation;
2. upward mobility and embourgeoisiement;
3. urban migration and cash income for the rural people and social mobility in the village; and
4. rural non-agricultural income and mobility within the village.

Caste has also therefore become weak as a system of social ranking because of these emerging patterns of social mobility. There are both losers and gainers of the macro-structural changes as well as micro-infrastructural inputs in the countryside. Caste and class cut across each other as is evident from these patterns, but in different contexts 'caste' is appropriated, though not in equal measure, by various castes and their members. A caste looks like a class and a power bloc, and yet it remains a caste. It was not so in the past, hence today a great deal of social mobility among various castes at different levels is observed, but not in the same measure. Caste is no more an object or an end in itself; it has changed, it has discarded some of its dysfunctional elements in today's context and has also become a 'resource', a means for some of its members. What is needed today is an appropriate conceptualisation of this complex situation rather than an undisputed adherence to the conventional concepts of 'caste', 'class' and 'power'. Caste-class-power nexus needs to be accepted as a concept signifying the dynamics of the interconnection between social, economic and political dimensions of India's social reality particularly since independence. Now let us see what the contributors to this volume have articulated on this complex but very significant theme.

Of the three papers on West Bengal, the first one is by Sekhar Bandyopadhyay on caste, class and politics in colonial Bengal covering the period between 1872 and 1937. Social movements among the lower castes initially aimed at upward cultural mobility; and the same castes/groups in course of time longed for material and political advancement. In their case, the well-off from among the lower castes were involved in the efforts for achieving higher status. The Namsudras of Bengal thus articulated through these efforts: (i) disapproval of their low ritual status and socio-economic and political alienation; and (ii) rejection of persisting social humiliation and economic exploitation. They thought of the high caste Hindus as their caste-oppressors and class-adversaries, and in this outburst the Namsudras received encouragement from the colonial rulers not because they espoused their cause but because the British wanted to show down the upper caste Mandarins in their own interest.

The second paper on Bengal is also on the related theme of 'caste and power' by Ranbir Samaddar. The author argues that class and caste merge in the articulation of aspirations for higher social status by the *dalit* (depressed) communities. The struggle of the scheduled castes is social as well as political. The continuity of caste and class together indicates persistence of the caste-class nexus that existed in the British period. The left-front government has not done much to break this rigid nexus as the middle peasantry has acquired a stable place in the system. Though the poor peasantry has not pauperised further during the left-front regime, but class contradictions have not sharpened further as expected during the regime of the present government under the leadership of Jyoti Basu.

The theme of the third paper on West Bengal is also the same, namely, caste and politics. The author, Srijnan Halder, examines how the rural middle castes have become a political force to reckon with due to improvement in their economic position. The gains in economic and political fields have prompted them to get access to higher education. But the situation in West Bengal is somewhat different from that of the neighbouring state of Bihar and some other states like Maharashtra, Karnataka and Tamil Nadu. Despite economic betterment and some political clout, the middle castes in Bengal are not able to deentrench the upper castes from the control of superior positions in professions, bureaucracy and higher educational institutions. In fact, the middle castes have not been able to come up to a level that they could challenge or compete with the near monopoly of the upper castes.

Based on a survey, Shaibal Gupta examines interconnections between caste, class and land in the context of agricultural production and technological inputs in Bihar. Gupta finds that to a considerable extent large landholdings are still owned by the upper castes, but the modern inputs into agriculture are not properly appropriated by them, hence low productivity. This is not true about the middle castes as they have even production with smaller landholdings and lesser. Thus, social background of the people engaged in agriculture becomes one of the most significant factors in agricultural production.

The situation in Orissa is somewhat different from Bengal and Bihar although the three states formed the state of Bengal until 1905. Referring to Orissan society, Bhairabi Prasad Sahu observes that its backward agriculture and aborted industrialisation have helped in consolidating the pre-capitalist social formation. The advancement of the productive forces could sharpen class-antagonism and hence transform social relationships. However, this is not happening at the moment because of the suppression of class relations by the hegemony of the caste structure. The author argues that the existing social structure and the economic under-development reinforce each other, hence only a break in this nexus could bring about social transformation. One of the obvious results of such a situation is the emergence of a considerable degree of social harmony and the politics of consensus. Apparently, Orissa has therefore not witnessed violence, riots and communal hatred despite deep-seated roots of discontentment among the deprived sections of the society. The middle class people living in urban areas have their roots intact in the villages, and the upper stratum of urban people is entrenched into the positions of power in the government, bureaucracy, professions, trade and business. This sort of sectoral control by the upper and middle classes has also prevented the lower classes to come up in revolt against their oppressors.

Drawing from his experience of field studies in the three adjacent states of Bengal, Bihar and Orissa, Anjan Ghosh highlights that perspective on caste and class needs reformulation keeping in view the dynamics related to these in contemporary India. Mobilisations based on the categories like 'backward classes', '*dalits*', 'Bahujan Samaj', 'Dravidas', etc., suggest that caste is no longer used just as a local endogamous group or a group enjoying a given ritual rank in caste hierarchy. Ghosh argues that caste has not disappeared but rather has reconstituted itself. Caste operates as a system of social hierarchy in some backward areas, but as a means of social identity it persists throughout India. The emergence of the class of *kulaks* and rejuvenation of caste as the basis of social identity have harmoniously co-existed. Economic prosperity has not necessarily resulted in the rejection of caste as an evil, rather, caste is being accepted in its new forms.

Gail Omvedt's paper on Kanshi Ram and his Bahujan Samaj Party is placed here because Kanshi Ram has largely drawn his followers from Uttar Pradesh and the surrounding areas. The Bahujan Samaj Party is a unique political innovation on the Indian political scene as it claims to bring together all the *dalits* of the country under a single banner. Since most of the political parties have not been able to express and articulate ideologically as well as practically the interests and concerns for the overall development of the *dalits* and lower castes, Kanshi Ram found it politically expedient to form a party known as Bahujan Samaj, literally, a party looking after the interests of the largest number of people who have remained *dalits* for centuries. Initially, the party adopted an 'anti-party' stance by refusing alliances with other parties and participation in political activities. Its professed single most important aim was to break the shackles of the caste system, hence it advocated a new and secular ideology. It also launched campaigns against untouchability, inequality, social injustice and inhuman treatment meted out to the lower castes. The main aim of the Bahujan Samaj Party is a scathing attack on the policies of the Congress and the state whom it holds responsible for perpetuation of rural feudal lords and slum *dadas* (toughs) in urban areas. The party is also against the rhetoric of the left.

The paper by Imtiaz Ahmad and N.C. Saxena provides details about caste, land and political power in Uttar Pradesh. It seeks to examine the interplay between caste, control over land and political mobilisation in rural Uttar Pradesh. The issues taken up for discussion are: (1) nature of dominance based on landownership and political power; (2) reasons for the continuity of dominance of Brahmins or Thakurs and of the backwardness of the intermediate castes; (3) impact of the abolition of the *zamindari* system on various caste groups; (4) reasons for the lack of class-based polarisation and mobilisation of the landless and poor peasantry; and (5) effect of the economic policies of the government, particularly in the context of the green revolution and the programme of land distribution. Ahmad and Saxena observe that the lower castes have been able to make a headway towards upward mobility because of the persisting caste-based hierarchy in rural Uttar Pradesh. However, the urban trading and professional castes like Banias, Kayasthas and Khatris who had acquired *zamindari* rights in the eighteenth century, lost it due to the abolition of the *zamindari* system after independence. These castes entered into politics and for some time they were quite strong, but their power declined with the increasing tendency of seeking support on the basis of caste. Numerically, these castes were not strong and hence lost out on the support which was simply based on education and other secular criteria. The middle castes are making a dent in politics, but are way behind compared to their counterparts in Bihar, Andhra Pradesh and Karnataka. However, a caste or a féderation of castes has become the basis of social identity for mobilisation among the power-seeking members of different castes.

K.L. Sharma, in the paper entitled "Feudalism, Caste and Class in Rajasthan", argues that Rajputana which comprised of nineteen Rajput, two Jat and one Muslim princely states along with several *thikanas*, *jagirs* and other forms of feudal establishments, represented a distinct mode of polity and administration compared to the one in the British India. It is this distinct character of the princely states that provided a definite structure and direction to caste and class relations relegating caste to a subordinate position. Despite caste being second to feudalism, it remained a vital and complex social formation comprising different layers, levels and units. Although feudalism occupied a superordinate position, it rarely interfered with the day-to-day functioning of different caste groups. In fact, class was determined on the one hand by feudalism and on the other by caste. Both caste and class were inextricably interrelated phenomena of Rajasthan's social formation and were somewhat differently structured and interfered with by the feudal system. After the abolition of feudalism, caste and class have come closer because of the absence of the mechanism which affected the two systems in a graded manner. The positive results of the abolition of feudalism are seen in various sectors of social life in Rajasthan including agrarian relations, politics and social mobility.

Since all the members of a caste do not enjoy a similar economic position, caste and class cannot be equated. Ghanshyam Shah makes this observation while examining the nature of political dominance vis-a-vis caste and class in post-independent Gujarat. The economic destinations within a given caste are not necessarily antagonistic, and the political elite of this caste generally have the support of upper economic stratum from within and outside their caste. Shah highlights that the merchants and the *zamindars* dominated the social life of Gujarat before the British established their rule in India. A class of rich peasants and industrialists also emerged by the turn of the last century. However, in course of time, the *zamindars* have either disappeared or turned into rich peasants and industrialists after independence. Thus, the business class (merchants and industrialists) and rich peasants enjoy dominance in contemporary Gujarat. The fact is that these two classes do not hold formal positions of power and yet together they form the real power elite.

The businessmen and rich peasants belong to the upper and the middle castes of Banias, Brahmins, Rajputs and Patidars. The latecomers are the Patidars who arose to political eminence after the mid-nineteenth century. However, all these castes are highly differentiated internally. The poor and the exploited strata of society are becoming increasingly conscious of their economic interests. Very often they have protested against the mechanisms by which they are exploited and the injustices that are inflicted upon them.

The State of Maharashtra is represented maximum in this volume as a total of five essays has been contributed by Sharad Patil, by Rajendra Vora and Suhas Palshikar, by Surendra Jondhale, by S.P. Punalekar, and by Gopal Guru.

In a very forthright manner, Sharad Patil reports that the debate on caste and class has made a big headway in Maharashtra because the anti-caste *dalit* movement is strong, and the left movement is somewhat weak. Patil blames the Marxist scholars and the traditional Communist parties for their failure to provide a satisfactory explanation for the resurgence of religious fundamentalism in the form of the Shiv Sena and cultist ideology in the name of neo-Buddhism/Ambedkarism. Although the rest of the country is witnessing religious and communal convulsions to a considerable extent, Maharashtra is facing more problems emanating from the caste-class nexus. Patil shows persistence of the nexus by drawing evidence from historical as well as contemporary sources.

Rajendra Vora and Suhas Palshikar, like Sharad Patil, discuss the problem of caste-class nexus vis-a-vis ideology in contemporary Maharashtra. The 1980s were marked by two sets of confrontations: (i) between the Hindus and the Muslims; and (ii) between the upper caste Hindus (*savarnas*) and the scheduled castes/scheduled tribes (*dalits*). The authors emphasise on the increasing Hindu militancy and the changing character of the Hindu identity in Maharashtra. The phenomenonal upsurge of the caste-communal violence has also paved the way for the emergence of a number of casteist and communal organisations. Further, Vora and Palshikar point out that caste-based conflicts must be analysed in terms of the class hierarchy in the state. Caste conflicts between the Marathas and the lower castes or between the caste Hindus and the *dalits* cannot be said to be simply caste or ritual conflicts because they are deeply rooted in the material interests of the warring groups. A process of class formation has set in, cutting into the hegemony of the upper castes. The appropriation of the state and its policies for development by the upper and upper middle castes/classes has come under severe attack from the 1960s onwards.

The Marathwada region of Maharashtra witnessed a prolonged intense agitation in 1978 against the proposal of renaming the Marathwada University after Dr. Babasaheb Ambedkar. Surendra Jondhale observes that this agitation was followed by a short lull but soon the silence was broken by an anti-reservation movement. Since then the left and the democratic organisations have been trying to build their credibility among the *dalits* and the nomadic tribes by organising them on different issues like the Minimum Wages Act, agrarian reforms, etc. However, the communal and casteist organisations have discovered a new device by attacking the *dalits* collectively with a view to hide/misguide the identity of the culprits. Besides this social boycott of the *dalits* and forcible grazing of animals on their fields have become a routine affair. The root cause of violence and atrocities against the *dalits* is their exploitation and the denial of minimum wages to them.

S.P. Punalekar analyses the nature of socio-economic development, its complexities and contradictions in Sangli district of Maharashtra. The study examines two questions: (i) who are 'developing' and in what kind of a political-economic milieu and with which supportive structures; and (ii) what tensions and contradictions have emerged in rural Maharashtra? Uneven development in Sangli district has resulted in disparities in levels of production, income levels and lifestyles of the people. The district can be divided into 'developed' and 'underdeveloped' zones. Punalekar names these two as Sangli I and Sangli II, respectively. In the case of Sangli I, there has been a great deal of development during the last thirty years. It is endowed with infrastructural resources like good soil and sub-soil water deposits. Human and technological surfeit is also available in abundance. Successful and profit-making co-operatives have come up on the basis of this. Punalekar is all praise for the progressive farmers of the district through whose efforts institutional support structures like the co-operatives concerning water, milk, poultry and sugar have acquired a great significance and play an important role in the economic development of the district. Strategies of the state regarding growth and its pro farmer policies have immensely contributed to the development of agriculture, trade, commerce, education, etc. However, Sangli II has remained backward and undeveloped because of the non-availability of natural endowments and recurrence of successive droughts. Even drinking water is not suitably available to many villages. People are quite agitated regarding this pitiful situation. They are organising themselves and are making demands for water, fodder and employment. The people believe that they have been neglected by the political heavyweights with regard to even their minimum needs.

The last paper on Maharashtra in the volume is by Gopal Guru on "Caste, Class and Politics in the Tanneries of Kolhapur". How caste and class reinforce each other is discussed by Guru in the context of the people engaged in the training of leather. Whether interactions between caste and class diffuse the class character of the community or not? Does caste camouflage the class character through the exploitation of the lower class tannery-workers? Guru observes approvingly the inherence of class in caste as the big tannery-owners appropriate a great deal of surplus based on the work done by the poor tannery-workers of their own caste. Since both owners and workers belong to the same caste, the class distinctions within the caste remain unexpressed and unarticulated under the cover of the same caste identity. How long can such a situation continue? Perhaps not for a long-time.

Three papers on South India by A. Nagaraja Naidu, A. Satyanarayana and Rajan Gurukul analyse caste, class and land relations from a historical perspective. Naidu highlights that in the colonial period, in South India, the lower castes were *dalits* and perceived the upper caste landlords as their enemy and not the British as the latter were not directly exploiting them. The upper castes, being the early beneficiaries of education, first entered into the British revenue administration and later on became entrenched in politics. They were nominated to the legislative council representing the landed aristocracy. In such a situation 'freedom' for the country had hardly any meaning for the *dalits.*

A. Satyanarayana discusses the relationship between land and caste in Andhra Pradesh during the colonial period. He also analyses changes in caste and class composition of the rural rich and the articulation of political power and its various forms. There has been a gradual decline of the power and authority of landed class as a whole. The *zamindars* and Brahmins have lost their hegemonic authority since the late 1950s, when land reforms were introduced in the State of Andhra Pradesh. Consequent upon the land reforms, a class of rural rich emerged from among the principal agricultural castes which in fact became a threat to the *zamindars* and Brahmins. Soon this 'new class' began to displace the traditional dominant castes/groups, and also received the support of a large number of people as its members belonged to the numerically preponderant castes.

Caste goes beyond the boundaries of kinship and family ties as it involves specialisation of labour/work on a wider corporate basis. Rajan Gurukul traces the genesis of the caste system in Kerala and observes that the actual formation of castes took place in the temple-centred Brahmin villages having agrarian activities. Brahmins, landlords and temples played a crucial role in the multiplication of castes and sub-castes. The peculiar systems of land relations and service tenure were responsible for the creation of the system of hereditary occupational groups. The Brahminical ideas of 'ritual status' were instrumental in converting these groups into 'endogamous castes'. Ultimately, the society was stratified in terms of higher and lower groups based on the ritual status accorded to various castes/sub-castes. Such a stratified society based on Brahminical prescriptions had the tacit approval of the king (ruler) as it was in his interest too to appoint officials and secure professional services on a hereditary basis to ensure the stability of his rule.

A.B. Bardhan opines that casteism and caste-conflict retard India's socio-economic and political development. He cites examples of confrontations, atrocities and violence based on caste prejudices. Caste is a force that polarises the people. It is used as an unscrupulous means for self-aggrandisement by a minority of people at the cost of the innocent, poor and unconcerned masses. It is such a class of people which has upheld the ideology of caste, and has kept it alive even in most adverse situations. Bardhan hopes that the mystification of caste upheld and propagated by the ruling classes would not stand ground much longer because of the tenacious militant struggle against it being waged by the revolutionary toiling masses.

Lastly, Javeed Alam looks at the constitution of social consciousness in contemporary India with regard to caste and class. Rapid shifts in the consciousness of the same very people ranging from democratic struggles to communal and sectarian fights have been observed. In fact, communal and sectarian mobilisation have become a dominant mode of political activity. Such communal, regional, caste or creed based tendencies have become a threat to India's unity and its secular and democratic fabric. Alam also feels that revivalist forces and communal politics hinder the emergence of class struggles and secular oppositional movements. The questions regarding caste or class or caste and class have to be seen today as Alam observes in the light of such communalised political mobilisations and activities. Though the development of capitalism in India has weakened caste and caste-like structures to a considerable extent, and yet they remain potent politically and culturally. Keeping this in view, Alam considers class, caste and social consciousness as aspects of a *totality*, that is, the social being. These are being transformed via retarted capitalism as Alam argues vehemently.

1

Caste, Class and Politics in Colonial Bengal: A Case Study of the Namasudra Movement of 1872-1937

Sekhar Bandyopadhyay

Social awakening and the political movements that were taking place among some of the ritually lower castes in India since the late nineteenth century have been interpreted mainly in two different ways. According to some scholars, such movements were the result of the economic prosperity and social ambitions of certain upwardly mobile communities that were merely looking for higher ritual positions in keeping with their newly improved secular status.[1] In the first stage of their movement, these people aimed only at acquiring the symbols of high status. But, in the second, their attention shifted to the more material sources of high status, i.e., education, employment and political power.[2] In contraposition to this analytical framework, which ignores the element of protest involved in all such movements,[3] there are some other historians who have seen only deprivation and protest in such caste movements. Built-up resentments against the implications of social inferiority resulted, according to them, in all such articulate caste agitations in the early twentieth century. And these they think were expressions of protest against all sorts of social and economic oppressions and a means to get rid of them.[4]

Both these explanations are, however, based on the same fundamental assumption that a caste represented an undifferentiated group of people who lived in the same conditions and behaved in a uniform manner in either of the two directions. The major purpose of the present essay is to question this very assumption of a monolith. It has been argued here that such caste movements originated neither solely from prosperity, nor from deprivation alone, and these were not the exclusive expressions of either ambition or protest. On the contrary, in a single caste movement, we may find the convergence of both the trends, though this does not of course preclude the possibility of divergence at a later stage, resulting in the weakening of the movement itself.

As a convenient methodology to understand these caste movements, it is, therefore, essential first of all to situate such communities within the broader class structure of the region. And then it is also necessary to look for the internal differentiations within each group. For differential achievements in a new institutional set-up had led to class divisions within each caste and created divergent interests and aspirations. Thus, while the masses remained preoccupied with the perceived threats to community honour, resentments against social disabilities and protests against economic exploitation, a tiny and relatively more prosperous section within the same group cared more for ritual symbols and looked eagerly for institutional concessions in order to be at par with the traditionally privileged higher castes. The relationship between the two sections could be symbiotic, rather than antagonistic, at a particular historical juncture and they might participate in the same movement. But such movements, instead of being homogorbous, reflected two different levels of consciousness, two distinct sets of goals and sometimes two different modes of operation. Yet there could be a conjunction of the two streams, which was sometimes due to a temporary communion of interests and sometimes in common opposition to the nationalist movement. But this conjunction did not mean that all internal tensions and conflicts were abjured. On the contrary, at a later stage when the colonial government began to patronise such movements, their leaders also started forgetting the masses and got involved in a politics of backwardness. They merely used the depressed socio-economic conditions of their respective communities for obtaining some concessions that could hardly benefit the entire community. The masses, still hoping for a better world and having much less faith in the high caste Hindu nationalists, continued to support their caste leaders, but certainly not with the same keen enthusiasm as before.

The present essay would illustrate these trends through a detailed study of the socio-political movement among the Namasudras, an untouchable peasant caste that constituted the largest Hindu caste group in Eastern Bengal. This particular movement attracted our attention not only being the most powerful among all the Scheduled Caste movements in colonial Bengal, but when a distinct Scheduled Caste politics

were in the higher professions. This backwardness, the Namasudra leadership believed, was due to the existing dominance of the privileged high caste Bhadralok in these fields.[37] And this could be broken only with the active assistance of the colonial government. The policy of protective discrimination in favour of the Muslims, initiated since 1906 by the authorities of the new province of Eastern Bengal and Assam, had encouraged similar aspirations among the better class Namasudras. In a number of meetings, therefore, in 1906, they resolved to collaborate with the Muslims in opposing the *Swadeshi* movement and expected the authorities to "bestow the same rights and privileges upon the Namasudras as have been done upon the Mohammedans".[38] For this purpose, the Namasudras of Dacca and Orakandi also sent several delegations to different Lieutenant Governors, apprised them of their degrading socio-economic conditions and demanded special privileges in education and employment.[39] In one such petition in 1911, they stated categorically that they had "not the slightest connection with any of the Hindu communities" and hence they desired "to be recognised by the government as an entirely different community having separate claim to political privileges like the Mohammedans."[40]

This separatism was not simply the outcome of selfish ambitions of a self-seeking elite, but in a real sense, a kind of protest against the existing social injustices. For the educational backwardness of the Namasudras was not just due to their lack of aptitude. Discrimination, both covert and overt, in matters of admission and hostel accommodation, was also an important factor behind this.[41] And this was acknowledged by the nationalists as well. While Ambika Charan Mazumdar and Aswini Kumar Datta spoke against this in different public meetings, Surendranath Banerjee and Nilratan Sarkar raised the issue on the floor of the legislative council.[42] But their appeals could hardly change the reality of social relations in Bengal. A number of indigenous social organisations, like the Depressed Classes Mission, later called the Society for the Improvement of the Backward Classes, also did commendable work for the educational advancement of this community.[43] But what they achieved was insignificant compared to what the Dacca Baptist Mission or the Australian Baptist Mission of Orakandi did for these people.[44] Finally generous patronage flowed in from the government in the form of special grants for their schools, free studentships, stipends and scholarships for their students and special hostels for them in different parts of Eastern Bengal and Calcutta.[45] By 1921, 8.5 per cent of the Namasudras aged five and above could read and write, and this indicated at least a modest improvement.

But "the young men, from among the Namasudras even when educated, cannot enter government service"—this had been one of the major complaints of their leaders. And this, they thought, was one of the impediments that restricted the advancement of learning among their caste members and consequently their upward social movement.[46] So far as the higher government services were concerned, a colonial official acknowledged in 1917 that there was only one Deputy Collector and one Sub-Deputy Collector from this community.[47] To redress this situation, in 1922, the government allowed certain special privileges to such communities to compete for the provincial services and the selection committee included a representative of their caste as a nominated member. But when even this arrangement failed to produce any result, the following year, the government decided to nominate qualified candidates from among them.[48] So far as ministerial services were concerned, an inquiry in 1930 revealed that in the major Namasudras concentration areas, the depressed classes were very poorly represented in such jobs. In Faridpur, they held only 5.47 per cent of the sanctioned posts, in Bakarganj 1.83 per cent, in Jessore one per cent and in Khulna 1.26 per cent, although they constituted 23,15,22 and 35 per cent of the population of these four districts respectively. And it was found that this low representation was mainly because it was "notoriously very hard to penetrate the barriers of those who now hold the fort", i.e., the high caste Hindus. The latter constituted only 13.5 per cent of the population of Faridpur and 14.5 per cent in Bakarganj, but monopolised 66.6 per cent of the appointments in these two districts. Hence, in 1931, the government decided to recruit depressed class candidates, in this case the Namasudras, in at least one out of every three non-Mohammedan vacancies in these two districts. In other districts, the recruiting authorities were only asked to give special encouragement to such candidates, but no reservation was provided.[49] But, in spite of this arrangement, only three Namasudras all over Bengal got into any government service during 1931-32. This was partly due to the dearth of suitable candidates, but was partly also the result of non-compliance with such orders by the local officials.[50]

This constant struggle against discrimination and deprivation naturally compelled the Namasudra leadership to look for political power. The Morley-Minto Reforms (1909) by granting special electorates for the Muslims, had stimulated similar aspirations in the minds of the Namasudras as well and this was evident in their petition of 1911, referred to earlier. But such tendencies became much more manifest when the Montague-Chelmsford Reform proposals were announced in 1917. In the winter of that year, they decided for the first time to stage a political demonstration in Calcutta. The meeting that took place on November 3, 1917 at Dalhousie Institute, allegedly with the help and encouragement of the European businessmen, accepted the reform announcement, but resolved that "if any additional power is withdrawn from the government and vested in the hands of a few leaders without giving any share of power to us, it will make the future progress of the backward classes impossible". The nationalist press reacted sharply to this demand for communal representation, allegedly manipulated by the "Anglo-Indian wire-pullers". The Bengalee, for example, called the Namasudras a bunch of "idiots" who were trying to "jump to the top of the tree."[51] But the Namasudras felt that they had little choice. In another meeting in the following year on the same date, they resolved that if the future electorate did not consist of "all the 190 castes of the Hindu society in proportion to their respective members," it would lead to the establishment of "the oligarchy of a handful of limited castes." If this was not prevented, a slow but continuous discontent, after gathering strength would dethrone the oligarchy and the whole constitutional experiment would "fall with a sound more violent in character than what the Bolsheviks have caused in Russia." For them, therefore, "communal representation" seemed to be the only possible measure that could safeguard their political interests.[52]

The Government of India Act of 1919 also formally recognised the "special needs" of such depressed classes and provided for the nomination of one non-official member from among them in the Bengal Legislative Council. The provision of separate electorate was not considered necessary, for the Namasudras, who were the most articulate group among these people, were likely to gain three or four more seats in the general constituencies where they had been decisively superior in numerical terms.[53] But the results of the election of 1921 proved this calculation wrong. Their numerical superiority mattered less, as most of them being poor cultivators did not have the voting right that depended on property qualifications. As a corollary, almost all the Namasudra candidates, except only one at Barisal, lost the election in spite of the fact that the Congress had decided to boycott it. Later, Bhishmadeb Das, who had lost the election in a general constituency, was nominated to represent the depressed classes in the legislature.[54]

This hapless plight of the Namasudras became much more evident in the election of 1923, when the Swarajists had got back to fight the electoral battle. In their annual conference at Pirojpur in June 1922, the Namasudra leadership had decided to launch a voter-registration movement as a step to "capture" the council.[55] But despite this electoral campaign all the Namasudra candidates, except the Swarajist Mohini Mohan Das, lost the election and this time a non-Namasudra was nominated to the legislature. This debacle may be partly explained in terms of the greater electioneering skill of the Swarajists and partly by low voter "turnout caused by the poor peasants" ignorance of the niceties of the electoral system.[56] The same story was repeated in the elections of 1926 and 1929, when the nominated members and the Swarajist Mohini Mohan were the only representatives of this community in the legislative council. In 1929, however, the government had nominated two instead of one member from this community. Later, when the Swarajists came out of the council in the bye-election of 1930, three more Namasudras were elected and this to some extent redressed the imbalance.[57]

Thus, most of the Namasudra majority constituencies prior to 1930 had returned high caste candidates. Therefore, it was ultimately the special constitutional provisions, i.e., on government patronage, that the Namasudras had to rely upon to secure representation for themselves in the legislature. They were more successful at the local level, where their numerical superiority in districts like Bakarganj, Faridpur, Jessore and Khulna ensured them larger representation in the elected self-governing bodies, like the municipalities of the district, local and union boards. In other districts, their failure to secure adequate representation in proportion to their number, as the Collector of Dacca observed, was mainly due to a lack of "instinct for organisation which would enable them to make their numbers felt" by outmanoeuvering the caste Hindus.[58] The implications of this phenomenon were not certainly favourable for the high caste Hindu nationalists.

The continuing frustration of their political ambitions led to the development among the Namasudra elite of a deep sense of loyalty to the colonial government and a feeling of suspicion about nationalist politics which appeared, in their perception, to be an exclusively high caste affair. The identification of the Swadeshi movement, the first major nationalist agitation since the beginning of the Namasudra protest, with the high caste gentry of Eastern Bengal was quite obvious as most of the leaders as well as volunteers came from their ranks and used their coercive powers quite often.[59] Hence, the Namasudra leadership, Guruchand Thakur and his associates for example, began to believe that the partition of Bengal would not affect the Namasudras, while its annulment would not bring any special benefit to them. In conjunction with the Muslims, they decided to offer a joint resistance to the Swadeshi movement and for this purpose Guruchand's son Sashibhushan also got in touch with Nawab Salimullah of Dacca, the leader of the East Bengal Muslims. The alliance between the two communities was viewed as the combination of two social underdogs, equally despised and exploited by the high caste Hindu gentry. After the Durbar declaration of 1911, Guruchand was rewarded for his loyalty[60] and Namasudra political separatism became far more firmly entrenched.

The two trends in the political behaviour of the Namasudra elite, i.e., loyalty to the British and alignment with the Muslims, became far more evident during the later years. When the Home Rule Movement began in Bengal around 1915, the *Moslem Hitaishi* predicted that sooner or later it would lapse into Hindu rule. Similarly, the Namasudras also believed that the higher castes had become much perturbed by the rise of the lower castes who were now challenging their previous social dominance. As it was made possible by the introduction of British rule, the higher castes were agitating for home rule, so that the upcoming lower castes could be brought back to their former subordinate position in society. Hence, the Namasudras not only did stay away from the agitation, but also held articulate demonstrations against home rule in different mofussil areas, especially in Dacca. Their association in July 1917 organised a deputation to the Governor to express their loyalty and to ask for fresh state patronage.[61] Finally, the two meetings in Calcutta in November 1917 and 1918, referred to earlier, may also be recalled in this connection.

This Namasudra loyalism and their lingering suspicion about the ulterior motives of the high caste nationalists became once again strikingly apparent at the time of the Non-Cooperation Movement, which is often believed to have been marked by an increased participation by the mofussil elite who had hitherto remained outside the political system.[62] But as the biographer of Guruchand tells us, C.R. Das himself had tried to persuade him to join the movement along with the members of his caste. But the latter turned down this appeal on the plea that though the Namasudras had respect for the concept of freedom, they were not in a position to join the movement to achieve it, for those who had nothing could not afford to sacrifice. Furthermore, there was a danger involved in this kind of movement. As it was being led by the high caste Hindus, once independence was really achieved its benefits would be monopolised by them alone, at the expense of the rank and file belonging to the lower castes.[63] A similar fear was also being voiced by the Namasudra legislators in the Bengal Legislative Council. "I know the term 'nation' in India is a misnomer", declared Nirod Behari Mullick in March 1921, by way of condemning the Non-Cooperation Movement. And a few months later, in view of the proposed visit of the Prince of Wales, the two Namasudra legislators expressed in no uncertain words their "loyal and dutiful homage" to His Majesty the King-Emperor.[64] It is true that not all the Namasudras were against non-cooperation and this dissident group had its protest registered at the Pirojpur annual conference in June 1922. But theirs was really a minority position and in the following year's conference at Khulna there was not a single dissident voice. The meeting, therefore, unanimously resolved that any such Non-Cooperation Movement against the British Government was against the interests of the Namasudra community.[65]

However, it was on the occasion of the Non-Cooperation Movement that the Namasudras and the Muslims for the first time had moved to opposite poles in politics and this had also caused considerable friction in East Bengal countryside.[66] But the two communities came closer again in opposition to the Civil Disobedience Movement in 1930. As the Swarajists had failed to provide any concrete programme for the social or economic upliftment of such people, they also steadily drifted away from the mainstream of nationalist politics and its principal proponents. By 1926, the *Barishal Hitaishi* was reporting that "the Namasudras and the Mohammedans are uniting against the upper classes."[67] In 1929, the Bengal Namasudra Association was formally recognised by the government and in the same year its leaders greeted the report of the Simon Commission which the Congress had so vigorously criticised and condemned. In August 1930, the Namasudra members of the Bengal Legislative Council voted against a resolution that demanded dominion status for India.[68] And finally, when the Civil Disobedience Movement was launched with its demand for *Purna Swaraj*, the Namasudra leaders, sometimes in collaboration with the Muslims, organised anti-civil disobedience meetings in the interioavas, particularly in the districts of Faridpur and Bakarganj. The colonial authorities therefore remained convinced that the "Mohammedans and the Namasudras are solidly anti-Congress" and "stoutly opposed to the present agitation and to those responsible for it."[69]

The Masses and Their Grievances

This rejection of the nationalist politics was not just an elite affair. This attitude was shared by the peasantry as well, since the leadership by constantly harping on the basic caste and class contradictions between them and the high caste gentry had successfully dissuaded them from joining the nationalist agitations that had come to be associated with the latter social group. During the Swadeshi Movement, for example, Guruchand and his associates successfully persuaded the Namasudra peasantry to believe that Swadeshi was a slogan of the rich, high caste Hindu *zamindar* class, which had always in the past socially oppressed and economically exploited the Namasudra peasants. The movement, as the Guru told his disciples, was entirely in the interest of the affluent class which wanted to transfer its burden onto the poor peasants by forcing them to buy more expensive Swadeshi goods. Never in the past had these nationalist leaders ever spoken against the inhuman treatment meted out to the Namasudras. So now, if they wanted their participation, they needed to first wage a battle against social inequalities, which they were not prepared to do.[70] In view of the composition of the leadership and its following, the association of the Swadeshi Movement with the high caste *zamindars* does not seem to be quite unnatural. Many of its celebrated leaders had *zamindaries* in areas where the Namasudras served as tenants and suffered as a result of the coming into vogue of *barga* tenancy and later high produce rent paying *dhankarari* tenancy.[71] Most of the Swadeshi volunteers in the Namasudra majority areas also belonged to the same social class. And many of them, as noted earlier, were freely using their coercive power to intimidate the peasantry to participate in the boycott movement.

The suspicions about the Swadeshi leadership became far more entrenched as it failed to provide any constructive programme for the social or economic improvement of the low caste peasantry. Certainly, the leadership was not ignorant of the problem particularly as the Namasudras constituted the largest Hindu caste group in the new province of Eastern Bengal and Assam. Leaders like Ambika Mazumdar through his Faridpur District Association and Aswini Kumar Datta through his Swadesh Bandhu Samiti, with its 159 rural branches in the district of Bakarganj, "made the most sustained and vigorous effort" to mobilise the Namasudra peasantry by promising them various social benefits such as the services of the barbers and washermen.[72] But such inconsequential and empty promises, seldom backed up by adequate follow up action, could hardly change the actual social relations in rural society and therefore could scarcely be expected to win over a self-conscious peasant community. As a result, by the end of 1907, the majority of the Namasudra peasants had started regarding the Swadeshi Movement as "something that the *babus* are doing."[73] In many areas in Faridpur and Bakarganj, they were freely buying foreign.goods, even when these were more expensive. And where they faced obstruction, they decided to set up their own has. In neighbouring Jessore and Khulna, they were more militant, as they threatened to burn the houses of those of their own caste who would not use foreign made articles.[74]

This alienation of the Namasudra peasantry and their intense hatred towards the high caste nationalist leadership could not be broken even by the "charismatic appeal" of Gandhi who himself visited Barisal during the Non-Cooperation Movement but failed to break "the apathy of the general public". Since the Nagpur Congress had resolved "to rid Hinduism of the reproach of untouchability", this was reiterated again and again by Gandhi in his various speeches. There was a widespread belief among many of the lower castes of Bengal that caste equality was one of the goals that the Non-Cooperation Movement was seeking to achieve. But their hopes were soon frustrated, as the leadership in Bengal did nothing in this direction, nor could it offer any major economic programme.[75] This really helped Guruchand and others to convince the cultivators in their community that the nationalist movement was really to further the interests of the wealthy upper caste Bhadralok. How Guruchand explained the situation to his disciples may be worth-mentioning here. In an average educated high caste family, he mentioned, usually one brother would be a lawyer, the second a·clerk and the third a trader. So while the lawyer brother would leave the court and join the Non-Cooperation Movement, the clerk would retain his job to maintain the family and the businessman brother would actually make profits by selling *khadi*. Hence, the Namasudra peasants, who had no connection with offices, courts or trades, should not be a party to this game.[76]

As a result, areas with a large Namasudra population, like the districts of Bakarganj and Faridpur, remained much less affected by the Non-Cooperation Movement. In Bakaraganj, the Namasudras actively resisted the Congress volunteers and co-operated with the authorities in breaking the *hartal* of 24 December, 1921.[77] In Faridpur, where the Muslim Khilafatists forcibly insisted on the boycott of foreign made goods, it led, as mentioned earlier, to violent friction between the two communities in a wide region. Elsewhere, the response of the Namasudra peasants was more muted, being only that of indifference and silent disapproval. But in general, as the government claimed in February 1922, the Namasudras did not participate in the Non-Cooperation Movement.[78] The same story was repeated during the Civil Disobedience Movement of 1930-31, when the Namasudra peasants all over East Bengal kept themselves away from picketing while in Bakarganj and Faridpur they actively resisted the Congress picket trying to dissuade them from buying foreign made goods.[79]

However, this rejection of nationalist politics by the Namasudra peasants should not be regarded just as a manifestation of their loyalty to the British Raj. This was really an expression of their protest against the social and economic injustices perpetrated on them by the landed classes belonging to the three upper castes of Bengal, who also dominated the nationalist politics in the province. In this sense, this rejection was more due to an antipathy towards the landed classes rather than sympathy for the colonial authorities. The peasants had little understanding of institutional politics and were much less concerned about the concessions that their leaders were demanding. This implies that they were less aware of the material prospects of loyalty of political separatism. Nor did they know anything about the concept of political independence for the nation. Their attitude towards the government was rather ambivalent. They preferred the distant ruler to the oppressors nearby, particularly as the former promised protection against the latter. But whenever in the name of maintaining law and order the authorities sided with the landed classes or the higher castes, the Namasudra peasants did not hesitate to take up arms against the state machinery. What was really constant in their behaviour was an articulate demand for what Kathleen Gough has defined as "ethnic freedom".[80] And to achieve this, they sometimes colluded with the Muslims against the high caste Hindus, sometimes collaborated with the government against the nationalists and sometimes stood against all.

The protest of the Namasudra peasants, as already mentioned, had started in 1872 with a no-work campaign aimed against the higher castes of Bakarganj and Faridpur. This trend continued well into the first decade of the twentieth century. In September 1907, about a thousand Namasudras in a meeting at Narail in the district of Jessore had resolved not to serve the higher caste Hindus. By 1909, they had joined hands with the Muslims and the two together had decided not to accept menial jobs in the houses of the higher castes and not to eat food cooked by them. In the adjoining Magura sub-division, they even decided not to cultivate their lands.[81] In the neighbouring district of Khulna, in May

1908 in village Tilak, the Namasudras backed by the Muslims had tried to enter the rostrum erected for *Bhawanipuja* and attempted to perform the *puja* themselves with the help of their own priests. To prevent this, the local Brahmins and Kayasthas appealed to the district authorities. When the police force arrived, a combined Namasudra-Muslim mob, about five to eight thousand strong, attacked it with spears and *lathis* and did not disperse until armed police arrived and opened fire on them.[82] In Faridpur, the Namasudras once again met in April 1909 at village Machkhali and resolved to boycott the higher classes who denied them social privileges.[83] In Mymensingh, around September 1909, the Namasudras of Katiadi decided to discontinue their services as *palki*-bearers and early next year in the Tangail sub-division they resolved not to serve the Kayasthas in any way.[84]

But apart from such specific incidents of protest, the Namasudras all over Eastern Bengal in the early twentieth century refused to accept certain types of menial jobs like those of scavengers or palanquin bearers for example, and this led to a good deal of social tension between them and the higher classes. By the end of the 1920's, in many areas the Namasudras had almost totally given up menial services and were after resorting to much wider *hartals* to harass their high caste adversaries.[85] This tension came to a head in 1929, when the Namasudras organised a prolonged *satyagraha* to secure their entry into the Kali temple at Munshiganj in Dacca. This time they even accepted the leadership of Swami Satyananda of the Hindu Mahasabha, as their traditional caste leaders did not come forward. But the disgraceful defeat of the movement and the stubborn orthodoxy of the local high caste Hindu society that was responsible for it, only widened the social breach even further.[86] This frustrating experience, by the beginning of 1930, once again brought the Namasudra masses closer to their leaders of the more sectarian caste movement.

This widening of the social breach was also the result of a conflict of classes. In the first decade of the present century the tension between the high caste Hindu landlords and their Namasudra tenants had come to the surface through the commutation proceedings under the settlement operations in Bakarganj. In this district, produce rent was uncommon except in marshy areas where the Namasudras served as tenants, and at the turn of the century the rapid introduction of the *dhankarari* tenures, "in which the rent was fixed at a definite amount of produce and by which measurement and fluctuations were equally avoided," put both the burden and the hazard of cultivation on the shoulders of the tenants, ensuring a steady and fat income for the landlords. But when the settlement operations started in 1904 many of these oppressed tenants applied for commutation of their high produce rents into reasonable cash rents under Section 40 of the Bengal Tenancy Act of 1885. And this they did in spite of considerable physical intimidation and legal harassment by the landlords, many of whom were also closely associated with the Swadeshi Movement, such as the Dattas of Batajore, the Dases of Goila, the Sarbajnas of Bakal and the Guptas of Chandshi. It is true that such commutation proceedings affected only seven per cent of the total area paying rent in kind, but the cases were numerous only in the marshy regions of Gournadi and Mehendiganj *thanas* (police stations) where the Namasudra tenants had successfully used their caste solidarity to organise a concerted resistance to the oppressive devices of the all powerful high caste landlords. This time they actively co-operated with the settlement officials who appeared to be God-sent angels coming to protect them against "the rapacity of the wolves".[87]

But this co-operation again was not a universal phenomenon. Around this time, in the neighbouring district of Faridpur also, such agrarian tension had become rife because of rapid proliferation of *dhankarari* tenancies in Namasudra inhabited areas. Here the disgruntled tenants sometimes unsuccessfully tried to get a cash rent substituted for the produce rent.[88] And when frustrated they often resorted to bazar-looting and house-breaking in order to harass their obtrusive landlords. When the police arrived to restore peace or conduct searches, it was violently attacked and assaulted by the local Namasudras.[89] By the end of 1909, such turbulence and lawlessness had become almost common place among the Namasudras of southern Faridpur.[90] In the adjacent areas of the districts of Jessore and Khulna also, such agrarian conflicts were not infrequent. And this became a continuing trend, as in 1928-29 we find the Namasudra and the Muslim sharecroppers combining to refuse to cultivate land as *bargadars* unless they were given two-thirds share of the produce,[91] a movement that indeed anticipated the Tebhaga Movement of the 1940's.

However, the relationship between the two peasant communities should be described more properly as a love-hate relationship. While at the grass roots level the Namasudras and the Muslims often united against their common enemies, the high caste Hindus, and at the upper level too there were occasional alignments to oppose the nationalist agitation, such as the Swadeshi or the civil disobedience movements but on the other hand, a series of riots also broke out between the two communities from 1889 onwards, the most serious incidents being those of 1911, 1923-25 and 1938, and this recurrent "hatred", as the District Magistrate of Khulna in 1911 rightly diagnosed, was more "due to feeling rather than to material matters."[92] In course of the nineteenth and the early twentieth centuries an articulate community consciousness had developed among the Bengali Muslims and the Namasudras both. The two large compact bodies of people, both zealous about the honour of their communities, were thus living side by side. Each regarded itself to be a superior people and the slightest offence to any member was regarded as an affront to the entire community and required immediate redress. The Namasudras gave offence to the Muslims by calling them *Nereys*, while the latter often despised the former as *Charls*. There was also constant friction between them over land and *hats* and at the slightest provocation they took up clubs and spears to spill each other's blood. This provocation in most cases was provided by the "haughty attitude" of the Namasudras, although later the Muslims usually got the better of their adversaries. On occasion, about five to ten thousand armed people were mobilised on each side at the shortest notice, and often the peace keeping forces, arriving to restrain the warring parties, became the targets of attack.[93] This shows that the Namasudra peasantry of Eastern Bengal, recently imbued with a militant caste consciousness and proverbially known for its martial qualities, preferred to vindicate the honour of the community through direct armed showdowns, instead of appealing to any law keeping authority. And when the latter sought to prevent them from using such direct methods, they did not spare even it. The Namasudra-Muslim riots in Eastern Bengal thus add an interesting dimension to the manifestation of the new consciousness of the Namasudra peasants in the early twentieth century.

The Parting of Ways

The Namasudra peasants, it thus appears, had their own perception of the socio-political realities around them and behaved accordingly. The fact that they often rallied round their leaders was because the latter could successfully project themselves as the champions of the peasants' cause and could fruitfully highlight the basic caste and class contradiction in the secondary group relations among the East Bengal Hindus. Not only did Guruchand through his dispensations constantly harp on the exploitation and harassment of the Namasudra peasants by the high caste landlords and the bhadralok politicians, the same theme appeared again and again in different caste meetings and the speeches of the Namasudra legislators. In this connection, one may recall the presidential address of Rajani Kanta Das in the Bengiya Namasudra Conference of 1922, in which he not only urged the government to pay more attention to the improvement of agriculture, but also demanded a comprehensive legislation to determine the landlord-tenant relationship. If possible, he declared, the tenancy legislation should be so amended as to declare the peasants the owners of the land.[94] Similar demands for amendments to the Bengal Tenancy Act were being raised in the legislative council as well. In July 1921, the Namasudra legislator Bhishmadeb Das had demanded suitable amendments to protect the rights of the *raiyats* and the under-*raiyats*. The "movement of time", he argued, "has rendered it necessary to give a higher and better status to the raiyats." Apart from this, other agrarian demands, such as the prevention of crop-failures in Faridpur or amelioration of food scarcity in the Namasudra villages of Khulna also figured frequently in the speeches of Das and his colleague in the legislature, Nirod Behari Mullick.[95] As a result, the Namasudra peasants also believed that their leaders had a concern for their interests. A symbiosis between the more well-to-do sections (to which the leadership belonged) and the less fortunate peasantry could thus be forged on the basis of a common community identity.

But from the beginning of the 1930's, this leadership began to forget their peasant followers. Occasionally it still continued to mention such peasant issues, as the necessity to clear an irrigation canal or a minor amendment to the tenancy legislation.[96] But the demands which it raised more frequently were for more educational facilities, employment opportunities and special constitutional rights.[97] It was, in other words, in pursuit of concessions that could only serve its own sectional interests. Consequently, it became more and more preoccupied with council politics and constitutional debates and began to propagate, like many other groups in India around the same time, an overtly separatist political ideology.

Meanwhile, important Namasudra leaders like Mukunda Behari Mullick, Birat Chandra Mandal, Bhishadeb Das, Dhananjoy Ray and Rasiklal Biswas had established contact with the All India Depressed Classes Association, which had been formed in 1917. The Bengal branch of this national body was established at a meeting at Kanchrapara in 1926, with Mullick as the president. In 1929, it was formally recognised by the government, while in the same year Mandal became a member of the executive committee of the All India Association, as the representative from Bengal.[98]

Thus, gradually by 1930, the Namasudras had come to the forefront of the "depressed classes" movement in Bengal. But as they became more and more embroiled in institutional politics, factionatism within the ranks of the leadership also increased. While the Bengal Depressed Classes Association remained closely attached to the Bengal Namasudra Association, both headed by Mullick, the Orakandi groups of leaders, like Amulyadhan Ray, Sarat Chandra Bal, Lalit Kumar Bal or Pramatha Ranjan Thakur (Guruchand's grandson, now an England returned barrister), who did not see eye to eye with the Calcutta based Mullick group, formed in 1932 a parallel organisation called the All Bengal Depressed Classes Federation. The difference between the two organisations was, however, only of personality and not of philosophy.[99]

Through all these fora, the Namasudra leadership was demanding a separate electorate and other concessions which, they believed, would ensure for them a fair share of the political power and official patronage. They welcomed the idea of a Round Table Conference and asked for their representation in it in order to ventilate their special demands and grievances. Through different meetings and resolutions, the association leaders demanded "their right as a minority to separate electorates" as a safeguard against high caste domination exerted through the Congress and condemned the joint electorate as being "positively harmful".[100] This position was amply vindicated by Mullick when he argued in his minute as the member of the Bengal Franchise Committee, that "the term 'Hindu' does not indicate any homogeneous race." At the one end, there were the privileged castes and at the other were the deprived millions of the depressed classes. To ensure a true, proper and effective representation of this latter group, it was desirable that "its representation should be from amongst itself and in proportion to its numerical strength."[101] This stand was shared by the rival federation leaders as well. When in 1932, the communal decision awarded ten seats to the depressed classes in Bengal to be filled in through special electorate, a special conference of the federation on August 28, thanked the British prime minister and his cabinet "for accepting the principle of separate electorate for the depressed classes of Bengal" and demanded for itself "at least thirty-seven" seats instead of just ten.[102]

Even Gandhi's decision to fast unto death to secure the abrogation of special electorate for the depressed classes seems to have had no effect on the Namasudra leadership. For in a meeting on 22 September, i.e., two days after the commencement of the fast, the Faridpur

Namasudras unanimously resolved to "support and approve of the communal award", by implication, even at the risk of Gandhi's life.[103] And then on the very next day, after the signing of the Poona Pact on 24 September, they communicated to the government that they were "not at all prepared to agree to the terms of the agreement",[104] which provided for only thirty reserved seats for the depressed classes to be filled in through joint electorate. Two days later, the federation formally condemned the Poona Pact as "Dr. Ambedkar's political blunder" and upheld the communal award as "a political advantage unprecedented and unparalleled in the constitutional history of India."[105] The Mullick group, however, had its dilemmas, partly because of its close association with Ambedkar and partly because one of their members, Rasiklal Biswas, was present at Poona at the time of the negotiations. Yet it had little choice but to join the chorus. On September 26, in an emergency meeting, the Bengal Namasudra Association and the Depressed Classes Association condemned the Poona Pact and criticised Ambedkar for his dictatorial manner in which he "practically gave away the real cause of the depressed classes."[106] A couple of weeks later, however, the two associations met again and decided to accept the pact as "the next best thing for them."[107] Subsequently, the federation leaders also came to the same decision, as the agreement, now also accepted by the government, seemed to be irrevocable. Moreover, the mounting non-Congress orthodox Hindu opposition to the pact and the growing antipathy towards the favoured depressed classes required an immediate mending of the fences. And then the other provisions of the Poona Pact, that secured special rights to educational and employment opportunities for the depressed classes, had also to be fought for against the high caste Hindu opposition.[108]

During all these years, when the Namasudra leaders were engrossed in constitutional debates and council politics, they had nothing on the cards for the peasantry. And as they began to neglect the peasants, the latter under the leadership of a little known man Jogendranath Mandal, rallied more and more round the Praja Movement. This tenants' movement, which had started around 1914-15 with the initiative of Fazlul Huq, had rapidly acquired a wide support base among the Muslim and Namasudra peasants of Eastern Bengal. But this alternative class-based political organisation was available for the Namasudra peasants only for a very brief period, as just before the elections of 1937 the Krishak Praja Party decided to abandon its Scheduled Caste base in order to compete with the League for Muslim votes.[109] At the same time, the Namasudra masses felt even less attraction for the Congress which offered no developmental programmes for the peasants and the untouchability removal movement had not been able to gain momentum in this province.[110] Indeed, the Namasudra peasants had nothing on the menu to choose except the politics of their caste leaders, who still enjoyed popular support, though it was only by default.

That the Namasudra peasants did not fully approve of the activities of their elite leaders is amply borne out by the fact that a number of established Federation leaders were defeated in the elections of 1937. Yet, of the twelve Namasudras who won the reserved seats, only one was a Congress nominee and he, too, was Rasiklal Biswas who had very lately changed his colours and probably most average voters did not even know of this. On the other hand, the Krishak Praja Party had decided not to contest in the general constituencies. Therefore, Jogendranath Mandal fought the election as independent candidate for an unreserved seat. In Bakaraganj North-East (General) constituency, which was predominantly a Namasudra area, he defeated a Kayastha Congressite in straight fight.[111] The results from this single constituency indicated the state of mind of the Namasudra peasantry, their determination to back up somebody of their own caste who had shown sympathy for their cause.

However, most of the thirteen victorious Namasudra candidates in the elections of 1937 belonged to the Mullick group. This compelled A.K. Fazlul Huq to include Mukunda Behari Mullick in his coalition cabinet and offer him the important portfolio of co-operative credit and rural indebtedness, by disregarding the claim of no less a person than Suharawardy. The Muslims also agreed to this arrangement, though after some initial protest.[112] But this political patchwork at the top did not stop the peasants of the two communities from getting involved in a fierce riot in rural Jessore in April-May of 1938. The situation only suggests that a political settlement at the top could hardly influence the affairs at the grass roots level, where the Namasudras as well as the Muslims were intensely conscious of their community identity and palpably sensitive about their community honour, which they were always prepared to vindicate with spears and guns, if necessary.

Conclusion

In the case of the Namasudras, therefore, their low ritual status had coincided with their subordinate class position vis-a-vis the three traditional upper castes of Bengal who, among the indigenous social groups, were still enjoying the largest share of the economic resources and political power within the new institutional set-up of the colonial period. This created among the former a sense of protest against the socio-economic inequities perpetrated on them by the latter both in the past and in the present. However, the Namasudra community itself had become economically differentiated, with two sections, one being relatively more successful than the other, having divergent perspectives and aspirations. In the Namasudra movement, we therefore find two levels of protest mentality, one against low ritual position and continuing exclusion from the source of wealth and power, and the other against social humiliation and economic exploitation. Their common object (of negation) was the social authority of the high caste Hindus, who were both their caste oppressors and class adversaries. And in their perception, the colonial government, the enemy of their enemy, appeared to be their natural ally.

It is true that while the leadership was more involved in institutional politics and more concerned about concessions and special privileges, the masses had little idea about the nuances of modern politics and often went against the government whenever they found it helping their enemies. But most often the government was on their side and this bred among them a sense of attachment and loyalty towards the *Raj*. The nationalists, on the other hand, failed to dispel this influence as they could not evolve an alternative political ideology rooted in mass consciousness. They were certainly aware of the problem, but the prejudices of the society they belonged to and the interests of the classes they came from prevented them from offering any effective social or economic programme for integrating these aggrieved lower castes with the rest of the nation. The relatively better-off sections of the Namasudras also found their economic and political aspirations unaccommodated within the nationalist politics. Hence, they preferred to stay away from it. They could also effectively mobilise the masses in support of their politics, by using on the one hand their caste and religious linkages and by articulating on the other the latter's socio-economic grievances. Towards the beginning of the 1930's, this leadership had become oblivious to the problems of the masses. But then the nationalists were even more distant from the latter and hence this lapse on the part of the Namasudra leaders did not result in any major shift in the political behaviour of the community as a whole.

The movement, however, lost its early radical potential in this way: in the absence of proper mediation, the discontent and the rebellious spirit of the Namasudra peasantry failed to make any imprint on either the wider social fabric or the broader structure of politics in colonial

Bengal. The movement had become most powerful when the aspirations of the leaders had converged with the grievances of the masses. It began to lose its strength when the process of divergence set in, gradually but unmistakably, divesting the leaders of their crucial mass base. While the latter became apathetic, the former could hardly look beyond the narrow confines of institutional politics. And after the partition of 1947, when the community lost its geographical anchorage in Eastern Bengal, their movement was weakened further and was reduced to [an inconsequential (existence)] a face not to reckon with.

Notes

1. See for example, F.G. Bailey, *Caste and the Economic Frontier*, (OUP, 1958), p. VII; Robert L. hardgrave Jr., *The Nayars of Tamil Nadu*, (Bombay, 1969), p. 263; Eleanor Zelliot, 'Learning the Use of Political Means: The Mahars of Maharashtra', in Rajni Kothari, (ed.), *Caste in Indian Politics*, (New Delhi, 1973), p.39; David Washbrook, 'The Development of Caste Organisation in South india, 1880 to 1925', in C.J. Baker and D.A Washbrook, *South India: Political Institutions and Political Change, 1880-1940*, (Delhi, 1975), pp. 176-177.
2. M.N. Srinivas, 'Mobility in the Caste System', in Milton Singer and B.S. Cohn, (eds.), *Structure and Change in Indian Society*, (Chicago, 1968), p. 194.
3. Demand for higher caste position or adoption of the so-called purer ritual symbols or 'Sanskritization' need not be taken as expressions of narrow social ambitions or mere emulation of the upper castes. For these also meant a protest against inferior social position and associated disabilities, as well as appropriation of certain symbols that had so long been the exclusive privileges of a few at the top. And the demand for a share in the economic resources and political power was indeed a challenge to the existing system of their distribution. For even in a supposedly changed situation under british rule, these were virtually monopolised by the upper castes.
4. See for example, Kathleen Gough, 'Indian Nationalism and Ethnic Freedom', in David Bidney, (ed.), *The Concept of Freedom in Anthropology*, (The Hague, 1963), pp. 174-175; Hetukar Jha, 'Lower Caste Peasants and Upper Caste Zamindars in Bihar (1921-1925): An Analysis of Sanskritization and Contradiction between the Two Groups', *The Indian Economic and Social History Review*, Vol. XIV No. 4, p. 556; Gyan Pandey, 'Rallying round the Cow: Sectarian Strife in the Bhojpuri Region, c 1888-1917', in Ranajit Guha, (ed.), *Subaltern Studies II* (Delhi, 1983). pp. 71-74.

5. See for example, John Gallagher, 'Congress in Decline: Bengal, 1930 to 1939', in John Gallagher, Gordon Johnson and Anil Seal, (eds., *Locality, Province and Nation: Essays on Indian Politics, 1870-1940*, (Cambridge, 1973), pp. 278-279; Sumit Sarkar, *The Swadeshi Movement in Bengal*, 1903-1908, (New Delhi, 1977), pp. 330-331, 392.
6. H.H. Risley, *The Tribes and Castes of Bengal*, (Reprint, Calcutta, 1981), Vol. I, p. 189; *Census of India*, 1901, Vol. VI, Part I, pp. 395-396; Vol. VIA, Part II, Table XIII, p. 246; *Bengal District Gazetteers*, B. Volume, (Calcutta, 1933), for the districts of Bakarganj, Faridpur, Jessore and Khulna; Naresh Chandra Das, *Namasudra Sampraday O Bangladesh*, (in Bengali), (Calcutta, 1368 B.S), p.1.
7. Report [of the enquiry made to investigate the desirability of appointing a special officer to look after the interests of the depressed classes in Bengal.] Appointment (Appointment), GB, File No. 5M-114 of 1928, A February 1930, Progs. Nos. 7-20, West Bengal State Archives, (hereafter WBSA).
8. H.H.Risley, op. cit., Vol. I, pp.183-185, 188; *Census of India* 1901, Vol. VI, Part I,P. 372; Digindra Narayan Bhattacharya, *Hindur Nabajagaran*, (in Bengali), (Calcutta, 1338 B.S.), pp.73-74
9. B.C. Allen, *et. al., Gazetteer of Bengal and North-East India*, (Reprint, Delhi, 1979),pp. 202, 300-301, 305, 342, 354-355.
10. H.H. Risley, *op. cit.*, Vol. I, pp. 185-186; Vol. II, Appendix I, p. 34.
11. Magistrate of Bakarganj to Census Supdt., Bengal, 7 October 1901; Magistrate of Mymensingh to Census Supdt., Bengal, 26 March 1902; Offg. Magistrate of Khulna to Census Supdt., Bengal, 16 October 1901, Risley Collection, (Microfilm), National Archives of India, (here after NAI), Roll No. 3; Mahananda Haldar, *Sri Sri Guruchand Charit*, (in Bengali), (Calcutta, 1943), pp. 119-120; Raicharan Biswas, *Jatiya Jagaran*, (in Bengali), (Calcutta, 1921), p. 1.
12. *Census of India*, 1911, Vol. V, Part II, pp. 370-373, Table XVI; J.C.Jack, *Bengal District Gazetteers. Bakarganj*, (Calcutta, 1918), p. 35; *Report on the Census of the District of Backergunge*, 1891, p. 7; *Report on Census of the District of Faridpur*, 1891, pp. 12-13; *Report on the Census of District of Dacca*, 1891, p.14; *Report on the Census of the District of Jessore*, 1891, p. 7; J.C. Jack, *Final Report on the Survey and Settlement Operations in the Bakarganj District. 1900 to 1908*, (Calcutta, 1915), pp. 46, 87; H. Beveridge, *The District of Bakarganj: Its History and Statistics*, (London, 1876), p. 190; Ratnalekha Ray, *Change in Bengal Agrarian Society. c 1760-1850*, (New Delhi, 1979), pp. 210-211.
13. *Census of India*, 1911, Vol. V, P. 379, Appendix to Table XVI, Part II.
14. *Report on the Census of the District of Backergunge*, 1891, p.8; *Bengal District Gazetteers. Bakarganj, op. cit.*, p. 73; L.S.S. O'Malley, *Bengal District Gazetteers, Jessore*, (Calcutta, 1912), p. 83; *Final Report on the Survey and Settlement Operations in the Bakarganj District 1900 to*

1908, op. cit., pp. 70, 168; J.C. Jack., *Final Report on the Survey and Settlement Operations in the Faridpur District. 1904-1914*, (Calcutta, 1916), pp. 20-22, 29, 31-32, 39; M.A. Momen, *Final Report on the Survey and Settlement Operations in the District of Jessore. 1920-1924*, (Calcutta, 1925), pp. 113, 123.

15. *Final Report on the Survey and Settlement Operations in the Faridpur District, 1904-1914. op. cit.*, p.25; *Bengal District Gazetteers. Jessore. op. cit.*, pp..84-85, 119; H. Beveridge, *op. cit.*, p. 192; Radha Kamal Mukherjee, Bangla O Bangali, (in Bengali), (Calcutta, 1347 B.S.), p.77; Mahananda Haldar, *op. cit.*, pp. 266, 473-475; Sitanath Biswas, *Jatitattva O Namasyakulodarpan*, (in Bengali), (Dacca, 1931), pp. 132-148; Ratnalekha Ray, op. cit. p. 211.
16. C.S. Mead, *The Namasudras and Other Addresses*, (Adelaide, 1911), p. 59; Mahananda Haldar, *op. cit.*, pp. 61-65, 98-100; Naresh Chandra Das, *op. cit.*, p.4.
17. *Census of India* 1911, Vol. V, Part II, Table XVI, pp. 370-373; Sitanath Biswas, *op. cit.*, pp. 132-154; Naresh Chandra Das, op. cit., p. 33.
18. H.H. Risley, *op. cit.*, Vol. I, p. 187; H. Beveridge, *op. cit.*, pp. 260-265.
19. For a recent study on the emergence of a Bengali Muslim identity, see Rafiuddin Ahmed, *The Bengal Muslims, 1871-1906: A Quest for Identity*, (Delhi, 1981).
20. Raicharan Biswas, *op. cit.*, pp. 4, 48-49; Rashbehari Ray, *Namasudra Darpan*, Vol. I, (in Bengali), (Khulna, 1910), p. 159; Buddheswar Biswas, *Kuloddeepan Namahchandrika*, (in Bengali), (Barisal, 1328 B.S.), pp. 1-2, 20-30; Sitanath Biswas, *op. cit.*, pp. 117-118.
21. Raicharan Biswas, *op. cit.*, pp. 1, 17, 48-49, 124.
22. Revd. P. Noble, Baptist Mission, to Commissioner of Dacca Division, 15 October 1917, Political (Political), GB, File No. 8A-10, B November 1917, Prog. No. 65, WBSA; C.S. Mead, *op. cit.*, pp. 9, 11, 14, 17, 22, 63, 116, 123.
23. Dist. Supdt. of Police to Magistrate of Faridpore, 18 March 1873, Judicial Dept., GB, A March 1873, Prog. No. 179, WBSA.
24. Magistrate of Faridpur to Commissioner of the Dacca Division, 8 April 1873, Judicial Dept., GB, A May 1873, Prog. No. 57, WBSA.
25. Offg. Commissioner of the Dacca Division to the Secretary to the Govt. of Bengal, Judicial Dept., 14 April 1873, Judicial Dept., GB, May 1873, Prog. No. 56, WBSA.
26. Tarak Chandra Sarkar, *Sree Sree Harileelamrita*, (in Bengali), (Faridpur, 1323 B.S.), pp. 13, 59-60, 66-67, 107.
27. Mahananda Haldar, *op. cit.*, pp. 567-574; Naresh Chandra Das, *op. cit.*, p. 15.
28. Magistrate of Khulna to Commissioner of the Presidency Division, 5 June 1911, Political (Police), GB, File No. P5R-1, B July 1911, Progs. Nos. 326-328, WBSA; Inspector General of Police to the Chief Secy.,

Govt., of Bengal, September 1911, Political (Police), GB, File No. P3P-34, B February 1912, Progs. Nos. 43-48, WBSA.
29. Naresh Chandra Das, *op. cit.*, pp. 16-17.
30. C.S. Mead, *op. cit.*, pp. 12-14; Mahananda Haldar, *op. cit.*, pp. 110-114, 119-120; Naresh Chandra Das, *op. cit.*, p. 38.
31. Sitanath Biswas, *op. cit.*, p. 157; Nirmal Kumar Bose, *The Structure of Hindu Society*, translated from Bengali by André Beteille, (New Delhi, 1975), p. 158.
32. *Bengal District Gazetteers, Jessore, op. cit.*, p. 50.
33. Revd. P. Noble, Baptist Mission to Commissioner of Dacca Division, 15 October 1917, *op. cit.*, Sitanath Biswas, *op. cit.*, pp. 157, 160.
34. General (Miscellaneous), GB, File No. 10C-4, B August 1901, Prog. No. 1, Notes, pp. 1-2, WBSA; Mahananda Haldar, *op. cit.*, pp. 255-258; Naresh Chandra Das, *op. cit.*, pp. 37, 68.
35. *Census of India*, 1901, Vol. VI, Part I, p. 250; 1911, Vol. V, Part I, Subsidiary Table V, pp. 351-355; H.H. Risley, *op. cit.*, Vol. I, pp. 184, 186; Sasikumar Badoi Biswas, *Namasudra Dwijatattva*, (in Bengali), (Barisal, 1911), pp. 90-99.
36. *Census of India*, 1911, Vol. VVI, Part I, pp. 309- 310; 1911, Vol. V, Part I, pp. 359-360; Rashbehari Ray, *op. cit.*, p. 155; Mahananda Haldar, *op. cit.*, pp. XIV, 100-102, 108, 123; Naresh Chandra Das, *op. cit.*, pp. 48-49.
37. *Census of India*, 1911, Vol. V, Part II, Table XVI, pp. 370-373; Mukunda Behari Mullick, Forward, in Raicharan Biswas, *op. cit.*, p. 6.
38. Quoted in Sufia Ahmed, *Muslim Community in Bengal*, 1884-1912, (Dacca, 1974), p. 257.
39. Mahananda Haldar, *op. cit.*, pp. 205-206; Sitanath Biswas, *op. cit.*, p. 157; Naresh Chandra Das, *op. cit.*, pp. 36-37; Nirmal Kumar Bose, *op. cit.*, p. 159.
40. 'Report on the political situation in Eastern Bengal and Assam' for February 1911, Home (Political), GI, A April 1911, Prog. No. 20, NAI.
41. General (Education), GB, File No. 11C-9-1, A April 1913, Prog. No. 67; File No. 11C-47, A September 1913, Progs, Nos. 14-15, Notes, pp. 1-2; File No. 1E-8 (1-2), A January 1917, Progs. Nos. 14-17 WBSA.
42. Fortnightly Report on the agitation in Eastern Bengal and Assam for the period ending 16 June 1907, Home (Political), GI, A July 1907 , Prog. No. 188; Fortnightly Report.... for the second half of August 1908, Appendix II, Home (Political), GI, A October 1908, Prog. No. 104, NAI; General (Education), GB, File No. 11C-9, A April 1913, Prog. No. 67 WBSA.
43. Hem Chandra Sarkar, Secy., Depressed Classes Mission to Registrar General Dept., 15 July 1916, General (Education), GB, File No. IE-8, A January 1917, Progs. Nos. 14-17, WBSA.
44. See Note 22.

45. General (Education), GB, File No. 1H-34, A June 1912, Progs. Nos. 34-50; File No. 11C-64, A September 1917, Progs. Nos. 111-112, Notes, pp. 1-2; File No. IH-2 B May 1920, Progs, Nos.34-44, WBSA; *Bengal Legislative Council Proceedings*, (hereafter BLCP), Vol. 46, 1 September 1914, p. 840; Vol. 50, 14 March 1918, p. 306, 28 March 1918, p. 491.
46. *Namasudra Suhrid*, May 1911, 'Selections from Vernacular Newspapers in Eastern Bengal and Assam for the week ending 24 June 1911', WBSA.
47. General (Education), G, B File No. 11C-112, A December 1919, Progs. Nos. 244-245, WBSA.
48. Appointment (Appointment), GB, File No. ID-1, A November 1922, Progs Nos. 114-417, Appendix E, p. XVII; Notification No. 7721A, 30 July 1923, Appointment (Appointment), GB, File No. 1D-1, A October 1923, Progs. Nos. 3-19, WBSA.
49. Commissioner, Dacca Division, to Chief Secy. Govt. of Bengal, 22 November 1930; Collector of Bakarganj to Commissioner, Dacca Division, 11 September 1930, Appointment (Appointment), GB, File No. 4-D-10 of 1930, A June 1931, Progs. Nos. 36-41, also Appendix A & B and Notes, p. 3, WBSA.
50. 'Statements', Appointment, GB, File No. 8L-35 of 1932, B April 1933, Progs. Nos. 429-430, WBSA; BLCP Vol. 41, No. 2, 28 March 1933, pp. 634-635.
51. *The Bengalee*, 6, 10, 11 November 1917.
52. *The Statesman*, 6 November 1918; Naresh Chandra Das, *op. cit.*, p. 38.
53. Appointment (Reforms), GB, File No. 6R-2, A April 1920, Progs. Nos. 3-10, Notes, pp. 13-14, also Appendix B, WBSA.
54. 'Notes on the Communal Award.....' by Rai Sahib P. Barma ; 'Note' by Sarat Chandra Bal, Appointment (Reforms), GB, File No. IR-90, B August 1933, Progs. Nos. 870-886, WBSA; *Report of the Bengal Franchise Committee*, (Calcutta, 1932), p. 23; Mahananda Haldar, *op.cit.*, pp. 284-285.
55. Rajani Kanta Das, *Bangiya Namasudra Conference*, (in Bengali, Firozpur,1922), pp. 17-18, 23.
56. *Report of the Bengal Franchise Committee, op.cit.*, p. 24; BLCP, Vol. 14, No. 1, 24 January 1924, pp. 39-40.
57. 'Minute on the Depressed Classes by Mr. M.B. Mullick', *Report of the Bengal Franchise Committee, op.cit.*, pp. 23-24.
58. Letters from various district officers in Appointment (Appointment), GB, File No. 5M-114 of 1928, A February 1930, Progs. Nos. 7-20, WBSA.
59. 'Memorandum on the National Volunteer Movement, Bengal and Eastern Bengal and Assam' by C.J. Stevenson Moore, 11 September 1907, Home (Political), GI, Deposit, October 1907, No. 19; Fortnightly Report..... For the second half of November 1907, Home (political), GI,

A January 1908, Prog. No.53; 'Report on Samitis in Dacca Division, Eastern Bengal and Assam, 1908', Home (Political), GI, Deposit, April 1909, No. 2, NAI.

60. Mahananda Haldar, op.cit., pp. 168-176, 262, 403; Raicharan Biswas, *op. cit.*, pp. 72-78.
61. 'Annual Report on Indian Papers Printed or Published in the Bengal Presidency during 1917', Home (Confidential), GB, File No. 129(1-6) of 1918, WBSA; BLCP, Vol. I, No. 5, 14 March 1921, p. 43; Buddheswar Biswas, *op.cit.*, p. 31; Raicharan Biswas, *op. cit.*, pp. 85-90.
62. Judith M. Brown, *Gandhi's Rise to Power*, (Cambridge University Press, 1972), pp. 346, 353, 356.
63. Mahananda Haldar, *op.cit.*, pp. 413-415.
64. BLCP, Vol. I, No. 4, 2 March 1921, pp. 158-160; Vol.4, 29 August 1921, pp. 113-115, 121.
65. Mahananda Haldar, *op.cit.*, pp.442-443; Rajat K. Ray, 'Masses in Politics: The Non-cooperation Movement in Bengal, 1920-1922' *The Indian Economic and Social History Review*, Vol. XI, No. 4, December 1974, pp.406-407.
66. Dist. Magistrate, Faridpur to Commissioner, Dacca Division, 21May 1923, Police, GB, File No. P5R-11/23, B May 1924, Progs Nos. 110-149, WBSA.
67. Quoted in J.H Broomfield, Elite *Conflict in a Plural Society: Twentieth Century Bengal*, (California, 1968), p. 273.
68. Appointment, GB, File No. 15A-2, B September 1929, Prog. No. 81, Abstract, WBSA; Reform Office, GI, File No. 163/III/30-R, NAI.
69. Home (Confidential), GB, File Nos. 599 of 1930, 597 (1-3) of 1930, 345 (1-3) of 1931; Fortnightly Report... for the second half of June 1930, WBSA; Sitanath Biswas, *op. cit.*, pp., 117-118.
70. Mahananda Haldar, *op. cit.*, pp. 168-176.
71. *Final Report on the Survey and Settlement Operations in the Bakarganj District, 1900 to 1908, op. cit.*, Appendix G-V.
72. Telegram from Govt. of Eastern Bengal and Assam to the Secy., Govt. of India, Home Dept., 26 September 1907, Home (Political), GI, B October 1907. Prog. No. 31: 'Report on Samitis in the Dacca Division, Eastern Bengal and Assam, 1908', op. cit., Fortnightly Report...for the second half of August 1908, Appendix II, Home (Political), GI, A October 1908, Prog. No. 104, NAI.
73. Resume of affairs in Bakarganj for 1907, Home (political), GI, A April 1908, Prog, No. 24, NAI.
74. Confidential diary of the Supdt. of Police, Bakarganj, for week ending 6 July 1907, Home (Political), GI, A August 1907, Prog. No. 110; Fortnightly Report .. for the first half of October 1907, Home (Political), GI, A November 1907, Prog. No. 18; Diary of Mr. Higjes-Buller, District Magistrate of Bakarganj for the month of January 1908, Home (Political), GI, A April

1908, Prog. No. 24; Weekly Report of the Director of Criminal Intelligence, 11 April 1908, Home (Political), GI, B May 1908, Prog. No. 38, NAI.

75. 'History of Non-cooperation Movement in Bengal', Home (confidential), GB, File No. 395 of 1924, WBSA; also Rajat K. Ray, 'Masses in Politics: The Non-cooperation Movement in Bengal, 1920-1922', *op. cit.*, passim.
76. Mahananda Haldar, *op. cit.*, pp. 413-415.
77. 'History of the Non-cooperation Movement in Bengal', *op. cit.*, p. 10; District Magistrate, Bakarganj to Commissioner of Dacca Division, 26 December 1921, Home (Confidential), GB, File No. 39 (129-137) of 1921, WBSA.
78. BLCP, Vol. 7, No. 20 February 1922, p.9.
79. See Note 69.
80. Kathleen Gough, *op. cit.*, pp. 174-175.
81. Weekly Report of the Director of Criminal Intelligence, 21 September 1907 Home (Political), GI, B October 1907, Prog. No. 47, NAI; *Bengal District Gazetteers, Jessore, op. cit.*, p. 50.
82. *Mussalman*, 29 May 1908; Magistrate of Khulna to Commissioner of the Presidency Division, 5 June 1911, Political (Police), GB, File No. P5R-1, B July 1911, Progs. Nos. 326-328, WBSA.
83. Report on the political situation in Eastern Bengal and Assam for April 1909, Home (Political), GI, A June 1909, Prog. No. 125, NAI.
84. Weekly Report of the Director of Criminal Intelligence, 7 August 1909, Home (Political), GI, B September 1909, Prog. No. 47, NAI.
85. Chief Sec., Govt. of Bengal to Secy., Govt. of India, Home Dept., 4 November 1926, Home (Confidential), GB, File No. 516 of 1926; Commissioner of the Presidency Division to Chief Secy., Govt., of Bengal, 9 January 1929, Appointment (Appointment), GB, File No. 5M-114 of 1928, A February 1930, Progs Nos. 7-20, WBSA.
86. District Magistrate, Dacca to Commissioner of Dacca Division, 18 October 1929, Home (Confidential), GB, No. 610 (1-5) of 1929, WBSA.
87. For details of the commutation proceedings, see *Final Report on the Survey and Settlement Operations in the Bakarganj District, 1900 to 1908, op. cit.*, pp. 167-168 and Appendix G-I, G-II, G-V, G-VII, G-IX.
88. *Final Report on the Survey and Settlement Operations in the Faridpur District, 1904-1914. op. cit.*, pp. 32, 94, 103.
89. Forthnightly Report..for the latter half of January 1909 Home (Political), GI, A March 1909, Prog. No. 105; Fortnightly Reports month of February 1909, Home (Political), GI, A April 1909, Prog, No. 52; Fortnightly Report... for the first half of March 1909, Home (Political), GI, A May 1909, GI, A May 1909, Prog. No. 131; Weekly Report of the Director of Criminal Intelligence, 9 October 1909, Home (Political), GI, B November 1909, Prog. No. 34; Chief Secy., Govt. of Eastern Bengal and Assam to Secy; Govt. of India, Home Dept., 20 October 1909, Home (Political), GI, A December 1909, Prog. No. 16. NAI.

90. Report on the Political Situation in Eastern Bengal and Assam for November 1909, Home (Political), GI, A January 1910, Prog. No. 127, NAI.
91. Commissioner, Presidency Division to Chief Secy., Govt. of Bengal, 9 January 1929; Magistrate of Jessore to Commissioner, Presidency Division, 2 January, 1929; District Magistrate, Khulna to Commissioner, Presidency Division, 2 January 1929, Appointment (Appointment), GB, File No. 5M-114 of 1928, A February 1930, Progs. Nos. 7-20, WBSA.
92. Magistrate of Khulna to Commissioner of the Presidency Division, 5 June 1911, Political (Police,) GB, File, No. P5R-1, B July 1911, Progs. Nos. 326-328; District Magistrate, Faridpur to Commissioner, Dacca Division, 21 May 1923, Police, GB File No. P5R-11/23, B May 1924, Progs. Nos. 110-149; Superintendent of Police, Faridpur to Asst. Inspector General of Police, Bengal, 23 July, 1925, Police, GB, File No. P5R-2 (4-12)/25, B March 1926, Progs. Nos. 95-103, also Home (Confidential), G.B, File No. 248/38, WBSA.
93. District Magistrate, Jessore to Commissioner of the Presidency Division, 2 June 1911; Commissioner of the Presidency Division to Chief Secy., Govt. of Bengal, 9 June 1911, Political (Police), GB, File No. P5R-1, B July 1911, Progs. Nos. 326-328, WBSA.
94. Rajani Kanta Das, *op. cit.*, pp. 9-11, 20 23.
95. *BLCP*, Vol. 1, No. 6, 1 April, 1921, p. 79; Vol. 3, 4 July 1921, p. 72, 7 July 1921, pp. 306-308, 12 July 1921, p. 495-496; Vol. 7, No. 3, 27 February 1922, p.3.
96. BLCP, Vol. 34. No. 3, 31 March 1930, p. 632; Vol. 41, No. 1, 20 February 1933, p. 44,
97. Education (Education), GB, File No. 2P-57 of 1925, B July 1926, Progs. Nos. 715-719, Abstract; File No. 10C-8, B July 1926, Progs. Nos. 256-257, Abstract; File No. 3p-11, B July 1926, Progs. Nos. 263-264, Abstract; File; No. 2p-35, B June 1927, Progs, Nos. 895-896, WBSA; BLCP, Vol. 34, No. 3, 18 March 1930, p. 80, 19 March 1930, p. 158; 25 March 1930, pp. 432-433.
98. Appointment, GB, File No. 15A-2, B September 1929, Prog. No. 81, Abstract, WBSA; Reforms Office, GI, File No. 163/III/30-R, NAI; Naresh Chandra Das,. *op. cit.*, p. 39, 52-55; Sitanath Biswas, *op. cit.*, p. 160.
99. Amulyadhan Ray, Secy., All Bengal Depressed Classes Federation to Private Secy. to the Governor of Bengal, 11.9.32, Appointment (Reforms), GB, File No. 1R-90, B August 1933, Progs. Nos. 870-886, WBSA.
100. Reforms Office, GI, File No. 163/III/30-R and K.W. of 35/31-R, NAI.
101. 'Minute on the Depressed Classes by M.B. Mullick', *Report of the Bengal Franchise Committee, op. cit.*, pp. 21-23.

102. See Note 99.
103. Faridpur District Depressed Classes Association to the Government of India, 22 September 1932, Reforms Office, GI, File No. 199/R/1932, NAI.
104. Secretary, Faridpur District Depressed Classes Association, to Governor General and Viceroy of India, 25, September 1932, Reforms office, GI, File No. 199/R/1932, NAI.
105. 'Statement of the Bengal Depressed Classes Federation on the Poona Settlement,' 27.9. 32, Reforms Office, GI, File, No. 199/R/1932, NAI.
106. Rasiklal Biswas, Secy., All India Depressed Classes Federation to Reforms Officer, Govt. of India, 19 December 1932, Appointment (Reforms), GB, File No. IR-2 of 1933, A April 1934, Progs, Nos. 9-61, WBSA; R.C. Roy Jt. Secy., Bengal Depressed Classes Association to Viceroy of India, 27 September 1932, Reforms Officer, GI, File No. 199/R/1932, NAI.
107. R.C. Roy, Jt. Secy., Bengal Depressed Classes Association to Viceroy of India, 19 October 1932, Reforms Office, GI, File No. 199/R/1932, NAI.
108. *BLCP*, Vol. 41, No. 2, 14 March 1933, pp. 99-103, 109-114.
109. Md. Enamul Huq-Khan 'A.K. Fazlul Huq and Muslim League in Bengal, 1906-1947', Unpublished Ph.D. Thesis, Punjab University, Chandigarh, 1982, Chapter III, particularly pp. 54-56, 64-69; also Naresh Chandra Das, *op cit.*, p. 55.
110. 'Conference of the Commissioner. Draft of a Memorandum on the General Political and Economic Situation in Bengal...'. Home (Confidential), GB, File, No. 689/33, WBSA.
111. 'Statement II: Detailed Statement showing the results of election to the Bengal Legislative Assembly, 1937', 'Statement showing the strength of various parties in the Bengal Legislative Assembly', Home (Constitution and Elections), GB, File No. R 3E-27, A May 1937, Progs. Nos. 1-13; Report on the Political Situation in Bengal for the second half of January, 1937, Home (Confidential), GB, File No. 10/37, WBSA; Mahananda Haldar, *op cit.*, pp. 550-551.
112. *Star of India*, 1 April 1937; also Report on the Political Situation in Bengal for the second half of March 1937, Home (Confidential), GB, File No. 10/37, WBSA.

2

Caste and Power in West Bengal

Ranabir Samaddar

Don Quixote of Scheduled Caste Politics

I shall begin with an example from the area where I work as a teacher in a college. It is situated in the northern tip of the 24-Parganas district, predominantly inhabited by Scheduled Castes like Namasudras and Muslims. It is close to the border of Bangladesh, some sixty kilometers away from Calcutta. It is an area formerly having close connections with Jessore and Khulna, where the trauma of Pakistan has been direct, and where uprooted people from East Pakistan came. This is an area where the idea of an axis between low castes and Muslims against the domination of upper castes was tried without any result.[1] An alternative spiritual and religious identity has been articulated going by the name of 'Matua', but, this too, while being successful in its limited sphere like the holding of an annual fair, the setting up of a 'Guru', who originally was Teckchand Thakur,[2] has had no success whatsoever in providing a separate socio-political identity to the *dalits*[3] of the area. The subdivisions like Bangaon, Basirhat and particularly the blocks like Bangaon, Gaighata, Habra, Baduria, etc., had witnessed in the past mighty peasant struggles during the Tebhaga and the post-Tebhaga phases—all under the Red Flag leadership of the Kisan Sabha. The dominant groups that joined the struggle were the Muslims and the peasant castes like Namasudras—a low caste, who were not bonded labourers, but worked as sharecroppers. Bauris were poor peasants and rural labourers who too joined the struggle. The Sadgops, also a peasant caste, were in the struggle too.

Frankly speaking, to the best of my knowledge, the Kisan Sabha never made any analysis of caste-wise participation in the peasant struggles. Later on, during the land reform programmes of the United Front and the Left Front governments, the peasants and rural poor have benefited. However, nobody has referred to the castes of beneficiaries of the land reforms. I am also ill-informed about caste-arithmetic of the struggle, land reforms, distribution of land, literacy, and so on.

In this milieu emerged the Don Quixote of the Schedule Caste politics of that area. Since he is a real-life character, I shall refer to him as X. He teaches Bengali in a local college, has done his doctoral dissertation on folk-literature, and certainly is a somebody as a Ph. D. among the Namasudras. As a student, he founded the West Bengal Scheduled Castes and Scheduled Tribes Students and Youth Organisation in 1960. The same year he started the *Bharat Bani Patrika*—a fortnightly journal as the organ of the *dalits* which still continues. He is the chief organising secretary of the Backward Classes, Scheduled Castes and Scheduled Tribes Confederation formed in 1985. In 1979, he founded the Democratic Socialist Party as the forum of the backward castes, which however, has remained a virtual non-starter. He has written a book and several articles on the Matua religion. Along with these activities, particularly during the early stages of his active life, he was a prominent activist of the Youth Congress and student organisations. For the Left, he only has contempt. The Left political leadership, he feels, is spurious and high caste dominated. The Left peasant movements for land and sharecropping rights, he feels, are limited, for they do not touch the vital question of caste hierarchy. When the Maribjhanpi massacre was organised by the Left Front government to forcibly drive away the low caste Bengali refugees from West Bengal back to Dandakaranya, he found the pattern of events to be exactly conforming to his assertions regarding the Left Front and the Communist Parties as the parties led by high castes. He has connections with Kansi Ram of Bahujan Samaj Party and Raj Shekhar of Karnataka. He takes pride in such associations. You may think now that this is an ideal milieu from where he could have taken off for organising the Scheduled Castes on a political platform, but he has preferred to remain a 'son of the soil', a political activist, a social worker, and therefore has remained a Don Quixote uptil this day. In the 1982 assembly elections, he contested from Gaighata reserved constituency and secured 831 votes. In 1987, he shifted to Bangaon, another reserved constituency and secured even less 382 votes.

A section of Naxalites, the CPI(ML) led by Santosh Rana, has in recent times tried to fuse class and caste as a workable strategy. Muslims, as a separate religious identity, have also been included in that strategy. It has failed miserably. Though the articulation of demands has of course mobilised some *dalits* and Muslims, the demands like reservation of jobs, implementation of the Mandal Commission report, etc. in particular, have attracted the Muslims and the backwards. But as a political tactic, it has neither achieved support from traditional Left, nor from the Naxalite revolutionaries. The Muslim League won one seat in 24-Parganas in 1987 and received substantial votes in several other constituencies. But Santosh Rana's effort to oppose Jyoti Basu in Satgachia riding piggyback on the Muslim League, flopped and we are back to square one. The Scheduled Castes in Bengal do not have a separate political identity, nor are there indications that they desire it. Yet, there is caste hierarchy, caste inequality, and the low castes are identified with poverty, exploitation and destitution. Can we speak of caste oppression? Can we speak of caste struggles? There are symptoms of a 'caste question' getting tense here. However, there is no political articulation. As we saw, both our man X and Santosh Rana failed. The politics here is dominated by politics. That is the issue before us today.

The Current Situation

The election manifesto of one Scheduled Caste candidate[4] contesting as an independent for the West Bengal assembly elections of 1987 shows a glimpse of that twilight zone where class and caste realities merge in the articulation of the aspirations of the *dalit* community. It starts with the recommendations of the Mandal Commission in 1980 that fifteen per cent of jobs should be reserved for the Scheduled Castes, 7.5 per cent for the Scheduled Tribes and twenty-seven per cent for the backward communities and laments that the Left Front government in Bengal and the Congress government at the centre are ignoring the recommendations for the upliftment of the weaker sections. It then looks at the class scenario and finds the *dalits* numbering twenty-seven crores still below the poverty-line. The *dalits* living in cities are also poor. There is no ceiling as regards urban assets, and the backward communities, who are mostly peasants also suffer as there is no crop insurance, no remunerative price for cash crops, etc. From 1972 to 1980, 3,200 people belonging to Scheduled Castes and Scheduled Tribes were murdered, 4,400 women raped, 5,540 dwellings burnt down. The manifesto notes that these are in reality class oppressions—the result of a policy of denying democratic rights to the *dalits* who are today becoming vocal in their protest against oppression by the powerful upper castes/classes. Hence, a fight on a Scheduled Caste platform is not merely a social fight but a political fight as well. The manifesto argues that while of the all-India government jobs and services 5.6 per cent have gone to the Scheduled Castes and the Scheduled Tribes, and 4.6 per cent to backward communities, the West Bengal situation is even worse as only 1.8 per cent of the class I jobs and 2.6 per cent of the class II jobs are taken away by the Scheduled Castes and 0.3 per cent of class I and 0.5 per cent of class II jobs by the Scheduled Tribes.

No doubt, pressure groups are arising from among *dalits* and backward communities like Rajbansis in some areas of North Bengal. It seems that social tensions will take a casteist form in certain parts of Bengal. One can give an analogy. Surely there is no 'nationality' repression or 'tribal' repression as such in West Bengal. But did that prevent the Gorkhaland movement from being articulated as an assertion of self-identify of the hill people, of their democratic rights? We have to remember that an Uttarakhand movement in North Bengal has a high degree of caste content, the forerunner of which was the Uttarbanga Tapashili Jati and Adivasi Sangathan.

Let us look at some figures quickly before getting into more substantive questions. These figures will show that there is a substantive basis of a 'caste question' in West Bengal, which is denied explicit articulation in the present political situation. Out of the Scheduled Castes, eleven per cent live in West Bengal alone. In one district, Jalpaiguri in North Bengal, as much as thirty-four per cent are *dalits*. This is why, North Bengal is having all sorts of separatist tendencies like Kamtapuri movement etc. The district where I work only recently, has 21.68 per cent Scheduled Caste population of the total population of 24-Paraganas. There are fifty-nine *dalit* communities. These include Dhoba, Jalia, Kaibarta, Namasudras, Poundra, Hari, Lohar, Rajbanshi, Muchi Bagdi, etc. These communities are engaged in handicrafts, scavenging, tanning, fishing, etc. The literacy rate is 17.80 per cent. Most of the *dalits* are workers engaged as agricultural labourers known as Bagdi, Bauri, Bhangi, Mal, etc. A few are peasant castes as well like Rajbanshi, Surri, etc. Of the fifty-nine communities, thirty-six belong to the first category.

However, it has been found that 81.38 per cent of the Scheduled Caste families own homestead land. Regarding ownership agricultural land the details are as follows:

Owned	33 per cent
Shared	11 per cent
Owned and Shared	18 per cent
Landless	38 per cent
Total	100

Today, with land reforms initiated by the Left Front Government, the situation may have marginally been improved, though the number of agricultural labourers has definitely increased.

Of the total assembly seats, fifty-nine seats are reserved for the Scheduled Castes. The Government of West Bengal has spent a lot of money on the welfare of the Scheduled Castes based on the recommendations of various committees constituted in the 1980s.[5]

In 1956-57, the total expenditure on the development of the Scheduled Castes was Rs. 50 lakhs in 1976-77, it increased to almost Rs. 6 crores, and in 1985-86 it was Rs. 44 crores. Nearly Rs. 34 lakh were spent last year on housing for the *dalits,* of which Rs. 20 lakhs were for the Scheduled Castes. The literacy rate increased from 17.80 per cent to 24.37 per cent during the decade 1971-81. The percentage of Government jobs for the Scheduled Castes also increased from 6.2 per cent to 12 per cent. Out of 14,77,329 beneficiaries of the distribution of land by the government, 5,50,000 are from among the Scheduled Castes and 3,00,000 are from Scheduled Tribes. About 60 per cent of the beneficiaries of the *barga* programme have been *dalits.* But then, one need not be over-impressed by these official figures, since the land is actually passing into the hands of prosperous peasants in West Bengal in the form of lease or sale. Even the developmental activities help contractors, middlemen, the *dalit* elite and party *baboos.* The studies by Mahasveta Devi in Jhargram of Midnapore district show that often the results at the ground level are nil.

Thus, the paradox of Bengal can be clearly posited now: There is an apparent basis for a 'caste question' here. Yet there is no 'caste question' in a politically significant way. It is not a serious issue, a populist agenda for even the power-grabbing politicians. A 'caste question', yet not acquiring the significance of a political question-as to why this is so is the question before us today.

A Confused Answer

Asok Mitra, in a series of articles[6], tried to respond to this query but the answer has been confused. In his words :

"Being an upper caste Hindu, and a self-regarding Bengali at that, I had begun life with the fond notion that, at least in Bengal, caste conflicts yield to class conflicts when it comes to the crunch. But one soon realised one's mistake and was convinced that West Bengal was essentially no different from the rest of India."

This, I repeat, is confusing. The point is not whether there are castes in Bengal as elsewhere, but why the form is different, as Mitra himself suggests that it is essentially different. He also suggests that *essentially* it is no different, which is to say, *formally*. For political activists, this is vital as they cannot rest content with such enquiries only. Let us briefly follow his arguments.

Caste and class realities always went hand in hand in Bengal. The Great Revenue Survey of 1850s was thus soon followed by the Great Caste Inquiries in 1890s. Caste conferred hegemony over subordinate people. Land was converted into a marketable commodity, which meant an accentuation of the hold of the upper caste landed gentry over the low caste rural poor. Plus, the *Raj* provided the administrative channels and the rule of law to the upper caste rich—the two great weapons for holding down the poor. In Bengal, this harsh reality of caste exploitation was hidden by the middle class behind the 'icon of class'—liberal connotation that could ignore social realities. If in the nineteenth century Bengal, a 'new class', born out of permanent settlement and assured of leisure and a secure coupon-clipping income, addressed itself against Hindu orthodoxy, today also, a 'new class' born of middle castes—a non-Brahmin aristocracy—has claimed that there is no caste-based backwardness in Bengal, no caste hierarchy, no caste oppression. This class, Bengal's new middle class, owes its existence to the growth of the service sector. It has spread to towns and villages. Its emphasis is on high technology, meritocracy, modern management and organisational techniques. If the earlier middle class spoke against caste in Bengal, today the middle class pretends there is no caste hierarchy and uses the acade of class theory for this pretension. There is one vital difference between the old and new middle class: "This new class, after the 1820s, being assured of a secure income addressed itself to the promotion of culture, which Bengal is so proud of today. The new middle class after 1960s abhorred culture and bereft of any investment outlet is today sunk in cultural debauchery."

Further, as Ashok Mitra argues, caste associations have been noticeably absent in West Bengal. The whole socio-cultural milieu is such that the backward castes are not productively motivated and this is the difference between the strength of the lower castes in Bengal and Bihar.

Half or nearly three-fifth of 38,000 villages are not endowed with *mandis* and thus they are cut off from the national wage and price policies and fluctuations therein. Thus, all in all, it is an atmosphere of leisure, parasitism, where caste-wise the power groups do not form armies of muscle men. So deceptive is the appearance, that even the Naxalites, who more than any other group have raised the peasant question in India, have neglected the fusion of caste and class for political reasons best known only to them.

There is no doubt that the role of the middle class is very crucial in West Bengal, more crucial than it is in any other state. The growth of the service sector accounts for them, just as B.B. Misra shows how a similar scenario existed in the later half of the nineteenth century when professional avenues opened up quickly. But then the growth of the middle class is not merely social, but political too. The partition has cut off the Bengal middle class from the big landed gentry of Bakharganj, Rajshahi, Dinajpur, etc., of the erstwhile East Bengal, and the rise of the rich and middle peasantry to political power in the countryside was welcomed by Calcutta-based urban politicians. This trend continues till date. The panchayat elections have formally given the middle class access to power in the sprawling countryside and the 'caste-in-limbo' situation persists today.

Look again at another political factor. The Left Front government policy is to stabilise the sharecroppers and its overall impact has been the stability of the middle peasantry in the countryside. Though it has not checked the impoverishment of the poor peasantry and the swelling of the ranks of agricultural labourers, it has meant a relative absence of a sharp class struggle between the landed gentry and the rural poor. In Bihar, as we have seen, this implies the struggle of the *dalits*. Asok Mitra has missed this point. Further, the policy of the Left Front government is to discourage the struggles of rural labour for minimum wages. Successive droughts and floods have weakened the farmers and labourers both and this too counts for a muted caste scenario. When the Left Front government first came to power, rural struggles flared up in Midnapore and Burdwan for fair wages. But the lid was quickly put on after the first term was over. The middle class is again the crucial political factor here. In fact, the whole social reform movement and the 'Renaissance' of the nineteenth century, which laid the ground for twentieth century liberalism, had all the imprints of a middle class.

Politically, our analysis must go deeper. If the middle class has helped in blunting caste antagonism, the struggles for land and civil rights have been equally important. The Tebhaga, and subsequently the peasant movements of the sixties, were revolutionary struggles where the dominant participants were tribals and poor peasants of *dalit* origin. The continuous trade union struggles in coal mines, plantations, tannery, printing, shoe-making, civic services, construction industry, etc., where *dalits* work in large numbers, have increased democratic awareness. Durgapur, Chittaranjan, Burnpore, Howrah, Calcutta, Budge and the large industrial belts on the two banks of Hooghly are the centres of large-scale industry where middle class educated youth have taken up jobs in large numbers. So too has worked the political factor of a militant student and youth movement and not merely in the metropolis, but also in the outlying district towns like Siliguri, Baharampore, Krishnanagar, Nabadwip, Burdwan, Suri, etc. These movements too have helped in creating a general democratic awareness and muting the caste factor.

It is amazing how Asok Mitra could ignore these phenomena under the omnibus term of 'middle class'. In a detailed and perceptive study of the industrial city of Howrah,[7] the authors have shown how a traditional low status cultivating caste like Mahishya could emerge as the dominant entrepreneurial group in an urban setting. They have found that unlike the traditional upper castes or the trading communities like Sabarnabaniks, the Mahishyas did not keep themselves ensconced in the caste entrepreneurial associations, and thus class stratification set in. But here too the political factor is ignored. For nowhere in this anthropological-psychological study do we find a mention of such militant union struggles of Burn, Guest-Keen, Remington, Howrah, Jute Mill, etc., nor of such democratic struggles like the Food Movement of 1966. We know that the youth of Howrah, so many belonging to Mahishya, participated in those movements. What impact did those movements have on them? Was it only because that many Mahishyas became salary earners, as the authors seem to imply, that caste solidarity did not function as a political factor except in the early fifties? We do not know.

In a discussion on the distribution of power in Andre Beteille's study of a village in South India, we do not find any mention of politics, and it seems that in the changing patterns of stratification in a Tanjore village politics has no role to play. There is no class struggle, no class politics, no political power to be aspired for. Similarly, when one analyst is refuting the notion of Sanskritization, the issue is posited and refuted not from a political but from a sociological angle.[9] The whole paradigm of tradition and modernity so prevalent in discussions on caste is empirically a false one since it does not count for the specificity of political struggles of considerable importance.[10] But whoever analyses the numerous incidents of caste violence in India will surely agree with me that political factors have been no less important than social factors.[11]

In harping on the specificity of the political factor, I do not wish to belittle the historical and social factors. Behind the phenomenon of muted caste struggles in Bengal today stands the Renaissance, and behind the Renaissance stands the Bhakti movement.[12] But, the then Bhakti movement has been elsewhere as well. How come that in Bengal it came to full fruition, while elsewhere this popular-democratic tradition could not counter the capitalist-landlord exploitation of the caste factor?

You have to accept, then, the legacy of the Communist movement, the struggles of Communist parties and groups, and the political significance of the legacy of popular democratic tradition. It can certainly be asked, as the Karnataka *dalit* ideologue has said, why this class line cannot be effectively pursued elsewhere?[13] Whereas some basic social reasons helped such a line in Bengal, elsewhere it may prove mechanical, in effect, "hiding caste behind the icon of class". The social disparities with respect to caste are still social; they exist, though still debarred from the domain of politics. But for how long will they be debarred is an important question.[14] As the GNLF movement showed, we do not know when the social questions will take the form of exclusive identities in an attempt to break away from political impasse, in fact political passivity born out of a revisionist politics so congenial to the middle classes of Bengal. Caste strings are there, particularly chaining the Scheduled Castes. They have not warmed up much as still the vast masses of rural and urban poor are regularly receiving political leadership from mass parties and organisations, though once again the middle class is the conduit. If politics is in a state of limbo here, so remains the 'caste question' too. It is there but remains suspended. And nothing short of a political breakthrough is going to end the impasse.

Notes

1. See biography of Jogendra Nath Mandal, a leader of the scheduled castes in pre-partition Bengal, "Mahapran Jogendranath" by Jagadishchandra Mandal (In Bengali), Calcutta, Mahapran Publishing Society.
2. Centenary Souvenir on the occassion of the awakening of Namasudras in Bengal, "Namasudra Jagaraner Satabarsha Purti Smarani", (in Bengali), Calcutta.

3. On the Namasudra Movement, I have written elsewhere in a book on the role of minorities in the Freedom Movement, "Bharater Jatiya Andolan O Jatiya Sanghatir Samasya" (in Bengali), Calcutta, 1985.
4. Published from Bangaon by Pratul Roy and Ranjit Banik in support of Paramananda Haldar.
5. These figures from "Scheduled Tribes and Scheduled Castes of West Bengal", Government of West Bengal, Calcutta, 1978.
6. "Caste and Class in Rural India', by Asok Mitra, Telegraph, Calcutta, from 22.7.86 to 26.7.86.
7. "The New Vaishas" by Raymond L Owens and Ashis Nandy, Calcutta, 1977.
8. "Caste, Class and Power" by Andre Beteille, Berkely, 1965.
9. K R V Rao in M N Srinivas, S Seshaiah and Parthasarathy, ed. Allied, Calcutta, 1977.
10. See, for example "Caste in Indian Politics", ed. by Rajni Kothari, "Introduction", by Rajni Kothari, Orient Longman, Delhi, 1970.
11. For example, "Caste and Communal Violence in Independent India", ed. by A R Desai, Bombay, 1985.
12. "The Structure of Hindu Society" by N K Bose, New Delhi, 1975.
13. The Statesman, 2.11.87.
14. See for example, 'A Study of Marathawada Riots: Aspects of Class and Caste in Social Tension', by S P Punalekar, Surat, 1981.

3

Caste-Class Situation in Rural West Bengal

Srijnan Halder

The dominating presence of caste in modern Indian society and politics poses several baffling questions to researchers. Not a single part of India is free from caste complexities leading to antagonism and conflicts. Nevertheless, the intensity and pattern of its influence vary according to historically determined socio-economic conditions of different regions. In this article, the role of caste in the West Bengal society and politics has been discussed. Tracing its origin in the history of Bengal, I, on one hand, focus on the aspiration of the rural middle castes who, with gradual modernization of agriculture, have emerged with new manipulative power as an articulate peasant class, and on the other hand have examined their relation with the palpable issue of education. I have also tried to analyse the current trends and present the possibilities for the future.

Social division, according to caste hierarchy, is a phenomenon unique to India. "The essence of caste is the arrangement of hereditary groups in a hierarchy", observes M.N. Srinivas.[1] Irfan Habib defines caste as "a fairly well-marked, separate community, whose individual members are bound to each other through endogamy (and hypergamy), and very often also by a common hereditary profession or duty, actual or supposed."[2] The other prevailing features of caste include restriction on food, drink and smoking, distinction in custom, dress and speech, pollution, ritual and other privileges and disabilities, caste organisation and caste mobility.[3]

If we concentrate on the functional level, we may say that the two distinct functions of this social institution are: (i) to ensure a more or less static mode of production in a hierarchically stratified society, and (ii) to provide a structure of ideological dominance for perpetuating a pre-modern social order based on inequality. In short, caste has a major power perspective in terms of domination and subordination in an essentially pre-modern setting. Thus, Kosambi correctly observes that "the caste system is designed to preserve Indian society in a static mold."[4] But a meaningful understanding of caste, as an institution of social relationship, is impossible without proper understanding of its relation to the distribution of power and property.[5] Hence, for understanding it, the political dimension becomes absolutely necessary. Moreover, in modern India, caste conflicts and contradictions among different caste categories and groups have pronounced conspicuously sharp contentions for power in the political arena rather than more layers in the hierarchical order.[6]

To a social scientist, the phenomenon of caste tension leads to a particular question, that is, whether the answer to the causes of caste tensions could be traced within the structure of caste itself, or one would have to examine the class structures and class relations of the society as well? As far as the political question is concerned, the caste problem cannot be analysed meaningfully without examining its relationship with the articulation of class interests in a broader social perspective. The relationship between class and caste is complex and has never been static. Their interdependence and interrelation in rural India is so unique that they demand a common analytical framework.

In this regard, we maintain that in the modern period (since the British conquest of India) caste is an empirical reality as well as a theoretical problem and can hardly be approached merely as a part of the feudal superstructure. It has a direct relation with the mode of production and it goes beyond that to supply a very powerful and extremely effective ideological apparatus to the bourgeois-landlord state for dividing and suppressing the democratic movements of the people,[7] besides having an important role in articulation of class interests. In the following section, the changing role of caste is traced in the pre-modern and the modern the socio-economic formations.

II

In pre-British India, two distinct modes of power remained intertwined in the agrarian society. The first was a communal mode wherein different patterns of power were vested in society as a whole and were held collectively. "The crucial element here lies in the fact that land, which in this situation, is the fundamental basis of life and social production, appears not as a product of labour but as its pre-supposition, as something which must be given or found before the labour process can commence."[8] In such a society, individual right or anything like that on land "flows from the prior authority of the community over the entire land."

The second, the feudal mode of power, may be defined in terms of relationship of physical domination and subordination where the life processes of the producers were necessarily brought under direct physical control for the purpose of production in varied forms.[9] In pre-British India, the state formation[10] incorporated both the modes creating areas of tension between them. In other words, a tension between the state and the society always existed. Presumably the intensity of such tension was never constant. The ideological factor was chiefly responsible for it. In this respect, caste played a significant role. For example, in ancient India, generally the Brahmins enjoyed much more social power than the state-owner Kshatriya kings. As the ideological leaders of society, the Brahmins controlled the mode of social behaviour. In the Hindu society, their position had never been challenged by the state. On the contrary, a nexus between the ruler and the Brahmins was essential for the ruling class to retain power. But, with the advent of Muslim rule, it became rather difficult for the Brahmins to influence the non-Hindu state. That does not mean in the slightest that the Brahminical dominance over society slackened under the Muslim rule. It was just the opposite. On the one hand, the Muslim rulers never questioned the authority of the Brahmins over the society, and on the other they did not in fact have any centralised state machinery to enforce an ubiquitous power over the society. Nor did they seriously, with an exception of Akbar, challenge the Brahminical dominance over the society.[11] Nevertheless, the distance between the two increased. Although many social scientists have shown that the influence of casteism supressed the boundary of the Hindu society and influenced not only the Muslim society but also the Sikh, the Christian and the Jewish societies.[12]

The feudal state opted out from intervening in the caste-based Brahminical authority. But the latter had to undergo certain important "adjustments and changes"[13] for the sake of its own existence. The reason for the resilience of its social domination under feudal state is interpreted by Habib: "The caste system helped to generate larger revenues from the village and lower the wage-costs in the cities, the Indo-Muslim regimes had every reason to protect it, however indifferent, if not hostile, they might be towards the Brahmins as the chief idol worshippers."[14]

The history of the state-society tension in India shows many characteristic features. One is that the jurisdiction of the feudal state was more militaristic than social and political. The despot and his feudal agents were generally considered externals to the society whose relational bond with the society was mainly economic, i.e., tax-collection. The basis of reckoning of revenue was never ownership of land but production, assessed on community basis and collected from the headman or the panchayat of a village. Social authority rested with the Brahmins either physically or through ideology. The second feature emphasizes on the ideological importance of casteism. It remains to be so strong as to absorb every shock rendered to it from both outside and inside the society.

It could withstand the bourgeois onslaught thrusted upon it through a colonial state which crushed the social authority of casteism to a large extent by extended authority through all encompassing administrative judicial and legislative means. The new State introduced another mode of social relations, viz., the capitalist mode of power. This mode brings in individual rather than the family, as the unit in political and legal transactions. Here "society is conceived of as the result of a contract between individuals and all individuals irrespective of differences."[15] The capitalist dominance is ensured in such a mode by complete control over the labour process through individual property rights over land and other means of production and the impersonal operation of the market.

What is important for our purpose is to know that through the introduction of a battery of impersonal operations and transactions in economic as well as politico-administrative spheres, the whole gamut of social relationships triggered off complex and long range tensions between the old and the new modes of power. It was a challenge to the colonial regime to introduce the institution of representative government in India, whatsoever limited and apparent its power might be. It was necessary for the sake of the capitalist state formation to destroy the peasant community and its communal ideology.

Caste as an institution and ideological structure served as the sriving force for communal authority. Therefore, theoretically, the existence of caste and the bourgeois state is so contradictory in terms that it is not possible for the two to co-exist. But, in practice, it happens. The paradox becomes possible because the caste system and the bourgeois state apply force on each other and change themselves in turn substantially. Hence, through complex process, caste system changed the bourgeois mode of power so far as its application in India is concerned, and in the process caste changed itself. The process is on and since the transfer of power in 1947, it has become and is becoming more and more complex. In that perspective, we shall examine the complex dynamics of caste-class relation as is evident in Bengal. But before that some historically specific features of Bengal regarding caste may be noted.

III

Before the Aryan influence, ancient Bengal was chiefly inhabited by the Austric and Dravida tribes. In some ancient Hindu, Jaina as well as Buddhist literatures like *Aitareya Aranyaka, Mahabharata, Bhagavata Purana, Dharmasutra by Bodhayana, Acharanga-Ayaranga Sutra* and *Aryamanjusri Mula*, etc., these tribes are referred as 'Dasyu', 'Mleccha', 'Papa' and 'Asura'. Their languages were as foreign and unintelligible to the Aryans as those of the birds.[16] Introduction of caste system on the Aryan pattern did not start until the fifth century A.D. To be precise, the Gupta dynasty (300-550 A.D.) primarily patronised the stratification of Bengal society on *varna* and *jati* lines. In the period of Pala dynasty (750-1135 A.D.),[17] castes lower than Brahmin were prominent. The Brahminical order was reinforced at the close of the Pala dynasty through the ideological stewardship of a Brahmin scholar named Bhavadev Bhatta.[18] But it was the Sena kings of Bengal (1095-1205 A.D.), among whom Bhilla Sena (1158-1179 A.D.) and Lakshman Sena (1179-1205 A.D.) are to be named separately, who tried their utmost to Aryanise the entire Bengal society against the pre-dominant tribal and non-Aryan influences. They eleborated the code of conduct for every caste and sub-caste and made strict rules for their application and declared those elements *patit* (degenerate) with whom they came into conflict as a social group. What is interesting here is that, unlike the previous dynasties, they tried to control the communitarian character of the peasant society. There is no doubt that the phenomenon weakened their social base significantly and the Muslim invasion followed exploiting the erosion of Lakshman Sena's social support.[19]

Historically, Bengal can claim at least two special features in regard to caste. First, there was only one Dvija caste, which was the Brahmin. The other two Dvija castes, namely, Kshatriya and Vaisya hardly existed in Bengal. Other than the Brahmins, all the castes in Bengal originated from large-scale mixing of local people and tribes. Those castes were mentioned to in the early writings as "Sankara". Thus, the caste structure in Bengal was divided into four broad layers. At the apex, there were Brahmins, below them in the hierarchy were placed the upper Sudras (referred to as "Uttam Sankara" in the *Brahaddharma Purana* and as "Sat Sudra" in the *Brahmavaivarta Purana*), then the lower dras, i.e., "Madhyam Sankara" and "Patit" or "Asat Sudra", respectively. Below these castes were the untouchables ("Antyaje" or "Adhama Sankara"). In all, the castes numbered between thirty-six to forty-one. The Melecchas and some tribes from within and outside Bengal were kept out of the caste society.[20]

The second special feature of Bengal was manifested in the cultural and ideological practices. In spite of all the efforts of the Sena kings, exclusiveness of the caste features was never followed so strictly as outside Bengal. Inter-caste marriages, occupational mobility, horizontal and vertical social mobility, etc., were fairly evident between the eighth and the thirteenth centuries A.D.[21] Moreover, it is significant that the Suhma, Sabara, Andhra, Bhilla, Meda, along with many other tribes and local clans, were allowed to continue their communal authority within the feudal state. Many of them were gradually incorporated as the lowest or on the fringe rung of the Hindu society along with their communal autonomy.[22]

In ancient Bengal, many religious sects preached humanism against caste-based divisions and humiliation. In fact, there was a tradition of such thought propagated by the Bhagavat followers, Sahaja Yanis, Buddhist Siddhāchāryas and some other Hindu scholars. In the Middle Ages, Vaisnavism under the guidance of Chaitanya Deva and the rich folk-culture of the Baulas openly preached against caste and communal aparthied. In the *Dohakosa* by Sarahapada (between the tenth and the twelfth centuries A.D.), the Brahminical authority over social and religious life was challenged. It was claimed that any person from any caste practising the Brahminical rites should be looked upon just as a Brahmin. Moreover, it declared that there was no separate caste like Brahmin or Sudra. Every person belonged to the same *jati*.

[Tayā na sūdram brāhmanādi jāti visesam bhabati siddham. Sarve lokā eka jāti nibaddhasca sahajameveti bhāva.]

Bhabisya Purana and *Vajrasucikopanisad* (973-981 A.D.) and the Buddhists preached the same idea.[23]

In the Chaitanya cult, Sudras and even Muslims could be welcomed as *gurus*. Sudra Ramananda and Muslim Haridasa were two well-known examples. The Baula sect (including the Aula, Baula, Sain, Kartabhaja, Darbesh communities) has advanced a bit forward. It rejects caste divisions, idols and other conspicuous Hindu customs. Muslim, Hindu, Bauls and Auls obey persons as their *gurus* or *sains* surpassing the religious boundaries.[24]

In the state structure of ancient Bengal, the Brahmins received less eminence up to the Gupta period. Contemporary evidences prove that only after the seventh century A.D. did the state gradually come under Brahminical dominance.[25] Previously, the Kayasthas "Sat Sudra" caste enjoyed near monopoly in the state administration. Although the political power of the Brahmins increased gradually, culminating during the Sena period. The Kayasthas, and to some extent, the Vaidyas (Ambostha Vaidya) continued to occupy the bureaucratic ranks of the feudal state.[26] The Kaivartas (fishermen or boatmen), who were referred to as "Patit" or "Sudras" in the *Brahmavaivarta Purana* and who had a close association with the peasant caste Mahisya, had been considered as a strong, integrated and militant caste.[27] They rebelled at the close of the Pala dynasty and established a Kaivarta kingdom in the north-eastern part of Bengal (Varendra) between 1075-1100 A.D.[28] There is no evidence to believe that the lower caste Kaivarta kings tried to challenge either the dominating role of Brahmins in the mode of production or their monopoly of social authority.

Through our presentation of some selected historical facts and features of ancient and medieval Bengal, we wish to show: (1) historically the communal (communitarian) society had been very powerful in Bengal, it always resisted and never fell in line exactly in the North Indian caste structure as it could be in regard to some other societies; and (2) some peasant castes like Chasi Kaivarta, Mahisya, Aguri (Ugra), etc., have been striving for centuries to achieve higher social status and power in Bengal.

But the Hindu society, after Muslim occupation, gradually distanced from the state and insulated itself to a great extent. Such a closed society became more and more reactionary under the Nabadwip ideologues who vied with one another regarding how accurately they could fall in the North Indian Hindu mainstream. This ideology of abhorrence went directly against the humanitarianism found among the people of Bengal. In this Chaitanya's humanistic anti-apartheid religious movement comes as an important landmark.

The above mentioned struggles in the ideological and political domains had a direct relation with the caste-class situation in Bengal. In ancient Bengal, trade (both inland and overseas) and craft were two main sources of income. Up to the seventh century A.D., agriculture was less important. Hence, the "Banik" or merchant castes enjoyed importance in the state. But since the eighth century A.D., they retreated[29] and the Sena king Bhallala (1158 A.D.-1179 A.D.), who was hostile to them, demoted them (particularly the Subarna Baniks) to the "Patit" or "Asat

Sudra" status. To contain their hostility, it seems, he upgraded the Kaivartas along with some other service castes.[30] In fact, between the eighth and the thirteenth centuries A.D., the Bengal society, to match the growing importance of agriculture, came under the control of the feudal mode[31] which was complemented by Brahaminical dominance over the society. The artisans and the service classes were subsequently degraded.[32] Vivid caste divisions seemed to strengthen with the growth of feudalism in Bengal.[33] Still, the feudal state had to compromise with the communal mode of power and the caste structure reflected it on ideological as well as economic and political planes.

IV

The British colonial system was first introduced in Bengal. The peasant struggles in colonial Bengal were never devoid of communal fervour.[34] Such movements became popular where people from the peasant castes participated in them in large numbers. The demand for increased share for the sharecroppers and other anti-landlord demands got the support of the peasant castes who, along with some service castes, henceforth will be termed as the middle castes. Under British rule India underwent a series of most significant changes, of which a few are noted here. With the onslaught of colonial economy and industrial revolution, the numerous artisan castes were thrown out of their jobs. With the economic breakdown, most of the business castes were forced out of the market. A sizeable section crowded on land and had been forcefully tied to agriculture.[35] This involuntary mass scale mobility affected the middle castes badly. Another important phenomenon of the colonial period was the introduction of English education, and through it, bourgeois liberalism. Besides, a number of modern industries, though inadequate, flourished.

Such phenomenal changes weakened the already flexible caste structure of Bengal. But it still continued to exert itself in some important areas of social relations, more so in the village community. In this regard, the first and most important was connubiality. Marriage was solemnised as per the rules of caste endogamy and clan exogamy. Next came restrictions regarding food, water and smoking. The third was untouchability: it was never so rigorously practised in Bengal as the records of some other parts of India show. Food practices became less and less restrictive progressively. Since the transfer of power, things have changed a lot and such restrictions are far less pronounced in West Bengal.[36] With a liberal view, now-a-days inter-caste marriages are generally accepted and are sometimes even arranged traditionally.[37]

Therefore, in modern Bengal, caste structure has lost much of its earlier importance. It is to be noted here that in Bengal, caste rites and rituals have been narrowed down. Even a majority of the Brahmins have limited their caste rite only to *upanayana* (taking of the sacred thread). One can also find Brahmins, not only in towns and cities but also in rural areas, who have not at all taken the sacred thread or have left it afterwards. These deviations never invite social boycott, popular wrath or violent reactions. This is perhaps due to the liberal cultural tradition in Bengal which may be an offshoot of its humanistic religious movements, distinct western influence, and a positive heritage of the Left and democratic movements. Another feature which has shaken the roots of casteism in Bengal is the great disaster of the partition in 1947 and the consequent large-scale spatial mobility. The large-scale diaspora made the time honoured societal norms extremely flexible and fragile.

Still, caste remains as a valid social phenomenon in West Bengal however frail and weak its structure may be. Caste has become more of a psychological phenomenon. Its status-value is still recognised in society, more so in the rural community. Nevertheless, here caste relations cannot be interpreted directly in terms of power relations similar to the pattern of many states in India. If we go deep into its psychology keeping in mind the historical specificities of Bengal, we will find that the Bengali people in general attach much importance to two things, viz., culture and education. Education itself is considered as the standard of accomplishment. An educated person is highly esteemed by the illiterate people. This esteem is not without reason. From the colonial time onwards, people have experienced that a person, whosoever he may be, can try to get a salaried white collar job, and hence a secured life only if he is educated. Here, his caste position is not an obstacle. On the contrary, he may get some privileges in terms of scholarships etc., if he belongs to a Scheduled Caste. In the same way, he can get some promotional preferences in service. Thus, to get rid of the uncertainties of agriculture, he would first have to qualify himself educationally. Secondly, education enhances his prestige and status in society. Virtually every man in rural West Bengal has one or the other kind of transaction with local level agencies of administration or panchayat. The transaction ranges from the payments of taxes to participation in local panchayats to litigation and settlement of disputes. All the transactions require a minimum level of education to write petitions or to understand notices and other written sources of information. Therefore, those people who can read, write and keep accounts are in high demand in rural society. Such people enjoy much power and influence as the other people queue up to them for helf. It would not be an exaggeration to say that such persons command so much honour and influence that they can be compared to the privileges that a Brahmin enjoyed in the traditional society. Historically, education was confined to the upper castes. A growing tendency is found among the Bengali lower and middle caste people to compete with the upper caste people primarily in the field of education.

It is true that birth in a middle or lower caste does not bar a person from getting education at par with the upper caste students. There is no religious or social bar on a low caste person to deny him education. Therefore, if he is interested, at least passively, to get education then what hinders the spread of education among the lower and middle castes of West Bengal? Here arises the question of class and economy. In a broad sense, under the capitalist economy education is something to be purchased with money. But, in West Bengal, we know that no fee is required for education up to the secondary level. Even some text-books are also distributed free of cost. Moreover, there are scholarships for the Scheduled Caste and Scheduled Tribe students. So, apparently our statement regarding education may be relevant particularly when a person thinks of the scholarships and quota system in the professional training courses as well.

A family can afford the luxury of sending a child to school and leave him undisturbed if it does not have to depend upon the child's earnings for its survival. It does not become possible for forty to forty-five per cent of the population below the poverty line to send their children to school. In a village surplus, whatever its size may be, is accumulated by the big and the middle farmers and the non-agricultural rich and middle classes. Only they can afford to send to their children to schools (and some, according to their economic position, to colleges). This phenomenon leads us to say that craving for education as an effective demand is confined only to the upper and middle classes. Education is a means of power and prestige as well as economic security. It is a valid demand made by the upper and middle classes.

V

Now, to test our hypothesis, we may take the help of a sample survey. The survey was conducted over a period of one year in Burdwan district in 1986-87. The total population of the surveyed development block (Memari, Block-I) according to the 1981 census is 1,56,729.[38] The sample was chosen from five different *maujas* under five gram panchayat areas. The voter list of 1983 was taken as the sample frame. The sample size was 200 out of 14,465.

It is necessary here to explain the justification of selecting the above sample. A differentiation within the peasantry and the existence of reckonable rich and middle classes within it is a presupposition for our enquiry, because otherwise we would not be able to understand and compare the attitudinal differences between various castes and classes. Burdwan district and Memari possess some requisite features. Burdwan is said to be the "granary of West Bengal" because of its high agricultural production. The green revolution has found a place there. Within Burdwan district, Memari is an advanced zone both in terms of agricultural production and marketing. It is developing agro-based and other kinds of industries which ensure, in the specific context of Memari, a two-way flow of capital between the agricultural and the industrial sectors. A small but significant class of capitalist farmers and an agrarian middle class are emerging in the area. These classes are ambitious. They are not content with their present economic power. They want to share political power to elevate their social status and prestige. These peasant classes come from among the middle castes.[39]

The powerful rural rich and the middle class people are found clustered in farming, trading (both wholesale and retail) and industrial ownership. Our study has shown that the local monopolists (owners of industries, trade and farms concurrently) come from the middle castes. They have entered the service sector too where they still lag behind the upper caste people.

It is interesting to note that nearly sixty per cent of the traders come from the middle castes showing that almost forty-six per cent of the members of this category concentrate on trading. Moreover, the local monopolists come from this category. Unemployment rate is lower among them compared to the upper castes. Although they occupy about forty-four per cent of the service sector, their main contestants in this sector are still the upper caste people. In particular situations such competitions create rivalry. Another arena of competition is that of big capital involving obviously less people. The people at the top exercise control over industry, trade and agriculture at the same time. As this class is at the apex of the rural socio-economic structure, it is less likely to foment caste rivalry within its ranks. It is evident that the most economically powerful section belongs to the middle castes. To retain their social and political influence, they often speak in terms of community rather than class to evoke caste feelings for political support from their fellow-members.

Thus, we find the lower castes and the tribes in a deplorable condition. The agricultural work-force comes from these groups, whereas only four per cent of the farm labourers belong to the middle and the upper castes. Sharecropping is quickly disappearing in Memari (2.5%) due to the emergence of the new agricultural economy. But this small section of sharecroppers also depends upon farm labour who are from the lower castes, tribes or are Muslims. The Muslim respondents remain outside the scope of this discussion because caste differentiation within the Muslims could not be meaningfully traced out in our study. A substantial number of peasants have also taken up trade to supplement their incomes in addition to agriculture. This has considerably improved their economic position. It is evident that the percentage of the educated unemployed is highest (33.33) among the upper castes, followed by the middle castes (28.57). But it is much less among the lower castes and tribes. This is not because of a higher employment rate among the lower caste people, but is due to a lack of education among them. Generally, the farm labourers get employment only for three to four months in a year and for a maximum period of fifteen days in a month. Chronic and severe unemployment is a common phenomenon among them.

The upper castes, together with the middle castes, depend on the lower castes/tribes for productive labour, but the upper castes lag behind the middle castes in capital accumulation. The upper castes do not take part in the production process. The lone person in our sample, who does not work for his livelihood, depending solely upon his ancestral property, belongs to an upper caste. All the occupational patterns vis-a-vis different castes show that vertical caste divisions correspond with the vertical class divisions. But if a comparison is made between the upper and the middle castes, no such parallel could be drawn. Traditionally, the Brahmins along with other upper castes owned land and controlled other means of agricultural production. Under the British rule, they were also employed as white-collar workers. The middle castes, however, concentrated mainly on business. Education has a direct relation with occupation and class. A direct relation of education with caste is also evident.

Not surprisingly, the maximum number of illiterate people belongs to the lower castes and tribes (nearly 63.5% and 14%, respectively). When we examine the percentages of literacy among different castes, we see an astounding rate (about 82%) of illiteracy among the tribes. The majority (approximately 54%) of the lower castes are illiterate.

Tribal people educated beyond primary level were not found in our study. The powerful middle castes have an advantage over the upper castes regarding education proper. Both the upper and the middle castes concentrate at the secondary level (36% of the middle castes and 38% of the upper castes). At the intermediate level, the two make almost the same proportional representation (approximately 15% of the upper castes and 16% of the middle castes). At the graduate and post-graduate levels, the middle castes score a higher position. Therefore, it is evident that the middle castes are ahead of the upper castes. It shows only a slight decline of the upper castes, and a higher level of consciousness among the middle castes.

The study further shows that the relationship between the poor and illiterate lower caste people and the upper and middle castes who come from the better off stratum of the society is that of dependence and dominance. In such a situation contradictions at two levels are to be located. One is between the rich and the poor placed in the higher, middle and lower positions in the caste hierarchy. The other is between the rich and the middle classes competing for more privileges. The second contradiction is more complicated since it expresses itself through another dimension, i.e., the upper and middle castes configuration. There is no doubt that the rich and aspiring middle class people among each caste try to speak in caste idioms to win over the poor and lower middle classes of their respective castes, but in this respect the middle caste rich people are more successful because of two reasons. First, they have acquired sufficient economic power to conquer new arenas of dominance in village politics, and second, the community feeling and bond are a stronger among them compared to the upper castes. The main difference between the two castes is that the upper castes are on the decline and they are struggling hard to retain their traditional status to the maximum possible extent. The middle castes have emerged as a new power bloc in rural Bengal. They evaluate education as a mundane activity and a practical cherished goal.

VI

In this context, if we turn for a while to the all-India scene, we find that since the 1960s, caste dynamics have had a wider political dimension than ever before. It is mainly due to the emergence of a strong and rich middle peasantry. As the production and distribution of both agricultural inputs and outputs widened, the capitalist norms, namely, the terms of trade between the monopoists and multinational suppliers of inputs became a source of tension. Within the peasantry too changes occurred.

The green revolution made the capital-owning peasants important.[40] They control the process of production at the local level and the entire peasantry has no option but to follow their leadership. In this process, absentee landlords and money lenders are pushed to the corner. On the other end, a large number of marginal and poor peasants are also compelled out of the production process.

Caste plays its role in politics significantly. In their struggle for remunerative prices for agricultural produce, the capitalist farmers find ready-made bond of affinity with other peasants by evoking caste-based primordiality. Peasant leaders never hesitate to utilise this bond, however opposed it stands to class consciousness. With overt or covert state-support, the upper classes organise on caste-basis for political gains. The gains of such politics are harvested naturally maximum by those classes which figure in sharp distinction from and in contradiction with the lower classes of their own castes.

In West Bengal, unlike the general pattern of articulation, the fusion between caste and class politics has taken some different ways. Class consciousness on the surface level outweighs caste consciousness in West Bengal. This explains the failure of a separate Scheduled Caste movement in West Bengal. But does it mean that the communal mode of power does not operate in rural Bengal? At least our enquiry does not show it. Historically, the articulate agricultural classes come from the middle castes. In spite of the modernization effects, the presence of Brahminical domination over Hindu culture in general is still so strong that the powerful middle castes find it quite difficult to establish their authority in cultural terms. The near monopoly of the upper caste people over education persists. Therefore, as we have seen, rich, upper middle and middle class people of the middle caste have developed a strong aspiration for achieving higher education, considering it a privilege.

In Bengal, rural people support the government because of its manifest pro-people bias. In the process of judging their claim, people are influenced by the opinion leaders. The opinion leaders generally come from among the rural rich and middle class of the middle and upper castes. Hence, the government which provides facilities to the middle class and middle castes can claim to become a popular government. It shows how real is the undercurrent of caste rural politics of rural West Bengal. How far it influences state policy and in what way does the state react and to what extent does it provide a scope for new policies and programmes. All these questions can be answered satisfactorily only if we have more studies of the nexus between caste, class, education and politics.

Notes

1. M.N. Srinivas, *India: Social Structure*, New Delhi Publication Division, Government of India, 1969, p.5.
2. Irfan Habib, *Caste in Indian History*, (Mimeo), p.3.
3. M.N. Srinivas, *Op. Cit.*
4. D.D. Kosambi, *Caste and Class in India* (Mimeo), p.3.
5. Andre Beteille, *Studies in Agrarian Social Structure*, Delhi, Oxford University Press, 1979 (3rd imp.) p. 11.
6. *Ibid.* p. 143.
7. The most glaring examples may be taken from recent Bihar state terrorism in support of the Bhumisenas organised by the landlords. It generally takes the guise of caste battles only to hide the devastating socio-economic exploration of the poor. For a detailed account of the struggle of the poor peasants against the landlords and the oppressor state see *Reports from the Flaming Fields of Bihar: A CPI(ML) Document*. Calcutta, Prabodh Bhattacharya, 1986.
8. Partha Chatterjee, "Agrarian Relations and Communalism in Bengal, 1926-1935" in Ranjit Guha (ed.) *Subaltern Studies*, Vol. 1, Oxford University Press, p.12.
9. *Ibid.* p.13
10. Kosambi has traced out the state-formation in India as a reflection of "man's progress in satisfying his needs in cooperation with all his fellowmen, not the success of a few at satisfying them at the expense of most of their fellow men". See D.D. Kosambi, *An Introduction to the study of Indian History*, Bombay, Popular Prakashan, 1956.
11. When in the 8th Century the Arabs conquered Sind they approved all the caste oppressions upon the Jats which were imposed by the Hindu rulers on the basis of brahminical edict (Manusmrti). See Ifran Habib, *Op. Cit.* p.12. Later, the British East India Company wanted as far as possible to yield to brahminism, as it was always a convenient tool for subjection of the "natives"

    D.D. Kosambi, Myth and Realty: *Studies in the Formation of Indian Culture*; Bombay, Popular Prakashan, 1962, p. 45.
12. For example see Kosambi, *Op. Cit.* p.1, Srinivas, *Op. Cit.* pp, 6-8, Habib, *Op. Cit.* pp. 12-14.
13. Habib, *Op. Cit.* p. 13.
14. *Ibid.* p. 12
15. Chatterjee, *Op. Cit.* p. 15
16. Nihar Ranjan Ray, *Bangali Itihas: Adi Parba*, Calcutta Niraksharata Durikaran Samiti, 1980 (3rd ed.) Vol. I, pp. 256-7.
17. *Ibid.* pp. 259-67, 308.
18. *Ibid.* pp. 267-78, 280.
19. *Ibid.* pp. 249-50, 278-300, 306-8, 323, 325, 328-30, 486-89.

20. *Ibid.* pp. 248, 266-67, 291-97.
21. So far as inter-caste marriage was concerned, marriage between higher caste males and lower caste females (including the Sudras) was accepted. But the status of a Sudra wife of a Brahmin was lower than that of his Brahmin wife. *Ibid.* p. 301.

    It is evident that in the Pala-Chandra and Sena-Barman periods the Brahmins took different occupations other than their caste-based occupations, which included a whole range from the king to the peasant. Similarly, the Ambostha-Vaidyas were appointed as the ministers to different kings. *The Sudras were appointed as royal servants among whom the Kaivartas also ruled a part of Bengal for generations. Ibid.* pp. 250, 305, 472.
22. *Ibid.* pp. 299-300.
23. *Ibid.* pp. 308-9.
24. Kshiti Mohan Sen, *Banglar̈ Sadhana*, Calcutta, Visva Bharati Granthan Bibhag, 1904 Shaka, pp. 59-60. 73-74.

    D.D. Kosambi has assessed the social role of Bhakti movement in *Myth and Reality*, pp. 31-37.
25. Roy, *Op. Cit.*, p. 304.
26. *Ibid.* pp. 303-4, 306-8.
27. *Ibid.* pp. 294, 296-97.
28. *Ibid.* pp. 472-74.
29. *Ibid.* pp. 326-29.
30. *Ibid.* pp. 249-50, 328.
31. *Ibid.* pp. 324, 330-31.
32. *Ibid.* pp. 306-7.
33. In the Sena period two social phenomena developed at the same time. One was the emergence of peasantry as a distinct class and the subsequent development of feudalism. The other was division of society into numerous castes and sub-castes with strict restriction on food, drink, marriage etc. To get a detailed account of caste divisions under the Senas see *Ibid*, pp. 278-97.
34. Partha Chatterjee has analysed the peasant movement in Bengal between 1920-1947 including some satyagraha movements in eastern and south-western parts of Bengal and showed the pattern of the essential relationship between the communal mode of politics and differentiation within the peasantry. See Partha Chatterjee "Agrarian Relations and Communalism in Bengal, 1926-1935" and "The Colonial State and Peasant Resistance in Bengal 1920-1947" in *Past and Present*, No. 110, Feb. 1986. A previous example is that of the peasant rebellion led by Titu Meer in 1830-31. Titu was a bengali peasant who was deeply influenced by the fundamentalist wahabi ideology. The series of sanyasi rebellions between 1763-1800 can be referred to as another important example of communal essence of peasant struggle in the early and mid period of the

british rule. See Suprakash Roy, *Bharater Krishan Bidroha O Ganatantrika Sangram*, Calcutta, DNBA, 1980 (3rd ed.) pp. 20-53 and 261-82.

35. The ruinous effect of the decline of indian town handicrafts and village artisan industries has been discussed by A.R. Desai exhaustively. See A.R. Desai, *Social Background of Indian Nationalism*, Bombay, Popular Prakashan. 1981 (Repring) chapters V and VII.
36. It does not mean that restriction on food, drink etc. has vanished altogether from West Bengal. Certainly the restrictive superstitions influence different people to different levels including the majority people who are not expressly influenced by them. Therefore, it does not affect social relations significantly.
37. If one looks at the matrimonial advertisements carefully in the pages of newspapers over a span of time, one would be able to notice the gradual loss of importance of essentiality of endogamy in Bengal society. No doubt the urban areas lead this liberalisation, but the rural society does not show an opposite trend.
38. *Block Plan*: 1985-86, Memari I Development Block, Burdwan, p.5.
39. Through our survey in Memari the following castes are noticed-

    (A) **Upper Castes**

    1. Brahmin, 2. Kayashta, 3. Vaidya.

    (B) **Middle Castes** (including peasant, trading and service castes)

    1. Aguri, 2. Sadgop, 3. Tanti, 4. Teli, 5. Banik, 6. Goala, 7. Mahisya, 8. Pramanik, 9. Kamar, 10. Chasi (Kaivarta), 11. Kumar, 12. Gandhabanik, 13. Kangsa Banik, 14. Subarna Banik, 15. Tambuli, 16. Vaisya, Saha.

    (C) **Lower Castes**

    1. Dule, 2. Munchi, 3. Dhopa, 4. Vaishnab, 5. Bagdi, 7. Malo, 8. Nania (Non Bengali), 8. Other specified Scheduled Castes.

    (D) **Not ascertained caste**

    1. Dhatri.
40. For the analysis of productive and political role of the capitalist farmers see D.N. Dhangare, "The Green Revolution and Social Inequality in Rural India" and Gail Omvedt "The New Peasant Movement in India" in the *Bulletin of Concerned Asian Scholars* (No. 2, Vol. 20, Apr.-Jun., 1988). The debate is continued in the Frontier, between Gail Omvedt and Sharad Patil in 1988 numbers of the journal.

    T.J. Byres has discussed the politics of Charan Singh, the Champion of "peasant interest" in "The New Technology, Class formation and class Action in the Indian Countryside" in *The Journal of Peasant Studies*, Vol. 8, No. 4, July 81.

    Byres has further discussed Charan Singh's politics, his class origin, historical process of development etc. in "Charan Singh, 1902-87: An Assessment" in *The Journal of Peasant Studies*, Vol. 15, No. 2, Jan. '88.

    The mode of production in agriculture has been debated on since early

60s in India. Alice Thorner has presented a commentary of the debate along with an excellent bibliography in "Semi-feudalism or Capitalism? Contemporary Debate on Classes and Modes of Production in India", *Economic and Political Weekly*, Vol. XVII, 49- 51, Dec. 1982.

4

Caste, Class and Landholding in the Analysis of Technology and Agricultural Production in Bihar

Shaibal Gupta

The broad contours of the agricultural transformation in India' are capitalist in character, though with slight regional variations. The extent of capitalist transformation is identified usually on the basis of the extent of hiring of wage labour and the extent of production for the market. These two conditions together, however, are not sufficient for capitalist relations in agriculture. According to Utsa Patnaik, the "criterion of accumulation and reinvestment must be specified as well."[1] She further explains that "if holding employing wage labour does not reinvest and expand lower production costs and try to move up on the scale of competitive efficiency, then where is the element of dynamism which marks off this so-called 'capitalist' enterprise with its 'capitalist' production relations from other exploitative relations such as the landlord-tenant one."[2]

Unlike the European experience, the technological innovation or initiative in India was not a result of an autonomous private initative but was because of governmental impetus. Despite the overall backwardness of Indian agriculture, agricultural enclaves were developed like Ludhiana in Punjab, West Godavari in Andhra Pradesh where extensive selective irrigation was introduced by the British government long before India's independence. That is why, in the above mentioned areas, "inputs like fertilizers, threshers, seed drills, tractors and irrigation pumps were in relatively extensive use even before the introduction of the new high yielding varieties."[3]

While discussing the extent of technology in agriculture, it should be kept in the mind that technology does not descend from a void. The technical innovation based on a given stock of knowledge and its utilisation is dependent upon the social framework and the power structure. It would not be appropriate, therefore, to treat technology as a factor independent of the social and political framework within which it originates. It is a dependent factor.

Given the class structure of the state, widespread infusion of technology in agriculture was not in the agenda of the state immediately after independence. But a concerted and a comprehensive strategy for augmenting agricultural production was initiated by the central government after a series of crop failures in the sixties. The shortage of foodgrains aggravated dramatically. Since 1937, after the separation of Burma, India has remained dependent on food imports. However, the size of imports varied from year to year. "During the fifties, when the food situation was good, imports constituted about five per cent of the domestic production, but in the sixties, it reached nearly eight per cent, and in one year, 1966, imports were fourteen per cent of the domestic production."[5]

Apart from the high foreign exchange cost of food imports, the generous and liberal food import under PL 480 from America was considered humiliating as it hurt the national pride. Food dependence had serious implications for both domestic and foreign policies of the government. The government became vulnerable to pressure from the donor countries. The rupee was devalued in 1966. The uncertainties at the policy level on the food front were further aggravated with the prognostication by the Paddock brothers of the widespread famine in 1975. They advocated that in the eventuality of extensive famine, U.S.A., the only food surplus country at that time, should try to save only those countries which can be saved. The Paddock brothers listed India in the category of 'can't be saved' countries. The Paddock thesis, even though not taken seriously, in any case highlighted the alarming situation on the food front.

So the 'new agricultural strategy' encompassing HYV seeds, fertilizers, pesticides, controlled water supply and mechanical equipment was ushered in the mid-sixties in India to increase the agricultural output in selected pockets.

In the context of the preceding discussion, we shall examine the technology and production spectrum in different agrarian segments in Bihar. One methodological problem in assessing the impact of the new technology on various agrarian segments in our study is regarding separation of the pure effect of the new technology from the historical trends (particularly in areas where large farmers were active in modernising agriculture during the pre-HYV period). Here, we may present a brief description of the survey which forms the empirical base of our study.

Bihar is one of the backward states of India. Industrial development in the state is confined to small areas and agricultural technology remains backward compared to other parts of the country. The annual compound rate of agricultural production declined from 2.97 per cent in 1952-53 to 1964-65 to 0.49 per cent in 1969-70 to 1983-84. Ironically, the agricultural production declined during the period of the so-called green revolution. Despite this gloomy picture, considerable change has taken place.

The ANS Institute at Patna, with support from the ILO, initiated a detailed study of the dynamics of employment and poverty in Bihar in 1981.[6] The data on caste, class, landholding and technology in this paper are drawn from this survey. The survey was conducted from 1981 to 1983 in five rounds. The present data are from the first and second rounds conducted in 1981-82. For our analyses, we have divided the agrarian population on the basis of size of holdings, caste rank and by class (economic status).

Land, Caste and Class: Concepts and Definitions[7]

Appropriate specifications of land, caste and class are necessary for evaluating their explanatory power.

1. *Land*

Both caste and class are by definition classificatory, while land is not. Comparability would, in one sense, be increased by converting land to a classificatory category, but the relationship with land is conceptually not so. And so this option was not used except in tabulations (where it cannot be avoided).

This point apart, three major issues arise in the specification of a land as a variable: (i) Adjustment of the area for the number of users; (ii) quality of land; and (iii) variations in control over land.

2. *Caste*

The phenomenon of caste provides three bases of stratification: the traditional hierarchy; the perceived actual status and activity groups; and the model of difficult task, 'dominant caste'. None of these is entirely satisfactory. An attempt to range castes is grouping castes on the basis of similarities and differences is an equally controversial exercise, 'dominance' is not always objectively definable and often seems to be an *ex post* rationalisation and primarily based on class considerations, allied with numerical strength, effective control of land and a reasonably high ritual position.[8]

The simplest and universally acceptable categorisation in Bihar is three-fold: forward, backward and scheduled castes. Forward castes comprise Brahmin, Bhumihar, Rajput and Kayastha and these have been historically dominant, and continue to be prominent in both urban and rural areas. Scheduled castes are at the lowest level of the caste hierarchy, while the backward castes are a heterogeneous category in between the upper castes and the scheduled castes. In addition to these three categories, there are also Muslims. A fifth category, namely, the scheduled tribes, is not in the sample.

A more detailed disaggregation is used in the analysis below. Our class disaggregation identifies nine groups. Since the explanatory power of any scheme increases with the number of groups it identifies comparability requires in it a disaggregation of castes. Nine caste groups were, therefore, formed as stated below:

1. Forward I (Brahmins + Kayasthas)
2. Forward II (Bhumihars + Rajputs)
3. Backward I
4. Backward II-Yadavas
5. Backward II-Koiris
6. Backward II-Kurmis
7. Backward II-Others
8. Scheduled Castes
9. Muslims

There are a large number of ways in which nine caste groups could be formed. This approach attempts to take into consideration heterogeneity within groups with respect to economic differences. The most complex group in our classification is that of the backward castes because many of these castes are in no way backward. Three particularly prominent and numerous agricultural castes, generally locally dominant, are Koiri, Kurmi and Yadav. The remaining backward castes are again divided, using the official classification, as 'other backward II', and 'backward I'. Both these categories include service, trading and specific occupational castes, but 'backward I' is generally not well endowed with skills, land or capital, and they are often found working as agricultural labourers.

It was also considered necessary divide to the 'forward' castes into two categories because Brahmins and Kayasthas (there were very few Kayasthas in our sample) are traditionally non-agriculturists, and their ritual position seems to influence their economic activities.

The remaining two groups, the scheduled castes and Muslims, are also quite heterogeneous. The bulk of the scheduled castes are found as agricultural labourers, but some adhere to their traditional occupations (Dhobi, Dom, Halkhor). However, in our sample, the vast majority of the scheduled castes were Musahars, Dusadhs and Chamars, and there was no obvious basis for differentiation. It was, therefore, felt better to treat them as a single category. Similar considerations applied to Muslims, who are also mainly agricultural labourers, but are also dominant in some areas, and some are prominent as large cultivators and landlords.

3. *Class*

A definition of class in terms of antagonistic, conscious groups identified by their positions in a system of production relations is basic to the Marian thought.[9] But such an approach does not adequately explain the semi-feudal social formation which dominates much of rural Bihar.[10] Rural Bihar can be characterised by the co-existence of various forms of exploitation (rent, usury, different forms of labour) and social groups, quite distinct in the system of production relations, but not necessarily directly antagonistic to each other. And so far as group consciousness is concerned, it is caste rather than class which determines collective mobilisations. To understand the key characteristics of this social formation, a fairly comprehensive classification has been based on the generation of surplus value in agriculture and its appropriation through the labour process.

Those households that supply devised labour for agricultural operations on others' lands on the basis of payment either in cash or kind may be treated as 'agricultural labour' households. These households are directly exploited by their employers and command the lowest status in the agricultural community. Above them are those peasant households which neither hire-out labour nor hire-in labourers for agricultural operations and conduct their agricultural activities with the help of the members of their households or on the basis of exchange of labour. These are termed 'poor middle peasant' households. They are neither exploiting nor are directly exploited through the labour process. Some of them may nevertheless be exploited (i.e., the surplus value they generate may be partly appropriated) through rent [11] or usury or due to adverse terms of trade. Their status is higher than that of agricultural labourers.

The next category consists of peasant households which employ manual labour for agricultural activities. This can be divided into three sub-categories. First, there are those who lease-out some land. These are termed as 'landlords'. Non-peasant landowners who lease-out land and also other non-peasant households who do not work on the land themselves but cultivate only through hired labourers are also termed as 'landlords'. This group is somewhat mixed since it includes petty leasers-out as well as large landowners who lease-out only a few acres of land.

Among the remaining peasants, there are some who deem it below their dignity to allow female members of their family to undertake manual work even on their own farms. These are called by us 'big peasant' households. The remaining households as in which both men and women work are termed as 'middle peasant' households. The basis of this classification is the nature and use of family labour which is important both in itself and in terms of reliance on hired labour.

The important point to note about this classification is that it does not depend directly on the land owned or cultivated but on the way the households utilise labour and land. Some anomalies still remain. For instance, those who are forced to lease out their land because of old age or illness may be classified as landlords. Households with no female members in working age group cannot, by definition, be classified as middle peasants. Thus, further disaggregation would no doubt provide more refined classification, but given the need to limit the number of categories formed, we would argue that the categories like landlord, peasant and middle peasant can highlight the main features of the agrarian class system.

Agricultural labourers also need to be sub-divided because terms of their employment vary, as do their relations to the means of production. A crucial differentiation in the labour process is between the 'free' and the 'unfree' labour. Attachment to a single employer—work only for that employer accompanied with indebtedness or cultivating the land of the employer—is taken as an indication of a relative lack of freedom ('permanent' labour for a single employer alone is not sufficient because it may merely reflect a freely entered long term contract). As regards access to the means of production, 'proletarian' or 'free' labour is free from the means of production in a double sense, that he is not only free from bondage or serfdom, but he is also 'free' from the means of production. This distinction calls for a second diffentiation within the class of agricultural labour. The cultivation of self-owned land or cultivation as a tenant provides a critical dividing point. Thus, we may have the following four classes among agricultural labourers:

1. Attached, not cultivating (ALNA=agricultural labourer, not cultivating, attached)
2. Not attached, not cultivating (ALNF=not cultivating, free)
3. Attached, cultivating (ALLA=cultivating land, attached)
4. Not attached, cultivating (ALLF=cultivating land, free)

In the analysis, we have divided agricultural labourers into two categories, the agricultural labour tied and the untied. Our classification of peasants and landlords was:

— poor-middle peasants (POORMIDP)
— middle peasants (MIDP)
— big peasnats (BIGP)
— landlords (LANDLD)

Finally, we must add to this the class of the non-agriculturalists (NONAG) which makes it a total of nine classes.

Table 1
Annual Compound Rate of Growth of Agricultural Production

(percentage)

	1952-53 to 1964-65	*1969-70 to 1983-84*
1. Andhra Pradesh	2.74	3.31
2. Bihar	2.9	0.49
3. Gujrat	4.55	3.92
4. Kerala	2.27	0.23
5. Haryana	-	3.31
6. Karnataka	3.54	2.44
7. Madhya Pradesh	2.49	1.65
8. Maharashtra	2.93	5.59
9. Orissa	2.48	2.28
10. Punjab	4.56*	3.92
11. Rajasthan	2.74	2.47
12. Tamil Nadu	4.17	1.12
13. Uttar Pradesh	1.66	3.19
14. West Bengal	1.94	0.91

Note: Punjab and Haryana combined.

Source: Column (2) Ministry of Food and Agriculture, Government of India, Growth Rates in Agriculture, p. 31; Column (3) Commission of Agricultural Costs and Prices, Government of India, Report of the Commission for Agricultural Costs and Prices as Price for Kharif Crops of 1985-86 Season (mimeographed), p. 69.

Since the non-agricultural class does not fit in well here, it could be aggregated with the poor-middle peasants or with the class of middle and big peasants or it may be omitted altogether. We chose the last option (Table 1).

Interactions Between Caste, Class and Land

Although conceptually distinct, caste, class and landholding overlap statistically and in some respects definitionally. Tables 2, 3, and 4 provide the pattern of interactions between these three varibles observed in our survey.

Table 2 shows the breakdown of caste by class. It can be observed that forward castes are essentially big peasants and landlords, while the scheduled castes are essentially agricultural labourers. Backward castes are spread across various class groupings, but each sub-group identified tends to concentrate in one or more classes. Backward castes I are essentially agricultural labourers. Yadavs and Koiris are mainly peasants, especially poor-middle and middle peasants. Two-third of Kurmis are big peasants and landlords, but other backward II are widely distributed having a relatively high proportion of non- agriculturalists. Muslims are spread across the classes, with the largest concentration (about half) among the non-attached agricultural labourers.

The interrelation is therefore strong but is by no means perfect. Every caste is represented in at least seven classes out of nine, while certain groups are almost absent. Bhumihar and Rajput as agricultural labourers and scheduled castes as big peasants or landlords are not found. There is, therefore, plenty of variation, and one can quite sensibly look for independent effects of caste and class in multivariate analysis.

Table 3 provides landownership by using total household landholdings. The relationship between class and landownership is strong. Where agricultural labourers own land, they are concentrated in the less than one acre category, especially an attached labour. Big peasants own more land than middle peasants, and the latter owns more land than the poor-middle peasants. Landlords are relatively better represented in the larger landownership categories; they are found cutting across all landholding sizes, and indeed the same is true about big and middle peasants as well. Thus, there is a fair degree of differentiation. Obviously, it will be difficult to distinguish between the effects of landlessness and the effects of belonging to the classes which have ninety per cent or more landless, such as non-cultivating agricultural or non-agricultural labour. Since landlessness is also found among other groups, we may find, if any, the distinct effect of lack of landownership. Landowners are

Table 2

Land Ownlrship by Class Absolute Numbers and (in Brackets) Percentage Distribution of Households

Land Ownership Group (acres)	*Class*									
	ALNF	*ALNA*	*ALLF*	*ALLA*	*POORMIDP*	*MIDP*	*BIGP*	*LANDLD*	*NONAG*	*TOTAL*
0	527	74	98	212	22	5	15	1*	134	1087
	(48.4)	(6.8)	(9.0)	(19.5)	(2.0)	(0.4)	(1.4)	(0.1)	(12.3)	(43.1)
0-1	77	2	217	119	124	52	100	54	7	682
	(1.0)	(0.2)	(31.8)	(17.5)	(18.2)	(7.6)	(14.7)	(7.9)	(1.1)	(27.0)
1-2.5	1	0	42	13	37	36	115	46	1	291
	(0.3)	(0.0)	(14.5)	(4.4)	(12.8)	(12.4)	(39.5)	(15.8)	(0.3)	(11.5)
2.5-5.0	0	0	7	0	7	15	138	51	0	217
	(0.0)	(0.0)	(3.3)	(0.0)	(3.0)	(6.8)	(63.4)	(23.4)	(0.0)	(8.6)
5.0-10.0	0	0	1	0	2	2	99	41	0	145
	(0.0)	(0.0)	(0.9)	(0.0)	(1.2)	(1.5)	(68.3)	(28.1)	(0.0)	(5.8)
10.0-20.0	0	0	0	0	0	1	64	17	0	82
	(0.0)	(0.0)	(0.0)	(0.0)	(0.0)	(1.6)	(77.9)	(20.5)	(0.0)	(3.2)
20 +	0	0	0	0	0	2	6	12	0	20
	(0.0)	(0.0)	(0.0)	(0.0)	(0.0)	(8.5)	(31.4)	(60.1)	(0.0)	(0.8)
Total	534	76	366	344	192	113	536	221	142	2524
	(21.2)	(3.0)	(14.5)	(13.6)	(7.6)	(4.5)	(21.3)	(8.7)	(5.6)	(100.0)

No. of missing observations = 7

* One case of a "landlord" who leased in all the land that he leased out, and owned none.

Table 3

Land ownership by Caste Absolute Numbers and (in Brackets) Percentage Distribution of Households

Land Ownership Group (acres)	*Caste*									
	Brahmin + Kayasta	*Bhumihar + Rajput*	*Backward*	*Yadav*	*Koiri*	*Kurmi*	*Other Backward II*	*Scheduled Castes*	*Moslem*	*Total*
0	24	8	251	31	15	8	87	477	487	4087
	(2.2)	(0.7)	(23.1)	(2.9)	(1.4)	(0.7)	(8.0)	(43.8)	(17.2)	(43.1)
0-1	38	59	126	70	79	12	61	181	57	682
	(5.6)	(8.7)	(18.4)	(10.3)	(11.5)	(1.7)	(8.9)	(26.6)	(8.3)	(27.0)
1-2.5	52	68	26	20	30	11	22	22	36	291
	(18.0)	(23.4)	(8.9)	(6.9)	(10.2)	(3.6)	(7.4)	(7.4)	(11.5)	(11.5)
2.5-5.0	80	51	3	18	11	20	7	6	20	217
	(36,8)	(23.7)	(1.6)	(8.1)	(5.1)	(9.4)	(3.4)	(2.9)	(9.1)	(8.6)
5.0-10.0	77	23	0	3	4	16	7	1	14	145
	(52.8)	(15.8)	(0.0)	(2.1)	(2.8)	(10.7)	(5.1)	(0.9)	(9.8)	(5.8)
10.0-20.0	40	24	6	2	1	4	2	0	4	82
	(48.5)	(29.3)	(6.9)	(2.1)	(1.4)	(4.6)	(2.1)	(0.0)	(5.1)	(3.2)
20 +	8	8	0	0	0	1	2	0	1	20
	(41.5)	(41.2)	(0.0)	(0.0)	(0.0)	(4.1)	(8.8)	(0.0)	(4.4)	(0.8)
Total	318	241	412	144	140	70	188	692	319	2524
	(12.6)	(9.6)	(16.3)	(5.7)	(5.5)	(2.8)	(7.5)	(27.4)	(12.6)	(100.0)

No. of missing observations = 7

found with a considerable variation in several classes, and which means a distinct association between land and class.

The relationship between caste and land (Table 4) is much more diffuse. Forward castes are widely scattered over groups. Brahmins are particularly found owning large landholdings contrary to the general impression that Bhumihars dominate in Bihar. Kurmis show up strongly in the category of intermediate holdings—twenty-five to ten acres. Scheduled caste and backward caste I landholdings tend to be small.

We may thus conclude that the relationships between caste, class and land, while strong especially between class and land, are by no means absolute, and provide substantial scope for analysing their respective independent effects. The indicators of technology practised by the different agrarian segments of Bihar are irrigation, intensity of cropping mechanisation and the use of improved seeds and fertilizer. We have not examined all the factors which are inhibiting adoption of technology and affecting production. However, we shall examine land size, employment, expenditure and debt patterns in different agrarian segments that have some bearing on the use of technology and production.

Irrigation and Intensity of Cropping

Irrigation is the most important input for agriculture in India. Indian agriculture suffers from inadequacy of water. "Inadequacy of irrigation water is often held responsible for poor growth of crop, nutrient deficiency, pest and disease."[13] Sen has estimated that about fifty-four per cent of variation in agricultural output between different parts of India is associated with differences in irrigation facilities.[14] "Given the limited opportunities for bringing additional acreage of fallow lands under cultivation in future, irrigation is capable of playing a useful 'land-augmenting' role in India."[15] The critical importance of irrigation to the new technology is one of the factors why the government's HYV programme stressed heavily upon the selective introduction of new seeds in areas with irrigation facilities.

Most of the areas where the green revolution succeeded (like Punjab or West Godavari) were known for their developed canal irrigation in the pre-HYV period. "Irrigation is a pre-condition for successful introduction of new varieties even in areas known for heavy rainfall, such as the rice producing deltas of South India."[16] Even the study of several countries by Harami and Ruttan[17] indicates that irrigation and cropping intensity were more important in the early part of modern agricultural transformation. "Already at the beginning of the Meizi Restoration, al-

Table 4

Caste by Class Absolute Numbers and (in brackets) Percentage Distribution of Households

Caste	Class									
	ALNF	*ALNA*	*ALFE*	*ALLA*	*POORMIDP*	*MIDP*	*BIGP*	*LANDLD*	*NONAG*	*TOTAL**
Brahmin + Kayasta	11	1	13	0	6	3	189	86	14	322
	(3.4)	(0.3)	(3.9)	(0.0)	(1.8)	(0.9)	(58.7)	(26.6)	(4.4)	(12.7)
Bhumihar + Rajput	4	0	2	0	6	1	182	44	3	242
	(1.6)	(0.0)	(0.6)	(0.0)	(2.7)	(0.5)	(75.2)	(18.1)	(1.3)	(9.6)
Backward I	131	32	85	73	28	10	22	9	21	412
	(13.8)	(7.8)	(20.7)	(17.7)	(6.8)	(2.5)	(5.2)	(2.2)	(5.1)	(16.3)
Yadav	13	2	33	10	25	39	21	1	2	144
	(8.9)	(1.7)	(22.8)	(6.8)	(17.1)	(26.8)	(14.3)	(0.6)	(1.1)	(5.7)
Koiri	9	0	22	3	44	26	18	15	4	140
	(6.1)	(0.0)	(15.5)	(2.0)	(31.1)	(18.4)	(12.6)	(10.9)	(3.1)	(5.5)
Kurmi	3	0	7	1	7	6	40	7	1	71
	(4.7)	(0.0)	(9.3)	(1.1)	(10.5)	(7.9)	(56.0)	(9.2)	(1.1)	(2.8)
Other Backward II	18	0	22	7	29	15	22	27	48	188
	(9.8)	(0.0)	(11.6)	(3.7)	(15.2)	(8.0)	(11.8)	(14.1)	(25.8)	(7.4)
Scheduled Castes	239	37	127	229	20	10	5	9	18	693
	(34.5)	(5.3)	(18.3)	(33.1)	(2.8)	(1.4)	(0.8)	(1.2)	(2.6)	(27.4)
Moslem	106	3	57	20	28	5	41	26	31	319
	(33.3)	(1.0)	(17.8)	(6.4)	(8.8)	(1.6)	(13.0)	(8.3)	(9.8)	(12.6)
Total	534	76	366	344	192	115	539	223	142	2531
	(21.1)	(3.0)	(14.5)	(13.6)	(7.6)	(4.5)	(21.3)	(8.8)	(5.6)	(100.0)

* Percentages in this column are based on the column total elsewhere they are based on the row total likewise Tables 2 and 3.

most a hundred per cent of the paddy fields in Japan were irrigated. As far back as 1935, the proportion of area irrigated was seventy per cent in Taiwan, and sixty-nine per cent in Korea. The cropping intensities were 165 and 126. Only at a much later stage were HYV seeds or fertilizers introduced for increasing the farm yield."[18]

The progress of irrigation facilities in India has not been very encouraging. The percentage of net sown area under irrigation increased from eighteen per cent in 1951-52 to twenty-nine per cent in 1981-82. The vast underground and overground potential of irrigation remains untapped in India because of lack of proper water management. One of the objectives of irrigation is to facilitate double cropping for increasing the intensity of cropping. The cropping intensity in India in 1981-82 was 124. Though there is no direct correlation between cropping intensity and irrigation, we find that in most of the states having higher percentage of irrigation, the intensity of cropping is high, such as in Punjab, Haryana, and Uttar Pradesh. But, in some other states, cropping intensity is low even with relatively higher percentage of irrigation, like Tamilnadu, Andhra Pradesh, etc. Interestingly in the states of Kerala and Orissa, intensity of cropping is high even with a lower percentage of

Table 5

Extent and Sources of Irrigation and Cropping Intensity in Different States in India (1981-82)

States	% of area irrigated to net sown area	Intensity of cropping	% of total area irrigated by canal	% of total area irrigated by tubewell	% of area irrigated by other means
1. Andhra Pradesh	32.2	1.15	45.46	4.06	48.37
2. Bihar	36.0	1.34	38.99	26.96	34.05
3. Gujarat	22.3	1.13	19.54	13.18	67.24
4. Haryana	61.4	1.59	52.62	46.00	1.37
5. Karnataka	14.15	1.09	39.43	1.07	60.50
6. Kerala	11.05	1.34	44.16	+	55.83
7. Madhya Pradesh	12.8	1.15	44.77	1.82	53.41
8. Maharastra	10.5	1.11	21.68	-	78.36
9. Orissa	19.8	1.43	65.92	1.89	32.18
10. Punjab	80.9	1.65	38.79	59.57	1.64
11. Rajasthan	18.6	1.19	32.59	6.44	60.97
12. Tamil Nadu	47.2	1.20	33.26	4.61	65.12
13. Uttar Pradesh	55.2	1.43	33.57	54.18	12.25
14. West Bengal	26.7	1.33	64.47	-	35.53

Source: Fertiliser Statistics, 1981-82.

availability of irrigation. In Bihar, the availability of irrigation and cropping intensity are moderately higher than the all-India average.

In some states where the irrigation facility is adequate, there is no commensurate increase in the cropping intensity. Table 5 indicates that the states depending mainly on canals do not necessarily have a high cropping intensity. Maintenance of canals is poor, and as a consequence, silt accumulates and reduces their holding capacity. Thus, distribution of water between crops, seasons and farmers is often faulty and wasteful.

Tubewell irrigation is more reliable than canal irrigation. In many areas the new technology is judged by the increase in the use of tubewells. The success of irrigation and thus cropping intensity in Punjab, Haryana and Uttar Pradesh is mainly due to tubewells. The extent of cropping intensity, though moderate in Bihar, is mainly due to tubewell irrigation, which was introduced extensively after the 1967 drought. However, tubewell irrigation being privately owned, unlike canal irrigation, is available to a small number of people.

The overall picture of irrigation and cropping intensity in different states does not reveal a complete view specially of its effects on different sections, classes and castes. Though technology is scale neutral, accessibility to it is not. That is why we have examined the percentage of area irrigated and intensity of cropping in terms of the size of cultivated holding, class and caste. Table 6 reveals that there is no direct correlation between availability of irrigation and cropping intensity. The intensity of cropping is highest in case of landholdings of half acre with poor middle peasants, Brahmin and Kayasthas as cultivators, but irrigation is highest in regard to landholdings between five and ten acres, having tie agricultural labour and Koiris manning cultivation. The intensity of cropping among Kurmis is quite high with a relatively lower percentage of availability of irrigation. It is interesting that in the case of the Brahmin and Kayastha cultivators, intensity of cropping is high even with a lower percentage of irrigation facility. The intensity of cropping is also relatively high among Bhumihar-Rajput cultivators with a lower percentage of irrigation facilities.

Table 6 further indicates that both canals and tubewells are important sources of irrigation in Bihar. To the categories having highest availability irrigation the bulk of the irrigation is provided by canal. Tubewell irrigation is provided more to the categories having half to one acre and one to two acres, having poor middle peasants and big peasants, apart from Bhumihar and Rajputs. Tubewell irrigation is high among the

Table 6

Extent and Source of Irrigation and Cropping Intensity Among Different Types of Households (Bihar)

	% of area irrigated to net sown area	Intensity of cropping	% of total area irrigated by canal	% of total area irrigated by tubewell	% of total area irrigated by other means
	1	2	3	4	5
Size of Cultivated Land					
Up to 0.5 acres	40.12	1.93	52.30	37.69	10.00
055 to 1 acres	33.55	1.61	33.82	44.85	21.32
1 to 2 acres	43.76	1.62	42.64	47.64	9.71
2 to 5 acres	26.28	1.60	68.29	26.29	5.41
5 to 10 acres	44.93	1.69	52.97	41.32	5.71
10 to more acres	40.71	1.55	78.79	16.58	4.64
Class					
Agricultural labour not tied	52.45	1.49	83.80	12.15	4.05
Agricultural labour tied	59.01	1.58	61.51	38.49	0.0
Poor Middle peasant	32.61	1.84	28.67	56.86	14.46
Middle peasant	35.29	1.60	71.58	20.72	7.70
Big peasant	41.04	1.74	52.58	39.73	7.69
Land lord	38.57	1.75	69.16	26.93	3.92
Non Agriculture	0.0	0.0	0.0	0.0	0.0
Caste					
Brahmin + Kayasta	47.78	1.97	72.45	20.95	6.59
Bhumihar + Rajput	33.79	1.57	59.17	34.60	6.23
Backward I	37.08	1.58	84.94	13.08	1.98
Yadav	20.17	1.46	53.07	36.15	10.78
Koiri	70.32	1.60	55.05	28.55	16.40
Kurmi	63.48	1.92	2.39	91.54	6.07
Other Backward II	68.72	1.59	80.16	12.91	6.93
Scheduled Caste	58.54	1.67	70.54	29.20	0.25
Muslim	56.68	1.56	32.96	67.04	0.0

Table 7

Agricultural Implements in Different States in India (1977-78)

	Four wheeled tractor (per thousand hectare)	*Oil engine (per thousand hectare)*	*Electric pumps (per thousand hectare)*	*Wooden plough (in 000 number)*	*Iron Plough (in 000 number)*	*Carts (in 000 number)*	*Percentage of sugar cane crusher worked by power*
1	*2*	*3*	*4*	*5*	*6*	*7*	*8*
1. Andhra Pradesh	1.02	10.59	12.45	182.31	7.18	75.65	35.88
2. Bihar	1.22	15.39	10.84	497.61	39.98	83.23	8.88
3. Gujarat	1.17	43.47	8.29	144.37	25.20	79.59	48.98
4. Haryana	8.34	22.22	30.73	164.61	68.04	88.89	22.58
5. Karnataka	0.76	8.42	18.00	222.94	56.96	66.25	49.01
6. Kerala	0.77	12.77	11.81	144.02	31.35	6.81	35.71
7. Madhya Pradesh	0.80	6.28	7.98	260.82	7.55	128.84	15.49
8. Maharashtra	0.68	99.09	20.72	105.18	31.51	81.94	78.95
9. Orissa	0.23	0.50	0.17	523.76	25.35	34.85	18.66
10. Punjab	15.99	77.44	30.93	144.33	217.45	79.60	18.02
11. Rajasthan	1.63	5.54	5.47	167.06	13.58	58.48	2.53
12. Tamil Nadu	1.03	37.97	124.70	485.62	92.61	100.08	54.50
13. Uttar Pradesh	4.09	27.55	9.87	446.59	125.59	131.51	6.72
14. West Bengal	0.11	—	—	213.09	0.65	53.52	—

Source: Statistical Abstract-India 1984.

Yadavas, Koiris and Kurmis, the vanguard of the green revolution in Bihar.

Thus, there is a positive response from all class groups and castes as far as intensity of cropping is concerned, provided enough water is made available to them. None of them have displayed inhibition or an archaic attitude towards irrigation, which is an important component of agricultural production. The availability of irrigational facility or intensity of cropping is not conditioned by class, caste or land-size. In fact, irrigation and intensity of cropping are more or less evenly shared by different categories of landholders, castes and classes.

Mechanisation and Accumulation

Now we will analyse the emerging pattern of investment among different categories of cultivators, caste and class groups. We have defined investment (capital formation and accumulation) as creation of or addition to durable productive assets capable of generating an income stream over a period of time. In agriculture, capital expenditure consists of expenditure on land improvement, i.e., land development, soil conservation, land reclamation, agricultural implements and machinery, i.e., threshers, iron ploughs, tractors, trolleys, etc., irrigation which includes sinking, boring and deepening of wells, diesel and electric pump sets, tubewells, net purchase of draught animals, warehouse, cattle-sheds and so on. We do not consider cultivators' current outlay on seeds, fertilizers, insecticides, etc. An analysis of the expenditure of cultivators on such immediate inputs may be undertaken later on in relation to the major crops and total agricultural output.

In Western Europe, the impetus for mechanisation in agriculture stemmed from 'enclosure' leading to 'consolidation of holding' and shortage of labour. In India, mechanisation has occurred on a large scale in regions such as Punjab and western Uttar Pradesh where land to worker ratio is high. The irrigation and cropping intensities were already at a very high level in these regions before the introduction of large-scale mechanisation. In the extremely land-scarce and labour-surplus regions such as eastern Uttar Pradesh and Bihar, the need for land augmenting and labour absorbing techniques like HYV are more important than farm mechanisation. Despite the extremely favourable water table, the growth of private investment in tubewells has not been impressive. Experience shows that for the poor and the labour surplus regions profitability of investment is not a sufficient condition for the adoption of new techniques. Public investment and credit, in case of resource constraints, may have to be directed for improving the infrastructure such as irrigation which in themselves have a potential for increasing output apart from providing the necessary basis for widespread mechanisation.

Table 7 shows the extent of mechanisation and adoption of modern implements in agriculture in India in 1977-78. It reveals that as regards tractors, Punjab is followed by Gujarat, Haryana and Uttar Pradesh. In the oil engines, Punjab is followed by Gujarat, Tamil Nadu, Uttar Pradesh, Haryana and Bihar. As far electric pumpsets are concerned, Tamilnadu is in the lead, followed by Punjab, Haryana, Karnataka and Andhra Pradesh.

As regards the iron plough, Punjab is in the lead followed by Uttar Pradesh, Tamil Nadu, Haryana and Karnataka. In the case of wooden plough, Jammu & Kashmir takes the lead, followed by Orissa, Bihar, Tamil Nadu and Uttar Pradesh. The wooden plough indicates backwardness in the realm of technology. In regard to the carts, Madhya Pradesh takes the lead, followed by Uttar Pradesh, Tamil Nadu, Haryana and Bihar. In Punjab, carts are relatively fever because of higher usage of tractors. Carts bear the main brunt of rural transport. Even the percentage of sugarcane crushers operated by power (electricity) is the lowest in Bihar. Only Uttar Pradesh is lower than Bihar thus as far as power-driven sugarcane crushers are concerned. Table 7 provides the backdrop of mechanisation in India and that of Bihar in comparison to other states.

Table 8 deals with different types of capital accumulation among various groups. The modern capital goods, as an important indicator of accumulation, are highest among the Kurmi landlords owning ten acres of land. The total value of agricultural implements is also high among the Kurmis, but is the highest among the middle peasants who own land between five to ten acres. The per capita value of warehouses and cattle-sheds increases with increase in landholding. But the value of both drops in the category of the landholding above ten acres. The value of cattle-sheds goes higher as one moves from a lower to a higher class. Per capita value of godowns is uneven.

In the economy of agricultural production, bullock plays a very significant role. In fact, bullock is of multipurpose help for the cultivators. It is the major, if not the only, source used extensively in ploughing, harvesting, irrigation and transport operations. Thus, according to Raj, it functions as a capital goods producing as well as a capital goods providing service.[19] Table 8 displays that the distribution of draught cattle is extremely uneven. The value of draught cattle decreases with the increase in landholding. The higher the class of a household, the lower is

Table 8
Different Types of Accumulation Among Different Types of Households (Bihar)

	Per acre value of modern capital goods	*Total value of Machinary (per acre)*	*Per capita value of Grain stores*	*Per capita value of Cattle sheds*	*Per acre total value of Draught cattle*	*Per capita value of Bicycles*	*Per capita value of Radio*
1	*2*	*3*	*4*	*5*	*6*	*7*	*8*
Size Class of Cultivated Land							
Upto 0.5 acre	0.0	236.833	3.285	0.142	1340.756	2.532	0.529
0.5 to 1 acre	49.563	213.716	4.738	8.200	799.144	7.830	1.099
1 to 2 acres	38.122	469.632	6.583	51.010	606.316	11.963	3.219
2 to 5 acres	136.607	402.138	6.878	62.066	287.267	9.144	6.786
5 to 10 acres	187.524	533.332	31.733	159.906	273.313	16.229	12.214
10 & above	294.464	488.482	27.837	125.262	209.436	17.394	14.161
Class							
Agricultural labour not tied	34.789	171.514	1.433	11.375	771.144	2.589	1.381
Agricultural labour tied	29.729	157.831	2.648	14.534	1183.334	0.0	0.0
Poor Middle Peasant	90.143	629.283	8.419	31.594	645.754	6.670	4.857
Middle Peasant	160.528	512.211	5.422	50.141	343.555	11.455	6.060
Big Peasant	210.477	586.602	19.377	91.147	347.994	15.230	7.462
Land Lord	290.625	549.162	12.577	109.153	375.660	20.182	16.124
Non Agriculture	0.0	577.167	1.174	0.560	0.0	7.299	0.0
Caste							
Brahmin & Kayasta	139.711	466.148	13.202	81.696	362.349	17.710	9.575
Bhumihar & Rajput	296.667	562.730	14.869	46.703	372.703	14.261	6.713
Backward I	20.874	162.572	1.930	13.721	854.100	3.040	0.604
Yadav	0.0	184.496	5.822	97.410	243.384	10.833	6.561
Koiri	341.958	971.420	9.686	75.939	690.100	13.558	1.768
Kurmi	621.497	1662.243	74.175	278.906	438.997	15.514	16.378
Other Backward	15.107	182.009	2.472	37.598	474.305	7.298	6.132
Scheduled Caste	112.971	212.877	2.206	5.598	1124.191	2.465	1.505

Table 9
Land Improvements in Different Types of Households (Bihar)

	% Area Improved with Irrigation (All sources)	*Percentage Area Improved by Canal*	*Percentage Area Improved by Govt. Tubewell*	*Percentage Area Improved by Pvt. Tubewell*	*Percentage Area Improved by other Irrigation Sources*	*Land Leveling (Acres)*	*Other Improvements (acres)*
1	*2*	*3*	*4*	*5*	*6*	*7*	*8*
Size Class of Cultivated Land							
Upto 0.5 acre	0.0	0.0	0.0	0.0	0.0	0.005	0.0
0.5 to 1 acre	0.0	0.0	0.0	0.0	0.0	0.009	0.0
1 to 2 acres	1.32	0.0	0.0	100.0	0.0	0.009	0.0
2 to 5 acres	2.14	0.0	0.0	85.13	14.86	0.096	0.0
5 to 10 acres	3.25	8.75	18.43	72.35	0.0	0.050	0.0
10 and Above	0.57	0.0	0.0	0.0	100.0	0.060	1.56
Class							
Agricultural labour not tied	0.90	0.0	0.0	100.0	0.0	0.004	0.0
Agricultural labour tied	0.0	0.0	0.0	0.0	0.0	0.002	0.0
Poor Middle peasant	0.0	0.0	0.0	0.0	0.0	0.033	0.0
Middle Peasant	1.40	0.0	100.0	0.0	0.0	0.002	0.0
Big peasant	3.90	0.0	0.0	85.81	14.19	0.086	0.05
Land Lord	0.30	100.0	0.0	0.0	0.0	0.009	0.0
Non-agriculture	0.0	0.0	0.0	0.0	0.0	0.0	0.0
Caste							
Brahmin and Kayasta	0.20	100.0	0.0	0.0	0.0	0.117	0.0
Bhumihar & Rajput	3.50	0.0	0.0	85.71	13.64	0.20	0.96
Backward I	0.0	0.0	0.0	0.0	100.0	0.005	0.0
Yadav	1.00	0.0	0.0	0.0	0.0	0.031	0.0
Koiri	0.0	0.0	0.0	0.0	0.0	0.046	0.0
Kurmi	11.40	0.0	20.24	79.76	0.0	0.0	0.0
Other Backward	0.0	0.0	0.0	0.0	0.0	0.017	0.0
Scheduled Caste	1.20	0.0	0.0	100.0	0.0	0.0	0.0
Muslim	0.0	0.0	0.0	0.0	0.0	0.001	0.0

the value of draught cattle for it. The draught cattle are found more among both categories of agricultural labourers, but higher among the tied agricultural labourers. A large number of small cultivators have a single bullock shared between two cultivators but as the size of holding is small the per acre value of draught cattle is very high. The distribution of draught cattle is quite uneven in terms of caste. The per acre value of draught cattle is high among the scheduled castes. As draught cattle is not divisible, the scheduled castes with limited land show a very high per acre value of draught cattle.

We have included bicycles and radios also as indicators of the process of modernisation of agrarian technology in various aspects. Per capita ownership of bicycles and radios is increasing with the rise in the holding. Though the tied agricultural labourers do not possess either a radio or a bicycle but as one goes high in the class terms its per capita value is increasing. In the case of bicycle, Brahmin, Kayastha, Kurmi, Bumihar, Rajput and Koiri have higher per capita value, and in case of the Radio, it is highest among the Kurmis.

As is revealed from Table 9, land improvement in terms of new means of irrigation is very limited. However, the land improvement increases with increase of the size of holding, though the improvements drop in the case of holdings above ten acres. The percentage of land improvement is highest among the Kurmis, followed by Bhumihars and Rajputs. The proportion of improvement of land through private tubewells is highest, though canals and government tubewells have also play a limited role.

The pattern of accumulation through levelling of land and other improvements like drainage, clearing, etc., is uneven. However, land-levelling improves with the increase in the size of holding. Except for landlords and middle peasants, the accumulation through land levelling is low. In terms of caste, land-levelling is highest among Brahmins and Kayasthas. The other improvements like drainage and clearing are limited to landlords, Bhumihars and big Rajput peasants. In any case, land accumulation in Bihar is extremely distressing.

Improved Seeds, Fertilisers and Productivity

The core of the new agricultural strategy is high yielding variety (HYV) of seeds through selective breeding. HYV is fertiliser-intensive. This technology has brought about dramatic results in agricultural production since the mid-sixties.

Table 10 indicates the percentage of area under HYV of seeds and per hectare consumption of fertiliser (in kilograms) for the year 1981-

82, in different states of India. Percentage of area under HYV is highest in Punjab, followed by Haryana, Uttar Pradesh and Tamil Nadu. In the consumption of fertilizer, Punjab is again at the top followed by Tamil Nadu, Uttar Pradesh and Haryana. Bihar makes a moderate use of the HYV and fertiliser.

Table 10

Use of Improved Seeds and Fertiliser in Different States in India (1981-82)

States	*% of area under HYV to net sown area*	*Per hectare consumption of fertiliser (k.g.)*
1. Andhra Pradesh	35.3	58
2. Bihar	44.5	25
3. Gujarat	22.14	41
4. Haryana	65.24	69
5. Karnataka	18.8	37
6. Kerala	19.9	43
7. Madhya Pradesh	16.96	12
8. Maharastra	24.8	29
9. Orissa	22.8	13
10. Punjab	100.0	195
11. Rajasthan	14.3	09
12. Tamil Nadu	49.3	89
13. Uttar Pradesh	52.0	73
14. West Bengal	39.9	46

Source: Fertiliser Statistics, 1981-82.

In the survey, we have taken paddy, wheat and maize to examine the responsiveness of different agrarian segments to new technology. These are the most important crops of Bihar.

The result of technological adoption as reflected in the HYV and fertilisers of different categories is mixed. The relevant figures are presented in Tables 11 and 12 (for paddy), Tables 13 and 14 (for wheat). Table 15 (for maize), and Table 16 (for gross output). In case of paddy, the pattern of adoption of HYV and fertiliser in terms of landholdings and class divisions is not very clear, though the adoption of HYV is steadily increasing with a slight drop in the category of one to two acres. In case of per acre cost of fertiliser purchase, results in terms of landholdings are mixed. It is high among poor middle and middle peasants. But, the Kurmis have not only adopted HYV in paddy quite substantially, but are also ahead of other caste groups in investing in fertiliser. They are the second highest in per acre output after the

Table 11

Details about Cultivation of Paddy in Different types of Households (Bihar)

	Percentage area sown land all paddy	*Percentage area sown Irrigated paddy*	*Percentage of area sown improved variety all paddy*	*Percentage area sown HYV all paddy*	*Percentage area sown seed type miss. paddy*
1	*2*	*3*	*4*	*5*	*6*
Size Class of Cultivated Land					
Upto 0.5 acre	38.34	35.00	12.91	12.91	15.00
0.5 to 1 acre	50.34	28.00	41.16	13.85	18.72
1 to 2 acres	39.98	57.00	17.42	9.53	16. 60
2 to 5 acres	51.36	39.00	22.09	21.08	10.83
5 to 10 acres	50.60	52.00	23.09	28.49	14.58
10 or more	54.79	55.00	13.93	28.12	14.22
Class					
Agricultural labour not tied	50.67	38.00	21.15	26.06	13.38
Agricultural labour tied	44.40	69.00	7.15	48.94	11.05
Poor middle peasant	43.73	63.00	3.88	14.73	33.33
Middle peasant	51.05	42.00	21.40	10.35	20.79
Big peasant	50.18	54.00	27.31	23.03	11.23
Land Lord	51.04	24.00	8.40	12.56	9.67
Non Agriculture	11.76	0.0	0.0	0.0	0.0
Caste					
Brahmin + Kayasta	52.39	42.00	21.09	14.45	13.44
Bhumihar + Rajput	48.82	44.00	23.59	25.11	0.71
Backward I	45.77	39.00	11.76	39.70	9.48
Yadav	56.43	21.00	3.61	22.24	23.17
Koiri	47.02	71.00	35.96	0.0	25.35
Kurmi	51.68	61.00	9.78	46.00	20.50
Other Backward II	51.02	73.27	17.57	19.63	17.45
Scheduled Caste	47.60	66.48	11.81	29.33	16.00
Muslim	42.78	29.96	42.59	0.0	23.87

Table 12

Cost of Purchased Fertilizer, Productivity and Sale of Paddy in Different Types of Households (Bihar)

	Per acre cost of purchased fertilizer all paddy	*Per acre Gross output (k.g.) paddy*	*Per acre Gross output value paddy*	*Percentage value sold outside village paddy*	*Percentage value sold inside village paddy*
1	*2*	*3*	*4*	*5*	*6*
Size Class of Cultivated Land					
Upto 0.5 acre	62.36	794.350	1319.958	0.85	0.23
0.5 to 1 acre	63.95	645.285	1066.381	0.31	0.0
1 to 2 acres	85.81	666.676	1154.523	0.37	0.44
2 to 5 acres	72.24	695.460	1082.178	2.11	0.91
5 to 10 acres	71.66	673.963	1004.138	11.82	0.53
10 or more	47.27	800.628	1129.154	3.64	0.53
Class					
Agricultural labour not tied	60.90	589.819	938.658	3.78	0.34
Agricultural labour tied	85.99	809.685	1367.849	1.20	1.02
Poor middle peasant	117.28	855.687	1169.395	0.0	0.80
Middle peasant	100.45	525.488	901.929	2.78	0.77
Big peasant	59.64	790.318	1195.162	7.38	3.62
Land Lord	40.71	378.793	639.744	7.50	6.55
Non-Agriculture	0.0	0.0	0.0	0.0	0.0
Caste					
Brahmin + Kayasta	41.96	504.024	820.733	8.24	8.76
Bhumihar + Rajput	59.86	887.480	1349.159	6.90	1.64
Backward I	88.63	694.988	1158.166	0.31	2.26
Yadav	50.32	425.148	664.132	0.79	0.0
Koiri	109.47	471.388	754.569	0.0	1.29
Kurmi	138.55	832.247	1242.284	11.32	1.22
Other Backward II	54.54	602.908	920.806	0.71	1.41
Scheduled Castes	73.95	752.404	1177.977	4.97	0.59
Muslim	39.35	458.070	879.577	4.01	1.29

Table 13

Details of Cultivation of Wheat in Different Types of Households (Bihar)

	Percentage Area sown all wheat	*Percentage Area sown Irrigated wheat*	*Percentage Area sown Improved variety wheat*	*Percentage Area sown HYV wheat*	*Percentage Area sown seed type missing adjusted*
1	*2*	*3*	*4*	*5*	*6*
Size Class of cultivated Land					
Upto 0.5 acre	33.23	81.25	37.98	11.06	5.29
0.5 to 1 acre	21.45	77.50	19.64	26.07	35.71
1 to 2 acres	30.93	89.80	35.89	36.29	12.58
2 to 5 acres	17.28	78.12	29.16	29.05	24.11
5 to 10 acres	16.77	85.51	14.63	49.71	21.34
10 and above	15.33	92.97	5.83	6.28	74.11
Class					
Agricultural labour not tied	18.91	82.55	17.45	28.30	36.30
Agricultural labour tied	29.46	92.64	22.79	42.65	21.81
Poor middle peasant	28.15	82.53	13.91	21.95	31.84
Middle peasant	24.86	96.63	18.37	48.75	20.28
Big peasant	18.70	82.80	30.39	26.17	30.66
Land Lord	10.57	58.67	15.07	14.44	26.01
Non-Agriculture	23.53	0.0	100.0	0.0	0.0
Caste					
Brahmin + Kayasta	17.91	76.56	26.49	28.45	25.33
Bhumihar + Rajput	16.34	82.44	27.63	7.48	44.21
Backward I	27.37	88.16	29.81	41.01	9.94
Yadav	14.59	78.77	8.02	55.50	1.10
Koiri	32.64	96.06	12.29	73.15	0.83
Kurmi	16.15	99.03	6.73	51.66	25.17
Other Backward II	10.78	77.29	4.13	25.66	64.31
Scheduled Caste	21.84	67.97	16.18	7.46	57.26
Muslim	23.69	71.46	43.66	29.67	18.90

Table 14
Cost of Purchased Fertilizer, Productivity and Sale of Wheat in Different Types of Households (Bihar)

	Per acre cost of purchased fertilizer wheat	*Per acre Gross output (k.g.) wheat*	*Per acre Gross output value wheat*	*Percentage value sold outside village wheat*	*Percentage value sold inside village wheat*
1	2	3	4	5	6
Size Class of Cultivated Land					
Upto 0.5 acre	64.558	409.918	888.682	0.0	0.0
0.5 to 1 acre	116.211	709.357	1563.400	1.19	0.0
1 to 2 acres	121.151	588.752	1272.599	0.51	0.19
2 to 5 acres	150.680	617.062	1292.519	1.53	0.24
5 to 10 acres	163.732	624.761	1350.878	2.82	2.42
10 and above	194.849	691.002	1408.244	4.06	1.79
Class					
Agricultural labour not tied	143.066	511.349	1194.335	1.30	0.27
Agricultural labour tied	92.583	568.091	1231.919	0.62	0.0
Poor middle peasant	112.185	492.703	1070.890	0.0	0.0
Middle peasant	150.395	732.893	1590.350	0.67	0.53
Big peasant	172.587	632.353	1335.927	3.85	1.54
Land lord	116.106	466.861	1036.673	8.49	0.91
Non-Agriculture	0.0	0.0	0.0	0.0	0.0
Caste					
Brahmin + Kayasta	150.091	553.749	1190.091	3.22	2.83
Bhumihar + Rajput	176.648	710.336	1522.766	2.99	0.0
Backward I	88.326	476.962	1037.829	0.0	0.0
Yadav	138.226	618.332	1343.945	0.0	0.0
Koiri	184.760	869.751	1803.002	0.0	0.0
Kurmi	204.958	665.912	1460.691	11.52	0.0
Other Backward II	149.412	430.646	940.926	0.0	4.96
Scheduled cast	128.087	580.883	1262.618	2.25	0.30
Muslim	98.353	436.512	948.760	0.0	1.11

Table 15

Area Improved Seed, Cost of Purchased Fertilizer, Productivity and Sale of Maize in Different types of Households (Bihar)

	Percentage area sow owned land maize	*Percentage area under HYV maize*	*Per acre cost of purchased fertilizer maize*	*Gross output value maize (per acre)*	*Value marketed maize (per acre)*	*Percentage value sold outside village maize*	*Percentage value sold inside village maize*
Size Class of Cultivated Land							
Upto 0.5 acre	0.20	100.0	206.00	559.040	0.0	0.0	0.0
0.5 to 1 acre	1.30	45.94	92.297	1393.459	0.0	0.0	0.0
1 to 2 acres	1.40	23.91	59.52	511.814	9.152	1.75	0.0
2 to 5 acres	3.20	21.84	78.902	447.845	83.057	18.42	0.0
5 to 10 acres	2.00	24.78	144.177	1608.314	74.084	8.36	0.82
10 and more	0.90	0.0	115.417	822.688	108.142	8.36	0.0
Class							
Agricultural labour not tied	1.70	47.37	121.368	347.000	0.0	0.0	0.0
Agricultural labour tied	1.90	19.23	56.846	449.808	0.0	0.0	0.0
Poor middle peasant	1.80	54.76	216.548	1867.238	0.0	0.0	0.0
Middle peasant	1.70	83.10	114.268	1006.803	37.817	3.60	0.0
Big peasant	2.60	12.43	137.492	1155.451	88.254	6.12	1.51
Land lord	3.80	15.73	15.209	368.311	87.877	21.78	2.08
Non-Agricultural	0.0	0.0	0.0	0.0	0.0	0.0	0.0
Caste							
Brahmin + Kayasta	0.10	0.0	0.0	2089.000	0.0	0.0	0.0
Bhumihar + Rajput	2.70	0.0	75.423	569.670	33.077	5.81	0.0
Backward I	3.24	39.29	104.589	491.732	61.071	0.0	12.41
Yadav	0.10	0.0	0.0	2753.025	0.0	0.0	0.0
Koiri	2.30	52.54	191.678	1348.762	0.0	0.0	0.0
Kurmi	3.80	50.55	349.166	1577.546	336.030	21.30	0.0
Other Backward II	1.20	86.49	57.757	7242.405	364.216	4.46	0.0
Scheduled Caste	1.70	10.52	92.105	630.158	44.631	5.17	0.0
Muslim	7.20	14.38	24.350	226.431	12.175	0.0	5.38

Table 16

Details about Aggregated Input and Output (All crops) in Different Types of Households (Bihar)

	Total value Gross output (per acre)	*Total cost of purchased seed (per acre)*	*Total cost of Purchased fertilizer (per acre)*	*Total cost of purchased (other) (per acre)*	*Total input costs (per acre)*	*Total value of marketed (per acre)*
1	*2*	*3*	*4*	*5*	*6*	*7*
Size Class of Cultivated Land						
Upto 0.5 acre	2227.963	118.966	177.426	65.778	290.861	101.960
0.5 to 1 acre	2195.357	72.833	98.320	57.711	288.944	34.210
1 to 2 acres	1766.230	51.118	135.207	63.981	244.657	70.856
2 to 5 acres	1569.033	32.749	120.650	30.677	178.123	120.472
5 to 10 acres	1571.680	—	123.111	43.397	191.127	264.125
10 and more	1444.051	117.110	93.070	29.604	139.792	254.582
Class						
Agricultural labour not tied	1389.932	36.312	103.801	29.839	169.894	98.227
Agricultural labour tied	1978.150	42.549	122.298	44.570	207.594	60.905
Poor middle peasant	2177.361	101.325	177.620	66.275	314.448	66.070
Middle peasant	1731.939	20.442	150.354	44.987	215.970	48.603
Big peasant	1879.264	31.617	130.355	26.315	204.512	241.443
Land Lord	1264.796	27.392	73.211	48.207	147.606	223.539
Caste						
Brahmin + Kayasta	1624.367	27.949	108.131	49.204	183.625	257.726
Bhumihar + Rajput	1817.490	44.222	117.678	37.297	198.209	201.413
Backward I	1693.085	37.680	113.370	43.243	193.187	82.090
Yadav	1129.233	14.190	87.174	49.180	120.611	25.445
Koiri	2147.644	72.085	235.858	77.051	354.898	32.241
Kurmi	2727.615	23.904	299.346	108.181	413.811	572.056
Other Backward	1493.264	11.244	76.328	44.394	131.985	59.893
Scheduled Caste	1882.070	53.847	121.172	32.320	205.702	120.856
Muslim	1214.280	25.108	86.735	30.372	117.157	135.526

Bhumihars and the Rajputs. The gross output of all crops is highest among the poor middle peasants. The surplus production that is marketed outside the village is highest among those having holdings between five and ten acres, big peasants and landlords and among Kurmis followed by Brahmins, Kayasthas Bhumihars and Rajputs.

In case of wheat, the landowners with higher percentage of irrigation have adopted HYV of seeds like those who have one to two acres and five to ten acres, tie agriculture labourers and middle peasants and Koiris and Kurmis. But fertiliser use has increased in wheat corresponding to the size of holdings and is highest among big peasants and middle peasants and among Kurmis, Bhumihars and Rajputs.

In case of per acre gross output of wheat middle peasants, big peasants and Koiris and Kurmis are highest. Here again, the surplus wheat is sold maximum by Koiris, landlords and big peasants, who own ten acres and above cetegory.

The percentage of maize grown is very limited. However, the percentage of HYV maize is highest among those having holdings of up to half acre and among the middle peasants and poor/middle peasants. It is also high among Koiris, Kurmis and others who belong to the backward category II. Per acre cost of fertiliser is highest among Kurmis, Koiris and backward II and among tied agricultural labourers, poor middle peasants, middle peasants and big peasants. The per acre cost of fertiliser is higher in case of those having five acres, five to ten acres, and above. But in gross output the category of half to one acre takes the lead followed by land sizes of five to ten acres. In terms of gross output per acre, it is maximum among the poor middle peasants, middle peasants and big peasants. In terms of caste, other backward II are producing the maximum, followed by Yadavas, Brahmins, Kayasthas, Kurmis and Koiris. The value marketed, however, is maximum in the case of Kurmi landlords and landowners in the category of two to five acres.

It is also revealed from Table 16 that the total value of gross output per acre decreases with increase in the landholding. Its output is highest among the poor middle peasants, tied agricultural labourers and Kurmis and Koiris. Even in the case of total cost of fertiliser, other total costs and input cost, Kurmis and Koiris are ahead of other castes. Kurmis are also marketing their produce to the maximum. In case of the poor middle peasants, their investment in fertiliser and other inputs is higher than the other classes, though, in the marketing of produce, big peasants and landlord are ahead of others. In the investment in fertiliser, input cost is maximum in the case of those having half to one and one to two acres.

The surplus produce is marketed maximum by those having five to ten acres and above.

Land Size, Employment, Expenditure Pattern and Debt

Table 17 indicates the per capita landholding and employment per household. The per capita landholding among all the categories is very low. In terms of caste, Brahmins and Kayasthas have the highest per-capita landholding, followed by Bhumihars, Rajputs, Yadavas and Kurmis. Secondly, the total days of unemployment in a year for workers are very high though it does decrease with the increase in landholding. Thus, large parcels of land and labour scarcity, the necessary conditions for mechanisation, are absent in Bihar's agriculture. Unemployment is lowest among the middle peasants and it is highest among the tied labourers. As agriculture labour is tied its mobility is restricted. Unemployment is quite high among the landlords as the option for employment for them is limited. It is interesting that modern capital goods and total value of machinery increase with an increase in the size of holding, though value of machinery drops among those having landholdings above ten acres. Modern capital goods have increased among different classes with the highest being among the landlords, though the value of machinery decreased in this category. Per acre value of modern capital goods, and value of machinery is highest among Koiris and Kurmis, but incidentally their unemployment per day is lowest compared to other castes.

Agricultural surplus plays a decisive role in agricultural innovation. But, in India, specially in the former 'permanent settlement' areas, it is frittered away in the conspicuous consumption or archaic social practices, like *shradha* (a ceremony performed after death), sacred thread ceremony, marriage etc. Bihar is afflicted by all these social practices. Table 18 provides a broad expenditure pattern in rural Bihar. It reveals that loans from non-traditional sources were not generally available for spending on social occasions. The quantum of loans from relatives was also low, though it was available among almost all the categories of people to a limited extent. But surprisingly, loans from traditional sources were available in abundance to all the landowners except those who belonged to the category of half acre. Per capita social expenditure was found to be the maximum among the non-agricultural categories, followed by the poor middle peasants, both tied and untied agricultural labourers and middle peasants. This practice was maximum among the backward I and II, followed by Bhumihars, Rajputs, Kurmis and Brahmins. The per capita total expenditure and per capita social expenditure increase with the increase in the size of holding. Expenditure rise corresponding with position in the local class. There, the peasants were found spending more on social occasions. Although per capita expenditure is highest among Bhumihars and Rajputs, followed by Brahmins and Kayasthas, social expenditure was highest among Kurmis, followed by Brahmins, Bhumihars, Rajputs and Muslims.

Table 17

Per Capita Land and Per Capita Unemployment among Different Categories of People in Bihar

	Per capita land cultivated (in acres)	*Per worker total days unemployed in a year*
1	*2*	*3*
Size of Cultivated Land		
Upto 0.5 acres	0.065	44.554
0.5 to 1 acres	0.135	42.133
1 to 2 acres	0.211	29.598
2 to 5 acres	0.445	21.658
5 to 10 acres	0.829	20.002
10 and above	1.240	4.438
Class		
Agricultural labour (not tied)	0.133	36.697
Agricultural labour (tied)	0.159	39.813
Poor Middle Peasant	0.191	31.435
Middle Peasant	0.322	17.820
Big Peasant	0.523	20.727
Landlord	0.715	38.706
Non-Agricultural segment	0.012	55.302
Caste		
Brahmin+Kayasta	0.561	42.769
Bhumihar+Rajput	0.509	33.803
Backward I	0.174	35.218
i) Yadav	0.447	27.441
ii) Koiri	0.230	32.286
iii) Kurmi	0.429	23.451
Other Backward II	0.323	46.626
i) Scheduled Castes	0.124	40.302
Muslim	0.251	38.092

Agricultural surplus is mainly spent on clothing. Apart from being a necessity, an elemènt of luxury is also present. Secondly, expenditure on medicines indicates the poor state of health services in rural Bihar. Percentage expenditure on tobacco is very high among small

Table 18
Different Types of Expenditure Among Different Types of Households (Bihar)

	Per capita exceptional expenditure (Both rounds)	Percentage expenditure in clothing	Percentage expenditure in fuel	Percentage expenditure in Bidi	Percentage expenditure in Medicine	Percentage expenditure in liquor
1	*2*	*3*	*4*	*5*	*6*	*7*
Size Class of Cultivated Land						
Upto 0.5 acre	60.026	53.15	2.46	5.68	18.20	0.72
0.5 to 1 acre	53.191	51.58	2.77	3.95	18.84	2.88
1 to 2 acres	156.845	51.66	1.66	8.33	16.56	2.55
2 to 5 acres	178.337	54.64	1.73	2.73	23.80	0.68
5 to 10 acres	224.221	60.80	1.98	2.73	13.69	1.88
10 and above	253.110	68.58	1.35	1.91	11.74	0.64
Class						
Agricultural labourer not tied	51.017	45.18	1.92	9.78	16.09	2.80
Agricultural labourer tied	29.225	44.07	1.01	10.71	25.21	1.23
Poor middle peasant	82.260	58.82	2.22	4.71	18.18	0.15
Middle peasant	185.977	57.61	1.05	4.74	17.06	1.35
Big peasant	244.085	63.64	1.55	2.23	17.90	0.32
Land Lord	192.602	52.76	4.99	2.44	18.30	0.35
Non-Agriculture	114.789	41.90	3.80	5.91	15.25	0.19
Caste						
Brahmin + Kayasta	252.811	64.79	2.90	1.56	12.10	0.30
Bhumihar + Rajput	193.260	56.47	1.79	3.20	21.99	0.01
Backward I	66.707	42.78	0.75	10.13	25.87	2.13
Yadav	31.187	51.72	0.37	6.05	19.42	3.64
Koiri	108.819	56.03	3.15	3.67	41.37	0.23
Kurmi	507.385	56.16	3.91	4.30	17.27	1.83
Other Backward II	93.312	52.36	5.29	3.78	78.84	0.23
Scheduled Caste	34.120	46.25	1.35	9.54	16.14	3.04
Muslim	128.413	51.12	1.95	4.80	18.18	0.21

landholders. Among the agricultural labourers, both tied and untied, the percentage expenditure on tobacco and liquor is very high. Among the backward castes, specially among Yadavas and scheduled castes, the expenditure on tobacco and liquor is quite substantial.

Tables 19 and 20 show that a high rate of interest inhibits accumulation and productive investment. Table 20 further indicates that traditional interest rate is as high as sixty-eight per cent in one of the villages under the survey. The rate of interest on loans from public agencies is relatively much lower. It also indicates that if it is available, it facilitates investment in agriculture. Even amongst the lowest stratum owning up to half acre of land, loans for agricultural purpose are high. Here again, Kurmis have utilised to the loan facility to their maximum advantage. The poor middle peasants have utilised the loan facility more than other classes.

Table 19

Rate of Interest on Loan in Sample Villages

Village	*% Rate of interest on loan from public agencies*	*% Rate of interest on loan from traditional sources*
Alalpur Bishunpur	12	57
Salempur Rupuspur	14	40
Paharpur Dayal	15	27
Diwan Parsa	13	20
Mahesan	10	50
Khangaon	22	46
Chandkura	12	56
Mohiuddin pur	16	65
Jitwarpur	12	68
Belabadan	12	59
Samahuti	15	63
Amrhi	13	28

The analysis of the data in this paper is tentative. It will be premature to come to a definite conclusion about the adoption of technological devices and production relations between different agrarian segments. The pattern of the adoption of technology and augmentation of production is found among landowners of all categories, classes and caste groups in varying degrees.

One important point that emerges from our data is that people with large landholdings, who are generally from among the upper castes, have modern capital goods at their disposal, but these capital endowments are not properly appropriated to ensure maximum agricultural

Table 20

Utilisation of Modern and Traditional Debt Among Different Types of Households (Bihar)

	Per capita value of modern debts	*Per capita value of traditional debts*	*Per capita value of debts from relatives*	*Modern debt used for Agricultural operation (per acre)*
1	*2*	*3*	*4*	*5*
Size class of cultivated land				
Upto 0.5 acre	5.711	135.135	1.211	0.120
0.5 to 1 acre	12.263	135.229	4.067	0.206
1 acre to 2 acres	41.925	147.985	4.481	0.116
2 acres to 5 acres	102.561	170.742	13.132	0.019
5 acres to 10 acre	147.594	135.712	4.707	0.070
10 and more	203.460	194.580	20.706	0.037
Class				
Agricultural labour not tied	15.705	129.641	2.521	0.015
Agricultural labour tied	0.416	138.341	0.714	0.009
Poor middle peasant	54.461	195.643	5.278	0.137
Middle peasant	55.294	79.458	4.357	0.089
Big peasant	165.787	160.818	12.002	0.085
Land Lord	129.902	156.014	23.593	0.049
Non-Agricultural	38.604	204.462	6.501	0.0
Caste				
Brahmin + Kayasta	154.531	212.787	12.816	0.103
Bhumihar and Rajput	174.513	170.743	5.163	0.062
Backward I	4.509	133.677	0.681	0.017
Yadav	38.332	110.327	8.725	0.028
Koiri	44.920	79.678	5.074	0.146
Kurmi	188.181	256.381	21.664	0.117
Other Backward II	39.683	130.111	11.345	0.029
Scheduled Caste	23.168	118.376	1.765	0.030
Muslim	29.823	109.655	17.068	0.050

productivity. The Kurmis, two-third of whom are either big peasants or landlords, have, however, exhibited a good use of capital goods in maximising agricultural productivity. Irrigation can revolutionise agriculture in Bihar accompanied with the proper flow of HYV seeds and fertilisers. Certainly, it these are made available, a fair distribution only can ensure the realisation of the productivity envisaged under a given programme. Factors like caste and class have to be checked from being stumbling blocks in this process of social transformation.

Notes

1. Patnaik, Utsa, "On the Mode of Production In Indian Agriculture—A reply" *Economic And Political Weekly*, Vol. VI, No. 40, Septement, 30, 1972. P.A. 148.
2. Patnaik, Utsa, ibid, P.A. 148
3. Das Gupta, Biplab, *The New Agrarian Technology and India*, MacMillan Company of India, Bombay, 1977, p. 13.
4. Joshi, P.C. "Technology and Agricultural Transformation:Problems of Capitalistic Vs Peasant Agriculture". *In Peasant, Farming and Growth of Capitalism in Indian Agriculture*, Edited by Y.V.K. Rao, G. Parthasarthy, Ch. R. Rao, M. Yadav Reddy, Waheenddin Khan, Visha Andhra Publishing House, Vijayawada, 1984. p. 320.
5. Das Gupta, Biplab, op.cit. p. 2.
6. Prasad, P.H. Rodgers, G.B. Gupta S., Sharma A.N. & Sharma, B. The Pattern of Poverty in Bihar Population and Labour Policies Programme, working paper No. 153, I.L.O. Geneva.
7. Prasad, P.H. and Rodgers, G.B., Class, Caste and Landholding In the Analysis of Rural Economy, Population and Labour Policies, Programme-Working Paper No. 140, I.L.O., Geneva.
8. Srinivas, M.N. *Social Change in Modern India*, University of California Press, Berkelay, 1968.
9. Rudra, Ashok, "Class relations in Indian Agriculture". *Economic and Political Weekly*, June 3-17, 1978.
10. (a) Prasad, P.H. "Caste and Class in Bihar". *Economic and Political Weekly*, Annual Number, February, 1978.
    (b) Prasad, P.H. "Towards a Theory of Transformation of Semifeudal Agriculture", *Economic and Political Weekly*, August 1, 1987.
11. However, it should be noted that not all those paying rent necessarily belong to the exploited class because a tenant may cultivate his leased in-land by employing labourers and pay rent out of the surplus thus obtained. Alternatively, a tenant can sublease his land and thereby becomes and exploiter. Therefore, tenants as such do not constitute a class in the

Marxian sense and have not been distinguished in our scheme.

12. Thorner, D. & Thorner, Alice, *Land & Labour in India*, Asia Publishing House, Delhi.
13. Kanwar, J.B., "From Protective to Productive Irrigation", *Economic and Political Weekly*, Vol-IV, No. 13, March 29, 1969.
14. Sen. L.K. "Role of Irrigation in Integrated Area Development Planning", Paper presented to the Seminar on 'The Role of Irrigation in Agricultural Development', Institute of Social and Economic Change, Bangalore, 1974.
15. Das Gupta, Biplab, op.cit, pp. 86
16. Das Gupta, Biplab, op.cit., pp. 86.
17. Hayami, Yujiro & RUttan, Vernon, *Agricultural Development: An International Perspective*, Johns Hopkins, 1971, pp. 114.
18. Rao, C.H. Hanumantha, 'Factor Endowments, Technology, And Farm Employment in *Reflections on Economic Development And Social Change* Edited by C.H. Hanumantha Rao, and P.C. Joshi, Allied Publishers Private Limited, New Delhi, 1979, p. 213.
19. Raj, K.N. 'Investment in Livestock in Agrarian Economies, Mimeographed, 1968 (unpublished).

5

The Orissan Society: Past Trends and Present Manifestations

Bhairabi Prasad Sahu

In the recent past, some articles focusing on the social roots of Orissa's backwardness have been published.[1] What has eluded the notice of scholars is the apparent continuity that the Orissan society presents in terms of its basic structure including aspects of dominance and power monopolised by certain sections in the domain of social relations with an apparent picture of harmony and stability that the social morphology exhibits.[2] These attract attention, because in the generally vitiated social atmosphere of the country, characterized by antagonism and strife between the 'entrenched' and 'ascendant' castes and/or the 'forward' and 'backward' castes in the north and the Brahmin and the non-Brahmin castes in the south,[3] the Orissan society bears the print of relative order and cohesion. We are not suggesting the persistence of an unchanging static society, for one is aware of the work of Bailey in Bisipara, conscious of the growing consciousness and latent assertion of the Khandayats and Chasas in pockets of rural Orissa and also willing to take cognizance of the possible challenge to the Brahmin-Karana domination by the Khandayats. Not that there are no caste tensions but what is more striking and important is that they do not assume and manifest violent forms.

It can be argued that backward agriculture and aborted industrialization have helped in consolidating the pre-capitalistic social formation, and that the advancement of productive forces has resulted in the transformation of social relationships which may possibly sharpen class antagonism, in many instances subsumed under caste categories and latent caste antagonisms. This neat hypothesis—the social structure and the under-developed material forces reinforcing each other—may appear convincing in its broad essentials but, nevertheless, leaves a few questions unanswered. It may account for the element of continuity but fails to answer for the prevailing apparent stability and cohesion, more so because Orissa is a part of the larger paradox, i.e., the Eastern Indian economy. Such a setting calls for a historical analysis and explanation. Further, the caste system, as suggested by Omvedt,[5] has to be viewed not simply as something belonging to the domain of the superstructure but as interwoven with and shaping the very relations of production in society.

II

The history of Orissa between c. 300 B.C. and c. fourth century A.D. is the history of the internal transformation of a tribal/autochthonous society. This transformation was partly autonomous and partly induced and impelled, owing to contacts with the Sanskritic culture of the Gangetic plains, the beginnings of which can be traced back to the Mauryan times.[6] The subsequent period, i.e., the fourth to the ninth centuries, experienced the emergence of a series of sub-regional states in different pockets of this macro region.[7] This can largely be explained in terms of the land grants to Brahmins, their role as harbingers of socio-cultural change, the peasantization of tribes and the associated ritual elaboration and consequent absorption of tribal deities into the Hindu pantheon.[8] Interestingly, however, the period and process of secondary state formation, coincided with the beginning of the parcellization of state sovereignty, which ultimately led to the emergence of a feudal structure. The specificities of the emerging pattern were well laid by the tenth century. The details of these trends, which can be explained as feudal both in the political and socio-economic sense, assumed a clear shape in the next three centuries. The picture that emerges thus is one of transition from tribalism to feudalism without any other stage intervening in-between.[9] The process, however, was not uniform and unilinear. The littoral zone experienced the transition to the historical phase earlier than the inland forest tracts and the rolling uplands.[10] The tribal situation accounted for the thwarted, uneven and halting nature of the process of transformation.[11] This, together with the physiography of the land, had a very important bearing on the nature and type of social formation in early medieval Orissa, the formative period of the development of the Orissan society, which was to determine and characterize the subsequent society. The king was emerging as the preserver and catalytic agent of change in the caste order within his domain.

The orthodox four-fold *varna* society which became the hallmark of Northern India in the early historical period and got entrenched in the socio-economic matrix in the Gupta and the post-Gupta periods was late to develop in Orissa. However, when it diffused and spread in this region, there was a difference in its character in so far as the broad essentials were concerned. The *varna* society did not assume the same form and operate with the same intensity in Orissa, as in the Gangetic plains. The regional variation could be explained first by the presence of a preponderantly tribal population and secondly, it could be accounted for, as suggested above, with reference to the physiography of the region. Assuming the coast as the base line, one can conveniently divide Orissa into three broad parts: (i) The coastal plains, (ii) the mountainous region and the plateau area of Central Orissa, dissected by a number of rivers, and (iii) the western rolling uplands, a product of interspersed rivers. The rolling uplands, in contrast to the plateaulands, are lower in elevation and have mostly an undulating topography. The area is less fertile than the coastal plains.[12] It may be mentioned that forty-four per cent of Orissa's land area is covered by forests. Thus, barring the coastal plains, there are no other widespread, resplendent alluvial plains which could uphold and sustain a social structure or stratified order of the northern type. The rich, fertile Gangetic plains supported a highly stratified feudal social structure, operating within the contours of the four-fold *varna* scheme, which provided the ideological rationale for surplus generation and extraction. The absence of a similar economic base was perhaps a serious impediment to the formation of a social order similar to that of the north. It appears that Orissa did not have a rigid, multi-tiered stratification pattern. The unproductive surplus appropriating elite had to be within workable limits in this formative period, characterized by the introduction of agriculture and rural expansion.

Land grants, as an instrument of socio-cultural change, heralded the immigration of Brahmins of various *gotras* and *caranas* from circa fourth century A.D. The Matharas, Sailodbhavas, Bhaumakaras, Sulkis, Bhanjas and Tungas made liberal grants of land to Brahmins.[13] In the ninth and tenth centuries, the Somavamsis intensified the practice and it continued to thrive under the Gangas. Beginning with the Rithapur plates of the Nalas, we have a number of inscriptions indicating that many grants were made in forest regions, under the Bhajans, Somavansis and Gangas.[14] There are inscriptional references to the habitation of tribals. The history of the origins of the ruling dynasties in early medieval Orissa unambiguously demonstrates that most of them originated from among the local tribes.[15] This explains the logic of the land grants to Brahmins in settled and forested regions. Grants in backward areas must have been made to bring virgin soil under cultivation and also to acculturate the tribal people. Sharma rightly argues that the land[16] grants to Brahmins in tribal areas led to inner colonization and the extension of agriculture.

Early medieval Orissa witnessed considerable agricultural expansion. A large number of land grant charters indicate the land grants would surely account for only a part of the total area under agriculture. The rise of numerous sub-regional states in the same period in different pockets of Orissa also presupposes the spread of agriculture to some extent. The Brahmins played a seminal role in the process of royal legitimation. They opened up new areas for cultivation and helped the process of peasantization of the tribes and allowed the Hinduized rulers to siphon off the surplus produce of the aboriginals. The infant regional kingdoms were not only dependent on the support and loyalty of the people but also needed their land for gradual extension of peasant agriculture, which alone could provide enough surplus for the maintainance of the dominant sections (ruling families, Brahmins, officials etc.).[17] The state was also dependent on the support of the tribal militia. Thus, it is only within the framework of state formation that the social scenario can be fully appreciated. The tribes were roped into the Hindu system for surplus generation and gradually into a new system of production relations characterized as 'feudal'. The key to the process was the peasantization of the tribes. The Brahmins indoctrinated them so as to ensure their subservience.[18] It is clear that the Hindu society had been assigning them a certain place within itself. Tribal absorption and integration was a desideratum, for Hindu social institutions which were imported into tribal areas needed a minimum of Hindu social context to survive.

This brings us to the problem of social stratification in Orissa. Land grants to Brahmins and the extension of agriculture had the attendant consequence of the conversion of the autochthonous tribes into Sudra castes, a process which was carried out simultaneously along with their peasantization.[19] Sharma's postulation that in the early medieval period in course of Brahminization in the backward areas the local tribal people were transformed into Sudras and their chiefs absorbed as Kshatriyas into the Hindu fold seems to be valid in the Orissan situation.[20]

This apparently two-tiered social structure needs to be further explained. Jiaswal writing about the absence of a Kshatriya *varna* in South

India notes that the tribal chieftains and/or Hinduized kings claiming Kshatriyahood lost their status as soon as they lost their political dominance.[21] A similar thing seems to have happened in Orissa too. The numerous autochthonous ruling families in early medieval Orissa were mostly of tribal origin,[22] and their pretensions of Kshatriyahood seem to have fizzled out with the loss of power. They did not give rise to a viable Kshatriya *varna.* In Orissa, there were no ancient Kshatriya clans to provide the base and hence the *varna* could neither take deep roots nor it could flourish.[23] The present-day Khandayats (the wielders of swords) who stake claim to Kshatriyahood are after all a militia-cum-cultivator caste, whose origins may be traced to the medieval period, possibly to the Ganga-Gajapati times.[24]

Similarly, there are references to Karanas claiming a Kshatriya descent[25] and more recently some Gaudas have claimed ancestry from the Yaduvanshi Kshatriyas. But what seems historically valid is that the Kshatriya *varna* never really crystallized in Orissa. In the period under discussion, some Orissan rulers had matrimonial relations with the Pallavas, Chalukyas, Cholas and Haihayas.[26] It may, however, be noted that these dynasties themselves were of very humble origins and so these marriages do not really prove anything on the issue of Kshatriya ancestry. Similarly, in subsequent times, many ruling families, especially in western Orissa where state formation actualized at a relatively later period, claimed a Kshatriya-Rajput origin.[27] However, as K.S. Singh posits, "the manufacture of spurious genealogy involving the conferment of the status of Kshatriya is an important indication of the Brahminization of tribes."[28] In short, the way in which the ruling dynasties of Orissa claimed Kshatriya status is not much different from the way in which "the great builders of Khajuraho temples emerged as Rajput Kshatriyas of Chandel clans out of a tribal base."[29]

The socio-economic change in Northern India had much to do with the decline of trade and the decay of towns, which led to the decline of the Vaisyas, who gradually had come to be associated with mercantile and town based activities. In the meantime, the Sudras had risen to be farmers and agriculturists. The blurring of the distinction between the two *varnas* is perceptible in Smriti literature. Taking a clue from the postulation of Sharma,[30] it may be suggested that the Vaisya *varna* did not arise in Orissa because during the period when Orissa experienced Brahminization, the distinction between the Vaisyas and the Sudras had already got blurred in Northern India. What seems possible in the Orissan context is that the indigenous tribal population was integrated in the

Brahminical social order mainly as Sudras and low castes. Jaiswal points out that the tribes were brought into the Brahminic fold at this stage mainly as Sudras rather than as slowly as Vaisyas in order to ensure their servility.[31] However, it may be added that the blurring of the distinction between Sudras and Vaisyas and the absence of a viable Vaisya *varna* might have made the Sudra status acceptable to the aboriginals without much reluctance. As Jaiswal posits the shift in the concept of the Vaisya *varna*[32] which got increasingly identified with trade and commerce in the early Christian centuries, was also responsible for the categorization of peasants in Gupta and post-Gupta times as Sudras. Besides, in the Orissan situation, as we shall notice in the following pages, there was no rigid polarization of the society, quite unlike the picture that one obtains for the south in the same period. In contrast the ruling class made conscious efforts to integrate and cultivate the tribals. The absorption of the tribal deities into the Hindu pantheon and their consequent rise to high ritual elaboration bear testimony to the fact.[33] This in turn gave rise to the cult of *shakti* worship, the numerous manifestations of which one finds in Orissa, during this period.[34] Tantricism was another by-product of the process. This cunning device sought to "bridge the gulf between the folk and the elite". Further, it may be of interest to note that in later centuries, especially in medieval times, the *panchamahaya*jnas which were earlier prescribed for and performed by a Brahmin were suitably adapted and recommended for a Sudra.[35]

Despite the absence of a viable Kshatriya *varna* or a Vaisya *varna* for that matter, we still find references in the charters of the regional ruling families where they vociferously proclaim themselves to be the defenders of the four-fold *varna* order and also *varnashramdharma.* This is more pronounced in case of the Bhaumakaras and the Somavamsis. What is strikingly absent in all the charters is the categorical mention of the four varnas. It may be deduced that in doing so they were clearly trying to gain vertical legitimacy in society and the acceptance for their rule. In Orissa, while the four-fold *varna* order continued to remain the ideal, i.e., what ought to be, the two-tier structure with its division into castes and the numerous intermediary occupational castes came to constitute the functional reality. Similar imprecise and vague references to the four-fold *varna* order are also encountered in the Ganga[36] and Gajapati records.[37] Two clearly indentifiable *varnas* evolved in the region, based on their functions—the Brahmin and the Sudra. The Vaisyas surfaced only occasionally in times of trade and the Kshatriyas never had local roots.

Turning to occupational castes it is deemed superfluous to elaborate upon the divisions and sub-divisions among the Brahmins. A.P. Shah,[38] U. Subudhi,[39] B.Das,[40] S.C. Behera,[41] B.K. Rath,[41a] S.K. Panda[42] and a host of other scholars have abundantly reflected on the various Brahmanic *Gotras Pravaras, Caranas* and *Sakhas.* The predominant position of the Brahmins in Orissan society since the days of the Matharas is a well established fact. What needs to be emphasized is that as in Northern India here too there was a proliferation of Brahmin castes on the basis of different indentities. The *Gotras Pravaras, Caranas* and *Sakhas* might have provided one basis. The migration of Brahmins from different areas of North and South India must have created divisions in their ranks owing to a difference in their levels of ritual purity and pollution. As Jaiswal suggests many of the Brahmins in Orissa, in course of the tribal acculturation and peasantization process, might not have been able to avoid physical labour completely and such Brahmins then must have stood degraded in the eyes of those who did not engage in manual labour.[43] The presence of the tribal priests and their recognition as degraded Brahmins must have further complicated the Brahmin stratum. Besides, there is evidence of Brahmins being engaged in many occupations. They officiated in different capacities, e.g., as *Mantrin, Aksapatalika* (record keeper), *Dutaka, Utkirnaka* (engraver), *Mahattara* (village headman), *Lekhaka, Ranaka* (a feudatory status) and *Mandalika* (governor).[44] These diversified occupations must have been of great relevance in triggering off stratification within the Brahmin-fold and consequently it must have stimulated sub-caste proliferation within this category.

The evidence concerning the other occupational castes is very scanty. However, their existence cannot be denied. They did exist and proliferate, occupying possibly at times an ambivalent position in the seemingly two-tier *varna* structure. D. Das, on the basis of certain terms used in the inscriptions, infers the existence of a section of people who in their occupation correspond to the record-keepers or Kayasthas.[45] We have reference to terms like *Lekhaka, Karanika* and *Pustapala.* A.P. Shah, however, notes that the inscriptions of Orissa do not indicate the existence of a separate caste such as the Kayastha prior to the tenth century A.D.[46] It seems that during the Somavamsi and Ganga rule, with the acceleration in the number of land grants and the intensification of the feudal system, the Kayasthas as a distinct caste came to take shape. Mohanty draws our attention to the existence of the Kayasthas under the Somavamsis.[47] It is learnt that a number of Kayasthas were attached to the office of the *Sandhivigrahika.*[48] The Narasapatnam plates refer to a term *Kayastha-Sandhivigrhika* and similarly another record uses a term *Mahakayastha-Sandhivigrahika.*[49] These terms have two meanings. First, it suggests that the office of the Kayastha and that of the *Sandhivigrahika* were held by one and the same person. Secondly, it may mean that a man of Kayastha caste held the office of the *Sandhivigrahida.* If the second was true, then it could be suggested that the Kayasthas, besides keeping records, also served in other capacities. We have references to Kayasthas occupying high offices under the Gangas. Some inscriptions mention the Karanas (Kayasthas) along with Brahmins. B. Das refers to two inscriptions where the form runs as *Brahmin-Karana-Puroga-Nivasi.*[50] The mention of Karanas together with Brahmins suggests their rank in society. In medieval Orissan records, we come across terms like *Shri Karana, Chhamu Karana, Deula Karana,* etc., indicating important assignments.[51] Like the Brahmin state functionaries, the Karana/Kayastha high officials were also allotted land revenues as remuneration for their services.[52] The Karanas emerged not only as important state functionaries but also excelled in the *sastras* and theology.[53]

We have terms like *Grihasvami* and *Grihadhyaksha* in the Jayarampur copper-plate[54] which seem to be synonymous with the expression *Grahapati* in Northern India. Similarly, in other records of the fifth and sixth centuries A.D., we find mention of the term *Kutumbin.*[55] These terms may refer to the householders and/or the well-to-do peasant householders. Among the other castes, mention may be made of the potter (*Kumbhakara*) and the bronze-smith (*Kamsyakara*) for they are referred to in the inscriptions.[56] The Bhaumakara epigraphic records mention three more castes, viz., weaver (*Tantravaya*), cowherd (*Goktuta*) and distiller (*Saundhika*).[57] In the Somavamsi records, we have references of goldsmith (*Suvaranakara*), engraver (*Vindhani*), mason (*Sutradhara*) etc.[57a] The inscriptions, sculptural relics and temple architectural remains of the period endorse the existence of engravers, sculptors, masons and quarrymen. What attracts attention is the fact that we have no definite record of the untouchables in this period. This indicates the relatively less stratified nature of Orissan society. The Dambas, Panas and Candalas of today might have made their beginnings in a later period. Those aboriginals who remained on the fringes of the Hindu society seem to have been reduced to these categories. Records of the thirteenth century mention thirty-six occupational castes which were deployed to render services in the temple. Mahapatra rightly argues that there is no justification to infer that these castes did not exist earlier.[58] On the basis of local tradition, he infers the presence of the preceptor (*Acharya*), garland arranger (*Pratihara*), flower-arranger (*Puspalaka*) washerman and barber (*Dyatas*) and gate-keeper (*Duarapalaka*). It may be added that the Ganga charters mention a number of other castes, such as perfumer (*Gandhika*), dealer in conch-shells (*Sankhiak*), brazier (*Kamsyikah*), goldsmith (*Svarnakara*), maker/ dealer of jaggery (*Gudika*), florist (*Malika*), milkman (*Gopala*), oilman (*Tailika*), craftsman (*Silpi*), etc.[59] Most of the above delineated castes seem to fall in the Sudra category. Their association with the temples and the deities had very important implications for the structure and evolution of Orissan society.

As regards the position of women, the available evidence is far from sufficient. From the sculptural representations on the Satrughuneswara group of temples, it may be inferred that women excelled in the art of dance and singing. Kalyana Devi of the Sailodbhava family is known to have patronized the Jaina saints.[60] Bhaumakara records reveal that widowed queens and daughters of deceased kings ascended the throne and ruled in full vigour with legitimate royal status.

Bhaumakara queens did grant villages to Brahmins and religious establishments.[61] The evidence for *sati* is conspicuously absent. Not before the eleventh and twelfth centuries do we come across evidences of *sati*.[62] In case of the Bhaumakaras it is visibly absent. The Sailodbhava records simply refer to the bereavement of the widowed ladies.[63] On balance, women in Orissa seem to have enjoyed a better social status than their counterparts in Northern India. This may be explained in terms of the tribal heritage and legacy, which unmistakably took time to break. Several Ganga charters reveal that donations were made to ensure the happiness and welfare of mothers and wives.[64] Some women of the royal family were well versed in the *Vedas, Sastras* and *Puranas*. Contemporary art among other things depicts women as co-participants with men in the observance of festivals.[65] There is evidence for the employment of women in the construction of the Sun Temple at Konarka. They were employed for lighter auxiliary work and were paid lesser wages than men. However, there is mention of one woman being employed as a sculptress.[66] Such instances are absent in the Gajapati records. Moreover, Sarala Dasa's *Mahabharata*, a work of the fifteenth century, reflects on child marriage, *sati* and the suffering of widows.[68] Admittedly, though *sati* does not seem to have been practised among the common people, yet these institutions amply suggest the deteriorating of women, the beginnings of which possibly may be traced to the Ganga period. The introduction of the *devadasi* system and dancing as a daily ritual in the temples is credited to the Gangas.

The scenario so far perceived suggests a case of regional variation and deviation from the North Indian social pattern. Nevertheless, the proliferation of Brahmin, Sudra and several occupational castes and the rise of the Kayasthas/Karanas have to be viewed in the perspective of the emerging feudal context,[69] although there may be regional differences in matters of details owing to the specificities of the macro region.

The South Indian social structure with its division into Brahmins and non-Brahmins, together with the attendant antagonism between them, failed to take roots in this macro region. The early medieval period in South India is conspicuous by the emergence of temples as landed institutions.[70] The temples came to represent the Brahminic dominance—social, political and economic. Kesavan Veluthat posits that these temples became centres of mighty agrarian corporations of a class of non-cultivating and landowning upper caste people placed over a toiling peasantry.[71] The Brahmins both controlled the property and officiated over the service of the temple. This created a cleavage between the Brahmins and the non-Brahmins, especially those non-Brahmins who belonged to the dominant peasant caste. R.N. Nandi has recorded epigraphic references pertaining to conflicts between Brahmins and peasants in early medieval *agrahara* villages of South India.[72] The Bhakti movement that swept the south is a reflection of this reality. It was an endeavour to gloss over the prevailing contradictions. In this perspective, it has been suggested that the Bhakti movement had a temple-base in South India,[73] and exuded an elitist bias.[74]

The present study shows that the patronage extended to the autochthonous tribal population by the dominant sections considerably mitigated the inherent antagonism in the existing social relations. Early medieval Orissa experienced a process of Hindu-tribal continnum and not a 'sustained displacement' of the aboriginals from their homeland, a process which formed the basis of the regional kingdoms.[75] In search of legitimacy and to redress the sense of deprivation of the tribes-turned-peasants religious compensations were offered by the ruling class. The rise of Shaktism or the cults of various mother goddesses, tantricism and the Buddhist Tara amply reflect on the emerging and existing realities. Most of the tribal deities underwent a process of Hinduization along with the parallel development of chieftainship to Hindu kinship.[76] Both tradition and practice indicate the tribal origin of Lingaraja (Bhubaneswar) and Jagannatha (Puri), the two famous Hindu deities of Orissa. Both these temples have two categories of priests. The *Badus* in Lingaraja and the *Daitas* in Jagannatha temple are said to be of tribal origin. They come into close and intimate contact with the deities whose personal attendants they are. The cases of the *Badus* and the *Daitas* along with the thirty-six functional castes in the service of the temples of Orissa, referred to above, present brilliant illustrations of the conscious attempt by the ruling classes to patronize and win over the subject tribals.[77] In Orissa, the issue of Brahmins monopolizing the Gods and the temples is thus strikingly missing. Even today, mother goddesses (*Thakuranis*) in numerous temples of Orissa are attended to by priests of humble origins like the Malis and in some cases even aborgines. The ikons of Pancha Varahi in village Satvaya on the sea shore of Cuttack district, for example, are being serviced exclusively by a tribal woman.[78] Aspects such as these suggest that Orissa has retained elements of its autochthonous culture despite Brahminization/Hinduization through the ages.

Apparently, the Brahmins and Kayasthas/Karanas were the dominant social sections after the members of the ruling houses in terms of their monopoly of social prestige, high offices, royal patronage and attendant economic power. In the absence of a viable Kshatriya/Rajput category, these two appear to be stable dominant caste groups. However, we have some interesting evidence from the Ganga period, a period characterized by rich agrarian surpluses, revival of intra-regional and inter-regional trade, rise of merchants and the introduction of gold coins[79] referring to Vaisya *agraharas*[80] and also suggesting the appointment of Vaisyas in high offices, including that of *Mahasenapati*.[81] The distribution of landed property seems to have been broad based spread over the Hinduized ruling houses, the Brahmins, Karanas and the Vaisyas, besides the peasants. Further, we learn that during the Gajapatis from among the five great exponents of Oriya literature, four were non-Brahmins.[82] Sarala Dasa was a Sudra, and agriculturist by caste. Moreover, in the same period many temple officials, such as the examiners of offerings (*Bhoga Pariksha*) in the Simachalam temple, were non-Brahmins.[83] The surnames such as Mohanti, Jena and Khajia are a clear indication of such a situation. What emerges is the absence of a state of status-summation in any given caste category. Simultaneously, the persistent, protracted efforts to cultivate and win over the tribals[84] in a largely tribal setting also seem to have shaped the course of the evolution of Orissan society. These may explain the apparent stability in structural terms of the regional caste system of Orissa.

The period of secondary state formation was characterized by the peasantization of the tribes and the universalization of the local tribal cults to a high level of elaboration. Hinduization of tribal deities not only served to legitimize the Hinduized kingships but also tried to divert attention from the social contradictions emanating from production relations. Social stratification, admittedly, does not seem to have been complex or rigid at this early stage owing to the strong tribal legacy. Not surprisingly, therefore, the evidence of cleavages is wanting. However, it appears reasonable to infer that the relations between the non-producing landowning Brahmins and the so-called Kshatriyas and the actual toiling peasantry were not entirely harmonious.[85] They seem to have entered into a relationship that may best be described as antagonistic-cooperation. By the end of the first millennium A.D., with the emergence of full-fledged peasant societies and the formation of regional kingdoms, the social setting appears to have experienced changes which are manifest in the emergence and proliferation of temples and temple-centered rituals, which finally culminated into the cult of Jagannatha. The temple as an institution provided validation to temporal authority and legitimized the social structure.[86] In that capacity it ensured the habitual subservience of the peasantry and perpetuation of the order. Elsewhere, we have argued that the temple, thus, was an instrument that helped to gloss over antagonisms and social contradictions and served to scotch social conflicts.[87]

With the emergence of the Jagannatha cult which increasingly assimilated elements of popular culture and folk religion,[88] the use of religion by the state to maintain and perpetuate the socio-political system entered a new phase in medieval Orissa.[89] Various deities at different levels such as the village, locality and sub-region came to be bound to Jagannatha in a relationship of subordination.[90] The belief is that even the *Yoginis* could not cause epidemics without his consent. The conspicuous absence of social protest in the garb of religious movements as a serious alternative, or if there were any, their tenuous existence reflects not so much upon the absence of social contradictions (although not of a very serious kind) very much inherent in the production relations of the times, but the inbuilt capacity to absorb and assimilate that was characteristic of the Jagannatha cult.[91] The emergence of the *Pancha-Sakhas* in the middle of the sixteenth century is interpreted as some form of social protest against the Brahminical dominance of the socio-religious order, for they expressed their contempt for Brahminical exclusiveness and rituals, emphasized the tribal origin or Jagannatha and to loosen the monopoly of the Brahmins over the scriptures, which were in Sanskrit, rendered many of them in native Oriya. However, they do not appear to have won many admirers/followers or brought about any readjustment and transformation in society.[92] Similarly, the advent of Chaitanya too does not seem to have had any serious bearing on social relations or realities.[93] It may be pertinent to mention that the stories such as *Manika Gauduni* and *Sriya Chandaluni* which are related to Jagannatha were creations of this medieval period and tried to promise illusory equality or breed a false sense of (non-existent) egalitarianism by portraying the Gajapati ruler as a sweeper during the car festival (*Ratha Yatra*) showing how Lord Jagannatha and his brother Balabhadra accepted curd from a Gauduni suggesting that Lakshmi, the deity of wealth and prosperity, was equally accessible to one and all including the untouchables. Kulke cites a passage from a script of the Rajaguru of Keonjhar amply illustrating the necessary participation of tribes like the Bhuiyans and Juangs in the *Ratha Yatra* in the late medieval feudatory states of Orissa.[94] Today, during the *Ratha Yatra* at Puri, every summer, the tribals go on to play a very important role in all the rituals concerning Lord Jagannatha, who is, during that period, accessible to all sections of society, high and low. What a tremendous effort at social reconciliation! Thanks to the ruling elite's understanding and appreciation of the social realities and material foundations!

III

In a different context, Marx wrote that "men make their own history, but they do not make it just as they please; they do not make it under circumstances chosen by themselves, but under circumstances directly encountered, given and transmitted from the past. The tradition of all dead generations weighs like a nightmare on the brain of the living."[95] These prophetic words objectively in the Orissan case seem to be quite apt. The social morphology and physiology of the present-day Orissa can be appreciated in terms of its historical background for much of the tendencies and patterns we have discussed live and manifest themselves even today. The present-day Orissan society has a massive content of the old mode of production. A cursory look around reveals the broad division of Orissan society between the Brahmins and non-Brahmins. The latter incorporates a wide range of people including the Karanas, Khandayats, Chasas and many occupational castes among others. It is difficult to identify people in the two middle *varnas* theoretically though one may work out some equation. Andrew Sterling had observed the prevalence of such a social situation in Orissa even in the early part of the nineteenth century.[96] In most villages of Orissa, the cultivating Chasa caste or the Khandayats are the landowning and the economically powerful castes. In places they largely conform to the significant features of dominant castes. There are villages where other castes like braziers (*Kansari*), oil-men (*Teli*) etc., are significant landowners and or dominant castes. The Khandayats in the coastal districts and the Kulaks in the inland districts are the emerging rich peasants who are throwing challenges to the ruling classes[97]—the Brahamin-Karana combine domination. Brahmins and Karanas are respectable upper castes considerably monopolizing the administrative and middle class professions and playing a disproportionately larger role in the decision-making process in the state. Yet, they are not necessarily the dominant castes in the economic or social sense of the term.[98] Turning to the question of landholdings, one notices that small and modest sized holdings are the general pattern. Instances of large landed estates or magnates are relatively very few.[99] The point is further driven home by the absence of the permanent settlement, i.e., the *zamindari* type of land revenue system in a major part of the state of Orissa, under the *Raj*. The permanent settlement reinforced the feudal system until recently in areas where it operated. Its absence in this case not only suggests the physiographic specificities of the land but may also explain the pattern of social formation in the region. The settlement in the Garjat states of western Orissa was of a different kind, and it was in a different setting which does not alter this understanding.

On the issue of social mobility the district gazetteers are quite suggestive.[100] Between 1901 and 1931, there are large-scale instances of Chasas rising to the status of the Khandayats. The same period witnessed an upward mobility of some Khandayats into the rungs of the Karanas. Similarly, there are instances of Gaudas claiming a Yadwansi Kshatriya status, putting on the sacred thread and refusing to work as *palanquin* bearers. One may refer to Bailey's work at Bisipora which delineates a similar process of upward social mobility among the lower castes.[101] Moreover, the numerous tribes inhabiting northern, western and southern Orissa, such as the Bhuiyan, Gond, Kond, Savara and so on have come to be increasingly assimilated to the Hindu peasant-base and are considered equivalent in status to clean castes.[102] Many of them have replaced the practice of burial by cremation, given up the eating of beef and recruit the services of the Brahmin for observance of rituals. These forms of social mobility acquire meaning in the context of the weak roots that caste features like social distance and exclusiveness have in this region. This relative openness may account for the apparent stability of the caste system in Orissa.

Wherever the Kulaks have emerged as a significant class, caste has become an idiom for them, which they have utilized for the fulfilment of their class demands. In Orissa, however, the very nature of the landholdings, which are small and modest sized, has held back the rise of an economically powerful and assertive Kulak class willing to make use of the caste idiom for class gains. However, the presence of a Kulak category in coastal Orissa and the intermittent western riverine plains can be visualized from the faction mongering in the ruling Congress and other political parties. In Northern India, the predicament of this section can be best summarised by citing one of the popular election cliches:

"Forward-Harijan bhai-bhai
Yeh Backward Kahan se Aai"

In the south, this class has systematically assured its ascendency at the cost of the Brahmins, who have paid the price for having manipulated their dominance so well until recently, and in the north it is unenviably sandwiched between the traditional upper castes and the Harijans leading to all sorts of caste-class tensions. In addition to the high tribal concentration in Orissa, the scheduled castes and other backward Classes constitute 17 per cent and 28.4 per cent of the total population, respectively,[103] and yet antagonisms of the above type have not vitiated the social atmosphere. The absence of organized caste politics points in the same direction. This can possibly be accounted for by the relative openness of the Orissan society and not so favourable agrarian base.[104] The major division here is not between castes but regions. Social antagonisms tend to get subsumed under sub-regional rivalries and elite conflicts.[105]

There is a great degree of social harmony and politics of consensus in Orissa. The increasing assertion of Khandayat-Chasa power has not clipped the wings of the Brahmin-Karana combine, what to speak of seriously undermining it. Politics continues to be urban-based, and not rural. It has been an overtly inert, non-violent state without any riots and communal carnage raging in it.

The absence of any radical programme can be appreciated by probing into the character of the Brahmin-Karana dominated middle class. Unlike the Bhadraloks of Bengal, they still retain their association with land and have their roots in the villages. This may partially explain the problem. But how does one explain the relative secular politics in the state? Orissa does not have the advantages of the legacy of a nineteenth ury Renaissance or sustained organized Left Movement as does ngal. Nevertheless, there have been no caste movements in Orissa of the kind in Maharashtra, Karnataka, etc. Although caste is socially present, it does not manifest itself politically. Thus, one may explain the situation by resorting to the historical evolution of the caste system in the region and emphasize the regional specificities, which have shaped and continue to a shape to large extent the very relations of production in the society. Ghurye was obviously stating a truism when he suggested that there is hardly a single caste system, but several, each specific to a linguistic-cultural region.[106]

Notes

1. See Manoranjan Mohanty, 1984, 'Social Roots of backwardness in Orissa (A study of class, caste and power), in *Social Science Probings*, Vol. 1. no. 2, June, pp. 184-228; M. Mohanty, 1985, 'Arguing with Bailey by proxy', in *Social Science Probings*, Vol, 2, no. 2, June, pp. 263-67; R. Barik, Caste system and economic backwardness of Orissa', (in the same issue), pp. 254-62 and M. Mohanty, 1986, 'Adrift middle class', in *EPW*, vol. xxi, no. 33, August 16.
2. Ibid.
3. Pillai provides a god account of the caste antagonisms and the social distance that is practised in south India, especially in Tamil Nadu and Kerala. See S.D. Pillai, 1976, The Draridian milieu, in S.D. Pillai, 1976, The Dravidian milieu, in S.D. Pillai (ed), *Aspects of changing India, Studies in Honour of G.S. Ghurye*, Bombay, pp. 129-35.
4. F.G. Bailey, 1958 *Caste and Economic Frontier*, London: also 1960, *Tribe, Caste and Nation, London.*
5. Gail Omvedt, 'Development of the caste system in South Asia: Notes Toward a Theory (mimeographed), I am thankful to George Chira of TDSS, Pune, for having sent me this article.
6. See S. Seneviratne, 1980-81, 'Kalinga and Andhra: The Process of Secondary State Formation in Early India, in *IHR*, Vol. 7, nos. 1-2, pp. 54-69: also see B.P. Sahu, 1984, Ancient Orissa: The Dynamics of Internal Transformation of the Tribal Society, in *PIHC*, Annamalai Session, pp. 148-160: also in K.M. Shrimali (ed), 1987, *Essays in Indian Art, Religion and Society*, Delhi, pp. 169-80.
7. H.Kulke, 1977, Early State Formation and ROyal Legitimation in late Ancient Orissa, in M.N. Das (ed) *Side-Lights on History and Culture of Orissa*, Cuttack, pp. 104-14; L.C. Hota, 1979, Some Aspects of the Social Life in Orissa from A.D. 800-1200, M.Phil dissertation submitted to

the Centre for Historical Studies, J.N.U., New Delhi (unpublished); also: B.P. Sahu, Social Changes in Early Medieval Orissa: The Case of Tribal Integration and Absorption (circa 6th-12th century A.D.), paper presented at the 1982 session of the Orissa History Congress, Baripada (revised version forthcoming).

8. H.Kulke, 1977, op. cit., B.P. Sahu, 1982, op.cit.
9. Sharma hints in the same direction in the concluding portion of the appendix on Orissa. See R.S. Sharma, 1980 (second edition), *Indian Feudalism*: c. 300-1200, Delhi, p. 236.
10. B.P. Sahu, 1987, op.cit., p. 177.
11. Tribals constitute 23.11 per cent of Orissa's population even today, as against the national figure of 7.5 per cent. See *Annual Plan 1982-83 Orissa (draft)*, Government of Orissa (Planning and Co-ordination Department), 1981, Bhubaneswar, p. 109.
12. B.N. Sinha, 1971, *Geography of Orissa*, New Delhi, pp. 146-62; also B.N. Sinha, 1977, Land and people of Orissa, in M.N. Das (ed), *Side-Lights on History and Culture of Orissa*, Cuttack.
13. See R.S. Sharma, 1980, op.cit. pp. 227-36; B. Das, 1978, *The Bhaumakaras and Their Times*, New Delhi: U. Subuddhi, 1980, A Study of the Brahmins of Ancient and Early medieval Orissa from Epigraphic Sources (c. 350-1100 A.D.), in *Proceedings of the Orissa History Congress* (hereafter POHC) pp. 18-24; A.P. Sah, 1976, *Life in Medieval Orissa (circa A.D. 600-1200)*, Varanasi.
14. Sharma, Ibid, pp. 233-34: Sah Ibid, pp. 133-38: Sahu, 1982, op. cit., Land grants in tribal frontiers have been referred to by Suvira jaiswal. See S. Jaiswal, 1979-80, 'Studies in Early Social History; Trends and Possibilities, in *IHR*, vol. VI, Nos 1- 2, p. 25.
15. Kulke, 1977, op.cit.; P.K. Mishra, 1985, Deities and State Formation in Ancient Orissa, *Jour Orissan Hist.* (hereafter *JOH*), vol. V, No. 2-Vol. VI. No. 1, pp. 6-13.
16. Sharma, 1980, op.cit.; pp. 33-34; D.D. Kosambi suggests that the *Brahmins* grasp of the calendar was useful for regulating agricultural operations in the peripheral areas. See Kosambi, 1956, *An Introduction to the Study of Indian History*, Bombay, pp. 236-37.
17. Kulke, 1977. op. cit., p. 108.
18. The Brahmin donees played a more important role than the rulers themselves in the diffusion of Hindu ideas and in the process of state formation which Kulke refers to as "Kshyatriyaization" or a process "from above". H. Kulke, 1976, Kshyatriyaization and social change: A Study in Orissan Setting, in S.D. Pillai (ed) *Aspects of Changing India, Studies in Honour of G.S. Ghurye*, Bombay, pp. 398-409.
19. Suvira Jaiswal makes a copious discussion of the problem in general. Jaiswal S. 1979-80 op.cit., pp. 37-38.

20. Sharma, R.S. 1969. *Social Changes in Early Medieval India,* New Delhi, pp. 15-16.
21. S. Jaiswal, 1977 (Second Edition), Studies in the Social Structure of the Early Tamils, in R.S. Sharma (ed) *Indian Society: Historical Probings,* New Delhi, p. 145. Also see Jaiswal, 1979-80 op. cit., pp. 36-37.
22. For the tribal origin of different dynasties in early medieval Orissa see Kulke, 1977, op. cit., also see P.K. Mishra, op.cit.
23. Burton Stein's hypothesis in the South Indian context (cited in Jaiswal 1979-80 op.cit., page 34) that the Brahmin-Peasant alliance was "voluntary" and of mutual benefit and therefore there was no need for the Brahmins to collaborate with the warriors, a fact chiefly responsible for the absence of a viable Kshyatriya caste in South India does not seem to be tenable, at least in the Orissan context, Here the Brahmins were the donees and the ruling chiefs or hinduized kings were the patrons. The Brahmins repaid their obligation by accelerating rural expansion and promoting social confirmism. It is more a case of Brahmin-Kshyatriya collaboration than one between peasants and Brahmins. Again, as Jaiswal rightly points out, it really sounds absurd that the peasant communities supported a non-producing priestly class without internal differentiations.
24. We get the earliest reference to terms like *Nayaka* and *Paik* denoting military and/or police functionaries, during the Gangas. There is inscriptional evidence suggesting that the *Nayakas* belonged to the Vaisya caste. Interestingly, surnames like Nayak/Naik and Paikray are common among the Khandayats today.
25. B. Das, 1980, 'Kayastas and Karanas in Orissa-a Study of Inscriptions, in *PIHC*', Bombay session, pp. 940-44.
26. Sah, op.cit., p. 127.
27. See R.D. Banerji, 1931, Rajput Origins in Orissa, in *History of Orissa, Vol. II,* Calcutta, Appendix VI, pp. 421-36.
28. K.S. Singh, 1977 (second edition), A Study in State-Formation Among Tribal Communities, in R.S. Sharma (ed) *Indian Society:Historical Probings*, New Delhi, p. 331.
29. Surajit Sinha has provided a very good account of the same process in the context of Central India, although pertaining to a slightly later period. See Sinha, 1962, State Formation and Rajput Myth in Tribal Central India, in *Man in India*, vol. 42; pp. 35-80.
30. Sharma, R.S. 1969, op. cit., pp. 11-12.
31. Jaiswal, 1979-80 op. cit., p. 39.
32. Suvira Jaiswal, 1980, 'Changes in the Status and Concept of the Sudra Varna in Early Middle Ages in PIHC, Bombay Session, p. 144.
33. See Kulke, 1977. op.cit., and B.P. Sahu, 1983. 'Social Morphology and Physiology of Early Medieval Orissa (C.A.D. 400-1000)' in *PIHC*, Burdwan Session, PP. 133-144; and Mahapatra, L.K. 1978. 'Gods Kings

and the Caste System in India', in B. Misra and J. Preston (ed) *Community, Self and Identity,* Hague-Paris, pp. 21-24.

34. B. Das gives a detailed picture of Saktism in this period and discusses its various manifestations. B. Das, Yogini cult in Orissa, in *PIHC*, 1979, pp. 91-98. Also see by the same author, Saptamatraka cult in early Medieval Orissa-A Socio-Economic Study,' in *JOH* vol. 4, No. 1. 1983, p. 19-24. 'The Kapalika sect in Early Medieval Orissa', in *JOH,* Vol. 2, no. 1, 1981, p. 6-9: also A.P. Sah op.cit., pp. 180-83.
35. Jaiswal, 1980, op. cit., p. 118
36. H.C. Das, 1981, 'Socio-cultural Life During the Rule of Imperial Gangas', in *Orissa Historical Research Journal* (hereafter *OHRJ*), vol. 27, nos. 1-4, p. 62.
37. M.P. Dash, 1981, 'Some Aspects of the Social Life under the Surya-Gajapati Rule (1435-1540), in OHRJ, p. 91.
38. A.P. Sah, op.cit.
39. Subudhi, U. 1978, *The Bhauma-Karas of Orissa*, Calcutta, Also see by the same author, 'A study of the Brahmins of Ancient and Early Medieval Orissa rom Epigraphic Sources (c. 350-1100 A.D.) in *POHC* 1980, pp. 18-24.
40. D.Das, op.cit.
41. S.C. Behera, 1982. *Rise and Fall of the Sailodbhavas*, Calcutta.

41a. B.K. Rath, 1983, *Cultural History of Orissa*, Delhi, see Chapter on Administration and Society.

42. S.K. Panda, 1978-79, 'Brahmins in Medieval Orissa (c. 1000-1500 A.D.)' in *Journal of Ancient Indian History,* Vol. 12, pp. 25-35.
43. Jaiswal, op.cit., 1970-80 p. 26.
44. Subudhi, U. 1980. op.cit., p. 21.
45. D. Das, 1977, *The Early History of Kalinga* Calcutta, p. 263-64.
46. A.P. Sah, op.cit., see Section on Society.
47. A.K. Mohanty, 1981, 'Social Life of Orissa under Somavamsis-An Epigraphic Study', in *POHC*, p. 78.
48. D.N. Chopdar, 1981. ROle of Mahasandhivigrahika in Orissan Polity, in *POHC*, p. 36.
49. Cited in D.N. Chopdar, 1981, ibid.
50. B.Das, 1980, op.cit., p. 942.
51. Ibid.
52. Sharma, 1980, op.cit., p. 230.
53. op.cit., also see p. Mukherjee, 1981 (second edition), *The History of the Ganjapati Kings of Orissa*, Cuttack, p. 152.
54. Cited in D. Das, op.cit., p. 268.
55. Ibid.
56. D. Das, op.cit., pp. 268-69.
57. U. Subudhi, 1978. op.cit., p. 114.

57a. B.K. Rath, op.cit. p. 123.

58. L.K. Mahapatra, op.cit., pp. 11-14.
59. H.C. Das, op.cit., p. 66; also see S.K. Panda, 1981, 'Orissa: Its Geography and Patterns of Settlement Under the Later Eastern gangas, A.D. 1038-1434, *JIH*, pp. 160-161.
60. S.C. Behera, op.cit., p. 187.
61. U. Subudhi, 1978, op.cit., pp. 115-116; also see relevant portions from the chapter on Political History of the Bhaumakaras.
62. Sah, op. cit., see Chapter on Society.
63. Behera op.cit., p. 188.
64. H.C. Das, op.cit., pp. 66-67.
65. Ibid.
66. A. Boner, 1970, 'Economic and Organizational Aspects of the Building Operations of the Sun Temple at Konarka', *JESHO*, Vol., p. 265.
67. P. Mukherjee, op. cit., p. 147.
68. Ibid, pp. 148-49.
69. The emergence of a class of powerful intermediaries and superior landlords on the one hand and the reduction of peasants and artisans to the position of semi-serfs on the other in Orissa as a result of land-grants to Brahmins has been clearly dealt with at length by A.P. Sah. Sah, op. cit., pp. 83-94; Binodini Das reflects on the vested feudal interest in land and the problems of hereditary succession to different offices in Orissa in the early medieaval period. Das Binodini, 1982, Administrative succession in a Feudal Structure in Ancient Orissa, in JOH, Vol. III, No. 1. pp. 24-27; also see Sharma, 1980, op. cit., pp. 227-30.
70. D.N. Jha, 1977 (Second Edition) '*Temples as Landed Magnates in Early Medieval South India*' (c. A.D. 700-1300), in R.S. Sharma (ed) *Indian Society: Historical Probings*, New Delhi, p. 202-216.
71. K. Veluthat, 1979. 'The Temple-Base of the Bhakti Movement in South India', in *PIHC*, pp. 189-90.
72. R.N. Nandi, 1984, 'Presidential Address, Growth of Rural Economy in Early Feudal India', *PIHC*, Annamalai Session, pp. 72-73.
73. For a deeper understanding of the Bhakti Movement, see Kesavan Veluthat, op.cit. and M.G.S. Narayanan and K. Veluthat, 1987, The Bhakti Movement in South India, in D.N. Jha (ed), *Feudal Social Formations in early India*, Delhi, pp. 348-75.
74. S. Jeyapragasam, 1980, 'Aspects of Caste System in Tamil Nadu During the Imperial Cola Times', in *PIHC*, bombay session, p. 202.
75. Reflecting on South India Stein argues that the tribally organised, pastoral and hunting societies suffered a sustained displacement at the hands of the caste organised socieities, Burton Stein, 1969, Integration of the Agrarian System of South India, in R.E. Frykenberg (ed). *Land Control and Social Structure in India History*, Madison, pp. 175-216.
76. H. Kulke, 1978, Royal Temple Policy and the Structure of Medieval Hindu Kingdoms, in A. Eschmann, H. Kulke and G.C. Tripathi (ed) *The*

Cult of Jagannath and The Regional Tradition of Orissa, New Delhi, p. 130.

77. For the tribal origin of Lingaraja and Jagannatha and the role of the *Badus* and *Daitas* see A. Eschmann, 1978, Hinduization of Tribal Deities in Orissa: The Sakta and Saiva Typology, in Eschmann et al. (ed.) op.cit., pp. 79-97. Also see A. Eschmann, 1978, The Vaisnava Typology of Hinduization and the Origin of Jagannatha, in Eschmann et al. (ed.) op. cit., pp. 99-117. For Hindu-tribal continuum see L.D. Mahapatra, op. cit., pp. 21-24.
78. See H.C. Das, 1982 (January), 'Cult of Varahi in Orissa', *Orissa Review*, Special Issue, pp. 146-47.
79. See S.K. Panda, 1980, 'Trade and Commerce of Medieval Orissa c. 1000 A.D.-1500 A.D.', *JIH*, pp. 21-28; S.K. Panda, 1982, "The Temples of medieval Orissa: A Socio-Economic Study," *JAIH*, PP. 140-42: The Ganga kings issued small gold coins called Ganga Fanams in considerable number. See A. Boner, op. cit., p. 270 and P.K. Misra, 1981, 'The Story of Orissan coins, in *New Aspects of History of Orissa*, Vol. III, Sambalpur University, p. 30.
80 Sharma, 1980, op. cit., p. 231.
81. H.C. Das, op.cit., p. 65.
82. M.P. Dash, op.cit., p. 94, also see Mukherjee, op.cit., p. 152.
83. Mukherjee, Ibid.
84. See H. Kulke, 1978, op.cit. pp. 125-37. H. Kulke, 1980, 'Rathas and Rajas, The Car Festival at Puri, in *JOH*, Vol. I, no. 2, pp. 28-39, and L.K. Mahapatra, op.cit., p. 21.
85. An analogous picture has been obtained for the social history of South India in the same period. For a convincingly argued and lucid presentation of South Indian Society in the Early Medieval period see D.N. Jha, 1981-82, Relevance of "Peasant State an Society" to Pallava Cola Times, in *IHR*, Vol. 8, nos. 1-2, pp. 74-94.
86. Spencer, similarly, in the context of south India has argued that temples in fact enhanced the very uncertain power of the ruler and the ruling class. He also observes that the patronage of temples and "The mantle or religious devotee, then, gave the kind additional persuasive power with which to control the destinies of men". George W. Spencer, 1969, 'Religious Networks and Royal Influence in Eleventh Century South India', *JESHO*, pp. 45 and 54.
87. B.P. Sahu, 1985, "The Brahminical Model Viewed as an Instrument of Socio-cultural Change—An Autopsy, in *PIHC*, Amritsar Session, p. 185.
88. Striling in 1825 echoed similar feelings and observed "there is one cause sufficiently obvious why all sects should here unite in harmony in the performance of their religious ceremonies, viz., that the temple instead of being consecrated exclusively to some form of the deity Vishnu alone,

is in fact occupied, in joint tenancy, by forms of three of the most recovered divinities of the Hindu faith. All other deities too are allowed to occupy niches or temples within the precincts of the great Pagoda, and are treated with so much respect, that the most obstinate secretary could not with any decency or consistency refuse to join in the general worship of the place." See A. Stirling, 1980 (reprint), "Orissa: Religion, Antiquities, Temples and Civil Architecture in N.K. Sahu (ed) *A History of Orissa*, Vol. II, Delhi, pp. 277-78; A Eschmann, op. cit.; also see kulke, 1982, 'Fragmentation and segmentation versus Integration:Reflections on the concept of Indian Feudalism and the Segmentary State in Indian History, *Structure in History*, vol. IV, no. 2, pp. 260-62.

89. For the political use of Gods and temples and the *interelation* between the legitimation of temporal authority and the structure of medieval kingdoms see Kulke, 1978, op.cit., Kulke, 1979, *Jagannatha-Kult and Gajapati-Konigtum*, Wiesbaden, pp. 223-39, Kulke, 1980, op.cit. and L.K. Mahapatra, op.cit.
90. Kulke, 1982, op.cit., pp. 260-62.
91. Even Chaitanya's preachings for almost two decades made no dent in people' love for and faith in Jagannatha. Some just came to perceive Jagannatha as the symbolic form of the Union of Radha and Krishna. See A.K. Deb, 1984, *The Bhakti Movement in Orissa*, Calcutta, p. 256.
92. See R.K. Das, 1980, social Protest in Medieval Orissa, *PIHC*, pp. 340-45; C. Das, 1982, *A. Climpse into Oriya Literature*, Bhubaneswar, pp. 62-85 and A.K. Deb, op.cit., pp. 34-37.
93. Deb, op.cit., pp. 256-57. Interestingly, a survey of the list of followers of Chaitanya in Orissa indicates that he had a substantial high caste following and that the lower castes remained largely untouched. Surnames of his followers such as Pandit, Pattnaik, Mahaty, Acharya, Misra, Dwija, Bipra etc., are very suggestive. See Deb, op.cit., p. 73.
94. Kulke, 1980, op.cit., p. 35.
95. Marx, Karl. 1976 "The Eighteenth Brumaire of Louis Bonaparte', *Selected Works*, Vol. 1, Moscow, (Third Printing) p. 398.
96. A. Strling, 1825, 'An Account, Geographical, Statistical and Historical of Orissa Proper,/or Cuttack', *Asiatic Researches*, Vol. 15, p.195.
97. M. Mohanty, 1986, op.cit.
98. The *Sasana* Brahmins, for example, are fighting a losing battle. They have not been able to adapt themselves to changing times. They are caught between the pull of tradition and its associated contempt for manual labour, superfluous arrogance and vague notion of self importance on the one hand and the rigours and challenges of the changing realities on the other.
99. The average size of more than 75 per cent of the holdings happens to be less than 2/2.5 acres. Holdings of 10 acres or more, which are considered to be large, comprise just about 10 per cent. The rest range between 5 and

10 acres. I am thankful to my friend and colleague B. Pati for this information as well as the information relating to social mobility in modern Orissa.

100. For example see *Orissa District Gazetter-Mayurbhanj,* 1967, Bhubaneswar, p. 110; *Orissa District Gazetter-Dhenkanal,* 1972, Bhubaneswar, p. 96.
101. op.cit.
102. Mahapatra, op.cit., p. 24
103. K.C. Tripathy, 1982, 'The People of Orissa', *Souvenir Orissa Sahitya Akademi,* Silver Jubilee, Bhubaneswar, p. 14.
104. Besides the small and modest size of the land holdings agricultural production has stagnated in the last two and a half decades. The Green Revolution does not seem to have had any effective bearing. The infrastructure is in bad shape. Only 16 per cent of the cultivated area is irrigated and the per hectare consumption of fertilizers is only 9 kg. See Mohanty, 1986, op.cit.
105. The rivalries between the people of coastal Orissa and western Orissa are too well known. Derogatory expressions like "Katakia" and Sambalpuria", for each other, are obvious examples. Further, there are contradictions not only between the Brahmin-Karana combine and the Khandayat-Chasa emerging alliance but also within these blocs.
106. G.S. Ghurye, 1961, *'Caste, Class and Occupation,* Bombay.

6

Caste and Kulaks in Eastern India: A Comparison of Bihar, Orissa and West Bengal

Anjan Ghosh

In the sociological and social anthropological lexicon, caste has become the ubiquitous insignia of Indianness. The proliferation of literature that has ensued on the subject has, however, had a reductionist effect considerably eroding the complexity of Indian civilization perhaps for the benefit of the purveying 'other'. This has been characterized as 'reverse orientalism' by Arjun Appadurai (1986:357) who has perceptively deserved that amenability to structural simplicity is a necessary prerequisite for finding a place in 'metropolitan theory'. He elaborates this in terms of his notion of 'gatekceping concepts':

> The fact is that the anthropology of complex civilizations does exist, but in a peculiar form. In this form, a few simple theoretical handles become metonyms and surrogates for the civilization or society as a whole: hierarchy in India, honour-and-shame in the circum-Mediterranean, filial piety in China are all examples of what one might call gatekeeping concepts in anthropological theory. Concepts, that is, that seem to limit anthropological theorizing of the place in question, and that define the quintessential and dominant questions of interest in the region.

To accede to the pervasive influence of these 'gatekeeping concepts' is to circumscribe our self-identity in the mirror of others. This calls for not a denial of these concepts as irrelevant but a critical reconstruction in accordance with our situations and needs. The misappropriation of concepts needs to be countered by a reappropriation and pave the way for authentic endogenous theory building.

The present essay is only a small step towards such an ambitious project. Its purpose is to understand the dynamics of caste in the contemporary Indian context. It seeks to do this by reconstituting the perspective on caste and class with an overt emphasis on their meanings. To enumerate the attributes of caste and class in terms of their substance is not enough to reveal their significance. On the contrary, their 'thingness' has frayed their richness as social constructs. Much of the literature in India is encoded in either attributes of conceptual polarity debating the choice of caste or class (see Sharma, 1986 for an extensive citation of the literature) as the unilateral system of social stratification, or representing the presence of caste in politics (see Sheth, 1981; Hawthorne, 1982; Kolenda, 1986). The latter representation is couched in the vocabulary of mediation: 'casteization of politics' or the 'politicization of caste' (Kothari, 1970; 1986) of the organized domain of politics, particularly elections. Yet the significance of caste and class for defining the relations of power in the unorganized sphere still remains elusive. Weiner poses the questions: Why is it that in certain situations of conflict people take recourse to caste as their self-identity, while in other circumstances the same people are prone to uphold their religious identity or regional and linguistic identities? Is it merely a consequence of the state's administrative initiative which defines popular response? Or is it a means of establishing autonomy of the popular will from the state?

In a way Dumont's (1970) influential work on the caste system has both aided and impeded our understanding of caste. *Homo Hierarchicus* was an exemplary structuralist analysis of a world-view. In reconstructing this social ideology, Dumont brought together all the elements of caste within a frame. (This was achieved not without some violation of the autonomy of the elements, in a sense, atrophying them.) But it also held up in relief an integrated view of the totality of caste. However, a structuralist account was of necessity ahistorical and could hardly account for change of the system. The choice, as Dumont himself notes, is a terminal one. Thus, change of the system can be registered only when it has been supplanted. A continuous restructuring of the system is not decipherable from a structural presentation. Hence, structuralist analysis constrains an understanding of transitional movements.

Dumont is actually true to his own promise. For his objective is to throw light upon his own (western) culture through comparison with an apposite 'other'. Consequently, his construction is governed by his own necessity, though in the process it appropriates the Indian social order for this other-directed purpose. Thus, individualism and egalitarianism of the West (sic. as if they are universally prevalent in the West) is pitted against the holism and hierarchy of India (as if it prevails unilaterally inspite of centuries of colonial rule). In this binary positing the subject of the study is reduced to the object of the 'other' in an enchantingly orientalist frame but this transfixing allows no incorporation of the 'blurred genres' of change. This premise of immanence is a major impediment to an appreciation of the contemporary context of caste. Dumont (1970: 265) says:

> One thing is certain: the society as an overall framework has not changed. The castes are still present, and untouchability still effective, although it has been declared illegal. Therefore, as a first approximation, there has been change in the society and not change of the society (emphasis in original).

The vocabulary of presence or absence envisages change as cataclysmic and not incremental. It thus obliterates the historicity of process of change. The accumulation of the shades of grey in the transformation process is disregarded. The reiteration of this absolutist vocabulary, "a structure is present or absent, *it does not change*" (Dumont, 1970:266) indicates a conception of change as displacement and not successive shifts, especially in a structure which is overdetermined by an ideology (of hierarchy), *the distance from it in terms of ambivalence towards it,* ultimately culminating in its vacuity and the emergence of a new ideology is entirely ignored by Dumont. This is evident from the way he sidesteps the question of legality in the passage quoted above. Though the declaration of untouchability as illegal may not wholly stem its practice, it does delegitimise its practice, thereby indicating a shift in the normative structure of society. More rhetorically put: can there be a change of the society without a change in the society?

The emergence of corporate caste identities through a horizontal coalescence of endogamous jatis mentioned as the fusion process by Hardgrave (1986) or as caste blocs by Dumont (1970:269) along with competition for power and resources among them indicates an on-going process of restructuration. In recent times, mobilizations with omnibus official categories like 'backward classes', or self-designated ones like 'Dalits', 'Bahujan Samaj', 'Dravida', etc. suggest that the meaning of caste has been undergoing a change. It is no longer a locally endogamous group which earmarks one's social and ritual position.

Hence, in this essay it will be argued that while caste has not disappeared rather it has reconstituted itself. It does not persist as a system except in some backward areas though as a social identity it has wide currency. More specifically as public ideology caste is related to the political emergence and articulation of a Kulak class. In propositional terms caste interpellates with the Kulaks. To illustrate this, the situation in the three states of Bihar, Orissa and West Bengal will be compared. The focus is on the post-independence period and contemporary trends therein.

In West Bengal, caste is of little political significance. Though this does not rule out the influence of particular castes over specific areas like the Mahishyas in Madnapur, the Mahatoo in Purulia, or the Rajbanshis in Cooch Behar and Jalpaiguri (Basu Ray Chaudhury, 1976:376) over which they are concentrated. Yet caste-based agitations or caste conflicts resulting in massacres of the lower castes has been absent in the state. The state government believes that caste is of little importance and that economic disparties are the source of backwardness of specific communities. A committee set up by the state government to look into the question of caste backwardness in August 1980 maintained that "Poverty and low levels of living standards rather than caste should, in our opinion, be the most important criteria for identifying backwardness" (Mandal, 1980:11).

Further, the Chief Minister of West Bengal pointed out that there were two castes in the state—the rich and the poor. In the context of recent revelations, this appears to be an over-optimistic evaluation. But before that let us look at the caste profile in West Bengal and notice what kind of role it has played in the politics of the state.

Notes

1. Appadurai, Arjun (1986): 'Theory in anthropology: Centre and Periphery' *Comparative Studies in Society and History*, p. 356-61.
2. Basu Roy Chaudhury, N.C. (1976): 'West Bengal: Vortex of Ideological politics', in I. Narain (ed): *State Politics in India, Meerut*, Meenakshi Prakashan.
3. Blair, Harry (1980): 'Rising Kulaks and backward classes in Bihar: Social change in the late 1970's *EPW*:15:2:January 12.
4. Chatterjee, Partha (1982): 'Caste and politics in West Bengal' in G. Omvedt (ed): *Land, Caste and politics in Indian States*, Delhi, Authors Guild.
5. Dhar, Hiranmay (1980): (1980):'Bihar: Caste and Class tangle', *Frontier:12:38:may 17.*
6. Dumont, Louis (1970): *Homo Hierarchicus, London, Paladin, Granda Pub. Ltd..*

7. Hardgrave, Robert (1968): 'Caste in India: fission and fusion' *EPW.*
8. Hawthrone, g. (1982): 'Caste and Politics in India since 1947'D. Mc. Cilvray (ed) *Caste ideology and interaction* Cambridge Papers in Social Anthropology-9.
9. Kolenda, Pauline (1986): 'Caste in contemporary Indian society', in D. Basu and R. Sisson (ed): *Economic and social development in India* Delhi, Sage Publications.
10. Kothari, Rajni (1970): *Politics in India,* New Delhi, Orient Longman.
11. Mandal, B.P. (1980) *Report of the Backward Classes Commission,* Vol-1. New Delhi.
11a. Mohanty, Manoranjan (1984): 'Social roots of backwardness in Orissa (a study of class, caste and power)', *Social Science Probings: 1:2:June.*
12. Sharma, K.L. (1986):'Caste and Class in India', *Sociological Bulletin*:33:1&2:March-September.
13. Sheth, D.L. (1981): 'Caste and Politics', in R. Kothari, et.al. (eds): *ICSSR Survey of Research in Political Science, Vol-3 (Political Dynamics),* New Delhi, Allied Publishers.
14. Weiner, Myron (1986): Talk on 'Ethnicity and Politics in South Asia', CSSSC.

Table 1

Caste and Religious Divisions, 1931 (as Percentage of Total District Population)

	Uppercaste Hindus	*Middlecaste Hindus*	*Depressed Classes*	*Tribes*	*Muslims*	*Other Religions*
Burdwan	9.81	29.07	34.50	7.69	18.56	0.36
Birbhum	6.44	22.45	36.5	7.82	26.69	0.10
Bankura	11.29	39.70	31.81	12.51	4.59	0.10
Manbhum	7.07	47.50	22.42	16.29	6.01	0.71
Midnapore	6.31	58.17	19.15	8.54	7.59	0.24
Hoogly	10.33	41.84	27.00	4.56	16.17	0.10
Howrah	10.48	46.58	20.86	0.42	21.27	0.39
24 Parganas	6.04	27.61	29.95	1.97	33.65	0.78
Nadia	4.84	21.99	10.19	0.54	61.77	0.67
Murshidabad	3.79	25.31	13.24	2.00	55.56	0.10
Malda	1.41	25.84	10.21	8.25	54.28	0.01
Dinajpur	1.32	32.78	5.76	9.48	50.51	0.15
Jalpaiguri	1.80	43.82	4.06	22.50	23.99	0.88
						2.94
Darjeeling	3.12	14.50	2.38	14.51	2.63	13.62
						49.24
Cooch Behar	1.87	59.48	2.74	-	35.33	0.58

Source: Census of India, 1931, Vol-V (Bengal and Sikkim) and Vol-VII (Bihar and Orissa).

Notes:

1. Compared with the present districts of West Bengal 24-Parganas in this table excludes the Bongaon sub-division (now in Bangladesh) and excludes part of Purnea district in Bihar which were later transferred to West Dinajpur district in West Bengal. Cooch Behar was then a Princely state outside British India: Manbhum was in Bihar of which the Purulia sub-division was transferred to West Bengal to form the present Purulia district.
2. The figures for Jalpaiguri and Darjeeling excludes 2.94 per cent and 49.24 per cent, respectively, of the populations who were listed as Nepali Hindus the caste distinctions among whom cannot be meaningfully incorporated into this discussion of the Bengali caste structure.

[Both the table and notes are extracted from Chatterjee 1982:97].

Table 2

Districtwise Breakdown of the Principal Middle Castes and Depressed Classes in Bengal 1931. (as Percentage of Total District Population)

District	*Principal Middle Castes*	*Principal Depressed Classes*
Burdwan	Sadgop 6.31, Goala 4.34, Kalu/Teli 2.08	Badgi 11.75, Bauri 7.86 Muchi 4.05, Dom 2.22
Birbhum	Sadgop 8.20, Kalu/Teli 2.38	Bagdi 9.24, Munchi 4.79, Mal 4.32, Bauri 3.90, Dom 3.83
Bankura	Goala 5.82, Teli 493, Sadgop 3.95 Kalu/Teli 2.79, Khaira 2.42, Tenti 2.21, Kamar 1.93, Kurmi 1.86, Mahisya 1.82	Bauri 10.74, Bagdi 8.07 Lohar 2.30, Sunri 2.26
Manobhum	Kurmi 17.84, Kumhar 3.15, Teli 2.68, Goala 2.26, Kamar 1.95	Bauri 6.69
Midnapore	Mahisya 31.56, Sadgop 3.92, Kurmi 3.06, Tantil 3.03, Baishnab 2.20, Raju 1.96	Bagdi 5.49
Hooghly	Mahisya 15.74, Sadgop 4.89, Goala 3.89, Tanti 2.50, Teli 1.98	Bagdi 14.02, Bauri 2.33
Howrah	Mahisya 24.92, Goala 2.51, Sadgop 1.92	Bagdi 6.99
24 Parganas	mahisya 12.14, Goala 2.62	Pod (Paundra Kshatriya) 14.71, Bagdi 3.68, Kaora 2.28
Naidia	Mahiasv 6.49, Goala 3.56	Bagdi 2.62
Murshidabad	Mahisya 5.48, Sadgop 3.82, Goala 2.06	Bagdi 2.94
Malda	Rajbangshi 3.99	-
Dinajpur	Rajbangshi 20.53	-
Jalpaiguri	Rajbangshi 33.68	-
Darjeeling	Rajbangshi 8.44	-
Cooch Behar	Rajbangshi 53.96	-

Note: The Khaira and Rajbangshi castes were not included among the 'Depressed Classes in the 1931 Census. Both are now listed as Scheduled Castes in West Bengal.

Source: Compiled from *Census of India* 1931, Vols-V and VII as given in (Chatterjee 1982).

Table 3

Distribution of Castes in Cuttack, Puri and Balasore 1931

Caste	*Cuttack*	*Puri*	*Balasore*
Upper Castes	12.15%	13%	13.98%
Middle Castes I	32.27	33.19	21.33
Middle Castes II	25.33	22.85	25.17
Depressed Classes	17.76	14.25	16.98

Upper Castes : Brahmin, Karan, Kayasta, Rajput/Kshatriya
Middle Castes I : (cultivating castes) Chases) Chasa, Khandajat
Middle Castes II : (artisans) Baniya, Barhei, Bhandari, Gaur, Gudia, Kamar, Kewat, Kumbhar, Mali, Tanti, Teli.
Depressed Classes : Bauri, Bhuiya, Chamar, Dhobi, Dom Ghusuria, Gokha, Hari, Irika, Kandara, Kela, Mahuria, Mochi, Pan

Source *Census of India* 1931, as found in (Mohanty 1984:212).

Table 4

Castes of Congress Legislators in Orissa (1961-80)

Castes	*Year*					
	1961	*1967*	*1971*	*1974*	*1977*	*1980*
Brahmins	18	7	8	10	4	27
Kshatriyas	7	4	5	3	-	3
Karan	7	3	6	12	1	8
Khandayat	11	1	5	8	2	22
Scheduled Castes	17	6	12	15	6	20
Scheduled Tribes	9	10	11	18	10	31
Others	4	1	4	3	3	11
Total	73	32	51	69	26	122

Source: (Mohanty, 1984)

Table 5

Caste Analysis of Ministers of Orissa (1946-80)

Year	*Brah-mins*	*Karans*	*Ksha-triyas*	*Khan-dayats*	*SCs*	*STs*	*Muslims*	*Others*	*Total Strength*
1946	2	2	1	0	0	0	0	0	5
1948	2	2	1	0	0	0	0	0	5
1950	3	2	0	1	0	1	0	1	7
1952	2	2	3	3	1	1	0	1	13
1956	2	1	4	3	1	1	1	1	13
1957	2	1	3	2	1	2	0	1	12
1959	5	1	4	1	0	0	0	0	11
1961	2	1	1	3	1	3	0	2	13
1963	3	1	1	2	2	3	0	2	14
1965	4	1	1	4	1	2	0	2	15
1967	5	3	1	2	2	5	0	1	19
1971	5	2	4	1	3	9	0	2	26
1972	4	2	0	1	5	3	0	0	15
1974	5	1	1	4	3	3	1	0	18
1976	5	1	1	4	3	3	1	0	18
1977	2	2	1	4	1	4	0	0	15
1980	2	6	1	4	2	2	1	1	19

Source: (Mohanty, 1984).

Table 6

Caste Profile of Bihar, 1931

	Caste		Per cent of Total Population	
Upper Castes	Brahmin		4.7	
	Bhumihar		2.9	
	Rajput		4.2	
	Kayasta		1.2	
		Sub Total		13.0
Upper backwards	Bania		0.6	
	Yadav		11.0	
	Kurmi		3.6	
	Koeri		4.1	
		Sub Total		19.3
Lower Backwards	Barai		1.0	
	Dhanuk		1.8	
	Hajjam		1.4	
	Kahar		1.7	
	Kandu		1.6	
	Kumhar		1.3	
	Lohar		1.3	
	Mullah		1.5	
	Tatwa		1.6	
	Teli		2.8	
	Others		16.0	
		Sub Total		32.0
Scheduled Castes				14.4
Scheduled Tribes				9.1
Muslims				12.5
		Grand Total		100.00

Source: (Blair, 1980).

Table 7

Caste Conflicts in Bihar

	Place	AGGRESSOR		VICTIM		ISSUE
		Caste	Economic Status	Caste	Economic Status	
1.	Bajitpur	Bhumihar	Landlord	Harijan	Agricul-labourers & sharecroppers	Wage, sharecropers, right over land
2.	Belchi	Kurmi	Landlord	All Caste	Poor peasant as, labs, sharecroppers	Social oppression
3.	Beniapatti	Kurmi	Landlord	harijan	ag. labs.	Wage
4.	Bishrampur	Kurmi	Landlord	harijan	ag.lab. sharecroppers	Wage, sharecroppers' right
5.	Chaudadano	Kurmi Landlord	Harijan	Ag. lab.	Wage	
6.	Dharampuri	Brahmin	Landlord	Harijan	Ag. Labs. & sharecroppers	Wage, sharecroppers' Eight
7.	Daheya	Yadav	All classes	Bhumihar	Poor peasant & one big landlord	Retaliation
8.	Gopalpur	Kurmi	Landlord	Harijan	Ag.lab.	Wage
9.	Jarpa	Bhumihar	Landlord	Yadav	Poor peasants & share croppers	Land dispute
10.	Kalia	Kurmi Landlord	Harijan	Ag.lab.	Wage	
11.	Khijuria	Brahmin	Landlord	Harijan	Sharecroppers	Sharecroppers right
12.	Parasbigha	Bhumihar	Landlord	Yadav	Sharecroppers	Sharecroppers right.
13.	Pathada	Yadav	Landlord	Harijan	Ag.lab.	Wage
14.	Pipra	Kurmi	Landlord	Harijan	Ag.Lab.	Wage
15.	Pipri	Kurmi	Landlord	harijan	Ag.Lab.	Wage & possession over land.

Source: (Dhar, 1980).

7

Kanshi Ram and the Bahujan Samaj Party

Gail Omvedt

Kanshi Ram, a leader of the North India-based Bahujan Samaj Party (BSP), has become one of the most controversial political leaders in India today. Citing slogans such as "Brahman Bania Thakur Chor, Baki Sab DS-4", most progressives and leftists characterize the movement as "casteist". Reacting to the extreme leader-centered functioning of the BSP and to literature which itself presents Kanshi Ram as the "New Messiah", some would go even further and stamp it as "fascist". Yet aside from the fact that Kanshi Ram is becoming the hero of large sections of the most oppressed castes in India, it is clear that politically the main effect of the new party has been to call into question for the first time in decades the secure hold of the Congress over the "Harijan vote bank" in North India. In an interview, the Rashtriya Swayamsevak Sangh (RSS) leader Balasabeb Deoras named the BSP (along with Mahendra Singh Tikait) as one of the real problems for the RSS in North India (*Illustrated Weekly*, August 14, 1988).

Surely, a political force that can strike fear both into the Congress and the RSS cannot simply be stamped as reactionary. Nor, for that matter can a *dalit* (depressed) political leader who characterizes Shivaji as "ours" and claims to represent the constituencies not only of Babu Jagjivan Ram but also of Chaudhary Charan Singh and to so some extent, Syed Shahabuddin (*Illustrated Weekly*, March 8, 1977) be easily characterized as casteist?

In fact, Kanshi Ram's Bahujan Samaj Party represents one of the celebrated examples of a new political assertion by *dalits*, coming after decades of fragmentation and absorption/cooperation by the Congress-ruled establishment. The other good example, of course, is Prakash

Ambedkar's Bharatiya Republican Party. But rather than making a detailed comparison, this paper will focus on some aspects of the BSP and of its North Indian base.

Politics of the Ambedkarite Movement

Ambedkar's political direction was clear and consistent throughout his life, although changing circumstances and constraints led to different political formations. The direction was to maintain the autonomy and leadership of *dalits*, but at the same time to seek a broader alliance or coalition which would include peasants and workers (in class terms) and all middle castes—non-Brahmins/backward castes (in caste terms). Throughout, the Congress as the representative of Brahmins and capitalists, was viewed as the most dangerous political enemy of the exploited and oppressed.

In the 1930s, Ambedkar formed the Independent Labour Party (ILP) which came out with a bold peasant-worker action programme in the mid 1930s, a period of tumultuous mass movements. The ILP fought not only for *dalit* interests, but also organized joint struggles of Mahar and Kunbi tenants against the *khoti* landlord system in the Konkan as well as participated fully in the major textile workers' struggle of 1938. At the same time, Ambedkar sought to convince non-Brahmin leaders in Maharashtra not to join the Congress, and urged the Bihar *kisan* leader Swami Sahajanand to pull his movement out of the Congress orbit. Although the ILP had some respectable success in Maharashtra, at an all-India level the middle castes and the peasant movement were getting fairly firmly drawn under the Congress hegemony and were helped considerably by the illusory leftism of the Congress Socialists and by the Communist policy of seeing the Congress as a "national united front".

Thus, in 1942, the Scheduled Castes Federation (SCF) was formed as a party of *dalits*, though on an all-India level. Although this was seemingly a surrender of efforts to develop a broader movement, Ambedkar's political aspirations did not change the 1951 election manifesto of the SCF and declared that it would like to work with backward castes and scheduled tribes and would be willing to change the name to Backward Castes Federation. To make this possible, it also declared a willingness to accept a merger into a federal party like the Socialists, the Justice Party and the Kisan Mazdur Party (the latter mainly represented peasants castes), without jeopardizing its autonomy. Finally, before his death, Ambedkar gave a call to form a formally open party to represent all exploited groups which resulted in the creation of the Republican Party.

This broad political thrust towards forming an alliance/coalition with middle castes and non-Brahmins and often Muslim peasants was shared by other sections of the pre-independence *dalit* movement, in spite of the tensions that continued to exist between middle caste Hindus and *dalits*, between peasants and agricultural labourers. In Bengal, in the 1930s, Namasudras had a sporadic alliance with the Muslim peasant-based Krishak Praja Party. In Punjab, Mangoo Ram's Ad-Dharma joined the Muslim-Hindu-Jat peasant-based Unionist Party. Both the parties had the broader anti-Brahmin, anti-Bania, anti-Bhadralok rhetoric and tenor thrust.

However, the extraordinary absorptive power of the Congress managed to stifle such attempts at an alliance from below. In a way, this was spearheaded by Gandhi with his various Harijan programmes and his very strong assertion of not a national, but a Hindu unity. However, it has to be clearly recognized that Gandhi was not the only factor, that the Congress elite very consistently and over a long period of time had developed a capacity and willingness to appeal to Harijans and scheduled castes whenever they were threatened by the non-Brahmin peasantry. Put in other terms, the Congress capitalists tried to use agricultural labourers against peasants and the Congress Brahmins tried to use *dalits* against the non-Brahmin middle castes, and they were quite successful in doing so. Gandhi's Harijan Sevak Sangh was not the only (or even main) effort in 1930s to appeal to *dalits.* Perhaps just as significant, though overlooked, was the role of Jagjivan Ram. He founded an agricultural labourers organization to split the Bihar Kisan Sabha, and Depressed Classes League as a counter to Ambedkar's ILP and Depressed Classes Federation—both in the same year 1936.

Thus, Indira Gandhi's rhetoric of *garibi hatao* and appeals to the rural poor and Harijans was no new political creation. Coming in the late 1960s after the massive political alienation of middle caste peasants which had shaken Congress strongholds in North India, it was simply the perfection of many decades-long Congress strategy. Pro-Congress progressives (needless to say, invariably urban, salaried Brahmins) described "Kulaks" and the "rich and middle peasantry" as the sole beneficiaries of agricultural progress and the main exploiters of agricultural labourers and *dalits.* Indira Gandhi and Congress leaders perfected "KHAM" alliance in many states referring to Kshatriyas, Harijans, Adivasis and Muslims (where as Kshatriyas referred to various backward castes in Gujarat)—but the hidden, unnamed term of the KHAM alliance was the Brahmins. It was really a renewed effort to unite the upper castes with the lowest castes against the politically assertive middle castes.

In the face of this political strategy, the *dalit* movement by and large wilted. Even in Ambedkar's own time, of course, large sections of the scheduled castes were entrapped enough in their Hindu identity and traditional subordination and they were pulled into organizations like Congress and even Hindu Mahasabha. The appeal to *dalit* poor peasants/agricultural labourers to see the village dominant peasants/middle castes as their main enemies and exploiters did of course have a base in the day-to-day forms of subordination and exploitation—and the power of this appeal and the ideology of the "rural poor" took on even more force when backed up by the very substantive political/economic benefits which Congress had to offer (at least to *dalit* leaders). Congress did manage to capture the Harijan vote bank in most states, and most of the various factions of the RPI were pulled eventually into some kind of open or indirect alliance with the Congress. *Dalit* interests got expressed only in sectional lobbying. Even the explosion of the "Dalit panthers" in the early 1970s got dissipated into factionalism, with a good proportion of the leadership getting reabsorbed into Congress.

In this background, the rise, from the early 1980s, of an independent, largely anti-Congress political force, firmly based on *dalits* but with a broader appeal to all backwards and exploited, can in fact be seen as a renewal of the earlier political thrust of the Ambedkarite movement. Kanshi Ram's Bahujan Samaj Party and Prakash Ambedkar's Bharatiya Republican Party have numerous differences in strategy and rhetoric, but they both represent the new political assertion, in which *dalits* seek to emerge as leaders in a wider coalition of the exploited and marginalized. A comparison here can even be made with the phenomenon of Jesse Jackson and his "rainbow coalition" in the U.S., where perhaps for the first time in history a black leader emerged with an impressive degree of success. In this sense, whatever the differences and limitations, the harbingers of a new era seem to be with us.

The North India Background: Chamars as a Leading Force

However, it is necessary to see political phenomena in their specific socio-historical and geographical contexts. Though Kanshi Ram has an all-India appeal to *dalits*, and though his root organization, BAMCEF, is all-India in scope, so far the political base of the BSP has been limited to Northern India, North-West India, to be more accurate. In spite of the genuine ability to appeal to other backward and minority communities, the main social base has been the large Chamar caste-group just as that of Ambedkar and the Republican Party today whose social base is the Mahars of Maharashtra.

The *dalit* movement throughout India has tended to be based among the largest (and relatively most advanced) *dalit* caste of a particular region—Namasudras in Bengal, Malas in Andhra, Mahars in Maharashtra, Paraiyas in Tamil Nadu, and Chamars in North India. This invariably gives rise to criticism of the movement as being in fact a "single caste" movement, and it is true that it does lead to tendencies to enclose the movement within the limitations of what we might call the "foundation caste". *But given the nature of caste in India, it is inevitable that all movements including rural (and many urban) economic movements, should have such a "foundation caste" (or tribal group) as their base.* Criticisms of the fact that such a "foundation caste" exists are meaningless, and in fact destructive because they pose an abstract unreality against the concrete historical reality. The more realistic question is to what degree such a "foundation caste" in fact serves as a vanguard to help a movement move beyond its limitations and draw in oppressed/exploited sections of other castes?

The Chamars are perhaps the largest scheduled caste in India. With leather working as their traditional caste occupation, they can be compared with such groups as the Chambhars in Maharashtra, or the Madigas in the Telugu-speaking region. However, it would be erroneous to see the North Indian Chamars as simply or mainly leather workers. In fact, as the largest untouchable caste in their region, they hold a position within the agrarian structure similar to that of Mahars (in Maharashtra), Malas, Paraiyans, etc. as the main purveyors of agricultural labour, and the main caste responsible for "village service" work (*vethbegar*) of all kinds. As such, in West Uttar Pradesh, Punjab and Haryana, they confront primarily Jats as the traditional landholding and cultivating peasant caste while in East Uttar Pradesh and Bihar they have to face the power of Rajputs as a noncultivating, landlord caste and intermediary cultivating tenant castes like Kurmis, Yadavas, etc.

In return for performance of agricultural and other village services, it seems that the Chamars like Mahars and others traditionally, were given some land for cultivation. Therefore, they were not simply "landless labourers" but also had a small but important foothold as small peasants. This, along with some economic position as leather workers and an ability to claim other labour, gave them some economic basis to assert themselves against exploitation and casteism by the beginning of the twentith century.

Table 1, which is based on 1921 and 1911 census data on caste and occupation, gives a comparative look at the agrarian economic position of the Brahmins, the main peasant caste, and the major *dalit* castes in different provinces. Its categories are very broad, and do not, for instance, show such important

Table 1
Caste and Agrarian Occupations

Province and Caste	*Actual Workers*	*Income from Rent of Land %*	*Cultivators %*	*Field Labourers %*
Mysore State (1921)				
Brahmin	51,221	17.13	21.79	0.35
Lingayat	142,366	3.15	79.43	2.62
Vokkaliga	246,329	0.44	89.83	2.08
Holeya	157,289	0.97	35.95	37.72
Madiga	63,364	1.58	45.13	26.17
Hyderabad State (1921)				
Brahmin	79,345	7.37	17.52	0.32
Maratha	500,638	6.99	60.90	16.33
Kapu	291,130	1.60	51.56	26.15
Telaga	146,230	1.01	61.22	15.68
Mahar/Mala	130,008	3.79	8.40	8.25
(Menial Service)				(65.33)
Madiga	203,492	0.65	10.28	10.16
Menial Service)				(83.54)
Chambhar	37,591	1.07	4.21	7.69
Madras State (1911)				
Brahmin, Telugu	27,029	34.53	32.37	0.29
Brahmin, Canarese	10,647	13.96	71.89	0.08
Holeya	29,696	—	3.29	75.46
Mala	196,259	0.18	14.78	71.89
Madiga	79,924	1.17	10.71	54.71
Bombay Presidency (1911)				
Brahmin, Chitpavan	10,407	19.00	2.47	0.13
Brahmin, Deshashtha	14,494	18.68	64.55	2.69
Lingayat	205,813	3.24	83.54	22.39
Maratha	426,649	1.58	47.63	14.93
Kunbi	319,813	1.59	66.88	20.67
Mahar, Holeya, Dhed	69,542	0.75	48.79	22.63
Mang, Madiga	22,672	0.52	16.60	41.71
Central Provinces and Berar (1921)				
Brahmin	149,193	3.22	36.67	6.22
Maratha	65,520	4.29	46.00	27.78
Kunbi	385,268	55.00	—	34.08
Mahar/Mehra	380,101	2.09	22.37	41.02
(Cotton weavers)				(11.33)
Mang	26,007	1.25	3.42	47.73
(native musicians)				(21.97)
United Provinces (1921)				
Brahmin	1,636,446	2.17	77.47	1.78
Rajput	1,263,373	(34.19)**	49.57	0.56
Jat	275,753	—	78.21	5.31
Gujar	123,863	1.76	74.02	3.93
(herding)				(12.71)
Chamar	1,998,105	0.42	45.64	25.35
				(5.96)

* Figures given under "traditional occupation". In the case of Hyderabad Malas and Madigas these can legitimately be assimilated into "field labour".

** Figures for "traditional occupation"; almost all were most likely landlords.

Source: Census of India, 1921; Census of India, 1911; figures given only for male workers.

Cultivators also, in the case of castes such as Rajputs and perhaps some of the Marathas, include those who used hired labourers and did not work on the land themselves. However, in spite of such inadequacies, the pattern they show is interesting. Chamars and Mahars in particular, in Uttar Pradesh and Bombay presidency, did have a fairly significant foothold as cultivators and not simply as field labourers. One important difference, on the other hand, is in terms of the middle caste they were related to, namely, Jats, who had no agricultural labourers worth speaking of among them, whereas Maratha-Kunbis had a fairly significant number, in the context of a much higher proportion of agricultural labourers to cultivators in Central and Southern India. Thus, where Chamars made up by far the largest majority of field labourers in Uttar Pradesh, in the Marathi-speaking region, the Mahars shared the agricultural labourer role to a significant extent with castes such as the Kunbi-Marathas. This has perhaps made the economic differentiation/contradiction between Chamars and Jats in North-West India sharper than that between Mahars and Kunbi-Marathas in Maharashtra. However, the social similarities are equally important, and it has to be stressed that a full analysis in either case would take account of all the *jatis* and their interrelationships. Maharashtrian Brahmins, for instance, were traditionally a much more dominating elite as compared to Uttar Pradesh Brahmins.

A crucial historical difference was the role in Maharashtra of Jotiba Phule and the Satyashodhak Samaj in spreading among the broad rural masses a radical, anti-caste ideology and movement. In contrast, the Arya Samaj in North-West India was much more conservative in its approach of rationalizing and modernizing Hinduism.

Still, the pattern of development of the *dalit* movements was similar, and the Chamar-based movement in North India has as much historical importance as that based on the Mahars in Maharashtra. In both cases, early Christianizing attempts gave some outlets to the untouchables and helped to provoke similar Hindu attempts. In North India, it was the Arya Samaj that played the role, in a sense, took up the "challenge" on behalf of Hinduism of reincorporating those they had excluded for so long. A *shuddhi* programme initially undertaken in the later nineteenth century by Arya Samajists to convert or reconvert individuals was turned at the initiative of *dalits* themselves into a collective programme for upward mobility of *dalit* castes accompanied by incorporation into Arya Samaj activists. By 1910, between 60 to 70 thousand *shuddhi* ceremonies had been performed in Punjab and Uttar

Pradesh and the Aryas had risen from a small number to 205,000, mostly apparently "purified" untouchables. It is in fact this tradition that radical Hindu reformers like Swami Agnivesh represent today.

However, it was not and is not enough radicalism for *dalits*, who found that even after *shuddhi* their position in the caste system and their treatment by caste Hindus had undergone little change. A major revolt against Arya Samajist identification with Hinduism took place, and by the mid-1920s movements like Ad-Dharm and the Adi-Hindu were becoming the vanguard voice of the assertive Chamars. Similar movements elsewhere (Adi-Dravida, Adi-Karnataka, Adi-Andhra), asserted that *dalits* were part of an originally egalitarian and prosperous community of original inhabitants of India, turned into slaves in the caste system as a result of Aryan invasion and conquest. These Adi-Hindu groups began to hold conferences establishing links with emerging *dalit* leaders elsewhere. Through most of the 1920s they worked in some kind of coordination with other non-Brahmin groups and by the 1940s were drawn into Ambedkar's movement. Outside Maharashtra, it was the North Indian Chamars who provided the strongest base for the Scheduled Caste Federation.

Towards the Bahujan Samaj Party

By the middle of 1960s, India was enveloped in an all-round economic and political crisis. Strikes and all forms of political agitation took place from that period on and in the 1967 elections. The Congress lost heavily in several northern states as disaffected peasants and middle castes turned to the opposition. Disaffection hit every political party including the Communists as the apparently revolutionary message of Mao helped to spark the "Naxalite" revolt.

Dalits were affected by the crisis in a variety of ways. As rural agricultural labourers and poor peasants, they suffered both from overall rural poverty and backwardness, a legacy of the "Nehru model" of heavy industrial, overcentralized industrial development and from the increasing economic and social tensions between the landowning middle and upper castes and the lower caste rural poor. The fact was that those who benefited from agrarian development as "Kulaks" might have been, in fact, a small minority, and they were in reality the holders of rural political power and influence who ruled the villages. The large majority of middle castes and backwards were as much a victim of the system as the *dalits*. In any case the *dalits* were at the receiving end of most of the attacks, confronting aggressive backlash whenever they tried to move ahead. Atrocities on Harijans committed in practice by a wide range of caste-groups from traditional upper caste elites like Thakurs and Bhumihars, Brahmins to middle castes and lower middle castes (Kunbi-Marathas, Kurmis, Yadavas, Dhangars, Vanniyars), went on an upward swing.

Dalit middle classes were in an equally tension-ridden and in a more ambivalent position. As beneficiaries of the reservation policies that had resulted from the earlier *dalit* movement, they had a *bit more economic security than their lower-class brethren* and hence could aspire for considerable upward mobility. But they faced on a continual score, condescension and opposition from their upper caste co-workers. Their economic position was often fragile particularly with large number of *poorer relatives* around. Within the Indian caste-community context, it was in fact eternally difficult for a "middle class" or "petty bourgeoisie" to escape from the rural and urban working class conditions which enveloped the majority of the scheduled castes.

Table 2

Scheduled Caste and Scheduled Tribe Occupations, 1981

	SC		*ST*		*Others*		*Total*	
	Lakh	*%*	*Lakh*	*%*	*Lakh*	*%*	*Lakh*	*%*
1. Agricultural Sector (a+b)	289 (19.5)	76.4	192 (13.0)	87.1	999 (67.5)	61.4	1,480 (100.0)	66.5
(a) Cultivators	107 (33.8)	28.2	120 (13.0)	54.4	698 (75.4)	42.9	925 (100.0)	41.6
(b) Agricultural Labourers	182 (33.8)	48.2	72 (13.0)	32.7	301 (53.2)	18.5	555 (100.0)	24.9
2. Non-Agricultural Sector	89 (12.0)	23.6	8 (3.8)	12.9	628 (84.2)	38.6	745 (100.0)	33.5
TOTAL (1+2)	378	100.0	220	100.0	1,627	100.0	2,225	100.0
(Total in Population)	(17.0)		(10.0)		(73.0)		(100.0)	

Notes:

1. This table gives percentages both across and down, it shows *what % of SCs* are agricultural labourers (48.2%) and also *what % of agricultural labourers* are SCs (33.8%), thus giving an overall picture.
2. The largest section of both SCs and STs are, first, in the more impoverished agricultural sector. SCs are much more highly agricultural labourers than cultivators, though they still make up a significant proportion of cultivators. Here we should remember that the Census *underestimates* the proportion of cultivators by vastly undercounting *women* cultivators and thus probably underestimates also the proportion of SCs and STs who are at least small peasants.
3. Of course no official statistics are available which separate "backward" or middle castes or minorities from the upper castes in the "Other" category which makes it practically impossible to get data on the general economic and social section which the BSP seeks to appeal to.

Sources: CMIE Table 1 8-C.

Out of this situation, it was in fact middle class, educated or semi-educated *dalit* youth who provided impetus to most of the militant organizations that arose from the late 1960s—the *dalit* Panthers in Maharashtra, Bheem Sena and *dalit* Sangarsh Samiti in Karnataka, etc.

The Bahujan Samaj Party had its roots in the same period, but with an entirely different history. Kanshi Ram, a young Punjabi *dalit* from a Sikh Chamar background employed in a Pune laboratory resigned his job in 1964 following a long-drawn dispute on caste issues and following a discovery of Ambedkar, determined to dedicate his life to the movement. After seven years of working for the Republican Party, he apparently concluded that it was worthless, and with little temptation towards the type of militancy offered by the Dalit Panthers began working towards a different kind of organization. And when BAMCEF (Backward and Minority Communities Employees Federation) was officially formed on December 6, 1978, it was, in several clear ways, a unique exploit.

First, in contrast to almost all other *dalit* and *dalit*-based organizations of the time, its formation and structure appear as deliberate and not reactive, emerging fourteen years after Kanshi Ram's resignation from government service. It has consistently refused a "reactive" agitational stance which has meant, in practice, staying out of many major *dalit* struggles. Perhaps the biggest example of this was the Namantar agitation for the renaming of Marathwada University after Dr. Ambedkar, which Kanshi Ram characterized as dominated by Poona Brahmins. This refusal to join ongoing agitational struggles has been more of an orientation by BAMCEF to decide its own political direction than simply due to the fact that as a government employees organization, BAMCEF itself could not engage in struggle activities.

Table 3

Scheduled Castes and Scheduled Tribes in Central Government Service (as on 1 January, 1982)

Group (Class)	*Total Employees*	*SCs*	*% of Total*	*STs*	*% of Total*
Class I	54,265	2,980	5.49	633	177
Class II	66,221	5,970	9.02	947	1.43
Class III	1,909,805	255,730	13,39	66,278	3.47
Class IV (excl. Sweepers)	1,094,569	256,261	23.41	81,496	7.45
TOTAL	3,124,860	520,941	16.67	149,354	4.78
To population, 1981			15.8		7.80

Source: CMIE, Table 1.8D.

Second, while it had *dalits* (scheduled castes) as its strongest base, there was a concerted effort from the beginning to include all backwards and minorities; the term "scheduled castes" does not even appear in the name of the organization. While the scheduled castes probably have the majority among the claimed two lakh educated employees including 3,000 holders of MBBS/MD degrees, 15,000 scientists members of BAMCEF. It remains true that all public functions of BAMCEF have sought to include leaders of various backward castes and minority communities.

Kanshi Ram's major organizational and rhetorical thrust was, in fact, to develop BAMCEF as the major support organization for a later, if indefinite, political thrust. It is significant to know that it is conducted by the newly formed DS-4 (Dalit Shoshit Samaj Sangarsh Samiti) from September 24, 1982. It was a denunciation of the Poona Pact. This pact, signed in 1932 by Ambedkar as a result of Gandhi's fast unto death to achieve the integration of *dalits* with the majority Hindu community, resulted in changing the separate electorates allotted by the British into reserved seats although with a largely increased number. Its fiftieth anniversary had been intended by the Congress Party for a major celebration, and it is noteworthy that DS's denunciation campaign was condemned by almost all the other *dalit* organizations in Maharashtra. But Kanshi Ram's message published in perhaps his only book—*The Chamcha Age*—was simple: the Poona Pact was the beginning of a process in which the educated elites of scheduled caste and backward caste communities were turned into simple puppets (*chamchas*) of the upper caste, they must reject this role and instead direct their services and talents towards organization of their total community towards breaking caste heirarchy and inequality. In its own description, "BAMCEF is considered a brain-bank, a talent-bank and a financial-bank of the oppressed and exploited society to move its mission ahead. The basic objective of this organization is to pay back to the oppressed and exploited society to which they belong" ("The New Messiah", 1988, p. 5).

From this point, the direction towards political action based in Northern India developed quite rapidly. In what it called "limited political action", DS-4 put up forty-six candidates for assembly elections in Haryana in 1982 (*Oppressed Indian*, June, 1982). The BSP, founded on April 15, 1985, contested Lok Sabha elections in December 1984, and then UP Vidhan Sabha elections in March 1985. It lost all seats contested in both elections, but won over a million votes in the Lok Sabha elections, and in Uttar Pradesh it was thought to have played a decisive enough role in drawing votes away from Congress, throwing fifty-one seats to Lok Dal and Janata Party candidates (*Illustrated Weekly*, March 1987). It repeated this performance in the Punjab Vidhan Sabha elections six months later when it was thought to have played a decisive role in turning the tide for the Akali Dal. Then, in the Bijnore Lok Sabha by-elections in December 1985, the ruling party's prestigious candidate Meera Kumar (daughter of Jagjivan Ram) could barely manage to win the seat with only a five thousand vote margin over the BSP candidate. Throughout this period, the DS-4 and BSP were organizing increasingly huge rallies, and in the process increasing their hold over scheduled caste and backward caste government employees.

What really projected Kanshi Ram as a national figure was, of course, the crucial Allahabad Lok Sabha by-election of July 1987, when he decided to contest against Sunil Shastri of the Congress and V. P. Singh of the opposition. Kanshi Ram's objective was to make this into a genuine three-sided contest, and throughout most of the campaign in fact it appeared as if the BSP, with relatively low funding, had the most enthusiastic and vigorous campaign centered on the rhetoric of overthrowing upper caste political power: *vote hamara, raj tumhara nahin chalega, nahin chalega.* And he emerged with eighteen per cent of the total vote (compared to Shastri's twenty-four per cent and Singh's fifty-two per cent), including sixteen per cent of the backward castes. (*India Today*, July 15, 1988, p. 35). A new political force had indeed taken its root on the national scene.

Political Ideology: Advantages of Vagueness

In all of this, what is striking is the nearly total lack of any clear ideology in the programmes and functioning of BAMCEF, BSP, etc. The thrust is solely on breaking the caste system to overthrow the rule of the three upper castes by organizing the "oppressed and exploited" for "equality". "Changing" and "destroying the system" are stressed, but the system is described almost solely in social terms. An economic programme is absent, so is any concrete outline of what *dalits* and backwards might do once they gain political power, of what kind of society might be built. According to Kanshi Ram:

> We have not laid down an ideology for our struggle. We are in the process of formulating it. Our struggle for annihilation of caste has begun all over India. At the end of the campaign we will hold a seminar in Delhi where people from different caste groups, interests and political parties will be invited. We shall seek a common approach

on the basis of a consensus (*Surya India*, May 1987; quoted in "The New Messiah").

In this sense it can also be noted that all the agitational and other campaigns of DS-4, BAMCEF might have been at the symbolic and cultural-political level; they have not dealt with any economic issues; they have been *jagruti* (awakening) campaigns. Massive bicycle tours from the far ends of India into remote villages, *melas* and "people's parliaments" were organized. The only issue taken up has been the 1987-88 anti-drink (alcohol) campaign.

Another aspect of this might be stressed. There is also little negative aspect to the BSP propaganda and campaigning. In contrast to some other *dalit* publications (e.g., *Dalit Voice*) and its regional language variants there is a little tendency to vitriolic attack on upper castes as "Nazis" or whatever, and there is also a little specific attack on individual upper caste politicians and other leaders. The basic thrust is rather the positive one of the *dalits* and backward castes organizing themselves. This characteristic gives the literature a vagueness and even a certain amount of vacuity, with almost no commentary on specific events, movements, issues; it also leaves it much more open-ended.

Although the attempt is to unite the minorities with *dalits* and backward castes, Kanshi Ram does not show the kind of "prominority" line which condones all minority fundamentalism on the pretext that Hinduism is the main enemy; there is a wariness about Islam, for example, or rather the positive stress (and this is consistent with Ambedkar) on Buddhism (with some references to the bationalism, humanism, atheism of Phule, Periyar and all). Similarly, there is no ideological interpretation of the origins of caste and untouchability, specifically, little of the "non-Aryan" theory which interprets all of Indian history in terms of Aryan (white) conquest of originally non-Aryan equalitarian civilization; the most recent expositions of such a view have identified India's *dalits* with "blacks" the world over, they have also added a strong racist tinge to the *dalit* movement.

All of this ideological vagueness contrasts strongly with Ambedkar himself who had clear economic programmes, who wrote extensively on the origins and history of untouchability and caste. Nevertheless, it has some definite advantages which at least make it understandable in an era (very different from that of Ambedkar) in which the major ideologies (in particular; traditional Marxism) have been in a state of crisis for some time.

Ambedkar's economic ideology, for example, was by and large that of the Marxist Left, tempered with a firm commitment to political democracy. (This general, very broad type of Marxism, with commitments to heavy industrialization, state planning, land reform, etc., also lay behind the Nehru model of development). Thus his specific economic programmes at the time of the Independent Labour Party were broadly those of peasants and workers not different from (and certainly equally militant as) the Communist or Socialist Left of the period. His orientation to technological development, industrialization, mechanization of agriculture was seen as going along with and requiring nationalism and collectivization—the whole programme of "state socialism" was very broadly, along Marxist Left lines. And Ambedkar himself generally made it clear that his disagreements with Communism centered on issues of totalitarianism and violence, on *how* to reach the goal, not so much on the goal itself or the economics of its construction.

This orientation was quite understandable in Ambedkar's time. There was no practical, seemingly viable alternative to the Nehru model and the Left ideology underlying it. Gandhism, the practical, available alternative in India, stood forth (only as based) on backwardness, Hindu *vedanta* avoidance of life, and acceptance of caste hierarchy/inequality.

Today, however, the "crisis of Marxism" is quite specific and calls into question most of these orientations, including technological development (seen as environmentally destructive), heavy industrialization (seen as leading to an overcentralized, unbalanced, uneven development which leaves the majority in poverty and backwardness), nationalism and collectivizations, seen as creating statist bureaucracies). Since these uncertainties extend to post-revolutionary societies themselves, it is not so surprising that a current anti-caste movement should remain silent on such issues.

Further, there are some specific reasons why the currently available form of Marxist economic ideology should be unacceptable to an organization like BAMCEF/BSP. The first is the tendency onwards discussing atrocities on *dalits* or caste conflict in the village, to interpret these in terms of a basic class conflict between rich and middle peasants (Kulaks, capitalist farmers, but the emphasis on "property ownership" as basic to "class" leads to a tendency to lump together all landowning peasants) and agricultural labourers and poor peasants.

However, this assumed class conflict is in contradiction to the *caste* alliance which Kanshi Ram is seeking to build between *dalits* and backward castes. With some exceptions, the majority of "rich and middle peasants" (and certainly the majority of those actually involved in attacks on *dalits*—the "foot-soldiers" of atrocities) are those classified as Sudras and falling in the eithty-five per cent majority the BSP wants to represent.

The second issue is that the general "Leftist" solution to the problems of the rural poor and *dalits* has been in terms of land distribution and collectivization and nationalization of industries at the broader societal level. Now in one sense,this "statism" might be seen to be in the interest of the governmental (bureaucratic) employees who are the main "brain-bank, talent bank and financial bank" for the BSP. However, the fact remains that the scheduled caste and the backward caste government employees are subordinates and a minority force in the bureaucracy, a move towards "statism" in the Indian context clearly brings with it Brahminism, the control of the upper castes. It is not surprising that there would be an ambiguity on this issue. Nor is it surprising that the lower middle-class support base of the BSP with its strong urban foothold could be sceptical about the tendency of urban Brahmin salaried intellectuals to tell them that the *main* enemy of *dalits* are the rural "dominant caste" peasantry. They confront more immediately the "dominant caste" of the cities and the bureaucracy and its much subtler forms of daily domination.

In the face of these complexities and uncertainties, then, the lack of ideology of the BSP may be a kind of advantage—an open-endedness in an era of uncertainty. There is also something to be said for the assertion that bringing the low-caste "oppressed and exploited" into political power, into organizational leadership and intellectual competence, is a prerequisite to any real building of ideology.

Conclusion

In many ways, the Bahujan Samaj Party is a product of the contemporary era of profound ideological uncertainties and political crisis of all established systems. It can be said to be the political expression of *dalit* and low caste communities, standing shakily on the base of partial gains won as result of past movements.

In many ways also, the BSP appears as an "anti-party" rather than a party. Its refusal of ideology, refusal of alliances, refusal to "place" itself in the political spectrum, its assessment of all parties by the single criterion of their orientation to break the caste system prove it to be an "anti-party" entity. In this sense also it appears "modern", a not untypical example of many such "new social movements" world-wide. At another level, of course, it can be noted that the vagueness of rhetoric and lack of sharp political definition is helpful, perhaps even necessary for a party striving to *unite* the divided, even warring eighty-five per cent. It is a way of keeping options open for whatever may be necessary to move ahead.

To call the BSP "fascist" is clearly nonsense. Fascism of course has an ideology, and the racial appeals that are integral to fascism are also signally lacking in BSP rhetoric. It is erroneous to call it "casteist" unless appeals to break down the caste system and a recognition of the caste-divided reality are to be stamped as "casteist". Here the point is: does one accept the material reality of caste in India or not ?

Vague as its rhetoric may be, and may be lacking as a clear ideology, the whole thrust of the BSP nevertheless appears to be *anti-systemic* (to use Wallersteinian terminology), "left" in the traditional sense. Even the often bitter critiques of the Communists (The Communist parties have become the biggest stumbling block in this regard). They keep talking about change but work for status quo. The BJP is better, they never talk about change. So people never feel duped (Kanshi Ram, *Illustrated Weekly*, March 8, 1987). They are like almost all *dalit* critiques, which are not of Communist ideals but of Communist failures to live up to ideals or do anything really practical about them. Obviously, the claims to unite and represent the eighty-five per cent "oppressed and exploited", the massive far reaching awakening campaigns directed against "untouchability, inhumanity, injustice, insecurity, inequality", the continual attacks on the Congress Party and the state, the characterization of "rural feudal lords and slum *dadas*" as the enemy—all of these do not contain or easily fit the usual "class" rhetoric of the Left. But they should at least leave the ground open for a dialogue.

References

Centre for Monitoring the Indian Economy, (1985) *Basic Statistics: Volume I All India* (Worli, Bombay).

Kanshi Ram., (1982) *The Chamcha Age :An Era of the Stooges* (New Delhi).

Khare, R.S., (1984) *The Untouchable as Himself :Ideology, Identity and Pragmatism among the Lucknow Chamars*, London: Cambridge Press.

Nikhil Lakhaman, (1987) "Sudden Impact:" *Illustrated Weekly*, March 18.

Lynch, Owen, (1969) *The Politics of Untouchability.* New York: Columbia University Press.

Jorden, J.T.F., (1970) "Reconversion of Hindusim: The Shuddhi of the Arya Samaj" in G.A Oddie, ed. *Religion in South Asia.* London: Curzon Press.

Joshi, Barbara, (1977) "The Buddhist Movement of Western Uttar Pradesh" (mimeographed paper), March 27.

(1986) Editor, *Untouchable: Voices of the dalit* Liberation Movement. London: Zed Press

(1987) "Recent Developments of Inter-Regional Mobilization of *dalit* protest in India", *South Asia Bulletin 7.*

Juergensmeier, Mark (1979) *Religion as Social Vision: The Movement Against Untouchability in 20th Century Punjab.* University of California Press

Assorted issues of *Oppressed Indian,Bahujan Nayak (Marathi), Bahujan Sangathak (Hindi), dalit* Voice, Bheem patrika and others.

8

Caste, Land and Political Power in Uttar Pradesh

Imtiaz Ahmad and N.C. Saxena

This paper seeks to examine the interplay between castes, control over land, and political mobilisation in rural Uttar Pradesh. Specifically, our concern will be with the following issues: Which castes have been dominant in the villages as far as landownership and political power is concerned? What significant changes, if and, have taken place in the pattern of dominance in last hundred years? Why has there been no active emergence of the intermediate castes in politics against the continuing hegemony of the upper castes, especially Thakurs and Brahmins? What has been the impact of the abolition of the *zamindari* system on the ownership of land by various castes? On the class front, why has there been no polarisation of social classes and mobilisation of the landless and the poor peasantry which form the bulk of rural society? How have the economic policies of the government in the last thirty years, especially the green revolution and the land distribution programme affected them?

For the past ten centuries, Uttar Pradesh has been politically the most important state in India. Its vast, fertile Gangetic plains attracted invaders from West and Central Asia, and in many ways the history of Uttar Pradesh became the history of India. The impact of the Delhi Sultanate and the Mughal rule was most penetrative in this region. The mutiny in 1857 remained largely confined to the plains of Uttar Pradesh and later, most of the important leaders of the Indian National Congress and the Muslim League were drawn from this state. "The roots of many developments in twentieth century Indian politics lie not in nineteenth century Calcutta or Bombay, but in the nineteenth century Benares, Allahabad and Aligarh" (Brass, 1965). The introduction of democratic politics after 1947 has further increased its importance as it elects one out of every six Members to the Indian parliament.

Despite Uttar Pradesh being the nerve-centre of all-India politics for a long period, the structure of the villages in Uttar Pradesh has remained largely unaffected by the changes at the top. Brahmins and Thakurs, constituting only sixteen per cent of the population, today control more than fifty per cent of the political offices, just as they paid more than half of the total land revenue in the sixteenth century at the time of Akbar. As will be argued later in the paper, the agrarian changes introduced in 1921-26, 1937 and 1952 did benefit the intermediate castes which make a little over half of the population, but they could never successfully challenge the supremacy of the traditional proprietary castes, namely, Brahmins and Thakurs, in electoral politics. If the election results of the *Pramukhs* held in 1983 at the block level are any indication, there appears to be increasing dichotomy between control over land and political power, which seems to be more closely linked now with ritual and social status. Unlike the states of Tamil Nadu and Maharashtra, there has been no movement against the dominance of Brahmins and Thakurs in Uttar Pradesh, just as class polarisation has also been absent despite poverty and exploitation.

According to the 1931 census, the proportion of principal castes in the population of Uttar Pradesh was as follows:

Table 1

Castes in Uttar Pradesh

Caste category	*Name of the caste*	*Percentage in total population*
A. Brahmins, Thakurs Elite non-cultivation castes	1. Brahmins	9.2
	2. Thakurs	7.2
	3. Banias	2.5
	4. Kyastas	1.0
	5. Khatris	0.1
Total		20.0
B. Elite cultivating castes	1. Jats	1.6
	2. Bhumihars	0.4
	3. Tyagis	0.1
Total		2.1
C. Intermediate cultivating castes and other back-ward groups	1. Yadavs	8.7
	2. Kurmis	3.5
	3. Lodhs	3.2
	4. Koris	2.8

Contd...

	5. Gujars	0.7
	6. Kahars	2.3
	7. Gadaria	2.0
	8. Teli	2.0
	9. Barhai	1.5
	10. Kachhi	1.4
	11. Kewat	1.1
	12. Murao	1.3
	13. Nai	1.8
	14. Others	10.7
Total		41.9
D. Scheduled castes	1. Chamarsm	12.7
	2. Pasis	2.9
	3. Dhobi	1.6
	4. Bhangi	1.0
	5. Others	2.8
Total		21.0
E. Muslims	1. Sheikhs	3.2
	2. Pathans	2.2
	3. Julahas	2.0
	4. Syeds	0.7
	5. Moghals	0.1
	6. Others (Faqir, Shunia, Teli, Nai, Darzi, Qassah, etc.)	6.8
Total		15.0

Certain features of the geography of castes in Uttar Pradesh need to be noted. First, except in the hills where Thakurs constitute more than fifty per cent of the population, there is no caste with more than a quarter of a district's population. Only in the following five districts in Uttar Pradesh, does a single caste approximate to nearly twenty per cent of the total population:

Table 2

Name of the district	*Name of the caste*	*Percentage of total population*
Mainpuri	Ahir	22
Azamgarh	Chamar	20
Ghazipur	Ahir	19
Mathura	Jat	19
Saharanpur	Chamar	21

Second, larger castes like Brahmins, Rajputs, Ahirs, Chamars and Kurmis tend to be evenly spread throughout the state. Jats, Tyagis and Gujars in the West, Kachhis in South-Central, Kewats and Koris in a few

North-Eastern districts and Bhumihars in Varanasi and Ghazipur have regional concentration. Uttar Pradesh is thus a multi-caste state. The general belief about India having regional dominance of certain castes (like the Marathas in Maharashtra and Jats in Haryana) does not seem to be true of Uttar Pradesh. If Muslims are considered as a homogenous group, they do not form a majority in any district, and are more than twenty per cent of the total population only in eleven districts, namely, Rampur (46%), Moradabad (38%), Bijnore (37%), Saharanpur (27%), Bareilly (29%), Muzaffarnagar (29%), Bahraich (27%), Gonda (23%), Meerut (22%), Pilibhit (22%) and Basti (20%).

Third, while in any district (except the hill districts), the number of castes with over five per cent of the total population may be only five or six, there would be another fifteen to twenty castes each with more than one per cent share in the total population. The districts in Uttar Pradesh are thus multi-caste in nature. The same is true of most of the villages, although there are some predominantly single-caste villages. An average village with 150 to 300 households may have fifteen to twenty-five castes represented in its population.

Caste structure in the North Indian plains, where the Aryan people and Sanskritic culture made its deepest impact, differs from that of the south in a fundamental respect. In the south, the Brahmins were the only representatives of the twice-born castes (there being no counterpart of North Indian Rajputs and Banias in the south) which increased their social distance from the rest of the Sudra population. On the other hand, due to the presence of other groups with high social status in the north, Brahminism did not have to be tyrannical. Their is a greater continuity in the scale of ritual rank of castes in Uttar Pradesh which led to a general sharing of social status and political power. Anti-Brahminism seems to have flourished in regions characterised by steep and discontinuous traditional social hierarchies. Regions with relatively higher proportions of twice-born castes and having more gradual and continuous social handicaps seem to be less susceptible to horizontal mobilisations from below comprising ritually deprived castes seeking opportunities, status and political power (Rudolph and Rudolph, 1967).

Control over Land

The complex hierarchy of traditional rights over land existed in Uttar Pradesh, as in other parts of the country, even before the Mughal period. Between the actual cultivator and the state, there were several layers of intermediaries which can be broadly reduced to two, viz., primary and secondary *zamindars*. The primary *zamindar* usually lived in the village, had immediate proprietary dominion over the soil, regulated the settlement of newcomers in the village, distributed land for cultivation and controlled the produce. He also had inalienable rights over the village wells, wasteland and groves. He was generally responsible for payment of revenue from the village to the secondary *zamindar*. The latter, also called *Raja*, collected land revenue from the primary *zamindar* and paid it to the Mughal treasury. He also held proprietary right in a few villages (Stokes, 1978; Metcalf, 1967). The power of this intermediate class to collect revenue was dependent on the goodwill of the emperor, and because of insecurity in continuity of his authority he had no concern for the long-term prospects of revenue collection. He, therefore, oppressed the primary *zamindar* to the extent possible, who is turn exploited the peasant cultivator (Habib, 1974).

At the time of Akbar, Thakurs as secondary *zamindars* paid more than two-third of the total revenue in the districts of middle *doab* (now Agra and Allahabad divisions), Oudh and the eastern region (Ain-e-Akbari). In Rohilkhand and *uttar doab*, their hold was, however, weak. The Jats, Muslims, Tyagis and Gujars in the upper *doab* region and Muslim region, and Muslims, Kurmis, Ahirs and Loadhs in the Rohilkhand region held huge estates. East of Lucknow, the Thakurs were powerful landlords who after their expulsion from their old territories in the north due to Muslim invasion, moved eastwards and conquered the land from the Bhars, Doms and other early landowners (Connell, 1971) In some of the districts of Uttar Pradesh, the caste composition of the revenue payers (as percentage of total revenue payers) at the time of Akbar was as follows:

Table 3

	Agra	*Bulandshahar*	*Saharanpur*	*Jaunpur*
Rajputs	54.0	54.0	19.5	64
Brahamins	3.3	3.8	7.0	—
Jats	19.8	—	—	—
Muslims	5.1	—	—	11
Gujars	N.A.	11.6	7.9	—
Tyagis	—	3.0	27.0	—
Brahmin-Bhumihar	—	—	—	6
Brahman Rajput	—	—	—	18

Source: Trivedi, 1975 and Cohn, 1968.

In the medieval period, as land was abundant, there was no threat of eviction to the peasant from the *zamindar* (Habib, 1962). Because of scarcity of manpower, a tradition of hereditary rights in land developed.

This tradition continued in the dry parts of the state even till the end of the nineteenth century. The settlement officer for Hamirpur, for instance, observed in 1880: "The occupancy tenants are a large body for two reasons. First, land is superabundant and *zamindars* were, if indeed, they are not still, glad to get cultivators to remain on any terms. The resident tenant generally gets the best land and has to pay a fair rate for it, the non-residents are induced for much lower rates."

The caste composition of *zamindars* altered substantially in the eighteenth and nineteenth centuries due to three factors. The collapse of the central Mughal authority led to the expansion of land control by caste groups like Jats, Gujars and Tyagis in the districts of upper *doab* and the Brahmins in central Uttar Pradesh. Second, the revenue demand fixed under regulation IX of 1833 was high which resulted in many sales. Third, the moneylending and the official class who were mostly Banias, Brahmins, Khatris and Kayasthas, kept on acquiring *zamindari* rights through falsification of records, public auction, debt mortgage, etc. The percentage of area held by non-agricultural classes increased in Shahjehanpur from six in 1840 to nineteen in 1900. Such transfers in the proprietary titles did not affect the tenants as far as the right to cultivate land was concerned, although the new *zamindars* often tried to raise the rents. District-wise caste composition of the *zamindars* at the beginning of the twentieth century (Robinson, 1977; Metcalf, 1967) demonstrates the strength of the new class of *zamindars*. The establishment of the British judicial system hastened the transfer of land to the new merchant, banking and the urban professional class as now they did not have to depend upon brute force to enforce their claim. Under the early British rule, the new opportunity to earn money went to Brahmins, Kayasthas, Banias and Khatris which was utilised by them to get the landed status so highly prized in the society at that time. The hallmark of attaining *zamindar* status was enough compensation for the initial difficulties that they encountered in realising rents, as they lacked traditional authority and many of them did not live in the villages. Purely from the commercial point of view too, land was not a bad investment as agricultural prices were increasing rapidly while revenue remained almost static. Production of commercial crops and utilisation of wasteland increased over all returns from agriculture, and its benefits went to the *zamindars* and the cultivators, (Cohn, 1968; Neale 1962). In Ghazipur district, the price of rice more than doubled and the price of barley increased by fifty per cent between 1795 to 1850. The burden of rent and revenue in Muzaffarnagar changed between 1840 and 1920 as shown in the following table:

Table 4

	1840	*1920*	*% change*
Value of output Rs./acre	8.10	81.00	+ 9002
Revenue Rs./acre	1.60	2.60	+ 63
Population per cultivated acre	0.89	1.31	+ 47

Source: Neale, 1962.

The British viewed with concern the transfer of land from old proprietary castes to the new commercial class. Sir George Edmonstone wrote: "It is certain that the old hereditary landholders do exercise an influence in their own villages and in their neighbourhood, such as the men belonging to the mercantile classes can seldom acquire... In a political sense, therefore, it is in the interests of the government to protect the old hereditary proprietors in the possession of their ancestral estates."

In the districts of North-West Provinces, which came under British control quite early in the nineteenth century, land was settled with the primary *zamindars* during the settlements made in the 1820s and 1830s ignoring the claims of the *Rajas* and secondary *zamindars* (Metcalf, 1967). Hence, a cohesive aristocratic class with large estates could not develop in the province. Except in Etah, Allahabad and Benaras, in no other district, the share of land revenue paid by the *zamindars* paying more than five thousand rupees annually in the total district revenue was as much as thirty per cent and in fourteen out of the remaining twenty-six districts it was even lower than fifteen per cent (Stokes, 1978). On the other hand, roughly two-third villages in the Oudh which was annexed by the British in 1856, were settled with the secondary *zamindars*, called *taluqdars* (Neale, 1962). Not only the *taluqdars* were given unfettered ownership rights, but their estates were also protected against division and attachment or sale through enactments of 1869 and 1870.

Tenants

The castes of the cultivating tenants in some of the districts may be seen from Table 1. A comparison of the table with the information given about the caste of proprietors reveals a number of interesting features about land control in Uttar Pradesh. First, the Rajputs maintained a greater area under proprietary than under cultivating rights. Similarly, Banias, Kayasthas and Muslims owned more land than they farmed directly. On the contrary, the share of Brahmins was higher in many districts in the cultivated land as compared to their share in ownership. Thus, whereas Rajputs, Muslims, Banias and Kayasthas lost over land as a result of tenurial reforms, Brahmins gained security of tenure and finally ownership in 1952 as a result of the *zamindari* abolition. The fact that the Uttar Pradesh Congress Party in the crucial period 1930-1950 was dominated by the Brahmins* who as a group secured better rights through land legislation assumes significance in this context.

Second, roughly half of the cultivated land was farmed by the intermediate, backward and the scheduled castes. They were considered superior agriculturists and through higher production they could pay better rents. The upper castes abhorred manual labour and neglected their fields. The settlement officer of Sultanpur observed: "It is peculiarly unfortunate that fifty-two per cent of the holding areas should be in the hands of Brahmins and Thakurs, neither of whom are agriculturists by tradition." Similar was the comment in Bahraich: "Brahmins are generally inferior and careless cultivators, they do not handle a plough and have to depend upon hired labour. Thakurs and Kayasthas are also indifferent husband-men." Gilbert Eteinne, during his field visit to a village near Varanasi as late as in 1978, noticed a joint family of twenty-five Kayasthas living on four hectares of land, and despite many able-bodied men in the family they hired one permanent and several casual labourers.

Third, as a rule, the upper castes had the best quality of land in the village under their cultivation either as their own *sir* and *khudkasht*, or under ex-proprietary tenure. And yet, the incidence of rent on them was lower.

In Pratapgarh, in 1896, the Thakurs paid Rs. 4.91 per acre as rent where as the low caste cultivators paid Rs. 7. In Rae Bareli, in 1929, the Kurmi was required to pay roughly a third more in rent than the Thakur, while the Kachhi and Muras tenant paid almost double (Stokes, 1978). In Bareilly and Gonda, the rent paid by various castes of cultivators is given in Table 5.

The anomaly in the differential rate of rent on caste basis continued even after the *zamindari* abolition as the rent paid by each tenant before the abolition became the land revenue to be paid directly to the state after 1952. In respect of *sir* and *khudkasht* land, which was mostly held by the upper castes, incidence of rent for the same class of land by a tenant was thus not uniform. These anomalies were corrected to some extent by legislation introduced during the Emergency in 1976.

---

* See Brass (1965), in 1937 all of the Hindu ministers of the Congress ministry were drawn from this caste.

Table 5

Caste	Rent per acre in Rupees		Average area of holding in acres	
	Bareilly(1903)	Gonda (1903)	Bareilly	Gonda
Thakur	3.45	3.26	2.29	6.58
Brahmin	3.78	3.98	2.15	4.04
Kayasth	—	3.80	—	—
Upper caste	—	—	—	—
Muslims	4.00	4.32	2.13	—
Lower caste Muslims	—	4.92	—	—
Kurmi	4.52	5.05	2.96	4.90
Muraos	5.30	6.21	1.58	2.81
Scheduled castes	4.24	5.01	2.00	2.99

Security of Tenure

Before the British arrival, it was the custom that the immediate cultivator of the soil, paying his rent, should not be dispossessed of the land he occupied. Nothing was to be gained by ousting him, as land was in plenty and manpower scarce. As pressure on land increased, security of tenure became a live issue, at least in the Oudh and eastern districts of Uttar Pradesh, where land was more fertile but the per capita availability of land was low. Under the Act X of 1859 in North-West Province, each tenant who had cultivated or held land for a period of twelve years was given a right of occupancy on that land at market rates. In the long run, it did increase the number of occupant tenants, but the immediate result was a large increase in evictions of tenants in the eleventh year, before they could be entitled to claim the benefit of the twelve year rule (Neale, 1962). This particularly happened in the eastern districts where in the face of rising prices and increasing area under sugarcane during 1850-1920, cultivation was becoming profitable. The landlords also attempted to extend their own direct cultivation by ousting the tenants with the result that in Basti, by 1919, more than one-third of the cultivated area had become *sir* or *khudkasht* of the proprietors (Stokes, 1978). In Ghazipur, of the total 12,17,458 tenants, some 65,918 were still tenants-at-will in 1887. The number of unprotected tenants would be higher if the large class of sub-tenants on the land of high caste tenants was taken into account.

Worse was the plight of tenants in the Oudh region where by 1883 some eighty-eight per cent of all cultivators, tilling seventy-seven per cent of the cultivated area were tenants-at-will. The status of Kori and Chamar tenants in Gonda in 1877 was no better than the bonded slaves of the high castes. The deputy commissioner for Pratapgarh in 1896 lamented the fact that the rents of the low caste cultivators could be screwed up by the landlords without recourse to ejectment. "A landlord seldom takes the trouble to serve a notice on a low caste cultivator. In order to raise rent, he simply makes him pay the enhanced demand."

The districts of western Uttar Pradesh, specially upper *doab* and Rohilkhand, presented a markedly different picture. In Saharanpur, for instance in 1870, there was hardly any distinction between the rent-paying tenant and the revenue-paying proprietor. The *zamindar*, even when he belonged to upper castes, had no inhibition towards manual labour and often cultivated a substantial part of his holding with the help of family labour. In Shahjahanpur, the acquisition of occupancy right by tenants was freely permitted by the landlords because the "tenants are not so plentiful as to create much competition for land." For the entire North-West Province, the percentage of land cultivated by the tenants-at-will was only 38.5 per cent in 1892 (Neale, 1962), mostly in central *doab* and the districts.

The seven year rule in Oudh and the twelve year rule in the rest of the province were finally abrogated in 1921 and 1926, respectively, and as a result the tenants were granted life-tenure. The terms of tenancy could be altered every ten years only by a special officer and not by negotiation between landlord and tenant. The heir of the tenant inherited the holding and held it for five years on the same terms as the deceased, but after five years the land again reverted to the landlord. The 1939 Act introduced by the Congress ministry of Govind Ballabh Pant pursued the logic of the earlier measures and granted to all tenants in Agra and Oudh full hereditary rights to their holdings. It also took away the right of the *zamindar* to resume land for making improvements in the use of the land.

Thus, as early as in 1926, the law had almost completely divested the *zamindar* of land from his control, except for his *sir* and *khudkasht* and the small amount that became available five years after a statutory tenant died. The following table demonstrates the growth in the number of secure tenancies in Uttar Pradesh:

Table 6

Non-occupancy Tenants as a Percentage of all Tenants

Region	*1899-1990*	*1926-27*	*1935-36*	*194546*
Oudh	82.2	10.5	11.9	5.1
Agra	41.9	4.0	6.2	2.7

Source: Neale, 1962.

Land and Political Agitations

One of the immediate reasons for introducing land legislation in Oudh in 1921 to provide greater security to the tenants was the agrarian disturbances which engulfed the districts of Pratapgarh, Rae Bareli and Faizabad in the years 1920-22. These districts were quite close to Allahabad, which was the centre of Congress nationalist politics at that time. After 1915, the Congress had begun to realise the political importance of mass mobilisation, and between 1915 and 1920 a number of *kisan* rallies were organised under its aegis to draw the *kisans* (farmers) to the nationalist struggle (Dhanagare, 1983:117). At the same time, grass root peasant activity had also come into being in these districts against the *taluqdari* and *zamindari* excesses. It is significant that the agitation was not directed against landlordism as such but it was against its abuses. In one of the meetings of the Kisan Sabha, the following resolutions were passed: "We shall not brook beating or abuses from anyone. We shall not pay illegal cesses. We shall not work as labourers without payment. If any one abuses us, we shall jointly ask him to restrain himself. If he would not listen we would take him to our Thakur (Zamindar)" (Majid Siddiqui, 1973).

The steep rise in wholesale prices during the first two decades of the twentieth century resulted in a decline of landlords' real income as formal rents did not rise:

Table 7

Prices, Rental & Revenue Demands, and Wages in the Uttar Pradesh (1900-34) (Index Numbers 1901 = 100)

Year	*Wholesale Prices*	*Rental Secured Tenants*	*Demands Ordinary Tenants*	*Land Revenue Demands*	*Wages (Agricultural)*
1906	129	104	106	101	100
1011	120	106	115	103	100
1916	160	111	121	104	120
1921	258	114	134	108	—
1926	230	120	146	109	—
1929	218	120	165	110	180
1930	162	121	166	111	—
1931	112	121	165	112	—
1934	103	121	161	113	120

Source: Dhanagare, 1983: 116.

The *taluqdars* and their agents resorted to extortion and rackrenting in order to bring rents more into line with prices. Actual evictions in the first two decades increased by 100 per cent (Dhanagare, 1983), and another 37, 844 ejection suits were pending in the courts of Oudh in 1921 (Neale, 1962). Kurmi and Yadav tenants, who had the reputation of having greater paying capacity, were special targets of landlords' exactions. Being small landholders they had to buy their requirements from the market and thus their economic distress was very acute.

The Congress extended its support initially under the belief that the *kisans* would, by and large, confine their struggle to fight against British imperialism. When the movement got directed against landlords and developed an autonomy of its own the Congress tried to diffuse it by the calling of the Non-Cooperation Movement.

Gandhi repeatedly issued instructions asking the peasants not to agitate against the *zamindars.* "You should bear a little if the *zamindar* torments you. We do not want to fight with the *zamindars...* We may not withhold taxes from government or rent from the landlord. Should there be any grievance against *zamindars* they should be reported to Motilal Nehru and his advice followed. We should influence our opponents by kindness, not by using physical force nor stopping their water supply nor the services of the barber and the washerman" (Pande, 1977). In 1922, when the tenants' struggle was at its peak, the Congress Working Committee workers informed the ryots about withholding of rent payment to the *zamindars* in contrary to Congress resolution. The Swaraj Party was even more forthright in its support for the *zamindars.* Its manifesto in 1923 contained the resolution: " True it is that the party stands for justice to the tenant, but poor indeed will be the quality of that justice if it involves any injustice to the landlords" (Pande, 1977). Withdrawal of support by the Congress party and partial amelioration by way of life tenancies provided by the Oudh Act of 1921 were the two important factors because of which the movement petered out.

Despite the fact that the Congress was dominated by small *zamindars* and urban professionals with *zamindari* connections, its support for the no-rent campaign launched in 1930-32 was not inhibited. The economic depression and the fall in production and prices had adversely affected upper tenantry and small *zamindar*-producers who had joined the Congress during mass mobilisation of the last decade. The poor tenants, under tenants and landless labourers, with no stake in the market, did participate in the *civil disobedience* campaign under the influence of the substantial landholders, but the movement lacked militancy and it remained a non-violent agrarian movement limited to seeking remissions from the government in taxes and rents (Dhanagare, 1983).

In the face of government repression and upward buoyancy in prices after 1932 the movement petered out.

Congress

A dominant section of the Uttar Pradesh Congress and Gandhi opposed radical reforms in the early thirties. About the abolition of *zamindari*, the Swaraj Party in 1932 resolved: "The party cannot possibly dream of such madness as to undermine the very foundations of society as it has existed for hundreds of years in India by trying to eliminate an important and influential class from it" (Pandey, 1977). Gandhi wrote in 1931: "We may not dispossess the *zamindars* and the *taluqdars* of their thousands of bighas. And among whom shall we distribute the land? We need not dispossess them. They only need a change of heart. When this is done and when they learn to melt at their peasants' woes, they shall hold their lands in trust for them, will give them a major part of the produce keeping only sufficient for themselves."

Despite such abhorrence on the part of the Congress to arouse political consciousness among the tenants, along class lines a vocal section emerged within the party, which had direct experience of peasant distress and protest and it started acting as a strong pressure group to orient the Congress politics towards the interests of the tenants. They formed the Congress Socialist Party (CSP) in 1934, which had its strongest base in Uttar Pradesh. By 1947, it had captured a number of elective positions in the district and the state organisations. Important Congress leaders like Sampurnanand, Kidwai, C.B. Gupta, N.D.Tewari had at one time or the other been in the socialist movement. The party exhibited several amorphous and overlapping tendencies such as Marxism, social democracy of the British Labour Party, and democratic socialism tempered by Gandhian concepts of decentralisation and the use of non-violent techniques for national movement and class struggle (Choudhari, 1982). However, its activities remained confined to district and state level politics and even this group never seriously tried to build up grass root leadership at the village and the block levels; nor did it attempt to organise the intermediate castes, which remained largely outside the mainstream of politics in Uttar Pradesh till the beginning of the 1960s.

Threatened by the increasing influence of the CSP in Uttar Pradesh Congress, the big *zamindars* and the *taluqdars* formed their own political party—the Northern Agriculturist Party (NAP). In the 1937 assembly elections, it got twenty-two seats as against 136 Congress, twenty-six Muslim League, one Liberal and forty-three independents (Burgher, 1969). Insofar as protection of long-term interest of the landlords was concerned, the NAP experiment proved disastrous, as it forced the Congress to openly espouse the interests of the tenants, especially those paying a rent of fifty rupees or more cultivating roughly ten acres of land who had voting rights, to wean them away from the influence of the *zamindars*. The NAP got disbanded soon, and neither in 1946 nor in the post-independence elections did the *zamindars* try to organise a coherent opposition to the ruling party. They chose to pursue individual rather than class interests.

As already stated, by 1940, the *zamindars* had been reduced to the status of being intermediaries in respect of cultivated land, as the law had provided occupancy and hereditary rights to the tenants. They still exercised a great deal of social authority as they controlled common utility lands such as pastures, *abadi* (residential) plots and market yards. The right to levy *tehebazari* fees from weekly *hats* (markets) on open or grove lands was a great source of income for the landlords, as it is even these days for their successors: the *Pradhans* and the rich farmers. In central and east Uttar Pradesh, where due to small size of holdings the small farmer did not even have one cartload of produce for sale at the time of harvest to meet rent demand and immediate family needs, the landlord often bought his surplus at lower prices and reaped profits through entry in the market at the appropriate time. The tradition has now been given official recognition by the procurement agencies of the state government while making purchase of foodgrains at the support price directly from the farmers. The village *bania* is included in the category of farmer and not a trader.

As the *zamindars* were allowed to retain their *sir* and *khudkasht* lands after the *zamindari* abolition in 1952, determination of the total area under this category is an important issue to understand the nature of agrarian society in the post-independence period. After each piece of legislation which sought to provide greater security of tenure to the tenants, the *zamindars*, specially those living in the villages, extended the area recorded under their self-cultivation as follows:

Table 8

Year	*Approximate area with the zamindars recorded as sir and khudkasht in acres (in lakhs)*
Before 1921	42
1938-39	57
1946-47	71
1957	81

Understandably, the *zamindars* exercised a good deal of extra-legal powers over the bureaucracy and the poor tenants who lost occupancy rights every time laws intended to benefit them were enacted. Cohn's field study in Jaunpur (1968) describes how *zamindars* could successfully evict even tenants who had legal right to permanency. Intention to abolish the *zamindari* was known much before 1947. The committee's report was made public in 1949. The legislation was passed in 1952 and its implementation began in 1955. The *Patwaris* got an opportunity as had never before occurred to them. They tampered with the accounts to such an extent that one cannot go to a Uttar Pradesh village today without hearing from *ryots* about land over which they should have *sirdari* rights but which went to the former landlord as *bhumidari* land, courtesy of the *Patwari* (Neale, 1962).

Yet the total quantum of land which the former big landlords were able to keep with themselves was insignificant as compared to the total land under cultivation over which they had rights to collect rents. On the eve of independence, roughly 5,893 *zamindars* paid 41.5 per cent of the total revenue, each paying more than Rs. 1,000 annually but they could get only four lakh acres recorded under self-cultivation in 1946-47, which came to less than one per cent of the total settled land. The following table gives the break-up of *sir* and *khudkasht* for various categories of *zamindars* in Uttar Pradesh at the time of *zamindari* abolition:

Table 9

Class of zamindars by land area of revenue paid	*No. of zamindars*	*% share in total LR*	*Total sir and khudkasht in lakh acres*	*% share in toal sir and khudkasht*	*Average area of sir and khudkasht per zamindar in acres*
Less than Rs. 25	17,10,530	15.1	30.0	42.1	1.75
Rs. 25—250	2,76,111	27.1	28.9	40.6	10.47
Rs. 250—1000	24,249	16.3	8.3	11.7	34.30
Rs. 1000—5000	5,089	14.2	2.4	3.4	47.16
More than Rs. 5000	804	27.3	1.6	2.2	199.00
	20,16,783	100.0	71.2	100.0	3.53

Source: *Zamindari* Abolition Committee (ZAC).

The petty *zamindar* paying less than twenty-five rupees as land revenue was, generally speaking, owner-cultivator who remained unaffected by the *zamindari* abolition legislation. At the apex of the pyramid, the big landlords of the last two categories, were left with sufficient land with them and a generous compensation for the loss of intermediary rights to cultivate it on modern capitalist lines. Some of their tenants, especially belonging to Brahmin and Rajput castes, also received proprietary rights over substantial areas, although they had already received occupancy rights by 1926 and hereditary rights in 1939. The loss or gain of land for Brahmin and Rajput castes in some of the districts can be seen from the following table:

Table 10

Land Held by Each Caste as Percentage of Total Land

	Brahmins as proprietors			*Thakurs as proprietors*		
	Before	*After*	*% in population*	*Before*	*After*	*% in population*
Agra	23.0	19.1	13.2	26.0	21.4	11.1
Kanpur	33.2	22.8	15.5	30.3	16.6	8.6
Gorakhpur	28.2	17.1	9.9	17.7	7.7	3.5
Kheri	4.5	16.4	9.4	62.8	7.5	3.7

Socialists and Land Taxation

When the Socialists (with a strength of 44 MLAs) joined the Samyukta Vidhayak Dal (SVD) government of Charan Singh in 1967, they got their demand of abolition of land revenue for small farmers included in the fourteen point programme of the SVD. As Charan Singh was personally not in favour of exempting the small farmers from payment of land revenue, presumably on grounds of loss of seven crores income to the state exchequer, no formal proposal ever came before the Cabinet. In October 1967, the Samyukta Socialist Party (SSP) and the Communist Party of India (CPI) ministers resigned on this issue. Threatened by an immediate collapse of the government, a compromise formula was evolved to create an agricultural research fund out of realisation of revenue from holdings up to 6.25 acres, with a provision that the small farmers could borrow from the fund at nominal interests. The SSP agreed to reconsider the resignations of their ministers, which however were never formally withdrawn. Their resignations were formally accepted on January 5, 1968. A month later, Charan Singh also resigned (Kashyap, 1985)

The marginal farmers continued to pay land revenue till July 1977 when the Janata Party again came to power after the mid-term elections. The SSP which through its merger with the Bhartiya Kranti Dal (BKD) in 1973 had given a power base to the latter in central and eastern districts of the province, was not a formal constituent of the Janata Party, yet some fifty out of 350 Janata MLAs had socialist background. They succeeded this time in getting the marginal farmers having land-holdings up to 3.125 acres exempted from payment of land revenue. The real intention of the Janata government was to abolish the land development tax on medium and large farmers, imposed in July 1976 during the Emergency period, but in order to project a 'pro-poor' image, appeasement of the poor farmers became a necessity. Total land tax on various categories of farmers had been changing as shown in Table 3.

The modest increase proposed in 1981 which would have affected only ten per cent of the peasant community was not accepted. A senior cabinet minister was very frank in admitting that it would have hurt "our vote banks".

According to the 1931 census, literacy among various caste groups was as follows:

Table 11

Caste and Literacy

Caste	*% in population*	*% of literates in total*	*% of male literates in English in each caste group*	*Total male literates in English*
Brahmin	9.2	29.3	2.44	111,166
Kayastha	1.0	70.3	19.64	94,076
Bania	2.5	38.4	4.24	53,508
Rajput	7.2	18.3	1.18	44.332
Bhumihar	0.4	31.0	1.67	3.190
Jat	1.6	8.1	0.71	5,751
Chamar	12.7	0.6	0.02	1,262

Unlike Bihar, the Brahmins of Uttar Pradesh took to western education and urban professions quite early in the nineteenth century. Rajputs, on the other hand, remained tied to the land and did not avail of the opportunities for higher education. Their representation at the middle and top levels of administration continued to be low till about 1965. With the introduction of capitalist technology in agriculture, the Rajputs are also becoming efficient farmers and the gap between their economic prosperity and share in government jobs is declining.

In August 1977, the Janata government decided to introduce reservation for backward castes in government services. Thirty-five Hindu and twenty-one Muslim castes comprising about forty per cent of the total population for each religious group were declared as backward classes eligible for reservation along with other groups as given in Table 12.

Table 12

Group eligible for reservation	% of jobs reserved in each category			
	Class I	Class II	Class III	Class IV
1. Scheduled caste	18	18	25	30
2. Scheduled tribe	2	2	2	2
3. Disabled	2	2	2	2
4. Dependents of the freedom fighters	5	5	3	3
5. Disabled officers of the army, emergency commissioned, and public services commissioned officers and ex-armymen	8	8	3	3
6. Backward classes	15	15	15	10

Unlike in Bihar, the reservation policy did not evoke much of a public furore, except in some of the eastern districts bordering Bihar. The principal beneficiaries of this decision are likely to be Ahirs, Kurmis, Gujars and Muslim weavers. They possess the necessary means to educate their children. Even social consciousness among them is higher as compared to the 'other backward classes'. Caste composition of the officers of the state-level services has also changed as shown in Table 13.

Table 13

Caste	% in population	Recruited between			
		1950-76		1977-80	
		Total No.	%	Total No.	%
1. Brahmin	9.2	244	35.6	35	23.6
2. Kayastha	1.0	95	13.9	11	7.4
3. Bania	2.5	66	9.6	14	9.5
4. Rajput	7.2	75	10.9	17	11.5
5. Khatri	0.1	24	3.5	4	2.7
6. Muslim	16.0	21	3.1	5	3.4
7. Sikh	—	7	1.0	—	—
8. Christian	—	1	0.1	—	—
9. Scheduled caste	21.0	109	15.9	26	17.6
10. Jat	1.6	12	1.8	4	2.7
11. Yadav	8.7	15	2.2	9	6.1
12. Kurmi	3.5	6	0.9	5	3.4
13. Gujar	0.7	4.	0.6	3	2.0
14. Other backward castes*	29.0	6	0.9	3	2.0
		685	100.0	148	100.0

* Also includes backward Muslims.

In addition to direct recruitment to services, the Janata government decided to extend the benefit of reservation in promotions also. However, this concession was withdrawn by the Congress government in November 1981. The policy of reservation for backward castes in direct recruitment still continues despite the fact that in 1983 the Congress ministry chose to mildly oppose the reccommendations of the Mandal Commission for backward classes. Some excerpts from the state government's letter to the Government of India read as follows:

> Whereas the state government is fully committed to the welfare and economic upliftment of weaker sections and backward classes it is felt that identification of backward classes with certain castes may create more problems than it may solve. The benefits of reservations may be cornered by an advanced minority which does not require any protection to the exclusion of those who really deserve... To use "backward classes" and "backward castes" as mutually exchangeable terms is neither rational nor fair... It is time to examine carefully the appropriateness and adequacy of measures adopted so far by various states to improve the conditions of the socially and educationally backward classes. The nation's responsibility towards them does not end with reservation in jobs. Such a measure may not produce any significant difference in the lives of the vast majority of the socially oppressed and deprived sections of the community. Bolder and more radical measures are needed to create a just and equitable social system.

Structure of Landholdings in Uttar Pradesh

As already stated, the intermediaries lost control over a substantial part of the land as a result of legislations introduced during the period 1920 to 1955.

The names of actual cultivators were recorded in the land records, which were revised every year. This facilitated conferment of tenurial rights to the cultivators. The area held by the ex-*zamindars* and the new landowners in 1957 was as follows:

Table 14

Category	*Total area as owners in acres (in lakhs)*	*% of total area*
Ex-zamindars	81.35	18.1
New owners with secure rights	362.58	80.4
Tenants with inferior rights	6.72	1.5
	450.65	100.0

Source: Neale, 1962.

Two points need to be noted here. First, of the total settled area roughly 390 lakh acres was under cultivation and the rest 60 lakh acres consisted of barren land, private forest, pastures, etc. The bulk of this 60 lakh acres was with the ex-*zamindars* and cultivators with large holdings. Second, roughly half of the 81.35 lakh acres was with petty *zamindars* with total holding of less than 10 acres. At the same time, some of the ex-tenants also became substantial landowners. The number of households and area owned by them in 1953-54 and 1971-72 were as given in Table 4.

The structure of landholdings in 1945-46 and 1980-81 is given below:

Table 15

Size of Landholdings

Size of holding in acres	*1945-46*		*1980-81*	
	% in total landholdings	*% in total area*	*% in total landholdings*	*% in total area*
0-2.5	62.8	17.6	70.4	25.2
2.5-5.0	18.4	21.6	16.03	22.6
5.0-10.0	12.8	22.6	9.2	24.8
10.0-25.0	5.1	22.2	3.7	21.2
25.0 and above	0.9	12.0	0.4	6.2
Total	100.0	100.0	100.0	100.0

Land cultiveted by scheduled caste households is shown in the following table:

Table 16

Size in acres	*No. of holdings in 000s*			*Area of holding in 000s acres*		
	with SCs	*Total*	*%*	*with SCs*	*Total*	*%*
0-2.5	2149.3	12344.3	17.4	1766.2	11075.3	16.0
	(81.6)	(70.4)		(42.6)	(25.2)	
2.5-5.0	334.9	2819.7	11.5	1115.0	9907.3	11.2
	(12.7)	(16.3)		(26.9)	(22.6)	
5.0-10	120.1	1595.6	7.6	795.5	10896.2	7.3
	(4.6)	(9.2)		(19.2)	(24.8)	
10-25	28.8	658.0	4.4	390.5	9297.5	4.2
	(1.0)	(3.7)		(9.4)	(21.2)	
More than 25	2.1	71.2	3.0	79.5	2720.2	2.9
	(0.0)	(0.4)		(1.9)	(6.2)	
Total	2635.2	17563.8	15.0	4146.7	43896.3	9.5
	(100.0)	(100.0)		(100.0)	(100.0)	

The structure of landholdings in other states in shown below in Table 17:

Table 17

States	Upto 5 acres		30 acres and above		Giri co-offi-cient
	% ofholdings	% of area	% of holdings	% of area	
Kerala	95.1	64.8	.05	1.9	.53
Orissa	89.3	46.0	.31	3.6	.50
J & K	85.3	62.3	NEGLIGIBLE		.43
West Bengal	84.0	53.7	N.A.	N.A.	.46
Assam	82.6	56.5	.03	0.3	.44
Bihar	82.2	44.4	.28	4.3	.57
Tamil Nadu	81.3	44.6	.33	4.3	.53
Uttar Pradesh	76.0	40.9	.37	4.0	.51
A.P.	66.4	21.0	2.40	20.9	.61
Karnataka	51.6	15.8	3.60	20.7	.58
Gujarat	49.9	12.4	5.50	26.1	.58
Rajasthan	47.4	7.9	7.30	38.8	.66
Madhya Pradesh	46.4	12.3	4.40	23.0	.55
Maharashtra	45.5	11.4	5.60	27.0	.62
Haryana	35.9	9.1	4.00	17.3	5.40
Punjab	30.8	8.5	4.00	17.3	N.A.

The following points emerge from these tables:

1. As against their share of twenty-one per cent in the total population, the scheduled caste households operate only 9.5 per cent of land. Area involved in general holdings up to five acres is 47.8 per cent of the total area, whereas for the scheduled caste holdings it is as high as 67.5 per cent. Of those who operate on large holdings of twenty-five acres and above, only three per cent belong to the scheduled castes.
2. Of the total number of households in Uttar Pradesh, only 0.4 per cent owned more than twenty-five acres of land in 1971-72 and the area involved in such holdings was only six per cent of the total area. Thus, it can be said that unlike the states of Andhra Pradesh, Gujarat, Madhya Pradesh, Maharashtra, Karnataka, Punjab and Haryana, Uttar Pradesh is not a state of large landowners.
3. The absolute number of large landholders in 1971-72 was 72,000, and they owned 24,14,000 acres. If, on an average, twenty-five acres per family is taken as the limit for land ceiling, the state should have appropiated 6.14 lakh acres as surplus land from them, whereas total land taken in possession so far as a result of

ceilings imposed in 1971-72 is only two lakhs. This gives us some estimate of the extent of evasion from land ceiling legislation.

4. Data collected by the Giri Institute of Social Science, Lucknow, on sale of agricultural land, indicate that except in the Terai districts, elsewhere there has been negligible transfer of land through sales. Thus, it will not be fair to assert that small landowners are being forced to resort to distress selling. The pressure on marginal holdings has certainly increased in the last twenty years, but it appears to be due to the increase in population and lack of employment opportunities for the tiny landowners in the non-agriculture sector. Seventy per cent of the rural households in Uttar Pradesh owned less than 2.5 acres of land each. Another fifteen per cent had holdings between 2.5 and 5.0 acres. Thus, Uttar Pradesh is a state of tiny landholdings.

Sub-Tenancy and Sharecropping in Uttar Pradesh

One of the oft-repeated objectives of *zamindari* abolition in Uttar Pradesh was to provide land to the tiller. However, the Uttar Pradesh Zamindari Abolition Committee observed that "in many parts of this province considerations of social status prohibit high caste men, Brahmins, Kshatriyas from engaging in certain kinds of manual work such as driving the plough which is considered fit only for lower caste agriculture or field labourers. All the same, since times immemorial, they have been treated as "cultivators". If the performance of manual operations were imposed as an essential condition, a large number of such men, whose livelihood depends upon lands, would be excluded from the definition of "cultivator" (quoted in Thorner, 1976:23).

Thus, the law in Uttar Pradesh did not make participation in manual operation or residence in the village a necessary condition for conferment of tenurial rights. Further, leasing-out was banned but sharecropping was explicitly authorised by introducing the following clause:

> Any arrangement whereby a person is entitled to a right merely to share in the produce grown on the land in consideration of such person assisting or participating with the tenure-holder in the actual performance of agricultural operations is not a "lease" (explanation to section 156 of ZALR Act).

There used to be a provision in the Uttar Pradesh Land Records Manual for recording the names of sub-tenants during the annual updating of land records but this practice was abandoned sometime in the late sixties on the pretext that it gave rise to unnecessary harassment at the hands of lower revenue officials of the cultivator who may not have leased out his plot for a regular rent but might be getting it cultivated through a share-cropper.

The Government of India had been persistently pointing out to the state government that the above-quoted explanation to section 156 which legalises crop-sharing was against the spirit of *zamindari* abolition, and therefore should be deleted. Finally, it was dropped by the Act 34 of 1974. The Government of India had also suggested inclusion of the following clause:

> Provided further that cultivation through servants or hired labourers will be deemed to be a lease unless it is accompanied with practical supervision by the tenure-holder or a member of his family.

The state government turned down the suggestion but instead added the following clause through Act 30 of 1975:

> Where a tenure-holder has transferred possession over the whole or part of his holding under any arrangement whereby the tenure-holder becomes entitled to any money or to any share in the produce grown in such holding or part then the transferer shall be deemed to have let such holding or part to the transferee.

This amendment, unfortunately, did not last long. Pressure was put on the state government by the MPs, MLAs and many individual landlords that the new clause was resulting in hardship to the sharecroppers as they were being ousted from their tiny plots. It was on this pretext that the above mentioned clause was dropped through Act 35 of 1976. The present picture, therefore, is that leasing-out is specifically banned, the law is silent about sharecropping but through administrative instructions the field officials are precluded from recording the names of the sub-tenants or the sharecroppers.

What is the extent of sub-tenancy in Uttar Pradesh? According to the twenty-sixth round (survey of 1971-72), roughly one-quarter of the farmers owning more than ten acres are leasing-out land but of the total area owned by them only seven per cent gets leased-out. On the other side, of those owning no land or less than 2.5 acres, roughly one-third are leasing-in land which supplements their owned area to the tune of additional fifty per cent.

With the introduction of new technology in agriculture, labour has ceased to be the most important input. At the same time, the lure of higher profits has certainly improved the quality of personal supervision even by the high caste big farmers. They may not be still touching the plough, especially, in east Uttar Pradesh, but no such caste inhibitions exist in using the tractor or the thresher. Therefore, as far as the consideration of higher productivity is concerned, the need for prohibiting crop-sharing practices is not paramount today if the owner is also contributing towards the cost of inputs. If the landowner is living in village, administratively it becomes difficult to ascertain whether he is getting his land cultivated through hired labourers, or leasing it out on a fixed rent basis, or sharing produce with the sub-tenant with or without contribution to current inputs and entrepreneurship. One landowner may resort to all the above practices or may change the arrangement from crop to crop. In many districts of east Uttar Pradesh, wages are sometimes paid to the hired labourers in the form of leasing-out a small portion of plot from crop to crop. It also enhances the landlord's influence in the village. Collection of information, where such subtle differences in practice are in vogue, through official machinery may not always throw light on the village realities, besides it may give rise to complaints of corruption and harassment.

On the other hand, it is administratively simpler to collect information about such landowners who are not living in the village where their lands are situated. With a view to estimate the number of absentee landowners, a district-wise?

Absentee landlordism no longer seems to be a "built-in depressor" under the changed conditions. High incidence of non-resident cultivation in the upper *doab* districts may also be there because of increasing opportunities of urban employment in this region. In Haryana too (Bhalla, 1983), the literate and the well-off family in the village as well as the owners of sub-marginal holdings who have migrated to a nearby city tend to lease-out their lands. A few big landowners, although quite capable of cultivating their lands efficiently, lease out a part of their holdings to bring a few small holders within their political orbit.

Land Reforms, Bureaucracy and Political Will

It has often been asserted that progress in the field of land reforms has been thwarted because of the absence of political will. To quote Appu: "In no sphere of public activity in our country since independence has the hiatus between precept and practice, between policy pronouncements and actual execution, been as great as in the domain of land reform. With resolute and unambiguous political will all the other shortcomings and difficulties could have been overcome, in the absence of such will even minor obstacles become formidable road blocks in the path of Indian land reform. Considering the character of the political power structure obtaining in the country it was only natural that the required political will was not forthcoming" (Appu, 1975).

The degree to which radical land reforms have been promoted in Uttar Pradesh has been determined by a number of factors: class character of the MLAs and ministers, orientation of the bureaucracy, the pressure which the potential beneficiaries have been able to apply on the politicians and administration, policy of the central government, relationship between productivity, local power and land reforms.

The background of the MLAs in the first three Uttar Pradesh assemblies was studied by Meyer (1989). He found that about thirty per cent of the MLAs came from the families of *zamindars* or *taluqdars*. The percentage distribution of MLAs on the basis of their father's profession was as follows:

Table 18

Heritage	*% in Uttar Pradesh Assembly*
Large Zamindar or Taluqdar	11
Medium Zamindar or Taluqdar	5
Small Zamindar or Taluqdar	9
Zamindar of unknown size	5
Cultivator with proprietary rights	43
Landless Agricultural Labourer	3
Non-Agricultural Backward	24
	100

(Total sample size-1290)

* The classification of the *zamindars* into large, medium and small was on the basis of the number of villages they collected rent from, 25, between 10 and 24 and less than 10, respectively.

From his data, Meyer concludes that "the extent to which MLAs are drawn from the upper segment of rural society is phenomenal. Traditional, financial and status resources seem to have greater potency in this early stage of democratic experience... Of the two hierarchical factors, economic status and ritual status, the former seems to have been the most effectual in elite recruitment. The even representation of the high castes was by a factor of two or three, whereas the factor for the wealthy would certainly have been at least thirty, perhaps 300, depending upon whether the very rich comprised one per cent or 0.1 per cent of the society" (Meyer, 1989).

Although the *zamindars* and *taluqdars* were patronised by all political parties they were more dominant in the right-wing Jan Sangh and Swatantra. The party-wise character of the MLAs of 1962 assembly is shown in Table 19.

Table 19

	Percentage break-up of each political party						
	Cong	*SP*	*PSP*	*CPI*	*Jan Sangh*	*Swatantrsa*	*Inde-pendent*
Large Zamindar or Taluqdar	9	0	8	—	16	33	32
Medium Zamindar or Taluqdar	9	4	5	—	4	—	—
Small Zamindar or Taluqdar	9	17	16	—	16	13	—
Zamindar of unknown size	4	0	3	7	12	13	7
Cultivator with proprietary rights	39	63	63	57	35	7	39
Landless agricultural labourer	4	4	3	—	0	—	3
Non-agricultural background	26	12	3	36	16	33	19
Total	249	24	38	14	49	15	31

What changes have taken place in the background of MLAs and other important politicians in the last twenty years? With the creation of only one type of tenurial rights in 1974, the distinction between ex-*zamindars* and new proprietors has now become blurred. Ownership of land being the primary axis of differentiation in the rural areas, an effort was made to find out from each district the amount of land which the present MPs, MLAs, MLCs and the *Pramukhs* elected in 1983 had in their own names. Data on occupations other than agriculture were also obtained. The break-up of 722 politicians on the basis of landownership is shown in the following table:

Table 20

Category	*Total number in each group*	*Percentage of the Total*
No land	42	5.8
Between 1 to 5 acres	158	21.8
Between 6 to 10 acres	125	17.3
Between 11 to 15 acres	129	17.9
Between 16 to 20 acres	98	13.6
More than 20 acres	170	23.6
Total	722	100.0

Before interpreting these data, it must be kept in mind that many politicians keep only small holdings in their names and the rest may be in the names of their family members or servants. Secondly, those reporting no land should not be confused or equated with landless agricultural labourers or artisans.

Most of them are teachers, businessmen or lawyers. The same is true of those with holdings of less than five acres. Their number is higher in districts with a sizeable urban population. On the whole, roughly forty per cent politicians have businesses like brick-kilns, foodgrains processing industries, cold storages, petrol pump stations, kerosene or coal depots. A number of them also have urban property. Therefore, it is difficult to assess the economic background of the MLAs on the basis of recorded land or subsidiary occupation in their names.

It is observed that districts with high pressure on land, political awareness of intermediate castes and with a history of Socialist Party activity tend to have more MLAs/Block *Pramukhs* with small holdings than the districts of the west Bundelkhand and the Oudh. Figures from some of the districts are set out in Table 6.

When the landownership of MLAs and the MPs is compared with that of indirectly elected MLCs and Block *Pramukhs*, one observes that the latter group tends to own more land than the former.

Although the data regarding the occupational background of the MLAs in the first three assemblies are not exactly comparable with the landownership pattern of politicians presented above, one can easily conclude that politicians who succeed in elections continue to be drawn from the upper segments of the rural society. Such a pattern of recruitment is certainly dysfunctional for implementation of redistributive policies. A few case studies will help in understanding the relationship between political structure and political will for radical changes, in agranian relations. These relate to the period 1980-81.

(a) According to the 26th round of the NSS, the total number of households leasing-in land in Uttar Pradesh was about 3.5 million, out of which 3.4 million owned less than five acres of land. They were entirely at the mercy of the landowners, had no security of tenure, and their names were also not recorded in the revenue registers. As already noted, the NSS figures seem to be under-estimates, the actual number of sharecroppers and sub-tenants may be close to five million. Restriction on leasing-out of land has not reduced the number of sub-tenants, but it has only succeeded in driving sub-tenancy underground. Obviously, so long as the restriction on leasing-out continues, it is not possible to record the names of the sharecroppers.

It was suggested to the government that leasing-out of land be made lawful and a drive on the pattern of 'Operation Barga' in

West Bengal be launched, with the important difference that no rights would accrue to the sharecroppers. It was thought that such recording could be feasible only if it was clear to the landowners that they would not lose ownership as a result of the sharecropper's names coming into the revenue records. Another point was: what useful purpose would it serve if the sub-tenants were not to get any security? If the policy was accepted and implemented three to four million people might get registered as sub-tenants and they would immediately be eligible for short-term credit from financial institutions, and secondly, it may result in greater confidence among them. A pressure group of the identified sub-tenants may emerge and in due course of time the government may grant them permanent rights as was done by the British in stages between 1880-1940. The government was keen to remove the ban on leasing of land but was not interested in bringing the names of the sub-tenants on the official records. The proposal, in toto, was not accepted.

(b) It was premised that any proposal to lower the ceiling limit on land (as present about twenty-five acres per family for irrigated land) would neither be accepted by the government nor would it yield much land due to administrative and legal hurdles. Unlike the parasitic class of *zamindars* who were economically isolated from the production process, the present rural elite was enterprising and very much rooted in the socio-political system, and hence was much more difficult to remove. Perhaps the only way was to take land away from such urban-based people who had a good source of income from non-agricultural sources but were still holding land. But even this measure would not have been acceptable to the power elite as most of them fell in the category of land-owners.

(c) Most of the cultivated land in the *terai* area of Nainital was in the possession of tribals till 1950. Under the colonisation scheme, it was decided to extend cultivation through deforestation and huge farms of 100 to 5,000 acres were given on lease to outsiders and retired military and civil officers. The scheme benefited a number of displaced people, mostly Sikhs, who came from Pakistan. Gradually, they started occupying the land of the tribals too. In 1969, the central government asked the state to enact legislation to prevent alienation of land from tribals to non-tribals. Consequently, the state passed a law declaring further transfer of land from tribals to non-tribals unlawful. All transfers till 1969 amounting to some 1,50,000 acres were regularised in stages.

However, illegal transfer of land continued even after 1969. This was done in a variety of ways. In some cases, the tribal was evicted by force, in others, he was paid a paltry sum of Rs. 500 per acre for handing over possession of land which now costs Rs. 40,000 to Rs. 1,00,000 per acre. In all such cases, the revenue records still showed the tribals as owners because of restriction imposed in 1969. About 15,000 acres had thus changed possession.

Since the problem was localised and the number involved limited, it was thought that possibly land could be restored to the tribals without disturbing the power structure. The following new clauses were suggested in the Zamindari Abolition Act:

1. Where any land held by a tenure-holder belonging to a scheduled tribe is in occupation of any person other than such tenure-holder, the assistant collector may *suo moto* or on the application of such tenure-holder put him in possession of such land after evicting the occupant and may for that purpose use or cause to be used such force as may be considered necessary, anything to the contrary contained in this Act notwithstanding.
2. Where any person, after being evicted from any land under sub-section (1), re-occupies the land may be punishable with imprisonment for a term which may extend to three years but shall not be be less than six months and also with a fine which may extend to three thousand rupees but shall not be less than one thousand rupees.
3. Every offence punishable under sub-section (2) shall be congnizable and non-bailable.

An ordinance was issued in June 1981 incorporating these clauses.

The district administration was not keen to implement this ordinance. Many officers thought that the tribals would not cultivate land intensively and therefore production would suffer. They perceived it as a headache which could lead to problems of disorder and violence in the area. The state-level authorities visited Nainital a number of times, finalised the administrative details, and exhorted the officers to initiate action in five villages to begin with.

In the meantime, representatives of non-tribals met the central ministers and talked of harassment to minorities. There was a spate of letters from the ministers and farmers associations of Punjab. The Uttar Pradesh government was accused of making things difficult for the central and Punjab governments which were trying to solve the "Sikh problem". On the other hand, there was hardly any pressure from the tribals, who, even in the assembly segment of Nainital district, were now in a numerical minority because of constant exodus of tribals and influx of outsiders during the past twenty years.

The Government of India asked for a detailed report from the state government. Since restoration of land to the tribals was an important policy direction of the central government itself, and since the ordinance was approved by the state cabinet, the state government reiterated its stand repording the ordinance.

Despite the presence of force, the district administration was dragging its feet and kept on postponing the physical eviction of non-tribals on one pretext or the other. The informal forces working on the district were stronger than the formal orders of the government.

The central government appeared to be sympathetic but did not want confrontation with powerful non-tribals, especially in view of the deteriorating situation in Punjab.

Although the ordinance has now been converted into an Act, not a single acre of land has been restored to the tribals in the last three years. No question has been asked in the state assembly or the parliament about the non-implementation of the Act.

The above case study demonstrates that not only the politicians but also the senior civil servants, who otherwise have no personal stakes in landownership, are hostile to land reforms. Several factors account for this attitude. First is their belief in the inviolability of property, whether urban or rural. Second is their faith in production-based strategy of development via the rich farmers and hence the a version to distributive policies. Third is the lack of clarity and knowledge about exploitation in the rural areas because of which they see the poor as lazy and incompetent and the rich as enterprising and worthy of resources. Fourth is their lack of faith in the capability of the delivery system which makes them divert time and capital to such areas where short term gains can be maximised. Fifth is their ignorance of revenue law. Very few officers bother to grasp even the most important provisions of the land reforms or ceiling legislations which affects the quality of supervision. Sixth is the high priority given in the state to maintenance of law and order. As removal of illegal possession over lands allotted to the weaker section, or implementation of Minimum Wages Act, etc., entail apprehensions of breach of peace, such programmes often get neglected.

The Hindu society is based on the twin premises of caste and inequality. Not only are different groups unequally placed as far as access to wealth, status and power are concerned, but it is considered right, proper and desirable that they should be so. Despite egalitarian slogans, the poor are still not regarded as full members of the society, they are in fact treated as inferior human beings. Such feudal attitudes have affected the ethos of bureaucracy too. Even in programmes like rural employment, integrated rural development (IRD), etc., where political will was positive, bureaucratic interest had been flagging. The government servants choose their careers for reasons of security, social prestige and the authority that they enjoy. These considerations can be satisfied only in an inegalitarian society. It is idle to expect that they, as a group, will do anything which will hit at their vested interest which lies in the continuation of the present structure.

The politicians, on the other hand, are conscious of the publicity that they earn out of introducing pro-poor policies, and often political support for such legislation is not wanting. It may be worth mentioning here that before launching a campaign for distribution of alienated land belonging to the gaon sabha to the rural poor in 1980, it was proposed to the state government that such people who take adverse possession of the lands allotted to the agricultural labour should be criminally prosecuted and a minimum conviction of six months imprisonment be awarded to them. This proposal evoked hostile reactions from other civil servants in the official forum but when it went to the cabinet it was immediately accepted. It was, in fact, widely published in all the chief minister's press briefings as one of the important achievements of the government. However, till September 1983, only 158 prosecutions were filed in the entire state under this provision and not a single case resulted in conviction. These figures need to be contrasted with another order of the government in which the poor were the victims. Sometime in 1978, during the Janata regime, it was decided to oust the agriculture labourers from such *gaon sabha* lands where permanent cultivation was not possible or which were being used by the entire village community as pasture or grazing lands. Within six months, more than 60,000 cases were filed in the revenue courts against the rural poor. The government got alarmed at the high number of evictions it led to, and therefore, stayed further action. Finally, in 1981, the allotment was regularised and the eviction proceedings were abated. In short, progressive legislative measures are often brought to naught by an indifferent and hostile bureaucratic response to its implementation.

Summary and Conclusions

Uttar Pradesh has been the nerve-centre of all-India power politics for over ten centuries. Unlike other parts of the country, there has been no movement in the plains of Uttar Pradesh for the creation of a new province. The loyalties are either super-regional or sub-regional, based on caste, religion and area.

Most of the districts in the plains of Uttar Pradesh are multi-caste in nature, with no caste having more than twenty per cent share in population. There is a greater continuity in the scale of ritual rank of castes in Uttar Pradesh which makes it less susceptible to horizontal mobilisation from below of ritually deprived castes.

The urban trading and professional castes like the Banias, Kayasthas and Khatris acquired *zamindari* rights in the late eighteenth century, but lost it due to the *zamindari* abolition in 1952. Their share in political power was significantly higher than their share in population soon after independence but it kept on declining as they lacked both the advantage of numbers and control over land.

Much before the formal abolition of *zamindari* in 1952, the cultivators in Uttar Pradesh had been granted security of tenure and fixity of rent. Agrarian legislation between 1921 and 1939 reduced the *zamindars* to being only intermediaries, except in respect of the self-cultivated land. They still exercised a great deal of social power as they controlled common utility lands. This right was also taken away in 1952. The number of *zamindars* paying more than Rs. 250 annually as land revenue was about 31,000; they paid roughly sixty per cent of the revenue, but they could retain only twelve lakh acres with them out of a total 350 lakh acres of cultivated land. In 1971-72, the total area involved in ownership holdings of more than twenty-five acres was only twenty-four lakh acres, out of which roughly half belonged to the ex-*zamindars* and the other half to the new proprietors. Except in the Terai, large holdings of more than fifty acres are very few in Uttar Pradesh.

Unlike in Bihar, the land records in Uttar Pradesh were maintained by the official machinery which facilitated the conferring of ownership rights on the former tenants in 1952. As the large number of high caste tenants avoided manual work they were permitted to get their lands cultivated through sharecropping, which was explicitly authorised by law. The introduction of new technology in agriculture, as also the fear of more radical land reform laws during the sixties, induced the high caste cultivators to take greater interest in agriculture which resulted in large scale displacement of sharecroppers from land. This may explain the rise in the percentage of agriculture labourers in the 1971 census. However, as the Uttar Pradesh. Land Reforms Law did not permit resumption of land by the former *zamindars* or voluntary surrenders by the tenants in favour of the *zamindars*, there has been very little transfer of land after 1955 from the then recorded tenants to the former *zamindars*. They, as already mentioned, retained enough land which was recorded as under their "personal cultivation". Elizabeth Whitcombe (1977) sums up the impact of the new technology on this class in the following words:

> In the new capital intensive agricultural strategy introduced into the provinces in the late 1966s, the Congress government had the means to realise the imperial dread: progressive farming amongst the gentry. Government made ex-*zamindari* viable in practice. Within a year or two of the programme's inception, virtually every district could find a crop of demonstration—the Rai Sahibs with their thirty, forth and hundred acre holdings, their multiplication farms of the latest Mexican wheat and Philippines paddy, their tubewells gushing out 16,000 gallons of water an hour, much of it on highly profitable hire, their tractors, their godowns stacked with fertiliser, their cold-stores, and their groves, their rights over fairs and bazars, their brothers and sons in the civil service and industry, the army and the police sending regular remittances to swell the family accounts in premutiny fashion; in short, a tenth of the *zamindari*, but ten times the income.

Although the Brahmin and Thakur share in land is 1.5 to two times and 2.5 to three times, respectively, than their share in numbers. It does not follow that all medium-large landholders are Brahmin-Thakurs or that all Brahmins-Thakurs are surplus farmers. Roughly four per cent in holdings of more than ten acres was with the scheduled caste families in 1981, similarly more than two per cent Brahmin and Thakur families belonged to the landless agricultural labourers category. It prevents open indentification of the state government's economic policies with any particular caste group.

Although the interests of commercial crop-growers are better protected than that of paddy and other subsistence crop-growers, yet it is difficult to conclude that the policies of the government help only the rich peasantry. The importance given to maintaining price stability and putting restrictions on movement of foodgrains outside the state directly affects the surplus farmers holding capacity and help the middle peasant as well as the the urban and rural poor. The rich farmers are helped more by technological and market forces rather than by conscious policies of the government.

The absence of certain objective conditions like absentee landlordism, uncertain tenure, sharp fluctuation in output prices, rise of gentlemen farmers have prevented sharpening of differences between the high and middle peasants. The green revolution technology and the spread of co-operative/commercial credit structure has also helped in integrating the middle and upper peasantry. It is difficult to assert that the middle peasants belong to a different sector of the rural economy or are capable of acting independently of other classes. Together they form a socially and politically conservative class.

Although the rich peasants or the landlords have lost the power to appropriate surplus from the poor peasantry, the latter along with the agriculture labour, are dependent on the former in many ways. The urban economy has not been able to provide alternative means to the poor for securing livelihoods. Since a steady supply of goods and services like agricultural inputs, credit, kerosene, licenses, etc., is not always available, the poor depend upon the middle and rich farmers in their interaction with the bureaucracy and the towns. The role of a "broker" is played by several actors at various levels, the MLAs do it for rich peasants who in turn do it at lower levels for their poor clients. Paternalistic relations still persist, which make the task of political parties easier for mobilising votes through the hierachical structure of the traditional society.

Piecemeal agrarian reforms, through embourgeoisiment, have changed the erstwhile militant class of insecure tenants into a conservative petty property owners, thereby reducing the potential for further radical land reforms.

Unlike Thakurs, the Muslims and the urban castes, who lost land in all the districts of Uttar Pradesh, the Brahmins gained land in many districts, especially in the east. Their share in cultivated land was higher as compared to their share in *zamindari* in these districts. They also took to western education quite early and have maintained their hold over all walks of life, including politics, bureaucracy and land.

Unlike the Brahmins, the Thakurs remained tied to land, and are now slowly overcoming their inhibition to higher education. As *zamindars* they got isolated from the mainstream of the nationalist movement but proved their hold over the rural areas by winning elections on the tickets of other parties. In the districts of Oudh and eastern Uttar Pradesh, their share in political power to-day is much in excess of their ownership of land, especially in the indirect elections of Block *Pramukhs* where money power is an important factor. The intermediate castes in Uttar Pradesh can be broadly divided into three categories: Jats, Tyagis and Bhumihars, who have a considerable position in land, possess high ritual status and because of their regional concentration are dominant in the politics of a few districts. In the second category are the Ahirs, Kurmis, Gujars and Lodhs. They have benefited from the tenancy legislations and green revolution and are active in politics in about a one-third districts of Uttar Pradesh where the force of number are on their side. In the last category are a large number of backward castes, many with less than two per cent share in the district population, who have not made any headway in politics. They lack political consciousness, and are economically backward.

During the nationalist struggle, the Congress party never made any effort to mobilise the middle castes. It remained dominated by the Brahmins and the urban castes. The Left parties, especially the Lohia Socialist Party, made conscious efforts to woo the Ahirs and Kurmis in the eastern districts of Uttar Pradesh. Being former tenants, the memories of exploitation were fresh in their minds and the Leftist ideology appealed to them. But because these cultivators had secured ownership rights in land as a result of abolition of the *zamindari*, the socialist parties found it difficult to sustain an ideological fervour based on economic interests. Instead they shifted their attention to cultural and caste interests. The Lohia Socialist Party, by merging itself with the BKD, de-emphasized its linkages with the poor peasant groups and tried to become a broad-based peasant party speaking for all sections of the peasantry.

The rise of the intermediate castes in some districts seems to have alienated the "other backward castes" who have shifted their sympathies to the Brahmin-Thakur dominated Congress party and hence, despite some loss of its traditional Muslim and scheduled caste votes, the Congress party still succeeds in elections.

There has been some fusion between middle castes; Ahirs have become Yadavas, Koris and Koeris have become Kushwahas, but on the whole all castes are extremely conscious of their position in the vertical hierarchy. The lower backwards and the scheduled castes do not identify themselves with the aspirations of the faster mobilising Yadavas, Jats, Lodhs, Gujars and Kurmis.

The traditional process of caste mobilisation cannot increase the representation of the lower castes as they lack the status, economic power, political consciousness and numerical concentration in compact geographical areas that have provided the basis for the entry of other caste groups like the Jats, Yadavas, Kurmis and Gujars into the system.

Except for the Left parties in the 1960s, all other political parties in Uttar Pradesh have so far relied excessively on a continuation of traditional systems of social control by the ritually and socially dominant castes in the villages. The political system is therefore obliged to favour those individuals and groups which are already powerful. With the weakening of the party structure and the erosion in the control over factional leaders by the district and state leaders, there has been, however, some distinct change in the working of the political system. As the voters are no longer completely in the grips of the factional leaders, an attempt is made by all major parties to exploit local incidents and to precipitate "waves" at the time of the elections. In this context, control over bureaucracy, specially the police, has become a salient issue in state politics.

Several features of the bureaucracy in Uttar Pradesh deserve to be noted. First, although its per capita income has increased only by about twenty-five per cent in the last thirty years, the number of employees has bloated by about eight times. Second, the dependence of individual politicians on the intermediate level of government structure for political advantages has vastly increased. Third, barring exceptions, the civil service has no faith in distributive programmes of social justice and has often successfully prevented implementation of policies meant to benefit the poor. Fourth, since the function of policy making has almost been by the abdicated political masters in favour of the civil servants, the will of the government is not identical with the political will. Often, the government has been able to pursue policies irksome to politicians. Fifth, the police itself has become a major source of violence in the state (Meerut 1982, Narainpur 1980, Pantnagar 1979, etc.) providing a convenient tool to the opposition to sansationalize such atrocities and exhibit them.

Despite penetration of capitalist relations in agriculture, the process of differentiation by which the rich farmers expand their land base and the poor peasants become landless has not taken place in Uttar Pradesh. The land market has continued to be extremely rigid, partly because of tenancy laws, but largely due to the tenacity of the small producer to cling to his plot despite odds. The accumulated surplus of the big farmers is invested in politics, agro-based procession industries and trade in government-controlled essential commodities. The village population has thus become more polarised in wealth and power, not necessarily in land ownership.

Roughly half of the rural population has been living below the poverty line. They are the landless labourers, marginal farmers and the artisans. The reasons for the lack of organisation among them are:

(a) their eeconomic weakness which makes them totally dependent on the medium and large farmers;
(b) they are scattered and lack the advantage of being concentrated like the urban poor;
(c) the nature of contact with their masters is more personal and patriarchical which makes their mobilisation difficult;
(d) they do not form a distinct class with common economic interests on issues like wages, subsidies on agricultural inputs and output prices as they do not share a common outlook;
(e) they are unskilled and can easily be substituted by family labour and labour from outside the village;
(f) caste plays a divisible role and the poor belonging to the backward castes are not willing to associate themselves with the scheduled caste poor; and
(g) the government policies have tended to mitigate class differences between the small and medium/large farmers and therefore the purely landless workers forming only twelve to fifteen per cent of the rural population cannot get organised against the rest.

Agricultural production in Uttar Pradesh, since 1975-76, has been growing at a faster rate than the all India average. Spread of irrigation, low feudal-type tenancy, greater interest of the upper castes in cultivation, declining dependency of the farmers on agricultural inputs like seeds, fertilisers and water, the government machinery and easier availability of the inputs in the market are some of the factors responsible for the spurt in production. Despite this, agricultural wages have remained stagnant.

References

Appu, P.S, "Tenancy Reforms in India", EPW, VOL X Nos. 33-35, special No; 1975, PP. 1360-61.

Bhalla, G.S. and Chaddha, G.K. Green Revolution and the Samu Peasant, N. Delhi: Concept, 1983.

Brass, Paul, Factional Polities in an Indian State: The Congress Party in Uttar Pradesh, Berkeley, California, 1965.

Burgher A; Opposition in a Dominant Party System: A Study of the Jan Sangh, the Praja Socialist Party and the Socialist Party in Uttar Pradesh, India, Bombay, Oxford University Press, 1969.

Chaudhuri, B., 'Eastern India II' in Dharma Kumar (ed), Cambridge Economic History of India, Vol. II (1957-70), Cambridge University Press, 1982.

Cohn, Bernard, S., Notes on the History of the Study of Indian Society, and, culture in Milton Singer and Bernard S. Cohn (ed) Structure and Change in Indian Society, Aldine Publishing co; Chicago, 1968, PP. 3-28.

Connell, C.J. Our Land Revenue Policy is Northern India, Calcutta, 1876, quoted from Agrarian condition in Northern India, Vol. I by Elizabeth Whitcombe, University of California Press, 1971, PP, 237-38.

Dhanagare, B.N. Peasant Movements in India, 1920, 1920- 1950, OUP, Delhi, 1983.

Elizabeth Klhitcombe Agrarian Conditions in Northern India, Vol. I, University of California, 1977.

Habib, Irfan, The Agrarian System of Moughal India (1556-1707), Bombay; Asia Publishing House, 1967 p. vii.

Habib, Irfan, The social Distribution of Landed Property in Pre-British India in Indian Society Historical Probing (ed.) by R.S. Sharma, People's Publishing House, N.D., 1074.

Kashyap, Subash, The Eighth Lok Sabha-A Profile of its Members in India Foreign Review, May 31, 1785.

Metcalf, Thomas R., "Land Lords, Without Land: The Uttar Pradesh *zamindars* Today", Pacific Affairs, 40 (Spring & Summer), 1967.

Meyer, R.C., Political Elite in an Underdeveloped Society, the case of Uttar Pradesh Unpublished Ph.D. dissertation quoted from Dominance and State Power in Modern India, Vol. I by Frankel, Frand Rao, M.S.A, OUP; Delhi, 1989.

Neele Walter, C;, Economic Change in Rural India Land Tenure and Reform in Uttar Pradesh, 1800-1955, Yale Studies in Economies Series No. 12, Yale University Press, 1962.

Pandey, G., A Rural Base for the Congress: the United Provincess 1920-40 in D.A. Low (ed.) *Congress and the Raj.* Delhi: Amoid Heinemann, 1977.

Robinson, P; Untitled Notes on W.Oldham's Memorandum, bound with old him, cit Sup, British Museum cat. No. 8022922 1-9 (No. 2) quoted from Agranian Condition in Northern India Vol. I by Elizabeth klhitecombe, University of California Press, 1977, p. 223.

Rudolph, Uoyd and Rudolph, Susanne, The Modernity of Tradition, Political Development in India, Chicago, 1967.

Siddiqi, M.H., "The Peasant Movement in Partapgarh, 1920." *Indian Economic and Social History Review*, vol. IX, no 3, Sept 1973.

Stokes, Eric, Peasant and the Raj. N. Delhi Vikas, 1978.

Thorner, Daniel, The Agrarian Prospect in India, Allied Publishers Ltd. Delhi, 1976

Trivedi, K.K., 'Changes in Caste Composition of the Zamindar Class in Western U.P; 1595-1900. *Indian Historical Review* Vol. II. No.1, July 1975.

9

Feudalism, Caste and Class in Rajasthan

K.L. Sharma

An understanding of caste and class in Rajasthan requires a specific treatment due to the fact that it was a part of the Indian India, and therefore remained largely unaffected by the British *Raj*. Rajasthan represented a sort of *feudalism* which did not exist in British India. The princely states of Rajputana which were ruled by nineteen Rajput, two Jat and one Muslim clans were different in terms of their historicity, continuity and change from the rest of the country. It is this mode of polity and administration which gave a definite structure and direction to caste and class relations. Both caste and class are determined by prescriptive evaluations (birth, race and ethnicity), existential conditions and conflict-situations. Caste and class refer to social and economic injustices and inequalities, and these are rectified through protests and social movements. Re-adjustments with the existing situations and emergence of new ones norms indicate changes in the system of social stratification.

To depict a picture of caste and class in Rajasthan, it would be appropriate to understand them in terms of their multi-dimensional functioning, and vertical and horizontal layers and levels. The two are internally structured as formations, and are interrelated in terms of domination and interdependence. Thus, caste and class are found as a complex social formation comprising different layers, levels and units. Here, social formation can be defined as a system of hierarchically structured relationships with a particular mode of relations. In the pre-independence period, colonial/feudal mode(s) of production produced hierarchical relations which could be identified on the basis of the socio-cultural and material conditions of the people. The structures of caste and class after independence bear the strong marks of the colonial/feudal system. Despite a great deal of change, the continuity of the colonial/feudal relations speaks volumes of the specific nature of caste and class nexus in India.

Feudalism was a mode of polity, administration and social relations in Rajasthan. Both caste and class were determined by this mode of production in terms of their actual functioning. Autonomy of caste or class seemed hazy at times because of the overarching nature of the feudal polity. Thus, caste and class were inseparable from the feudal social formation. Feudalism was a social formation as well as a mode of production. Consequent upon the abolition of feudalism, there should have been more of its continuity in the form of "semi-feudalism", but unlike British India, in Rajasthan, there has been more of change, perhaps due to the very compulsions of the feudal social formation. Feudalism in Rajasthan was so near-absolute that it could not persist after independence. Since this was not the case in Eastern India, for example, hence semi-feudalism persists there. The princes and *Jagirdars/Thikanedars* could not retain the hold on the lands they controlled because of the vast size(s) of the *jagirs.*

The situation that emerged in the *zamindari* and the *khalsa* areas was somewhat different. The feudal lords were able to retain control on the maximum possible best lands declaring themselves as self-cultivators. In fact, in British India *zamindari* rights were generally restricted to small tracts of land and the *zamindars* had a substantial portion of land under self-cultivation ranging from thirty to fifty per cent of their landholdings. Since they retained large landholdings under self-cultivation, only a small part of their lands could be taken away from them for the tenants. However, those *jagirs* which were large territories, even as large as today's districts, had to part with most of their lands in favour of the peasantry. Rajasthan, being a land of *jagirs*, witnessed greater changes due to the abolition of landlordism than other parts of India where the *zamindari* system was in vogue. Scarcity of land has/had not been an acute problem in Rajasthan. This is one reason why there is a near total absence of excesses and atrocities on the marginal peasants and agricultural labourers in Rajasthan since independence. Hunger for land in states like Uttar Pradesh and Bihar has caused exploitation and oppression of the poor agricultural workers and sharecroppers.

In Rajasthan, caste was not a rigid system in practice compared to other states. There were several anomalies and incongruities regarding status of the *dwij* castes. These ambiguities in real life situations could particularly be found between Brahmins and Rajputs, Rajputs and Banias, and Rajputs and the principal agricultural castes. Caste was also a less rigid system because of the expression and articulation of rights and duties by the "functionary castes" whenever they were maltreated and were not paid as per customary rules by their patrons. Caste and village councils played an important role in settling of disputes between *jajmans* and *kamins*. However, feudal hegemony reigned supreme over all the decisions taken by these bodies. Feudalism in the princely states of Rajputana as described by James Tod resembled the features of "feudal society" as characterised by Marc Bloch in medieval Europe. A brief reference will be made later to the notions of the Asiatic mode of production and feudal social formation with a view to draw lessons for understanding caste and class relations in Rajasthan. Finally, structural and psychological changes, political rivalries and emergence of a new class structure in post-independence Rajasthan will be analysed.

II

Rajasthan's peculiarly complex situation, as it prevailed, provides a test ground for examining various formulations and approaches to the study of caste and class in India. The important ones are about the mode of production in agriculture and the differentiation of peasantry. The other formulations are related to nature of caste and class relations. The approaches to the study of social stratification (caste and class) can broadly be classified into: (i) ideo-historical, (ii) Marxian, and (iii) institutional-administrative reforms approach. The conceptions of caste and class have been guided by these approaches[1].

Emphasis in the ideo-historical approach is on the understanding of ideas and changes therein as a "method" of study for analysing social reality. To be specific, Louis Dumont's study of caste system may be cited as an appropriate example.[2] For Dumont, caste is "social" like religion. It is an ideational system as the ideas of pollution-purity, hierarchy and corporateness are basic to its structure and functioning. These ideas, if put together, make caste an ideology of a unique nature, hence its ideological particularism. The ideology of caste encompasses all other forms of social relations, particularly economic and political.

At least two questions can be posed regarding Dumont's ideational construction. Is the notion of Homo Hierarchicus synonym of India's caste system? Are there no elements of Homo Equalis in India's system of social stratification? There have never been uniform patterns of hierarchical relations in a mechanical form as Dumont's notion of

Homo Hierarchicus would imply.[3] The rank-order of castes such as Brahmins, Rajputs and Banias in Rajasthan has a number of anomalies and incongruities. These incongruities have the unwritten sanction of the people. Secondly, inequality does not essentially imply hierarchy of the sort Dumont envisages in his treatment of the caste system in India. Inequality is a relative phenomenon, and also entails equality of a sort. Caste system itself has inbuilt mechanisms of egalitarian relations which have not been adequately studied by the students of social stratification. The caste system is not simply Homo Hierarchicus, a system just opposite of Homo Equalis.[4]

The Marxian approach highlights the existential conditions. Marx speaks of "structure" of existential conditions as well as the "process" of change in these conditions. Structuring of social inequality is a continuous process. The life-process of definite individuals, as they are, as they operate, produce materially under certain material limits, presuppositions and conditions, refers to the quintessence of the Marxian approach to social inequality.[5] Marx writes: "Consciousness can never be anything else than conscious existence, and the existence of men is their actual life-process."[6] Men are seen by Marx in their actual processes.

The following statements drawn from Marx and Engel's *The German Ideology* provide a succinct view of Marxian frame of reference:

How is social life produced?
What is its mode of production?
What units are produced as a result of certain social conditions?
What is the nature of social interaction between the groups produced through such an evolutionary process?[7]

The Marxian approach finds its expression in several ways. But the dominant one is still the one mentioned above in the form of some selected questions. R.S. Sharma writes: "The mode of production involving the theory of surplus leading to class formation continues to be the best working hypothesis...."[8] Kosambi formulates his definitions of "history" and "class" in pursuance of the Marxian approach to the study of Indian society. He writes: "History is the presentation in chronological order of successive changes in the means and relations of production."[9] He further writes: "The proper study of history in a class society means analysis of the differences between the interests of classes on top and of the rest of the people; it means consideration of the extents to which an emergent class had something new to contribute during its rise to power, and of the stage where it turned (or will turn) to reaction in order to preserve its vested interests".[10] A.R. Desai and some other scholars too adhere to this broad Marxian approach.[11]

Indian society is characterised by the Asiatic mode of production (AMP) too. Ruben writes: "Thus, we may like to characterise Indian history as that of a society based on the Indian variant of the Asiatic mode of production with strong elements of slavery in antiquity and of feudalism in the middle ages, succeeded by capitalism which mainly came to India in the form of British colonialism till capitalist India became independent in 1947."[12] However, such a unilinear mode of change rules out the possibility of replacement/displacement of structural elements, and admits only slow differentiation of statuses and roles and adaptation to new situations and challenges. But, on the contrary, Romila Thapar observes "status mobility" in ancient India more among the elites due to foreign invasions and migrations. A hiatus between ritual status and actual status and emergence of "mixed castes" are also reported by her as evidences of status mobility and change.[13]

What is the AMP? Two notions, namely, oriental despotism and stagnation are attributed to the Marxian concept of AMP.[14] However, Krader periodizes the concepts of oriental despotism, oriental society and the AMP in Marx.[15] Thus, Marx evolved the concept of AMP in stages. Under the concept of AMP, Marx inquires into internal economic relations in a specific way. He relates the legal and political forms with economic relations. Thus, despotism and stagnation are not central features of the concept of AMP. Now the question is: Was there feudalism in Rajasthan? If yes, what was its nature? And how it was different from feudalism elsewhere in India? Does the concept of AMP apply to the feudal social formation in Rajasthan? These and some other questions will be taken up later on.

The institutional-administrative reforms approach explains the role of people's consciousness, socio-cultural movements and the state as an agent of social change. One can always question the nature and relevance of the change brought about by institutions, organisations and the state, controlled and managed by the elite. However, what is suggested here is that social and cultural factors are main obstacles in social change.[16] The entrenched castes and institutions prohibit radical transformation of the Indian society. The national movement for India's independence, the movements and organisations launched by social reformers and the Indian state have brought about social change.

The Indian Constitution, for example, guarantees fundamental rights, provides dirictive principles of state's policies, and makes provisions for the betterment of the weaker sections and the abolition of the caste system and untouchability. Five year plans, public sector enterprises, promotion of small scale industries, land reforms, etc., are other notable developments in post-independence India. The Indian state is a welfare state because it provides measures for the upliftment of the weaker sections of society and promotes "mixed economy". Social legislations have also been a special feature. Despite elitist policies, socio-cultural inequalities have decreased in the post-independence period. But, at the same time, economic disparities have also increased in some specific contexts.

III

D.D. Kosambi expressed reservations about Marx's concept of the AMP.[17] Marx and Engels made references to State-controlled irrigation, absence of private property in land, autarkic villages, absence of towns to explain the AMP and its despotic and stagnant nature. Kosambi and other social historians question the formulation of the AMP because there was existence of private property in land and of a ruling class which expropriated the surplus from the masses.[18] Kosambi holds the view that a process of "feudalism from below" developed in terms of a class of landowners between the state and the peasantry and it wielded armed power.[19] However, R.S.Sharma holds the view that feudalism in India began with the land-grants made to Brahmins, temples and monastries from the first century B.C. and developed into a well-entrenched system by the Gupta times. Both religious and secular grants became popular, hence the emergence of feudal property undermining the communal rights on land.[20] "The economic essence of Indian feudalism... lay in the rise of landed intermediaries leading to the enserfment of the peasantry through restrictions on peasant mobility and freedom, increasing obligation to perform forced labour (*visti*), mounting tax burdens and the evils of subinfeudation."[21]

D.N.Jha has rightly pointed out the anomaly and contradiction in the debate due to the rejection of the concept of AMP and the acceptance of the idea of feudal social formation. Jha sums up as follows: The hallmark of feudalism is not merely the "structured dependence of the entire peasantry on the lords", and equally importantly, there are different forms of exploitation, immobility, forced labour, ever-increasing burden of dues, etc., all arising out of the lord's superior rights on land, the evils of subinfeudation and the eviction of tenants.[22] It is important to note that feudalism was a social formation, it produced certain social consequences. Some of these features of feudalism were not simply confined to an economic mode of production, instead they encompassed the entire social fabric.

In the recent debate led by Byres and Mukhia on feudalism, facts regarding the situation in Rajasthan have been ignored.[23] However, Byres has rightly made some relevant observations in his opening article regarding the debate on feudalism.

He asks about the acceptability of the notion of an Asiatic mode of production, the applicability of feudalism in the context of pre-colonial, non-European societies, and finally, if the two, namely, the AMP and feudalism are not applicable, then within a Marxist analysis, what is applicable to these societies?[24] A majority of contributors to this volume are of the view that India had feudalism of its own variety, different from European feudalism.[25] However, Mukhia does not hold this view. Pre-colonial India was not feudal according to Mukhia. In Europe, there was *structured dependence* of the whole peasantry upon the lords, whereas pre-colonial Indian society was characterised by self-dependent or free peasant production.[26]

Byres is right in his observation that a proper analysis of a society can be undertaken with a careful treatment of both relations and forces of production. The question of dominance of either can also be settled, but not necessarily in terms of relations of a corresponding or mechanical nature.[27] Byres emphasizes on the nature of the dominant mode of production in a particular social formation. There may be other modes of production too. More important is the notion of a *social formation* in which there can be different modes of production under the *dominance* of one of them. In regard to Rajasthan, this is largely true, but feudalism as a mode of production was so dominant that other modes of production became nearly non-functional. It was so determining in nature that it shaped the whole of the Rajasthani society. Feudalism in Rajasthan was in many ways comparable to the feudalism in medieval Europe.

IV

Marx and Engels' notion of production is appropriate here. They write: "In the social production of their life, men enter into definite, necessary relations which are independent of their will, relations of production which correspond to a definite stage of development of their material productive forces."[28] Also relevant is Marc Bloch's conception of feudalism in Europe. The main features of European feudalism are, for example, a subject peasantry, widespread use of service tenement (i.e., the fief) instead of slavery, the supremacy of a class of specialised warriors, ties of obedience and protection vassalage, fragmentation of authority leading to disorder,etc.[29] There are several other meanings and notions of feudalism ranging from absolutist serfdom to expropriation and exploitation. Strikingly, most of these features of European feudalism were existent in the case of Rajasthan. Rajasthan was a feudal social formation in the true sense of the term.[30]

While drawing a sketch of feudal system in Rajasthan, James Tod observes: "It is more than doubtful whether any code of civil or criminal jurisprudence ever existed in any of these principalities; though it is certain that none is at this day discoverable in their archives. But there is a martial system peculiar to these Rajpoot states, so extensive in its operation as to embrace every object of society. This is so analogous to the ancient feudal system of Europe, that I have not hesitated to hazard a comparison between them, with reference to a period when the latter was yet imperfect."[31] Tod makes a mention of "feudal incidents" (duration of grants) as the more general obligations of the vassals in Europe and shows their existence in Rajasthan. These are: (1) reliefs, (2) fines of alienation, (3) escheats, (4)aids, (5) wardship, and (6) marriage.[32] Details of these practices and sketches of various princely states of erstwhile Rajputana speak of near absolute form of feudalism in Rajasthan. Undoubtedly, feudalism was both a dominant and determinant mode of production including its forces and relations.

The report on the land-tenures and special powers of certain *Thikanedars* of Jaipur State by C.U. Wills mentions that in six areas the *Thikanedars* exercised such unusual powers as might seem to support their claim to stand outside the ordinary administration of the state.[33] "All of them have been excluded from the scope of the recent settlement operations; all of them are outside the customs cordon and are treated for customs purposes as foreign territory (*ilaqua gair*); all the *Thikanedars* in these areas enjoy the privilege of manufacturing and selling intoxicating liquor, and all but one enjoy the vend right for opium and other intoxicating drugs; most of them take a royalty on quarries; three of them maintain their own police and exercise criminal and civil jurisdiction; and the one *thikana*, which has important mineral resources, has been conceded the right to the minerals produced. Each *thikana*, therefore, in these six areas, constitutes, in a greater or less degree, a *Raj*, so to speak, within the *Raj*..."[34] The State of Jaipur was under the British *Raj*, and these *thikanas* were under the State of Jaipur. One could very well imagine the state of feudalism and the nature of social relations in such a situation before independence.

Caste hierarchy in terms of (1) *dwij* castes, (2) principal agricultural castes, (3) lower castes, and (4) "untouchables" was prevalent in Rajasthan, more or less comparable with other parts of India. However, there was one basic fact about Rajasthan which perhaps did not exist elsewhere in the same manner. In principal, the Rajputs were ranked after the Brahmins and the Vaishyas occupied a rank below the Rajputs. In practice, it was not so. The Rajputs rarely behaved as a *dwij* caste, they did not wear the sacred thread, and only occasionally observed fasts, rituals and other religious practices. The Brahmins and the Vaishyas were quite particular about observance of all the sacred practices and ritual acts. Rajputs not only were non-vegetarian and non-teetotallers, they accepted food and water from castes lower to them in the caste hierarchy. Commensal distinction was nearly non-existent between the Rajputs and the agricultural castes like Jats, Ahirs, Gujars, Malis and Meenas. Thus, Rajputs did not enjoy a very high ritual status. On the contrary, being the rulers, the Rajputs enjoyed the highest status and power in the state. Even the educated *Kulin* Brahmins had to acknowledge the *Thikanedar's* superior status and power by offering blessings and good wishes, and only in response to this would the *Thikanedar* recognise the Brahmin's superior ritual status. The feudal mode of social relations was superior to caste hierarchy. The Rajput princes, *Thikanedars* and *Bhomias* sat on all judgements in which people from all castes including Brahmins were involved. Decisions of caste councils and village panchayats were superseded by the Rajput rulers. All castes offered functionary and other services to the Rajputs, but the Rajputs were not obliged to render any kind of service to other castes, including Brahmins. Rajputs presided over common village functions organised at the time of festivals of Gangaur and Dussehera. Being landlords, Rajputs collected land revenue, levied taxes and *lagbags*, and imposed *begar* (forced labour). The kinsmen of the ruling family and even ordinary Rajput families and their members were not subjected to any kind of taxes, forced labour and excesses which were normally imposed upon other castes, including Brahmins.

Feudal status (rank) of a princely state/*thikana* was the main consideration in matrimonial alliances. The Rajputs alone had domestic servants. The Golas (a caste group) served the Rajput feudal lords as slaves. Golas were even offered as part of dowry by some *Jagirdars*. Rajput women practised *purdah*. They did not move out of their houses except when they were required to visit their parental homes/villages and relatives. Moving out under the cover of dark was preferred to avoid exposure to the public. Even grinding of foodgrains and fetching of water from *panghat* (village well) were prohibited. All Rajput houses had toilets, specially for the use of the womenfolk. Thus, Rajputs were less of a caste as they were more of a ruling clan, an aristocracy, and a power-wielding group. In terms of ritual status, many caste groups considered Rajputs lower than Vaishyas. The latter observed not only rituals and practices associated with their caste, they also adhered strictly to the Brahminic values like vegetarianism and teetotalism. These were considered as virtues and a source of status emulation.

Feudalism blurred the distinction between caste and class because the system of land-grants and cesses and taxes reduced the hiatus between different castes on the one hand and between different classes on the other. Barbers, dancers, drum-beaters, potters, carpenters and Brahmins were given land-grants in lieu of their services rendered to the *Thikanedars.* All were "landlords" of a sort. At the same time, such grantees could not be equated with the *Bhomias* and kinsmen of the *Thikanedars.* For example, a barber was more of a *Nai* and less of a "landlord". However, there were always some favourite lower caste officials of the *Thikanedars* who enjoyed a "higher" status than the upper caste men who were not attached with the *thikana* administration. The system was such that everything revolved around the *thikana/jagir.*

V

Several "terrorist" and violent programmes and activities were organised to challenge the legitimacy of the feudal system. The Praja Mandals in various princely states carried out programmes of political and social awakening. These anti-feudal activities were led by the educated Brahmins in particular. Some Rajputs, Banias and Kayasthas were also associated with anti-feudal and peasant movements in the princely states. There was no uniform pattern of feudalism. As many as forty-five grades of *jagirs* existed in Jaipur State alone. The number of taxes and cesses were as many as 175. Exploitation and extortion reached the extent of eighty-seven per cent of the total agricultural production in some areas.[35]

Abolition of the *jagirdari* system was a case of withdrawal of status, and hence it was not taken with ease by the landed aristocracy. The *Jagirdars* involved the Government of Rajasthan in litigation with a view to delay the implementation of the Act to gain time to evict their tenants from the best lands and to transfer the same in their own names as self-cultivators. The Kshatriya Mahasabha launched *bhooswami andolan* for safeguarding the interests of the princes, *Jagirdars* and *Bhomias* by demanding more *khudkasht* (self-cultivation)lands, more compensation, less land revenue, rehabilitation of the staff of the princely states,*thikanas* and *jagirs*. Thus, the implementation of the abolition legislation was made a slow process allowing the landed groups and individuals to maintain partly, their traditional status and partly to adjust to the new situation arising out of the abolition of the feudal system.[36] We find a clear interplay between caste and class in case of the Rajput *Jagirdars* and *Bhomias*. Even earlier, in the 1930s and 1940s, peasant movements, for example, in Shekhwati region, were named as Jat agitations by people as well as by historians. "Jat" as a caste was not different from "Jat" as a class of peasants. It continues to be so even today to a large extent despite emergence of differentiation by means of education, migration and adult franchise.

The abolition of the *jagirdari* and *zamindari* systems and subsequent land reforms despite the initial setbacks caused by the obstacles created by the vested interests in their implementation, has, in fact, "revolutionised" the rural scene to a great extent. No doubt, the impact has been *uneven* on the emerging class structure. But the *Jagirdars* and *Bhomias* could not retain all the land that was in their possession. The granting of tenancy rights to the cultivators is something which has brought about a significant change in the mode of production and social relations in rural Rajasthan. Improvement of arable land, change in the cropping pattern and the very notion of owning land have raised the status of the peasantry. The other exploited groups, particularly those who had to render *begar*, reacted strongly against the continuance of some of the feudalistic practices even after the abolition of the *jagirdari* system. These include discarding of traditional callings, for example, by barbers, *chamars* and some other groups. These groups organised themselves through their caste associations.

A strong reaction by the exploited masses was expressed against the feudal elements in the early years after the abolition of the *jagirdari* system. To some extent, hostilities are expressed even today by the ex-feudal and the ex-tenant groups towards each other during elections and in some specific socio-cultural contexts. Clearly, such expressions by the new agrarian classes indicate their emergence as dominant groups, both economically and politically. Reactions to these by the traditionally powerful groups explain their concern for their heritage and efforts to restore the past glory. The Jats and other communities initially imitated the Rajput style of nomenclature and the Brahminic style of living. Today, they imitate mainly the urban white-collar groups for status-emulation. Both, education and migration have contributed to this trend. There are perceptible structural changes in the position of the ex-tenant castes. They have moved up and have become a more articulate and vibrant force in local and state politics. A small number of the ex-feudals have retained some of the elements of their traditional status, but most of them have adjusted to the new situations. A good number of them are pauperised and lead a miserable life.

My study of six villages, two from each of Sikar, Jaipur and Bharatpur districts of Rajasthan, shows that there were thirty-two castes in all the six villages, of which a maximum of nineteen were in one village and nine were in another.[37] Barring the upper castes, namely, Brahmins, Rajputs and Banias, the other castes depended upon their traditional occupations to a considerable extent. Four main classes were found: (1) ex-*Jagirdars* and *Zamindars*, (2) merchants, (3) peasants and artisans, and (4) agricultural and manual labourers.[38]

The study shows an overlap between caste and class. This is evident from the correspondence between caste, landholdings and positions of power enjoyed by members of different castes. About 12.5 per cent of the lower class people come from the upper castes, whereas sixty-three per cent of the upper class households belong to upper castes. There are also cleavages between caste and class. At least twenty families own more than a hundred acres of land, and have pumping-sets, tractors and sprinklers, etc. These well-off families were tenants-at-will before the abolition of the *jagirdari* system. Most of these families belong to the dominant peasant caste of Jats. Brahmins and Banias have moved out of their villages and taken up new/secular jobs. Rajputs have been somewhat slower in this process of change and adaptation as the setback caused by the abolition of *jagirdari* has upset them a great deal.

VI

Caste is both a normative system and a system of actual social relations. In certain areas, caste adheres to its normative sanctions, in some other spheres caste has taken up activities which have no traditional approval. Members of a caste compete with each other as well as co-operate depending upon the specific contexts in which they find themselves. At times they interact with each other as if they belong to two antagonistic classes. Thus, caste refers to social inequality in theory as well as in practice. Caste status is a "resource" as well as a non-functional dysfunctional label. As a "resource" it functions as an "interest group", as a means of mobilization, and becomes harmful when caste becomes the basis of oppression, exploitation and degradation. Caste has become weak in some respects, but has become strong in some other spheres. All these multilinear trends of change and adaptation show its adaptive capacity. Distinction between caste and class is of a marginal nature. The peasant agitation was known as a Jat movement in Shekhawati. The Kshatriya Mahasaba was not simply a caste organisation, but was an association of landlords. The Jat Sabha was not just a caste council, it was also an organisation of peasants. The Kisan Sabha is not simply peasant's organisation; it is very much an association of castes engaged in agriculture. This may be true about the Vaishya Sabha, Rajput Sabha and Bhooswami Sangh, etc. Caste struggle in Rajasthan was, in fact, class struggle, and vice-versa.

The separation of caste and class seems to be superfluous and mechanistic. Both caste and class are real dimensions of India's social formation, and they are by and large inseparable from each other. Class is not simply a construct or abstraction. Classes of landowners, landless labourers, traders and money-lenders are structural components of India's economic formation. These classes interact with each other and have a hierarchy of social relations. Caste is an infrastructural resource/liability in regard to forces and relations of production. *Jajmani* relations and kinship can be explained in terms of class relations and mode of production as well.

Caste and class represent the same structural reality. Caste sentiments have acquired a new form. Caste-based commensality and untouchability have withered away to a very large extent due to modern forces of social change. Castes function as classes because they are called upon to perform economic functions. Caste associations in towns and cities perform economic and political functions more than social and cultural activities. Caste is a very effective system of exploitation of the lower castes by the upper castes. A "class war" against *Harijans* by the upper castes and dominant peasant castes has been reported in parts of Bihar, Uttar Pradesh, Maharashtra, Andhra Pradesh, etc.

The following points may be considered for discussion:

(1) Whether the abolition of landlordism has brought about transfer of landholdings from one group to another, or not? If yes, are the new landholding groups different qualitatively from the ex-landlords?

(2) Whether technological devices have further consolidated the traditional inequalities or have reduced them?

(3) Whether political power has shifted from one group of people to another or not, independent of the change in the pattern of landownership?[39]

The following patterns of social change and mobility may be noted:

(1) downward mobility and proletarianisation,
(2) upward mobility and embourgeoisiement,
(3) urban income for rural people and mobility in the village, and
(4) rural non-agricultural income and mobility.[40]

The upper castes and classes were affected adversely due to the abolition of the *jagirdari* and *zamindari* systems. Some functionary castes too were affected negatively. The intermediate castes (peasants) were benefited immensely. However, the upper castes were able to seek alternate sources of livelihood. They made a quick beginning for reconsolidating their lost status and power. Some families from among the upper and middle caste groups began to draw income from new opportunities available within the village as a result of new institutions and structures introduced after Independence. The state has played an immense role in social transformation in the post-independence period.

Notes

1. Malik, S.C., Determinants of Social Status in India: Problems and Issues in (ed) Determinants of Social Status in India by S.C. Malik, Delhi: Motilal Banarsidass, 1986, pp. 1-27.
2. Dumont,Louis, London: Granada Publishing Company Ltd., 1970.
3. Sharma, K.L. 'Structuring of Social Inequalities in Rural India' Paper presented at the Workshop on Equality-Inequality, August 27-29, 1986, New Delhi (mimeo).
4. Ibid.
5. Marx, Karl and Frederick, Engels, The German Ideology, Moscow: Progress Publishers, 1968, pp.32-38.
6. Ibid.
7. Ibid.
8. Sharma, R.S., Material Culture and Social Formations in Ancient India, Delhi: Macmillan India Ltd., 1985.
9. Kosambi, D.D., Introduction to the Study of Indian History, Bombay: Popular Prakashan, 1975. See also R.S.Sharma's 'How Feudal was Indian feudalism', in Feudal Social Formation in Early India, edited by D.N. Jha, Delhi: Chanakya Publications, 1987, pp. 165-197.
10. Ibid.
11. Desai, A.R., Social Background of Indian Nationalism, Bombay: Popular Prakashan, 1948. See Charles Bettelheim, India Independent, London: MacGibbon and Kee Ltd., 1968.
12. Ruben,Walter, 'Outline of the Structure of Ancient Indian Society', in R.S. Sharma and Vivekanand Jha (ed.) People's Publishing House, 1974.

13. Thapar, Romila, 'Social Mobility in Ancient India with Special Reference to Elite Groups'; in R.S. Sharma and Vivekanand Jha (ed.) op.cit.
14. Bailey, Anne Mand, and Liobera, Josep R., General Introduction in The Asiatic Mode of Production: Science and Politics (ed.) Anne M. Bailey and Josep R. Liobera, London: Routledge and Kegan Paul, 1981.
15. Krader, Lawrence, Principles and Critique of the Asiatic Mode of Production in Anne M. Bailey and Josep R. Liobera (ed.)op. cit.
16. Myrddal, Gunnar, Asian Drama, Vol. I, Penguin Books, 1968.
17. Kosambi, D.D., Kosambi on History and Society: Problems of Interpretation, edited by A.J. Syed, Bombay: University of Bombay Publication, 1985.
18. Jha, D.N., 'Editor's Introduction' in Feudal Social Formation in Early India (ed.), op. cit., p.4.
19. Kosambi, D.D., op. cit.
20. Sharma, R.S., op. cit.
21. Jha, D.N., op. cit., p.6.
22. Ibid., p.12.
23. See T.J. Byres and Harbans Mukhia (ed.), Feudalism and Non-European Societies, London: Frank Cass & Co.,1985.
24. Byres, T.J., in Byres and Mukhia, op. cit., p.2.
25. See Kosambi, Sharma and Desai, op. cit.
26. Mukhia, Harbans, 'Peasant Production and Medieval Indian Society', and 'Was There Feudalism in Indian Society'? in Byres & Mukhia (ed.), op. cit.
27. Byres, T.J., op. cit.
28. Quoted from Byres, op. cit., p.6.
29. Bloch, Marc, Feudal Society, Chicago:University of Chicago press, 1964.
30. Tod, James, Annals and Antiquities of Rajasthan, New Delhi: M.N. Publishers,1983.
31. Ibid., p. 107.
32. Ibid., p. 128.
33. Wills, C. U., The Report on the Land-tenures and Special Powers of Certain Thikanadars of the Jaipur State. Delhi: T.M.H. press, 1933.
34. Ibid., pp. 6-7.
35. Sharma, K.L. Caste, Class and Social Movements, Jaipur: Rawat Publications, 1986, pp. 109-138.
36. Ibid.
37. Sharma, K.L., The Changing Rural Stratification System, New Delhi: Orient Longman,1974.
38. Ibid., p.104.
39. Sharma, K.L., op cit., 1986, pp.77-78.
40. Ibid., p.50.

10

Caste Sentiments, Class Formation and Dominance in Gujarat

Ghanshyam Shah

This paper seeks to examine the nature of political dominance in Gujarat in the context of caste and class during the post-independence period. The concepts of caste and class are vague. Though their relationship with the means of production provides the important criterion to determine classes in society, it has not been found to be adequate enough for explaining the complex empirical situation. Occupation and/or income are also not satisfactory criteria to determine the class to which an individual belongs. However, for convenience, I shall use occupation and/or ownership of the means of production and their scale and size (for example, quality and size of landownership) to identify the class to which the individual belongs. The economic stratum, though easy to identify, does not give the same meaning as does the term "class" which indicates the relationship between the classes in the mode of production. Class has a subjective significance as well as a social value for a given person. A person's value judgment and behaviour are influenced by his class position. Moreover, a sense of conflict is implicit in the term "class," whereas the term stratum is a descriptive category and does not help much in understanding the dynamics of socio- economic relations and change. I use the term "class" with all its limitations, which has the same meaning as, and something more than, economic stratum. One faces the same difficulty with the term "caste." Hierarchy, endogamy or marriage circle and social commensality (*roti* and *beti vyavahar*, i.e., food and marital transactions among the members) together are the main principles of caste. It is relatively easy to identify caste groups whose members are bound together by *roti* and *beti vyavhar*, at the village level. Their status in the village social hierarchy can also be identified. However, all castes are not endogamous. Some are exogamous and follow hypergamy. Sometimes the levels of hypergamy are so many that one finds it difficult to decide where one caste ends and the other begins, and difficulties are enormous when one takes up the analysis at the level of the state as a whole. The persons who claim to be members of the same caste but reside in different parts of the state, do not enjoy the same social status in the respective villages in which they reside. They also do not observe uniform social customs. Except identifying themselves with the same nomenclature of the caste, the persons claiming to be the members of the same caste, do not always have common social characteristics (occupations, customs, life style, etc.) with others residing in different areas. In fact, from the point of view of social characteristics, they are closer to the members of other caste groups of the same locality than to their own caste members living in different areas. As a student interested in the state's political process, I am more concerned with the political dimensions of caste than with its social characteristics which include kin and marriage relationships and the observance of social customs. The political dimensions of caste imply that the members identify themselves as belonging to one caste and share the same nomenclature of caste as against the members of other castes engaged in political action. In some cases, they invent a new name to encompass various caste groups. In that sense the term "caste" includes its sub-sub-sub endogamous unit, marriage circles called *ekdas* or *gols*.

I use the term "caste sentiments" to point out the subjective sense of its members (caste for itself), where they feel a sense of oneness as against the members of other castes. The sense of oneness is based on real or imaginery common historical heritage. It has the connotation of "status" involving the principles of purity and pollution, which has become redundant in recent years (Shah, 1984).

The main argument of this paper is that since all the members of a caste do not enjoy a similar economic position, caste and class cannot be equated. There are economic differentiations, though not always necessarily antagonistic, within each caste, and the dominant political elite of the caste by and large come from or with the support of upper economic strata. In order to seek the support of the caste members in political sphere, the elite appeal to caste sentiments and invoke caste consciousness so that harmony among the members is maintained despite economic differentiations. Thus, economic differentiations tend to develop classes within caste, and caste ideology, that is, a sense of the same social status of the members based on the principle of pollution and purity, attempts to blur the differentiations and to invoke a sense of oneness among the members. At the same time, the political elite of the upper economic class ally, whenever necessary, with the members of the same class outside their caste to attain and maintain politico-economic dominance.

The Background

The present-day Gujarat in Western India came into existence in 1960, as a result of the vivisection of the erstwhile Bombay State. The state can be broadly divided into two sub-regions on the basis of the historical and socio-cultural heritage as well as psychological make-up. One is mainland Gujarat and the second is peninsular Gujarat. Peninsular Gujarat consists of Kathiavad, known as Saurasthra and Kutch areas.

Gujarat has six per cent of the total area of the Indian Union, having 1,95,986 sq. kms. area. According to the 1981 census, the total population of the state was 33.96 millions. There are 255 towns and other urban agllomerations and thirty-one per cent of its population, as against 23.7 per cent of India's population in urban areas. It has also a higher rate of literacy (43.75%) more than that of India as a whole, which has 36.17 per cent. The per capita income of Gujarat was Rs. 1,623 as compared to India's per capita income of Rs. 1,267 at 1979-80 prices.

Caste Structure

Caste enumeration from the census data is not available for the last fifty years. In order to get a broad pattern, we, therefore, depend upon the 1931 census.

The Brahmins, Banias and Rajputs belong to the upper castes. They together form twelve per cent of the total population. There are about eighty main divisions among the Brahmins and forty among the Banias. (This also includes the Banias who follow Jainism). Many of the divisions of each caste are further divided into two or three sub-castes. For example, the Brahmins are divided into Audich, Bhargava, Anavil, Nagar, Khedawal, Modh, etc. Each of them is further divided into Grihastha and Bhikshuk Nagar, Desai and Bhathela Anavil, Baj and Bhitra Khedawal, etc. These are again divided into *dasa* and *visha* which are further divided into *ekade* (units) or *gols* (circles). And some *ekades* are again divided into *tads* (literally meaning factions) which are endogamous groups. The Brahmins and Banias are spread throughout the state. Traditionally, the Banias have been merchants and moneylenders. A large number of them are still engaged in these occupations.

Some are white-collar employees and a few are also cultivators. Besides following their traditional occupations as priests, Brahmins are also found in white-collar jobs. A few of them are in business and agriculture too. Unlike other parts of the country, Banias have overshadowed Brahmins in economic and political spheres for several centuries.

Table 1

Caste Break-up: 1931 Census

Castes	*Total*	*Percentage*
Higher Castes		
1. Brahmin	289.796	4.06
2. Bania	208,739	2.96
3. Rajput	345,727	4.85
4. Others	80,321	1.13
Middle Castes		
5. Patidars	868.030	12.16
6. Artisans	437.762	6.13
7. Mali	8,669	0.12
8. Bhat, Barot	23,549	0.33
9. Kharva	13,792	0.19
10. Bharwad	143,477	2.01
11. Koli	1,729,039	24.22
12. Machhi	39.382	0.55
13. Bhoi	26,992	0.38
14. Others	309,670	4.34
Lower Castes		
15. Depressed and Untouchables	511,866	7.17
16. Other Backward Castes	161,381	2.26
Others		
17. Aboriginals	1,260,374	17.65
18. Muslims	609,304	8.53
19. Christians	52,940	0.74
20. Parsis	15,086	0.21
21. Others	3,283	0.05
Total	7,139,179	100.00

Literally, "Rajput" means the son of a ruler. The members of the caste belong to or are related to the ruling families who enjoyed political power at one time or other in the past. Unlike Brahmins and Banias, there is no vertical division among the Rajputs. They do not follow endogamy. They practice hypergamy. Kingdoms and tenures were abolished after independence. Though a majority of them are now landholders, some are in white-collar jobs and a few are in business.

The Patidars used to be known as Kanbis. They are still known by that name in some parts of Saurashtra and North Gujarat. The change of name is a result of a marked improvement in their status. "Whereas other castes are by tradition associated with relative ease with one of the four *varnas* of classical literature, when we come to the Kanbi we are immediately faced with claim and counter-claim. Those Brahmins who have had no dealings with them and are not therefore dependent on their goodwill have categorised them as Sudras. They themselves in the past and still today make varying claims now to Kshatriya and now to Vaishya status" (Pocock, 1972: 56). They constitute around twelve per cent of the population. The main divisions among them are: Leuvba, Kadva, Anjana and Matiya. Each of them is further divided into several branches. There are fifty-two divisions of the Kadva Patidar. Each division is further sub-divided into some more divisions. Each division had its *panchayat*, i.e., caste council and customs for social commensality. But they are not endogamous, because they believe that they are descendants of one ancestor. They form marriage circles consisting of a cluster of villages, called *ekada*. These circles are endogamous. However, Leuvas follow hypergamy. The hypergamous tendency among them "was so powerful that each endogamous unit could not be perfectly endogamous even at the height of its integration. Each unit was ranked in relation to others, and many members of the lower units married their daughters into the higher units, so that almost every unit became loose in the course of time" (Shah, 1962:16).

The Patidars are the second largest caste in the state. Their number is relatively smaller in South Gujarat than in the rest of the state. Besides agriculture, the Patidars are also entering into business and industry, and taking to white-collar jobs. Among the migrants from Gujarat to Africa, Europe and America, the Patidars form the single largest group. All Patidars do not enjoy the same status. The Leuva Patidars of Charottar area (Anand, Borsad, Nadiad and Petlad talukas of Kheda district) enjoy highest status among them. The Kolis form the largest caste cluster in Gujarat, constituting around twenty-four per cent of the population. They are spread throughout the state. Today some of them do not like to be called Kolis. Instead they call themselves Kshatriyas in Central and North Gujarat and Patels in South Gujarat. The Kolis of South Gujarat prefer to be called just Kolis. Broadly, the Kolis can be divided into coastal Kolis and mainland Kolis. There are Chunavaliyas, Khants, Patanvadiyas, Talabdas, Dharalas, Machhis. Matias, Gulams, etc. These divisions are not clear and there is a great deal of local variation and overlapping. Different groups use different names to identify their castes.

Each of the social groups is divided into several local groups based on marital relationships. For instance, Thakardas of Kheda district are divided into three groups, namely, (1) one hundred and fifteen villages Thakarda Kshatriya panch (i.e., council); (2) fifty-two Thakarda Kshatriya panch, ; and (3) twenty-seven Thakarda Kshatriya panch. They are cultivators, small and big landowners, farm labourers, fishermen and sailors. In the past, there were a few principalities in North Gujarat and Panchmahal ruled by Koli chieftains.

The scheduled castes (SCs) or ex-untouchables constitute seven per cent of the population. They are also spread throughout the state. Besides being small and marginal farmers and landless farm labourers, they carry out traditional functions such as sweeping the streets, carrying carcasses, weaving, etc. In urban areas, many of them are now factory workers and white-collar employees. They are divided into several social groups such as Chamar, Bhangi, Shenama, Vankar, Mahyavanshi, Garoda, Dhed, etc. Like other castes, they are further divided for marital purposes.

Unlike the scheduled castes, the scheduled tribes (STs) which constitute fourteen per cent of the population (according to the 1981 census) of the state are concentrated in a few districts of East and South Gujarat. The majority of them are small and marginal farmers and agricultural labourers. According to the 1981 census, only 7.3 per cent of them live in urban areas. A large number of them are casual workers, a few are employed in factories and white-collar jobs. The major tribes in Gujarat include Bhils, Dhodiyas, Chaudhris, Gamites, Warlis, Kokanas, Kotwaliyas and Halpatis. They are also divided into several endogamous groups.

The Muslims are eight per cent of the total population. Like Hindus, they are also divided into several social groups such as Sayads, Shaikhs, Pathans, Mughals, Memans, Boharas, Khojas, etc. They are spread all over the state. They are cultivators, petty traders and industrial workers. Parsis are refugees from Persia. They have been settled in South Gujarat since the eighth century. They constitute less than half a per cent of the population, and are agriculturists and businessmen. A large number of them began migrating to Bombay in the beginning of the nineteenth century.

The Post-Independence Scene

The Congress party came to power after independence in Saurashtra,

Kutch and the Bombay State of which mainland Gujarat was a part. It has ruled in the decades since then except for a few years in the seventies. From the beginning, the party emphasized the need to develop industrial and agricultural sectors. For agricultural development, the government adopted two strategies: one was to bring about institutional changes, and the second was related to technological development. The former aimed at changing the feudal land relations by adopting land reforms, and the latter related to the development of infrastructure to increase productivity.

Soon after independence, the Congress government initiated the process of territorial integration. By 1948, all the princely states were merged with the Indian Union and the rulers were granted privy purses. The rulers of thirty-nine princely states of Gujarat received the purses. This reduced their income as well as political power. Having merged the states and formed the new states, the new government proceeded to bring about changes in the traditional land relationship in these states.

There were three types of land tenure systems in Saurashtra: occupancy, *girasdari* and *barkhali*. Land was held by the cultivator directly from the state under the occupancy tenure. Except in a few principalities, the cultivators did not possess ownership of land. Under the other tenures, there were intermediaries between the cultivators and the states. Such tenure holders were Girasdars who included Talukadars, Bhagdars, Bhayats, Mulgirasis and Barkhalidars.They were landlords enjoying property rights on land and collecting their shares of the agricultural produce from the cultivators without tilling the land. This system was also prevalent in mainland Gujarat.

On the very first day of the formation of the Saurashtra State in April 1948, the new government dominated by Banias and Brahmins granted occupancy rights to the cultivators in unalienated (*khalsa*) villages without compensatory payment.

For the first time, the cultivators got the right to transfer and inherit land. The government also abolished *velth* and *begar*, i.e., forced labour which the Girasdars had been extracting from the cultivators.

In regard to other tenures, the situation was complex as there were as many as 51,278 Girasdars, Barkhalidars and other landlords in 1,726 villages. As a first step, the Government of Saurasthra promulgated the Saurastra Protection of Tenants Ordinance in May 1948 which stopped arbitrary evictions. According to the ordinance, no landlord could obtain the possession of land held by a tenant except by the order of the government.

The landlord could terminate the tenancy of the tenant by giving six months' notice in writing expiring on 31st March, 1949, stating therein the reasons for such termination including whether the landlord required the land for bonafide personal cultivation. The government issued another ordinance called the Saurashtra Gharkhed Tenancy Settlement and Agricultural Land Ordinance in July 1949. Accordingly, the landlords were allowed to take possession of land from tenants only for personal cultivation. The landlords formed the Girasdar Association and started agitation against the ordinance. They started evicting the tenants from the land in the name of self-cultivation. Suffice it to mention here that the Kutch, Kathiawar, Gujarat Kshatriya Sabha (later on known as the Gujarat Kshatriya Sabha), a caste association, which came into existence in 1947 supported the cause of Girasdars.

On the reccommendation of the Agrarian Reforms Commission appointed by the Government of India, the Government of Saurashtra enacted the Saurastra Land Reforms Act, 1951, and the Saurastra Estate Acquisition Act, 1952. These Acts aimed at abolishing the intermediary system and giving occupancy right to the tillers. All the landholders could pay land revenue in cash, and were put on the same footing.

These Acts were implemented immediately. As a result, the landlords either became cultivators or they lost the land. According to a sample survey, in 1947-48, only 357 Girasdars had some land for self-cultivation, the number increased to 396 Girasdars who had *gharkhed* land in 1954-55. This means that forty-three Girasdars, who were not at all cultivating land themselves prior to the reforms started, cultivating land personally (Mishra, 1961). In effect, the Girasdars evicted their tenants in many cases and started tilling land themselves. These included many Girasdars who had never visited their farms earlier. Moreover, the pattern of landholdings also changed. Table 2, based on the sample survey, provides details of changes in the number of holdings of all categories between 1947-48 and 1954-55. It shows that the number of holdings in upper category, namely, above forty acres of land, declined and the number increased in the lower category, particularly between fifteen and twenty-five acres. Howard Spodek computed the Gini index of inequality for Saurastra and its neighbouring states. He found that Saurastra had "one of the most even distributions of landholdings in any region of India" (1976: 77). The Girasdars launched an agitation against the reform and some of them revolted against the state. Some resorted to dacoity, which was responsible for eighty to eighty-five deaths and thousands or even lakhs of rupees were looted in a series of some twelve major crimes between 1949 and 1952.

Table 2

Changes in the Number of Landholdings of all Categories of Cultivators Between 1947-48 and 1954-55

Size of Holding	*Period*			
	1947-48		*1954-55*	
	Number	*Percentage*	*Number*	*Percentage*
Nil	129	2.6	98	2.0
000-005	371	7.5	404	8.1
005-015	994	20.0	1250	25.2
015-025	965	19.5	1147	23.1
025-040	1207	24.4	1215	24.5
040-060	745	15-0	573	11.5
060-080	291	5.9	175	3.5
080-100	123	2.5	51	1.0
100-150	112	2.2	33	0.7
150-200	8	0.2	6	0.2
200 & above	12	0.2	5	0.1

The Government of Bombay State also passed several Acts between 1949 and 1955 abolishing various *girasdari* tenures which existed in some parts of the state. These Acts conferred occupancy rights on the tenure-holders, inferior-holders, registered occupiers or occupants and permanent holders without charging occupancy price. Rajputs and Koli Talukdars of Gujarat, like their counterparts in Saurastra, lost land to the tenant cultivators. Their power over villages declined. A few of them started cultivating land but they lacked training and aptitude for agriculture.

Simultaneously, the government enacted a comprehensive land legislation called the Bombay Tenancy and Agricultural Lands Act. Among other benefits, it gave to tenants a fixed tenure and protection from eviction. Later on, the Tenancy and Lands (Amendments) Act of 1956 gave land to the tillers, so that on a particular day (1st April, 1957) all tenants would be deemed to have come in possession of the land they cultivated as tenants. Unlike the Girasdari Abolition Acts of Saurastra, the tenancy legislations were not rigorously implemented in Gujarat. This was partly because of the implicit interference by the Patidar and Bania-Brahmin landlords who otherwise would have been adversely affected by the Act. They dominated the Congress Party and administration. At the same time, however, the Act did not flop altogether either. Desai (1971: 123), who carried out the sample survey in sixty-five villages, observes:

> The results of tenancy abolition, however, were not as expected. About half the area previously under tenancy passed into the ownership of their respective erstwhile tenants. About twelve per cent of the land held by nine per cent of the tenants continued under recognised tenancy. A little over two per cent of the lands of tenants slipped from them in default of payment of compensation amounts. The rest were cases in which the tenants either denied tenancy, surrendered their lands to the landowners or kept away from the hearings of the tribunals and, therefore, missed out, of their own volition, to be owners of the land they cultivated on lease. Thus, a sizeable tenantry escaped ownership under tenancy abolition.

We do not have data to identify the caste of the tenants who became the owners. However, we should note two facts. One, nearly half of the tenants belonged to lower castes including SCs and scheduled tribes (Desai, 1971). Since they were poor and less exposed to the outside world, they found it difficult to understand the intricacies of law. Moreover, in village society, they were subdued and found it difficult to raise their voice against the landowners of the dominant castes. Therefore, they were more likely than the upper caste cultivators to surrender the tenancy. They either did not declare themselves as tenants or did not present themselves before the tribunal to prove their claim. Many of them did not have the confidence that they would be able to pay off the instalments to the landowners. Second, among the tenants, as many as sixty-three per cent were owner-cum-tenants. Their number is larger among the upper and the intermediate castes than the lower castes. Table 3 provides information about caste-wise status of the tenants. This information as well as our own observations suggest that a large number of tenants belonging to the upper and intermediate castes took advantage of this Act. The land which they obtained was often at the expense of members of their own castes who had moved on to urban areas and did not wish to take to cultivation. The tenants belonging to the lower castes rarely got land from the high caste absentee landlords.

Concealed tenancy in different forms has continued. In order to provide land to the landless to narrow the gap in the landholding pattern, the government introduced the Land Ceiling Act in 1960. The Act was amended in 1974 which further lowered the limit of the ceiling. But it has remained largely on paper. The government received only 43,721 acres of land. Most of this land was of inferior quality, thus defeating the purposes of the legislation. Although various legislations related to land reforms led to the redistribution of land to some extent, they have not changed land relationship in terms of caste or class.

Table 3

Number of Tenants by Status and Caste

Caste	*Owner-cum-Tenants*	*Pure Tenants*	*Total*
Upper Caste Hindu	84	43	127
	(66.14)	(33.86)	(100)
InterMediate Caste Hindu	1428	536	1962
	(72.68)	(27.32)	(100)
Lower Caste Hindu	776	465	1242
	(62.53)	(37.47)	(100)
Scheduled Caste	54	86	180
	(52.22)	(47.78)	(100)
Scheduled Tribe	363	424	787
	(46.12)	(53.88)	(100)
Mohmmedan	101	129	230
	(43.92)	(56.08)	(100)
Christian	6	8	14
	(42.86)	(57.14)	(100)
Parsi	3	3	6
	(50.00)	(50.00)	(100)
Total	2853	1984	4547
	(62.74)	(37.26)	(100)

Note: Figures in the brackets are percentages to the total.
Source: M.B. Desai, 1971.

According to the 1981 census, sixty-one per cent of the workers in Gujarat are engaged in agriculture as the principal source of earning; thirty-eight per cent of them are cultivators and twenty-three per cent are agricultural labourers. Table 4 gives distribution of landholding by size. About sixty per cent of the cultivators own less than three hectares of land. On the other hand, 1.35 per cent households hold more than twenty hectares of land. The government had identified 1,30,000 small and marginal farmers in the state by the end of March, 1973. In terms of caste, Patidars, Rajputs, Kolis, Brahmins, STs are the main landowning groups. According to the sample survey carried out by the Centre for Social Studies, Surat, one-third of the Patidars and one-fourth of the Brahmins and artisans are rich peasants (see Table 5). A majority of the cultivators belonging to the Kolis, SCs and STs are small and marginal farmers. However, there are proportionately fewer landless labourers among Patidars, Brahmins and Banias than among the Kolis, Muslims, Rajputs, artisans, Sts/STs. The majority of the Banias and other upper castes such as Brahmakshatriyas, Luhanas, etc. are engaged in business. A larger number of persons coming from among the upper castes (except Rajputs) are in white-collar jobs and professions.

Table 4

Number of Operational Holdings and Area Operated by Size of Operational Holdings in Gujarat, 1970-71

(Figures in '000s)

Size Group (Hects)	*No. of Holdings*	*Per cent Share in total*	*Cumulative Percentage*	*Area (Ha.)*	*Percent Share in Total*	*Cumulative Percentage*
Below 0.5	284	11.7	11.7	79	0.8	0.8
00.5-01.0	295	12.1	23.8	220	2.2	3.0
01.0-02.0	464	19.1	42.9	621	6.8	9.8
02.0-03.0	325	13.4	56.3	802	8.0	17.8
03.0-04.0	229	9.4	65.7	704	8.0	25.8
04.0-05.0	176	7.2	72.9	790	7.9	33.7
05.0-10.0	424	17.4	90.3	2987	29.9	63.6
10.0-20.0	201	8.3	98.6	2708	27.1	90.7
20.0-30.0	27	1.1	99.7	621	6.2	96.9
30.0-40.0	1	0.3	100.0	151	1.5	98.4
40.0-50.0	1	Neg.	—	44	0.4	98.8
50.0 & more	1	Neg.	—	122	1.2	100.0
	2412	100.0	—	9999	100.0	

Source: Agricultural Census, 1970-71, 1975,32.

As mentioned earlier, the farmers of Gujarat were producing commercial crops ever since the seventeenth century. Cotton was then the main cash crop. Then they started cultivation of tobacco and groundnut. Slowly, the area under food crops declined and the area under non-food crops increased between 1910 and 1940. This process has been accelerated further during the last three decades as infrastructure facilities have increased. The irrigated area increased more than four-fold from 1950 to 1981. Canals watered only 3.4 per cent of irrigated area in 1951-52, which increased to seventeen per cent in 1970-71. The number of oil-engines, electric motors, pump-sets and tractors increased four to five times during the two decades. The use of various types of chemical fertilisers also increased from seventeen thousand tonnes in 1960-61 to 403 thousand tonnes in 1982-83 (Economic Intelligence Service, 1983). Credit facilities through co-operative societies and banks to the farmers shot up considerably. The All-India Rural Credit Review Committee pointed out that Gujarat was next only to Maharashtra in the whole country in the matter of (i) borrowings by cultivators from cooperatives,

Table 5

Occupation, Landholding, and Caste in Rural Gujarat

	Occupation								Landholding			
	Un-employed Retired	Profes-sionals	Service	Business	Agri. & Other Labour	Cul-tivators	Others	Total	Less than 5 acres	5 to 15 acres	15 acres & more	Total
Brahmin	16	2	11	3	4	52	12	100	41	32	27	298
Bania	14	1	5	45	45	30	—	100	55	24	21	144
Rajput	7	*	2	1	15	72	2	100	42	35	23	1963
Other Upper Castes	15	1	9	31	13	26	4	100	46	42	12	68
Patidar	6	1	3	1	7	81	1	100	25	42	33	1923
Artisans	8	1	3	1	36	48	3	100	42	33	25	854
Koli	8	*	2	*	24	62	3	100	66	23	11	3091
Other Backward Castes	7	*	2	1	33	45	12	100	43	41	10	
Scheduled Castes	7	*	2	*	39	43	8	100	69	26	5	
Scheduled Tribes	4	*	1	*	21	67	5	100	77	21	2	
Muslims	7	*	2	9	35	44	3	100	36	45	19	685
Others	17	—	9	3	38	30	3	100	66	17	17	66

* Less than 0.5 per cent

and (ii) the proportion of cultivating households which reported borrowings from co-operative societies to the total cultivator-households. In each district, there is a District Central Co-operative Bank. At the village level, agricultural credit societies also function. By the end of June 1976, 97.4 per cent of the 18,275 villages in Gujarat were covered by the primary agricultural credit societies.

With these inputs, the average level of output of a number of crops increased during the last three decades. But, at the same time, the average level of area under foodgrains has tended to decline during the period from 1961-62 to 1977-78 from 48.3 lakh hectares to 44.8 lakh hectares, while that under non-foodgrains increased from 53 lakh hectares to 59.1 lakh hectares. It should also be mentioned that the growth rate in agriculture is not stable. There is a great deal of fluctuation in output both of food and non-food crops. And the performance of crop cultivation in the seventies compared to the sixties was "not very encouraging" (Sharma, 1983).

As happened elsewhere, the economic condition of most of the small and marginal farmers has not improved as they are unable to take the advantage of "technological development" in agriculture. They do not get adequate credit facilities and inputs when they need them the most. The condition of the agricultural labourers has also deteriorated and their number has increased from 1951 to 1981. Real wages of the agricultural labourers and the total period of employment have not increased, forcing them either to join the army of unorganised urban labourers or live below the subsistence level.

Agriculture labourers are, by and large, not organised for asserting their demands, though clashes between the landowners and labourers are increasing in different parts of the state. The agricultural labourers occasionally display militancy and resort to stoppage of work, demanding higher wages or village common land for a housing site or grazing their cattle or protesting against raping of their women by the landowner. The landed class employ *rakhas*, i.e., watchman to protect crops in the farms, who use force against the militant labourers. The labourers are not only manhandled and beaten but also sometimes murdered, and their huts are set on fire. Labourers also retaliate. Many of the clashes are localised and sporadic, continuing for a day or two. However, a few clashes continued for many days and affected a number of villages. For instance, a militant *dalit* agricultural labour leader was mercilessly beaten and set on fire by the youths of the landowners, who was a Patidar by caste, in Jetput, the village near Ahmedabad, in December 1980, because he was mobilising labourers against the landed class. This infuriated the local labourers as well as the *dalit* (Harijan) leaders of Ahmedabad, adding fuel to the already volatile situation ignited by the anti-reservation riots spear headed by the urban upper caste, middle class students (Yagnik, 1981; Desai, 1981). Through their control over the media, the higher castes gave a casteist colour to the confrontation and to some extent incited, though not with much success, poor cultivators and labourers from other backward castes to attack members belonging to the STs/STs (Shah, 1983). Similarly, confrontation between the tribal labourers and Rajput and Patidar landowners in Valia, Bharuch district, in 1981 continued for several days.

In such situations, the state has invariably come to the rescue of the propertied class and failed to provide protection to the labourers. The instances of the confrontation between the agricultural labourers and landowning class were frequent in the sixties and early seventies in South Gujarat. There are only neneteen unions of agricultural labourers with less than one lakh members, which is barely four per cent of the total number of agricultural workers. One of the important organisations of the agricultural workers is the Halpati Seva Sangh (HSS), an organisation of the Halpatis (a scheduled tribe) who are agricultural labourers. It was an offshoot of the Gandhian activities among the tribals in South Gujarat. It came into existence in 1961 and advocated the implementation of the Minimum Wage Act, which played a catalytic role in encouraging militancy among the labourers. The leaders of the HSS, however, intervened when strikes by the labourers broke out to minimise the tension and made efforts to reach a compromise. Jan Breman (1974: 494) observes: "Self-respect and class-consciousness are not taught. On the contrary, the organisation does not aim at making the Halpatis able to stand up for themselves, aware of the social system without any fundamental change in their dependence". The HSS undertakes a number of welfare activities for the Halpatis, and whatever little catalytic role it could play in organising strikes by the labourers in its early phase has diminished now. In fact, recently the leader of the HSS has joined the hands with the Khedut Samaj, an organisation of the rich and middle farmers who were at one time his arch enemies. The Majur Mahajan, a Gandhian Textile Labour Association (TLA), has established the Khet Majur Mahajan Sangh in 1976 which had 5,446 members in ten districts in 1981. Some of the Congress leaders started Khet Vikas Parishad in 1975 which raised the issue of the implementation of the Minimum Wages Act when the Janata Party was in power between

1977-80. However, it did not organise and mobilise agricultural labourers after 1980, though it redressed the grievances of individual labourers, and influenced the government for raising wages under the Minimum Wage Act. Though the Minimum Wage Act has been revised in 1982, raising wages from Rs. 5.50 to Rs. 11 for a day's work, agricultural labourers rarely get the prescribed wages except in Saurashtra. The government has appointed 115 officers to enforce the law, but the officers rarely visit the villages. They expect labourers to visit their offices and report about low wages, which normally does not happen. Under the Act, the farmers are expected to keep records of wages paid, but such records are seldom maintained. "When farmers are big and powerful, they don't allow the officers to perform their duties by using political pressure." It is reported that at least two deputations of MLAs visit the labour minister of the state every month, seeking his intervention to prevent action against farmers. Occasionally, the officers prosecute the farmers for violation of the labour laws, but the courts seem to be lenient towards the landowning class. In 1981, 1982 and 1983, the amounts of fines imposed by courts for violation of labour laws like non-maintenance of records were Rs. 31,785, Rs. 92,897 and Rs. 2.06 lakhs, respectively.

The agricultural workers' unions and other organisations such as the HSS, Khet Vikas Parishad, and Majur Mahajan prefer to avoid confrontation between the agricultural labourers and the landed class. Therefore, they undertake a number of welfare activities, providing supplementary income to the labourers' families. A number of voluntary groups whose number has increased in the seventies, supported by the government, foreign funding agencies and business houses also carry out rural development programmes. These programmes are not economically viable. At the most they provide a dole and manage the prevailing tension in rural Gujarat (Shah and Chaturvedi, 1983). Because of welfare programmes, activities of the Khet Vikas Parsihad, rhetoric of *garibi hatao* (remove poverty) and sympathetic attitude of some Congress leaders towards the downtrodden, the agricultural labourers by and large support the Congress (I) in elections.

The rich and middle cultivators have built up their organisation to protect and advance their economic interests. Some of their organisations are the Cotton Growers Association, the Tobacco Growers Associations, the Vegetable Growers Association, etc. These associations enrol members, maintain offices and publish newsletters providing information regarding market trends, government policy, etc., to their members. Their publications are also the vehicles of ventilating their grievances against the government. They appoint part-time or full-time public relations officers based in Ahmedabad and Delhi who deal with the state and central governments. They pressurise the government to encourage export of their products, protect the price of their crops and distribute greater aamounts of inputs at subsidised rates to boost production. Such organisations are not directly associated with any one political party. They finance different non-left parties for elections. They felicitate the ministers and administrators irrespective of party or caste identity.

Besides these, the rich and the middle farmers form organisations of farmers under different banners from time to time. Bhailalbhai Patel of Kheda district organised a political party—the Khedut Sangh—in 1951 to oppose the tenancy legislations. He believed that the act of "land to the tillers" would create conflict in the village society between tenants and landholders. According to him, "the simple truth that the interests of all people working on land such as artisans, tenants, labourers are one and the same like a welded whole is not known. These interests do not conflict. They should be maintained in an integrated manner which can be done by considering the family of those working on land with the former as the head" (Amin, 1963: 17-18). He felt that the government was bringing in Communism by taking away land from large landowners (Bhalani, 1966).

The party put forward its candidates for eleven assembly seats in Gujarat and four in Saurashtra. It won only one seat in Saurashtra and one in Gujarat (Table 6). Bhailalbhai himself was defeated and most candidates even lost their deposit. Such a rout was due to two reasons. One, the majority of the farmers who were small and marginal landholders and tenants did not see any reasons to oppose land reforms. At least theoretically, the reforms were in their favour. Second, rich and middle peasants were not organised in one party. Moreover, many of them believed that strategically they should not oppose land reforms as they were advantageous to a large number of the farmers. They feared that they would lose the support of the mass of peasants if they opposed the reforms. At the same time, they were a confident that they could protect their interests by remaining with the party with a mass base, i.e., the Congress. It should also be emphasized that the farmers of Saurashtra in fact benefited from land reforms.

Bhailalbhai Patel and other leaders of the Khedut Sangh later on took the initiative in the formation of the Swatantra Party in Gujarat in

Table 6

Percentages of Votes Polled and Seats Won by Political parties in Gujarat Legislative Elections, 1952/1980

	1952		*1957*		*1962*		*1967*		*1972*		*1975*		*1980*	
	Seats	*% of votes*	*Seats*	*% of votes*	*Seats*	*% of votes*	*Seats*	*% of votes*	*Seats*	*% of votes*	*Seats*	*% of votes*	*Seats*	*% of votes*
Congress	141	56	101	57	113	51	93	46	140	51	75	41	141	50
Congress (O) (Camelinto existence after 1969)	2	—	—	—	16	24	56					24	21	22
Swatantra (Founded in 1959)				26	24	66	38	—		2	—	—	—	—
Lok Paksha	2	12	—	—	—	—	—	—	—	—	—	—	—	—
K B L P (Founded in 1974)	—	—		—	—	—	—	—	—	12	11	—	—	—
B L D (Founded in 1974)	—	—		—	—	—	—	—	—	2	1	—	—	—
Jan Sangh		—	—	1	—	1	1	2	3	9	18	9	9	13
Hindu Maha Sabha	—	3	—	—	—	1	—	—	—	—	—	—	—	—
Socialist	4	9	3	4	7	8	3	3	—	1	2	1	—	—
M G J P (Founded in 1956)	—	—	31	1	4	—	—	—	—	—	—	—	—	
Communist	—	—	—	—	—	—	—	—	—	—	1	1	—	—
Other Parties	—	1		—		—		—	—	1	1	1	—	2
Independents	10	19	—	7	7	10	5	10	8	12	15	12	10	10
TOTAL	157	100	133	100	154	100	168	99	168	101	181	100	181	97

Percentages are rounded, and therefore the totals do not add up to 100, Less than 0.5 per cent votes

(a) This included The Khedut Sangh, Krishikar Lok Paksha and Praja Paksha in 1952.

(b) This included The Ram Rajya Parishad

(c) This includes SP, SSP, and PSP.

(d) This includes CPI and CPM

(e) T7 Independents were supported by the Janata Morcha

(k) Janata Party

(i) Bharatiya Janata Party

* Coalition Partners in the Janata Morcha.

1959. They received the support of some ex-rulers and Girasias who suffered from the land reforms. The party also succeeded in attracting a section of the middle and rich farmers of the Patidar caste, who had improved their economic conditions in the fifties. But Bhailalbhai was aware of the fact that rich and middle peasants and Girasdars and ex-rulers themselves were not numerous enough to win elections. They needed the support of a large section of the masses. Therefore, they evolved a strategy of caste alliance between legislators for raising of the ceiling on land. The government rejected the suggestion of one MLA belonging to the treasury benches that agricultural land be taken over from the so-called farmers whose non-agricultural annual income was more than Rs. 15,000. The government also rejected even the simple suggestion of forming a watchdog committee to observe the implementation of the bill. Nor did the government take any other steps to gear up the administrative machinery so that surplus land could be surrendered for distribution among the landless under the Land Ceiling Act. A leader of the Khedut Samaj audaciously said at a public meeting that the Act was not going to be implemented as "the Congress governments do exactly the opposite of what they profess."

In the same year, the Khedut Samaj also opposed the levy of paddy imposed by the government under the 1973 Levy Act. Under this Act, the small farmers having one acre or less land were exempted from the levy payment and it was progressively applied, so that the bigger farmers had to contribute a larger share of paddy than the smaller farmers. For instance, in Surat district, out of 70,000 farmers, only 27,000, i.e., thirty-nine per cent, had to pay levy at differential rates. The farmers organised demonstrations, manhandled Congress leaders working for agricultural labourers and took the law into their hands, whereby the levy collection operation was disturbed. They stopped the supply of milk and vegetables to the cities for two days, and organised *satyagraha* when two leaders of the Samaj were arrested. Following the arrest of the leaders, disturbances occurred in the *taluka* towns of South Gujarat like Bardoli, Navsari, Buhari, etc. Meanwhile, the riots against corruption and price rise in the urban areas started. The urban middle class and students demanded the resignation of the chief minister, Chimanbhai Patel, a Patidar by caste. Though the leaders of the Khedut Samaj opposed the levy, they were not against Chimanbhai Patel. They, therefore, went to the rescue of the *khedutputra* (son of a peasant) Chimanbhai Patel. Opposing the demand for the chief minister's resignation, Vallabhbhai Patel, a leader of the Samaj said that the Central government was responsible for corruption and price-rise. "When the state is engulfed by food riots and the chief minister, the son of a peasant is in trouble, the farmers have not to think of anything but compromise with the government for the larger interest." They compromised with the government whereby their leaders were released. They withdrew the agitation. They went further and declared that the farmers would give more paddy in levy than what the government demanded. In fact, some of its leaders from Saurasthra and South Gujarat moved around villages for the collection of levy (Shah, 1977). Later, the Samaj supported the Janata Morcha, i.e., the non-Congress and non-Communists united front in the 1975 elections (Table 6). The Congress lost power and the Janata Morcha formed the government which scrapped the Levy Act.

In terms of caste, the Khedut Samaj is dominated by the Patidars. More than eighty per cent of its office-bearers are Patidars. However, its leaders do not speak in terms of Patidars from the platform of the Samaj. They use the term *khedut*, i.e., the farmer. On the other hand, various caste associations and journals of the Patidars use "Patidar" as synonymous with *khedut.* For instance, the names of their journals *Jagtat* (protector of land) or *vharti* (land) mean that they were farmers. Like the Khedut Samaj, the caste journals publish articles on the problems of the farmers related to irregularity of irrigation and electricity, scarcity of fertilisers and seeds, price protection to agricultural crops, etc. The general stance of the caste journals is opposition to land reforms. They advocate large holdings, arguing that small holdings are uneconomical. Such demands obviously do not affect the small and marginal farmers who are unable to use infrastructural facilities. Opposition to land reforms advocated by the journals is against the interests of most Patidar cultivators who are small and marginal farmers. Some of them were aware of the fact that they were being used by the big farmers of their own caste in order to advance the interest of the latter. A small farmer from the Patidar caste from a village in South Gujarat said:

> The farmers are unnecessarily blaming the government for their problems of irrigation, fertilisers, electricity or labour. Actually, the big farmers themselves are to be blamed. They accumulate and aggrandise like an insatiable hungry giant. Big farmers are like big fish, they simply disregard the smaller varieties. And when they want support for this or that issue, they come to us in the name of farmers' fraternity, solidarity and unity. For instance, take the issue of electricity for pumping water into fields. It is said that the rich, big and powerful farmers of Bardoli are influential in changing the

course of power distribution. They bribe the power-hungry people. Similar is the situation about the irrigation water. The stronger the lobbying is, the greater are the rewards. In such a situation, who really cares or bothers for the small farmers (Patel, 1982).

At the same time, paradoxically, like many other small Patidar farmers, he also supports the Khedut Samaj. This is because of a variety of reasons. One, they feel that their interests are not in sharp conflict with those of the rich and middle peasants. They hope that if the government concedes to the demands of middle or rich farmers and lowers the prices of agricultural inputs, they would also. Second, there is always a political party which organises the small and marginal farmers and expresses their grievances. The parties emphasize unity and harmony among the farmers. If any leader, even from the ruling party, raises the grievances of the poorer strata, he is immediately accused of creating a "class struggle", which is considered to be against "Indian culture". Third, caste organisations and their leaders repeatedly emphasize the unity of the Patidars for the development of the community. Any attempt to divide the community in terms of class, they fear, would lead to conflict and would give an opportunity to Communism which would turn "individuals in to animals without any freedom." Fourth, the small and the marginal farmers of the Patidar caste, like the members of any other caste, imbibe prejudices against other communities and thus create a cultural barriers to their unity across the castes. The small Patidar farmer who is critical of rich Patidar cultivators quoted above also expressed strong prejudices against the Dublas or Halpatis, who are agricultural labourers.

The Khedut Samaj has secured support against the imposition of land ceiling and paddy levy from the Koli, the Rajput, the Bareeya and the *adivasi* middle and rich peasants. By and large, neither the Khedut Samaj nor the various caste associations of the Patidars favour association with any party. However, such an anti-Communist party is almost an official stand of the leaders. On the other hand, the leaders of the Samaj are individually associated with the Congress, the Bharatiya Lok Dal, the Janata and the Bharatiya Janata Party. During the elections, they use their influence in mobilising the farmers for their own party, which creates stresses within the Samaj.

Industrial Sector

Gujarat occupies a prominent position on the industrial map of India. There were 9,722 factories, that is, twelve per cent of the total factories in the country, registered under the Factories Act in 1976-77. They generated Rs. 3,531 crores worth of output which accounted for a ten per cent share of the whole country. In terms of capital income generated in manufacturing activity, Gujarat stands second, next to Maharastra. In 1976-77, Gujarat generated Rs. 322 per capita as against the all-India average of Rs. 194.

Out of the two hundred top industrial giants of India, twenty-four are located in Gujarat. Among them, two are in the co-operative sector. Two fertiliser plants, one at Kalol and another at Kandla, run by the Indian Farmers' Fertiliser Cooperative Ltd. (IFFCO), are the largest single producers of chemical fertilisers. The second co-operative giant is the Kaira District Milk Producers' Union Ltd. (AMUL) It is India's largest unit in the dairy industry with sales of various products aggregating Rs. 58 crores. The Gujarat State Fertiliser Co is one of the largest joint sector projects in the country with sales of Rs. 89 crores.

Textile manufacturing is one of the major industries in Gujarat. Along with textiles, chemical and engineering factories were also started in the beginning of this century. After the formation of Gujarat State in 1960, its industrial structure has changed strikingly. By 1977, the share of the textile group in factory labour force had dropped sharply from seventy-six percent to eighteen per cent (Shah, 1979).

The Banias enjoy dominance in the industrial sector. There were seventy-two textile mills run by sixty-two companies in 1964 in Ahmedabad. Some companies owned more than one mill. As many as fifty-two companies were owned by Banias, eight by Patidars and two by non-Gujaratis (Spodek, 1965). Patidars who entered the industry as early as 1860s, now compete with Banias for the ownership of big and small industries. Rich and middle Patidar peasants who prospered in agriculture diverted their surplus to industry. They invested in agro-industries. The first sugar factory in Gujarat was started in 1957. No new factory was added till the end of 1960s. During the last decade, seven more factories have come into existence on co-operative basis. The same is the case with groundnut oil mills. Most of them are owned by Patidars. They also dominate AMUL and most of the other district level milk dairy co-operative societies such as SUMUL in Surat, Sagar Mehasana, Abad in Ahmedabad, Sabar in Sabarkantha, etc. Moreover, rich cultivators invest the surplus in the industrial sector by buying company shares and debentures.

As a few industrialists belong to the agricultural caste and still own land in their native villages, they express concern for agricultural development as well. They make special efforts and divert some of their earnings for agricultural development. For example, the Federation of Gujarat Mills Industries (FGMI), Baroda, carried out surveys regarding fertilisers and some pest control programmes, provided assistance to the farmers in securing a variety of agricultural inputs, in drilling wells, in marketing, etc. during the sixties. Various industrial houses formed as many as fifty-five rural development organisations during the early eighties. They provided technical and managerial know-how for agricultural production and marketing, and also carried out welfare programmes for small and marginal farmers. Thereby, they developed the rural market for their industrial output and increased the availability of foodstuffs in the urban area.

In terms of caste, though many Patidars and a few persons from the artisans castes have entered the business and industrial sector, the Banias still dominate this sector. At the outset it should be emphasized that caste consciousness is relatively weak among the businessmen and industrialists as compared to the peasants, thanks to their relationship with technological development, the competitive market and linkages with all-India and international business houses. Though there is a tendency to help their caste fellows, members of different castes belonging to the same business or industry freely meet and carry out business transactions. There is cut-throat competition even among the members of the same family or caste engaged in business or industry. For example, thanks to the competition among the industrialists of the Makarpura Industrial Estate, Baroda, hailing predominantly from the Patidar caste, dissociated themselves from the FGMI which is also dominated by the Patidar industrialists, and formed their separate organisation.

There are ten chambers of commerce. One is at the state level, known as Gujarat Vepari Maha Mandal, and nine are at regional and sub-regional levels. There are three industry-owners' organisations: (1) Ahemdabad Mills Owners Association; (2) Federation of Gujarat Mills and Industries; and (3) Saurashtra Mill Owner Associations. These were founded in 1891, 1918 and 1942, respectively, and are not affiliated to any political party. However, some individual businessmen or industrialists are closer to one or the other non-Left parties. They are in considerable agreement on political matters irrespective of their party affiliations. Both the Congress and non-Congress party members are critical of the labour policy, tax structure, licence policy, etc. of the Congress. Erdman (1971:36) observes: "In comparing formal affiliation and economic orientation, however, virtually the only discernible difference between supporters of the Congress and non-Congress (both independents and Swatantrites) was the more frequent mention of general notions of "social justice" on the part of the former. Yet, this was offset by the fact that the most vehement FGMI critics of the economic politics of the Congress were not Swatantrites but Congressmen. For example, no Swatantra member even remotely approached the vehemence with which FGMI Congressmen attacked the 1964 resolution on social control of banking as well as the party's labour policies". During the seventies, the Southern Gujarat Chamber of Commerce elected only those persons as its presidents who were affiliated to the party in power at the state level. They elected Congressmen when the Congress was in power. They elected Janata men when the Janata Party came to power (Parekh, 1982). They were primarily interested in maintaining and protecting their interests whichever be the party in power. While doing so, caste affiliation or groupings did not remain important.

Individual industrialists and their organisations play a very important part in local and state policies. The leading members of the business community are associated with several government committees at the district and state levels. They give financial "contributions" during and in-between elections to different non-Left political parties as well as to their office-bearers and MLAs. Though their informal contacts with the top political elite and business magnates they have achieved a "private understanding" with the ruling party to get their things done (Dandekar, 1972; Kochanek, 1974). They have also built up strong linkages to influence the bureaucracy, including the police, at all levels. Though they do not always succeed in preventing thc introduction of each legislation which may affect their business interests adversely, they more often than not succeed in sabotaging such legislations at the implementation level.

There are more than three million workers in non-agricultural establishments, inclusive of industrial and white-collar workers. We do not have the caste break-up of the industrial workers of Gujarat. However, a few micro studies suggest that a large number of them come from Koli, Patidar, artisan castes and SCs/STs. Forty-two per cent of the workers in Ahmedabad are immigrant from different states such as Rajasthan, Uttar Pradesh, Bihar, Andhra Pradesh, Orissa and Maharastra. Though it is not possible for any factory owner to employ only his caste fellows in the factory for skilled and unskilled work and supervisory jobs, many middle and small factories, owned particularly by Patidars, give preference to the members of their own caste in their recruitment policy. (Banias cannot adopt this policy because they do not get sufficient number of workers from their own caste). This is done, not primarily because of their loyality to the caste but because (as a workshop superintendent in a factory explained), "the stress on social links provides an insurance against and activities harmful to the production and general discipline of the factory" (Sheth, 1968: 77).

The workers in the large, organised sector are relatively better paid with a secured tenure than the workers in small scale industries and with the unorganised sector. Even in many large scale industries, particularly textiles, yarn, pharmaceuticals, etc., all the workers do not enjoy secured tenures. Quite a large number of them have been employed as temporary or shift workers for more than fifteen years. And thus they do not enjoy benefits like the organised workers do. The workers of the small scale industries are unorganised and get their wages on piece-work basis. To use Hein Streefkerk's (1981) phrase, they get "too little to live on, too much to die on". Most of the workers still work for twelve hours a day, with one unpaid holiday in a week. They do not have any security of tenure, sick leave, provident fund or insurance. Factory owners of small scale industries defy government rules and regulations including the labour officers who are supposed to protect the interests of the labourers. Instances of the factory owners or their henchmen beating the workers and compelling them to work for longer hours occasionally appear in the newspapers. Child labour is also found. In many ways, Engel's description of industrial workers in the England in the nineteenth century can still be compared with that of the workers in the unorganised sector and small scale industries in contemporary mills. Thirteen textile mills in Ahemdabad and eight in other cities have been closed down which made 40,000 workers unemployed compelling them to return to the village or opt for casual work whenever available or just starve (Jani, 1984).

The Textile Labours Association (TLA) is the largest and dominant trade union in Gujarat. It had 1,34,621 members out of the total labour face of 1,50,000 in the textile industry[15] in Ahmedabad in 1981. It has also sponsored its sister organisation known as Laghu Udhyog Kamgar Mahajan, covering chemical, engineering, pharmaceutical manufacturing, brick kiln, industries, etc. in 1961. It had 16,500 members in Ahmedabad. The TLA believes in the philosophy of class harmony rather than class conflict and adopts a conciliatory approach to solve the labour-management disputes. The TLA in Ahmedabad is a craft-based federation of twelve craft unions such as those of weavers, throstles, winders, engineers, mechanics, clerks, and so on. As mentioned earlier, after 1933, the TLA has concentrated more on welfare activities than on agitational activities. The welfare activities include co-operative banks, dispensaries, maternity homes, sewing classes, relief work during calamities, etc. It is "the only union in the country which has been carrying on such extensive welfare and educational work for its members and their families" (Karnik, 1978: 109). Though there are some trade unions led by the Congress and the Bharatiya Janata Party and a few led by non-party leaders, their ideology and functioning are not substantially different from those of the TLA. Hein Streefkerk (1981:755) observes: "For a number of union leaders the promotion of workers' interests was not their chief means of support, for them managing a union is like managing a business, for which they must be on good terms with both the bosses and the workers". There are a few Socialist and Communist trade unions but their influence has been insignificant so far. Though the number of industrial disputes have increased in Gujarat, industrial relations are still more peaceful compared to those in other states. Gujarat ranks lowest among various states of India "in relation to all available indicators of industrial conflict such as the number of workers involved per dispute, the proportion of workers involved per dispute, the proportion of workers involved in dispute to the total employment in industry and the number of mandays lost in industrial production per employee" (Sheth, 1983: 494).

Middle Class

With the growth of industries, public sector and urban centres, the size of the urban middle class engaged in white-collar jobs in public and private sectors, petty business and in small scale industries has increased during the post-independence period. We do not have statistical data to quantify its size, however, it is sufficient to indicate that the workers employed in organised and unorganised sectors have increased from 8.9 lakhs in 1966 to fourteen lakhs in 1982. A large part of the middle class consists of the Bania, the Brahmin and the Patidar castes. Members of the SCs/STs, artisan castes and other backward castes have also joined the middle class, though their proportion is small. The middle class people are more educated than the members of the working class. They are mobile and fired by higher aspirations. They are vocal and sensitive. They played an important part in the freedom movement. They led the Maha Gujarat Movement in 1956-57 demanding a separate linguistic state for Gujaratis. In 1974, the middle class, under the hegemony of students and teachers, launched the movement against price rise, scarcity and corruption. However, under the shrewd guidance of the interest groups and parties, the economic issues were sidetracked and the movement succeeded in ousting the chief minister and dissolving the state assembly. The leaders of the movement however maintained unity among the various castes and communities (Shah, 1977).

But on other occasions, the middle class gets divided on caste and religious lines. The anti-reservation agitations in 1980-81 and 1985 are cases in point. As mentioned above, in terms of caste, the middle class is not homogenous. Spread of education is not even among all the castes, though, relatively speaking, the upper strata of the lower castes have started taking advantages of the educational opportunities. A survey of rural Gujarat shows that the gap in literacy is wide between the upper castes including Patidars and backward castes including Kolis, SCs and STs. Only six per cent of the Patidars and eight per cent of the Brahmins, as against forty-seven per cent of the ST, thirty-five per cent of the Kolis and twenty-seven per cent of the SC families are illiterate, i.e., none of their family members have received even elementary education. Regarding college education, the Bania, the Brahmin and other upper castes excluding the Rajputs are better placed than the other castes.The Patidars, the artisan castes and the SCs are almost at par in college education. At least one person from each of about seven per cent households of these castes has received college education. The rise of higher education among the SCs, who are traditionally considered at the bottom of the caste hierarchy, is conspicuous. Besides several other factors, their rise can be attributed to facilities specially made available to SCs/STs by the government. Because of the rise in education and reservation of jobs in the government sector, the SCs have used the opportunities offered to them. The proportion of SCs/STs in class III positions increased from 4.8 and 4.4 per cent in 1971 to 10.7 and 8.9 per cent respectively in 1978 (Scheduled Castes and Scheduled Tribes Commission Report, 1980). This proportion should have increased further since 1978. That means, there are more than forty thousand clerks/typists from SCs/STs. This obviously meant a curtailment of the opportunities available to the upper and middle castes who had so far monopolised government jobs. Their condition has deteriorated further as a result of rise in unemployment. Between 1971 and 1982, the number of unemployed persons registered in employment exchanges has increased more than three times from 154 thousand in 1970 to 528 thousand in 1982. Among the unemployed persons as many as fifty-nine per cent were educated. The middle class of the upper and middle castes was adversely affected by the rise in the unemployment of the educated people. They thought that they were not able to get jobs because of the reservations for the SCs/STs. However, the presence of SCs/STs as colleagues as well as their relatively quick chance for promotion upset the upper and middle caste employees who were intoxicated with their own superiority and who harbour deep-seated prejudices against the SCs/STs. It should also be mentioned that in 1980, the Government of Gujarat recognised eighty-two caste/community groups as socially and educationally backward class (SEBC), and provided them ten per cent reservations in government jobs.* This has further reduced the size of the cake available to the middle and upper castes. The students belonging to middle and upper classes of the Bania, the Brahmin and the Patidar opposed the reservation policy of the government and launched an agitation in December 1980 against the policy of reservation of seats for SCs/STs and other backward classes in post-graduate studies in medicine. Later on, they demanded abolition of reservation in government jobs as well as admission to professional courses. The agitation continued for three months. Clashes broke out between students from the SCs/STs in general and SCs and upper castes in particular in Ahmedabad, Nadiad, and Vadodara and in some other cities. The riots touched the villages of Kheda, Mehasana, Ahmedabad and Surendranagar districts where SCs have improved their conditions and

* The Government of Gujarat appointed the commission under the chairmanship of Justice A.R. Baxi in 1972 to identify socially and educationally backward castes, races or tribes who deserve special treatment and grants of special concessions similar to those being granted to the SCs and STs. The commission identified eighty-two castes/classes/groups as socially and educationally backward. The commission submitted its report in 1976 when the Congress party was in power. The government of Janata Morcha accepted its recommendations and provided reservations in government jobs and admissions in educational institutions to the eighty-two castes/communities in 1978.

have become more militant than their caste fellows in other parts of the state (Bose, 1981). Huts of the SCs were set on fire in several villages. They were also beaten up. They were excommunicated by the upper and middle caste Hindus in the villages. More than one dozen Harijan youths lost their lives and several hundreds lost their huts and other belongings. The lower castes, covered under the SEBC, did not support the SCs against the upper castes though a few instances are available in which they provided shelter to the affected Harijan families. At the same time, they did not become instruments of the upper and middle castes for attacking the SCs. The government gave certain concessions to the agitated medical students, though the reservations were not abolished. Thus, in this agitation, the middle class was divided into upper castes and backward castes.

Once again the middle class of the upper castes resorted to direct action for more than four months in 1985 when the government raised the quota of reservation for SEBC from ten per cent to twenty-eight per cent in January 1985.* The government employees belonging to upper and middle castes as well as backward castes other than SCs/STs joined the fray demanding abolition of the roster system which provides relatively faster promotion to SC/ST employees. The anti-reservation agitation continued for more than four months. It was confined to urban areas. It took toll of more than two hundred persons and destroyed property worth several million rupees. The state was completely paralysed. Consequently, the government not only withdrew the eighteen per cent rise in the reservation for SEBC but also conceded the demand of the agitationists to review the reservation for the eighty-eight castes/com-

---

* After the introduction of the reservation of SEBC in 1978, members of some of those castes who were not considered by the Baxi Commission as socially and educationally backward castes made a representation to the government that their case may be considered. The Congress government, therefore, appointed a second commission in 1981 "to consider whether there were any other castes/communities/classes". Justice C.V. Rane was its chairman. The chairman rejected caste as a measurement of backwardness. It adopted income and occupation as criteria to determine 'backwardness'. It recommended twenty-two per cent reservations for occupational groups which are considered as backward. The commission submitted its report in 1983. The government rejected the major recommendations of the commission in 1985 on the ground that they were beyond "the terms of reference of commission". At the same time, the government accepted the recommendation of the reservation quota. And in January 1985 the quota was raised.

munitics which were considered as SEBC in 1988.

In both the agitations, the middle class of upper and middle castes had an edge over the middle class of the lower castes, and SCs/STs. The former are bigger in size and more united than the latter. They also get moral support of the rich of their castes. They are also more articulate and enjoy more control over the mass media than the middle class of the backward castes. Moreover, the middle class of backward castes, SCs and STs are alienated from their caste fellows who are poor and do not dream of getting the advantage of the reservations in their life time. Therefore, the poor strata of the backwards, SCs and STs were indifferent to the agitations. Furthermore, the backward castes which follow the path of Sanskritization for upward social mobility, look down upon the SCs/STs. They, therefore, hesitate to make a common cause with the latter. In the beginning, the SCs/STs were quiet because they thought that the agitation was against the SEBC whose reservation percentages were raised by the government. The employees of the SEBC joined the agitation against the roster system as it did not benefit them.

Nothwithstanding the intra-class differences, the Hindu middle classes of different castes unite against the Muslims in times of communal riots. A number of communal riots have increased in Gujarat from thirty-one in 1980 to eighty-four in 1982. The Hindu middle class instigated the Hindu working class against the Muslims in the 1969 riots in Ahmedabad and the 1982 riots in Vadodara (Patel, 1984). The anti-reservation riots of 1985 often turned into communal riots in Ahmedabad, Vadodara and other cities of Gujarat. However, it is very difficult to say at this stage what role the middle class of the SEBC, SCs and STs played in the 1985 communal riots when they faced onslaught of the upper and middle castes.

Caste Organisation

Some of the caste associations categorically declare that they have nothing to do with political matters. Diversity of political affiliations of the members, they fear, would create disharmony in the caste organisation. On the other hand, a latter type of caste associations have come into existence to influence caste members in elections. They direct members to vote for this or that party. Their leaders are politically active and are associated with one or the other political party.

Caste associations, political or otherwise, have come into existence to strengthen caste ties and to inculcate a sense of fraternity among the members. One of the caste journals advises its members: "It is the duty of cach caste member to consider all the members of the caste as brothers and each should help each other. He should be proud of his caste and should have reverence for it."[15] When persons migrate to a city for employment, they feel lost in the new environment. They need some support, both material and psychological, at the time to face the crisis as well as for recreational and social purposes. Such needs lead them to form caste organisations. Some castes form their own organisations to receive benefits from the government on the basis of their "social and educational backwardness". As many as 140 castes submitted memoranda to the Socially and Educationally Backward Class Commission appointed by the Government of Gujarat, showing their backwardness and requesting it to include them in the category of "backward class". The upper strata of these castes took the initiative in forming caste associations by emphasizing caste consciousness and caste unity among the members. For instance, the leader of one such caste appealed to his caste members in the following manner:

> We heartily appeal to all those who been born in this caste, in whose veins the blood of Prajapati flows. You should be proud of yourself and your caste. You should organise Prajapati Mandals in the area where you stay and unite all such organisations at the district level. All should physically, mentally and financially cooperate and assist to build a united strength. Let us forget all differences between the small and the big, the rich and the poor, the good and the bad and social divisions and strengthen ourselves (Pipaliya, 1982: 45).

Of late, most of the caste organisations—those of the upper as well as the lower castes—do not lay emphasis on the principle of purity and pollution. They no longer strive for raising or maintaining the traditional status of their castes in social hierarchy. Some of the lower castes which followed the path of Sanskritization to improve their status, do not give much importance to it. The struggle for higher and lower social status is becoming redundant for many urbanised caste members. At the same time, paradoxically, the caste system, as a unit of social interaction is not rejected. The principles of primordial loyalty and harmony among the members of the castes are emphasized.

In order to sustain the ideology of caste fraternity, caste organisations strive to develop co-operation among the members for their economic development. They undertake welfare programmes concerning educational and economic activities. They run schools and hostels, distribute scholarships, and give loans for higher studies. They conduct vocational training courses, run co-operative societies for caste members in general and women in particular for production and marketing of goods which generate income, provide medical facilities and financial assistance to needy caste members. They compile directories of caste members giving details regarding their occupation and education. These directories have two purposes. One, the caste members of the same profession come to know each other and may cooperate in business. Second, they provide information to the parents prospective brides and bridegrooms. Of course, all caste associations do not carry out these programmes because they do not command enough economic resources. Caste associations of many Bania castes are more prosperous than those of the lower castes. This is because quite a few Banias are engaged in business and donate money to their caste associations. The number of such wealthy persons is small among the low castes.

There is no caste organisation of the Patidars at an all-Gujarat level covering all their sub-subdivisions. Like other castes, they have a number of organisations, both traditional, i.e., caste panchayat, and modern, i.e., caste associations, confined to sub-divisions, regions or marriage circles. It was started by non-traditional caste leaders who were involved in the anti-imperialist movement. They combined social reforms and political activities. One such organisation was the Patidar Yuvak Mandal (PYM) of Surat district. It was founded in 1908. The founder, Kuvarji Mehta, a Congress freedom fighter, felt that social reform activities and caste organisations were the safest way of mobilising support for the freedom movement. The objective of the PYM was "the for spreading education among the Patidars, for social reform, for abolishing harmful customs and traditions in the caste, for mobilising and cultivating public opinion for protecting the interests of the farmers" (Bhatt, 1970: 302). As mentioned earlier, the Patidars often call themselves farmers, and use both words synonymously. The interchangable use of these words take care of social and economic interests of the members, though it has become defunct after independence. During the freedom movement, as mentioned above, most of the Patidars' caste panchayats were dominated by the middle peasant Patidars and they supported the various Gandhian struggles. After independence, a section of the middle and rich peasant Patidars opposed the land reforms introduced by the Congress in the Bombay State. But those middle and rich Patidars who remained in the Congress enjoyed a dominant position in the party till the 1960s. In order to develop their patronage networks they favoured caste members in the distribution of party and government positions, and other benefits, but they did not use caste organisations to support one political party or the other. Those political leaders who tried to use the platform of their caste organisations for issuing appeals to the voters were vehemently opposed by the Patidar associations and it was categorically mentioned that under no circumstances would the organisation participate in politics. Middle and rich Patidar peasants work through the Kehdut Samaj to protect their economic interests. Recently, when they lost their strength both in the state cabinet and state assembly, they felt the need for unity. They felt that they should unite to show their strength. Attempts are being made, though without success, to unite various Patidar caste associations into one unified organisation.

Besides working as a pressure group on such issues, the Sabha began to participate in politics directly from the early fifties. It supported the Congress in the fifties and the Swatantra Party in the sixties. In the 1952 elections, the leaders of the Sabha appealed to the Kshatriyas that it was their *dharma* (duty) to support the Congress Party. In 1962, they asked them to support the Swatantra Party.

During these and the subsequent elections, a number of Kshatriya leaders opposed the Sabha's decision and worked against the Congress in 1952 and against the Swatantra Party in 1962 and 1967. In the course of interaction with political parties during the three decades, the leaders of the Sabha got divided into different political parties. The Sabha lost its political appeal as the organisation of the Kshatriyas. Some erstwhile powerful leaders faced defeat in the predominantly Kshatriya constituencies. The organisation has become almost inactive except for issuing statements in the newspapers. Currently, some of the prominent leaders of the Sabha are with the Congress Party. The Kshatriyas who belonged to the Bharatiya Janata Party (BJP) formed another state-wide organisation called the Gujarat Kshatriya Sangh, and they organised two conferences of the Kshatriyas. The Kolis of Central Gujarat and North Gujarat also formed a new organisation confined to the Bareeyas, the Thakards and the Patanwadiyas. The leaders of these organisations bargain with the political parties for party nominations. Consequently, the Kshatriya's strength in the state assembly increased from eleven per cent in 1960 to eighteen per cent in 1980. It remained more or less the same in the 1985 assembly elections. It should be mentioned that the Kshatriya Sabha openly came out in support of the then chief minister, who was a Kshatriya, during the 1985 anti-reservation agitation.

Thus, along with the class-based organisations, various caste associations covering several sub-castes have come into existence during the last three decades. More often than not, the initiatives for such organisations have come from the upper strata of the castes who are interested in maintaining their hegemony in the socio-economic and poltical fields. They evoke caste sentiments for maintaining solidarity among the members. Most of the caste associations do not directly participate in electoral politics partly because they do not have a large enough membership and partly because their members are divided among various political parties. At the most they appeal to the voters at constituency level. The Gujarat Kshatriya Sabha (GKS), however, directly participates in electoral politics by bargaining with political parties and forming factions within the parties. Other caste associations also tacitly induce members to form factions within class-based organisations and political parties.

Caste, Class and Politics

As a short-cut to power, political parties have evolved a strategy of caste arithmetic, wooing the leaders of the numerically large castes for winning elections. As elsewhere in the country, the party organisation of the Congress had weakened in Gujarat by the late sixties. Party discipline and commitment have been increasingly replaced since the early seventies by individual factional loyalty, command over physical and financial resources and manipulative political skill. The party leaders have now no inhibition in using caste and/or religious setiments. The Congress and other non-Left parties including the BJP, which is considered to be a disciplined and ideologically committed party, increasingly succumb to caste pressures in successive elections. In the 1950s, the Congress party gave more weightage to party commitment and party work than to the candidate's caste in distributing tickets, other things being equal. At that time, the majority of the party members who could lay claim to party commitment and longer political experience than others belonged to upper and middle castes, as they had better chances to get recruited into the political arena than the members of the lower castes. Moreover, the main competitors were small in number and caste differences among them were not striking. Because of their numerical strength, the Patidars began to gain an edge over Brahmins and Banias. The opposition parties also did not penetrate into the lower castes. The majority of their candidates belonged to the upper and middle castes. However, the Swatantra Party changed the politics of caste dimensions in the 1962 elections. Bhailabbhai Patel, the leader of the Swatantra Party had evolved a "grand strategy" known as the Pksha ('P' for Patidar and 'ksha' for Kshatriya)—the alliance between the Kshatriyas and Patidars—to win the elections. As mentioned earlier, the Swatantra Party openly allied itself with the Gujarat Kshatriya Sabha (GKS) and gave party tickets to the Kshatriyas generously. It should be mentioned that the Congress Party was hobnobbing with the GKS since 1952, but did not concede all its demands.

The Congress lost the majority of the assembly seats for the first time in 1962 from Kheda district, the stronghold of the GKS. The party then realised that it could no longer take the support of the Kshatriya masses for granted. Therefore, after 1962, the party became more liberal than ever in offering poltical positions to the Kshatriyas. As the GKS was allied with the Swatantra Party, the Congress recruited the local influential Kshatriyas in the party. It sponsored a parellel Kshatriya organisation of the Koli Kshatriyas at several places, and attacked the GKS at its most vulnerable point, i.e., the cleavage between the Rajputs and the Kolis. As against seven in 1962, fifteen Kshatriyas (Kolis and Rajputs together) for Central and North Gujarat were given the assembly tickets by the Congress Party in the 1967 elections. Two parliamentary seats were also allotted to them. Consequently, the Kshatriyas split between the Congress and the Swatantra Party. However, the Swatantra Party, as mentioned earlier, could not keep the Kshatriya and the Patidar power-seekers united for long. The majority of the Kshatriya leaders left the party in 1971. By that time, the Congress Party also split into the Congress(R) and the Congress(O). As elsewhere in the country, the Congress secured a sweeping majority in the assembly elections of 1972 securing 140 out of 180 seats. Some of the prominent Kshatriya leaders who contested on the Congress(O) tickets were defeated for the first time in their election career in 1972. In fact, the Kshatriya strength in the state assembly was reduced from twenty-nine in 1967 to twenty-four in 1972.

Gujarat witnessed an unprecedented protest movement—Navnirman Andolan—dominated by the urban middle class against the Congress Party in 1974 (Shah, 1977). The popularity of the Congress Party receded in the country. The Congress lost power in Gujarat in the 1975 elections for the first time. The United Front(UF) which was later named as the Janata Party, came into power. In terms of caste, the UF was dominated by the Patidars. The Congress, which already had a support base among the Kshatriyas and the deprived social groups, formed the alliance called KHAM, an alliance between the Kshatriyas (K), the Harijans (H), the Adivasis (A) and the Muslims, and distributed party tickets and positions in the party among the members of these castes in the 1980 elections. It continued to indulge in the rhetoric of "Garibi Hatao" which began in 1971, and declared itself as the real Congress.

The leaders, particularly those who worked among the tribals and Harijans, depicted Mrs. Gandhi as *garib-ni-ma*, i.e., mother of the poor and the deprived social groups. The party conspicuously excluded Patidars from the leadership of the party and the ministry. The number of Kshatriya Congress MLAs increased from eleven per cent in 1967 to twenty-five per cent in 1980, whereas the strength of the upper castes—the Banias, the Brahmins and the Patidars—had been reduced from sixty per cent to twenty-eight per cent during the same period. The then chief minister (1984) was a Kshatriya from Kheda district. And, for the first time, as many as five Kshatriyas against three Patidars occupied positions in the ministry of twenty. None of the Patidars held a cabinet rank. Such discrimination against the Patidars alienated the Patidar political leaders from the Congress Party.

A similar pattern is also emerging at district levels, particularly in the zila panchayats. Of the forty-five members of the district local board in Kheda district, twenty-six per cent were from the Koli-Kshatriya caste in 1969. Their percentage has risen to fifty-four in 1983. However, members of the state assembly and zila panchayats belonging to low castes do not belong to economically poor strata of their castes. For instance, out of thrity-three Kshatriya zila panchayat members, in 1983 in Kheda district, nineteen (57%) owned ten acres of land or more and seven (21%) owned between two and nine acres, three members were professionals (lawyers) and four members did not disclose the amount of land they owned. Though we do not have the data for other districts and the state assembly, we have no reason to believe that Kheda district is an exception. Moreover, the Congress (I) has so far not fully succeeded in transferring political power to the members of the low castes at village level. For instance, in Anand *taluka* of Kheda district, which is a stronghold of the Gujarat Kshatriya Sabha, the Koli-Kshatriyas constitute fifty-five per cent of the population as against thirty-four per cent of the Patidars; the latter hold the position of sarpanchas in thirty-seven per cent of the village panchayats, as against thirty-four per cent offices of sarpanchas held by Kshatriyas, in 1984. It should also be noted here that a few persons belonging to the low castes initially gained political positions in panchayats, they lost ground subsequently. This is due to two reasons. First, the upper castes and classes succeeded in creating splits among the low caste leaders. Second, though the members of the low castes got poltical positions, they remained economically dependent on the higher castes who are also substantial cultivators. A few lower caste leaders who are economically well off do succeed in putting up a tough fight against high caste leaders. They have behind them the numerical strength of their castes, and moreover, they are not economically dependent on the high castes. P.N. Sheth (1976:247) observes: "In this village (Boriavi), the Baraiya sarpanch is a seasoned and articulate leader. In both the panchayat elections under the panchayati raj, he had managed to retain Baraiya majority in the village panchayat. In both the elections, the offices of sarpanch and upa-sarpanch went to the Baraiya and their allies. It may also be noted that the Baraiyas of this village enjoy some economic independence which has made the leader Sarpanch bold enough to challenge the Patidars". Thus, the elite of the low castes who are economically better off compete with high caste elite in the power game successfully.

Table 7

Caste Composition of the MLAs in the Assembly from 1957 to 1985

Caste	*First* 1957-62	*Second* 1962-67	*Third* 1967-72	*Fourth* 1972-75	*Fifth* 1975-80	*Sixth* 1980-85
Brahmin	18	25	20	17	14	20
	(16.35)	(18.38)	(14.08)	(12.32)	(7.73)	(10.9)
Bania	19	16	21	17	26	13
	(17.27)	(11.77)	(14.79)	(12.32)	(14.36)	(9.8)
Patidar	26	37	32	35	49	37
	(23.64)	(27.21)	(22.54)	(25.36)	(27.07)	(20.3)
Kshatriya	13	14	29	24	32	38
(Rajput & Koli)	(11.82)	(10.39)	(20.42)	(17.39)	(17.69)	(20.9)
Muslims	4	9	3	3	5	11
	(3.64)	(6.62)	(2.81)	(2.37)	(2.17)	(6.0)
Sch. Castes	10	11	11	11	14	13
	(9.09)	(8.09)	(7.75)	(7.79)	(7.73)	(7.1)
Sch. Tribes	15	21	22	22	27	29
	(13.64)	(15.44)	(15.44)	(15.94)	(14.92)	(15.9)
Other Backward Castes	5	3	3	9	14	16
	(4.55)	(2.20)	(2.12)	(6.53)	(7.73)	(8.9)
N.A	22	18	26	30	1	—
Total	132	154	168	168	182	182

Note: Figures in brackets indicate percentages.
Source: For the first to fifth assemblies (B.C. Shah, 1982).

The Congress selected as party candidates for the state assembly or zila panchayats mainly amongst these Kshatriya power-seekers who enjoyed a relatively better economic position than the majority of their caste members, enabling them to bear at least a part of election expenses. Ironically, the GKS failed to bring together all the so-called Kshatriyas -

in its fold, but the Congress succeeded to some extent in uniting as a block the Koli MLAs of the party in the assembly against the upper caste members. These different social groups of the Kshatriyas have however not united at the grass root level even for political purposes. Animosity between Rajputs and Kolis in Saurashtra has not been cemented by the politics of caste alliance. The latter are still closer to Patidars as far as economic and political interests are concerned. A Congress MLA of the Koli caste from South Gujarat may support and identify himself (as 'we') with other Koli MLAs of Central Gujarat within the party against other factions, but his followers in the constituency do not share the same sentiment of oneness with the Kolis of other parts of Gujarat.

Such a caste-based strategy of the Congress has created an odd combination of the ex-feudal lords and poor peasants within the party. They acquired political office, thanks to their numerical strength without controlling economic resources which are still controlled by the upper castes and classes—Bania, Brahmin and Patidar.

Discrepancy between political power and dominance has come to the surface in Gujarat. Not only trade and industry, but the co-operative sector which generates wealth and distributes resources are dominated by Patidars, Banias and Brahmins. Though political power has satisfied the ego of the Rajput and Koli Kshatriyas it has not improved their economic condition. In fact, the main public sector undertakings of the state such as Gujarat Fertiliser Corporation, Gujarat Industrial Development Corporation, Gujarat Housing Development Finance Corporation, State Transport Corporation, etc., are headed by members of the upper castes. This has led to frustration. The conflict between the Rajputs and the Patidars in Saurashtra is a glaring example of this contradiction. As the Congress supported the Rajput ex-landlords and rulers in Saurashtra, in the process it alienated the Patidar ex-tenants and now owner-cultivators, and the Kolis, the owner cultivators and labourers. As mentioned earlier, the Congress was responsible for the liquidation of the feudal interests in the 1950s. The Rajputs still suffer from the hangover of the past and consider the present rule with a Kshatriya as the chief minister as an occasion for the re-establishment of their earlier rule over the Patidars. But their economic condition has not improved. In fact, it has deteriorated. On the other hand, the Patidars have significantly improved their condition. The Rajputs are jealous of the economic prosperity of the Patidars. The Rajputs are ministers, MLAs, MPs and also the presidents of zila panchayats but the co-operative oil mills, co-operative milk Societies, etc., are controlled by the Patidars as these require investment and managerial skills. The Patidars, who enjoy dominance in this field, try to control the Rajputs which the latter resist and retalitate by using their political power. Hence, there are furious clashes between the two communities which frequently lead to murders of several persons of either community in broad daylight.

The political elite of some of the low castes like the Kolis or the *adivasis* have an edge over the other as far as numerical strength is concerned. After gaining office they try to strengthen their power base by providing patronage to the members of their castes. But the path is not smooth. The cake of their patronage is small and is confined to government jobs and welfare programmes. Even in the distribution of the government-aided programmes they face several handicaps. They cannot provide government jobs to all their caste fellows because of open competition and shrewd connivance of the upper caste bureaucrats. The administration which is dominated by the upper castes implement welfare programmes half-heartedly. Moreover,the welfare programmes have inherent limitations which hinder the improvement of the economic conditions of the deprived strata in a competitive market economy. And besides this, the political leaders of the low castes are primarily interested in strengthening their own economic interests as well as those of their caste. As most of these leaders belong to middle peasant or urban middle class, they support such policy measures which protect and advance their interests. While doing so, they compete against as well as join hands with the leaders of the upper castes belonging to their own class. We have already mentioned a case of rich and middle *adivasi* peasants who joined hands with Patidars against ceiling and paddy levy. The Kshatriya leaders who hold position of power in the Kheda district panchayat and the state have done very little to improve the economic condition of the small and marginal farmers and landless labourers of their own caste. They could not implement the Minimum Wage Act which has a provision to provide at least subsistence to the landless labourers, and the majority of which belong to the Kshatriya caste. As for the tribals, the tribal elite are interested in seeing a middle or rich cultivator or an educated person from among them as a cabinet minister in the state to get more reservations in white-collar jobs, to organise co-operative banks which can support *adivasi* entrepreneurs to get irrigation facilities, fertilisers, improved seeds, and so on. They make these and other demands in the name of the *adivasis*, but in practice, their concern for the ordinary *adivasi* is not only secondary but also instrumental (Shah, 1973). These elite bank upon caste support to bargain with political parties to get political power and to protect their class interests. If caste comes in the way of their economic and political interests, they ignore or split it.

Concluding Remarks

The merchants and *zamindars* dominated the social life of Gujarat before the establishment of the British rule in the early eighteenth century. Along with them and as an offshoot of their rule, a class of rich peasants and industrialists emerged by the turn of the last century. In course of time, the *zamindars* have either disappeared or turned into rich peasants or industrialists during the post-independence period. Thus, in contemporary Gujarat, the business class (merchants and industrialists) and rich peasants enjoy dominance. They together form the dominant power elite, though they do not hold formal positions of power. During the elections, their political support is divided among the non-Left parties. They financially support MPs and MLAs and also patronise bureaucrats at all levels. No cabinet can afford to antagonise them and also remain in power for a long time. There is competition and rivalry within and between business houses, businessmen, industrialists and rich peasants for protecting one's own individual or group (based on nature and type of business or industry) interests and accumulate larger profit than the rival groups. At the same time, they are relatively well organised in the context of particular business or industry, and are also united as producers (in the case of rich peasants), businessmen and industrialists at the district and the state levels. They close their ranks when their collective interests as perceived by them, are at stake. They often, but not always, play decisive roles in the formulation of policies of the state promoting their interests directly. However, they openly violate and sabotage various laws which affect their interests adversely at the level of implementation.

In terms of caste, the businessmen and rich peasants largely come from among the upper and the middle castes, viz., Banias, Brahmins, Rajputs and Patidars. The latecomers in the economically dominant group are the Patidars who rose to political eminence after the mid-nineteenth century. However, these and other castes are not homogenous. As many as forty-seven per cent of the Rajputs are agricultural or non-agricultural labourers and poor cultivators. On the other hand, fifteen per cent of the various artisan castes and eight per cent of the Kolis are rich cultivators. Economic differentiation on the one hand and competitive market economy and polity on the other have slowly dismantled the caste structure. The principle of pollution and purity on which the caste system is supposed to be based upon has become obsolete. At the same time, the dominant power elite group, and the government employees belonging to relatively higher strata of the lower castes who are is being coopted by the dominant power elite organise caste associations and invoke caste sentiments in order to gain political positions or to maintain their dominance in the political arena. In order to sustain caste sentiments, welfare programmes are sponsored by the well-off strata of respective castes. In return, they seek the support of the poorer sections of their castes in politics to gain power and to maintain status quo. This strategy has worked to an extent, as the class-based organisations of the industrial workers, agricultural labourers and poor cultivators are either non-existent or weak. Very little effort has been made by the state and the elite to develop class consciousness as opposed to caste consciousness. In fact, the dominant socio-political ideology in the state negates the ideology of class consciousness as "dangerous" for the development of society. Nevertheless, the poor and the exploited strata of society are increasingly becoming conscious of their economic interests. And they have often undermined directives issued by the dominant strata of their respective castes, and have overlooked caste sentiments when their economic interests have been threatened. They protest and revolt against exploitation and injustice. More often than not their agitations are sporadic and spontaneous, though occasionally they are widespread and organised. These agitations are crushed by the state machinery and dominant power elite, and their leaders are coopted into the power structure. Welfare programmes are launched to pacify simmering dissatisfaction amongst the exploited masses. Thus, the social situation in Gujarat is not quite clear. Caste, as a social organisation based on the principles of pollution and purity is crumbling, though not disappearing. At the same time caste sentiments prevail in the intra-class conflicts among the poor farmers, agricultural labourers and industrial workers as well as among rich peasants and business people. On the other hand, different classes are being formed, cutting across caste boundaries. But class consciousness as such is yet to develop. This situation works in favour of the dominant strata in perpetuating their hold over the society.

References

Ahmedabad: Gazetteer of the Bombay Presidency, Vol. IV, Bombay Government Central Press, 1879.

Amin, R.K., "Rural Renaissance And Sri Bhailalbhai", *Dr. Bhailalbhai Patel 75th Birth Sovenieur*, Vallabh Vidyanagar, Charotar Vidya Mandal, 1963.

Bates, Crispin, The Nature of Social Change in Rural Gujarat: The Kheda District 1818-1918, *Modern Asian Studies*, Vol. 15, No. 4, October, 1981.

Bhalani, Asmita, *Karma Yogi Bhaikaka* (Gujarati), Vallabh Vidyanagar, Charottar Gramodyog Sahakari Mandali Ltd, 1966.

Bhatt, Anil, "Caste and Political Mobilisation in Gujarat District" in *Caste in Indian Politics* (ed), Rajni Kothari, Delhi, Orient Longman, 1970.

Bose, Pradip Kumar, "Social Mobility and Caste Violence: A Study of the Gujarat Riots" in *Caste, Caste Conflict and Reservations*, Centre for Social Studies, Delhi, Ajanta Publications, 1985.

Breman, Jan, "Mobilisation of Landless Labourers: Halpatis of South Gujarat", *Economic & Political Weekly*, Vol. 9, No. 6-8, Feb., 1974.

Choksey, R.D., *Economic Life in the Bombay, Gujarat 1800-1939*, Bombay, Asia Publishing House, 1958.

Dandekar, V.M., Next Step on the Socialist Path, *Economic & Political Weekly*, Vol. 7, August, 1972.

Das Gupta, Ashin, *Indian Merchants and the Decline of Surat* Wiesbadon, Franz Steiner Vering, 1975.

Desai, I.P., "Anti-Reservation Agitation and Structure of Gujarat Society", *Caste, Caste Conflict and Reservations*, Centre for Social Studies, Delhi, Ajanta Publications, 1985.

Desai, M.B., *Tenancy Abolition and the Emerging Pattern in Gujarat*, Bombay, MS University, 1971.

Desai, Mahadev H., *A Righteous Struggle*, Ahemdabad, Navajivan Publishing House, 1951; Dobbin Christine, *Urban Leadership in Western India*, London, Oxford University Press, 1972.

Economic Intelligence Service, Basic Statistics Relating to the Indian Economy, Vol. 2, States, Bombay, Centre for Monitoring Indian Economy, 1983.

Frdman, Howard, *Political Attitudes of Indian Industry: A Case Study of the Baroda Business Elite*, London, University of London, 1971.

Forbes Alexander K, Ras Mala: *Hindu Annals of Western India*, New Delhi, A-Heritage Publishers, 1973 (first published in 1878).

The First Schedule of the 1950 Indian Constitution classified the units of the Indian Union into four categories viz., A, B, C and D. Under part A were included the former British Indian provinces; part B included bigger princely state or the union of such states; part C and D were centrally administered states, through the President.

The Moghal administration classified villages into two categories: (1) *rasti* (peaceful or loyal) and (2) *Mewasi* (turbulent). The rulers of the latter, mainly Rajputs or Kolis asserted their independence from any higher authority. They used to pay revenue only under force.

"Under the Marathas (1777-1817) the silk, taxed when raw, taxed as it passed through each process, and again taxed when ready for sale was so weighted... that its manufacture ceased to pay and almost died out". Ahmedabad *Gazetteer, Op. Cit.*, p. 135.

Panch is an old institution, which was known as *Mahajans* or guild. The main functions of the Panch was to maintain harmoney among the various business groups.

'Minimum Wage on Paper', *The Hindu* September 25, 1984.

Ibid.

Times of India, (Ahmedabad), November 13, 1973.

Gujarat Mitra (daily, Surat), November 25, 1973.

Khedut Vani (Fortnightly, Bardoli), Vol. I, No. 15, January 1, 1974.

See caste journal for example *Kadava Patidar Parivar*, published from Rajkot.

Some of the articles published in various caste journals such as *Dharati, Jagat*, *Kadava Patidar Parivar* express such views.

Jagtat, Vol. 3, (Posh Savant 1997), 1953.

Gandhi M.K., *Collected Works*, Vol XIV, Delhi, The Publication Division, 1965.

Gillion Kenneth L, *Ahmedabad: A Study in Indian Urban History*, Ahmedabd, The New Order Book Company, 1968.

Gopal Surendra, *Commerce and Crafts in Gujarat: 16th and 17th Century*, New Delhi, People's Publishing House, 1975.

Hardiman David, *Peasant Nationalists of Gujarat*, Delhi, Oxford University Press, 1981.

Jani Manishi, *Bekar Milmajdoor, Behal Milmajdoor*, (Gujarati) Ahmedabad, SETS, 1984.

Karnik VB, *Trade Union Movement and Industrial Relations*, Bombay, Allied Publishers, 1978.

Kachanek Stanley A, *Business and Politics in India*, Berkeley University of California Press, 1974,

Kothari Rajni and Tarun Sheth, Extent and limits of Community Voting: The Case of Baroda East in *Party Systems and Elecltion Studies*, in Kothari and other, Delhi, Allied Publishers, 1967.

Kothari Rajni and Ghanshyam Shah, Caste Orientation of Political Factions, in Party System and Election Studies, Rajni Kothari and others, Delhi, Allied Publishers, 1967

Mehta Makrand, *The Ahmedabad Cotton Textile Industry*, Ahmedabad New Order Book Co, 1983

Mishra R.R., *Effects of Land Reforms in Saurasthra*, Bombay Vora & Co, 1961.

Mishra S.C., *The Rise of Muslim Power in Gujarat*, Bombay, Asia Publishing House, 1963,

Parekh Jayshree, *Vepar and Rajkarn* (Gujarati), (Ph.D. Thesis).

Parekh Hiralal T, *Arvachin Gujaratnu Rekha Darshan* (Gujarati) Ahmedabad, Gujarat Vidhan Sabha, 1967.

Parikh R.D., *The Press and Society*, Bombay, Popular Prakashan; '65; Patel Sujata, the *Capitalist Class and Labour Politics: A Case the Ahmedabad Millowners' Association 1918-1938*, (Ph.D. Thesis)New Delhi, Centre for Historical Studies, Jawaharlal Nehru University, 1983.

Patel Priyavadan, *Impact of Irrigation on Power Relation ships in a village: A Case of Tundi* (Mimeo), Surat; Centre for Social Studies, 1982.

Patel Priyavadan, *Communal Plots in Baroda* (Mimeo), Surat, Centre for Social Studies, 1984.

Pathak D.N., M.G. Parekh, K.D. Desai and P.N. Sheth, *Dimensions of Political Behaviour in Gujarat* (mimeo), Ahmedabad, Gujarat University.

Pavlov V.I., *Historical Premises for India's Transition to Capitalism, Mosco, "Nakka" Publishing House, 1978.*

Pearson M.N., *Merchants and Rulers in Gujarat*, Delhi, Munshiram Manoharlal, 1970.

Pipaliya L.P. (ed), *Gujaratna Prajapatio: Ek Abhyas* (Gujarati), Boroda, Jaldhar Society, 1982.

Pocock David, *Kanbi and Paridar*, London, Oxford University Press, 1972.

Rabitoy Neil, System V! Expediency: The Reality of Land Revenue Administration In the Bombay, Presidency 1812-1820, Modern Asian Studies, Vol. 9, No.4, 1975.

Shah AM, Political System in Eighteenth Century Gujarat, *Enquiry*, Vol. 1, Spring, 1964.

Division and Hierarchy: An Overview of Caste in Gujarat, *Contributions to Indian Sociology*, (NS) Vol 16, No 1, Jan- June, 1982.

Shah BC, Evolution of Gujarat Vidhan Sabha, Journal of Political Studies, Vol XV, No.2 September, 1982.

Shah Ghanshyam, Traditional Society and Political Mobilization: The Experience of Bardoli Satyagraha (1920-1922), *Contributions to Indian Sociology* (NS) No. __, 1974; Shah Ghanshyam, *Caste Association and Political Processes in Gujarat*, Bombay, Popular Prakashan, 1975.

Shah Ghanshyam, *Protest Movements in Two Indian States*, Delhi, Ajanta Publications, 1977. (and Chaturvedi HR), *Gandhian Approach to Rural Development*, Delhi Ajanta Publications, 1985; (and Chaturvedi HR) Caste in Contemporary India, Caste, Conflict and Reservations, Centre for Social Studies, Delhi Ajanta Publications, 1985.

Shah Narottam, *Some Facets of Industrial Development of Gujarat*, Bombay, Centre for Monitoring Indian Economy, 1979.

Sharma Usha, Performance and Prospects of Gujarat Agriculture, *Gujarat Economy: Problems and Prospects* (ed), D.T. Lakdawala, Ahemedabad, Sardar Patel Institute of Economic and Social Research, 1983.

Sheth N.R., *The Social Framework of An Indian Factory*, Manchestor, Manchestor University press, 1968; Sheth NR,"Industrial Relations in Gujarat" (ed) D.T. Lakdawala, *Gujarat Economy: Problems and Prospects*, Ahmedabad, Sardar Patel Institute of Economic and Social Research, 1983.

Sheth Pravin, *Patterns of Political Behaviour in Gujarat*, Ahmedabad, Sahitya Mudranalaya, 1976.

Spodek Howard, The 'Manchesterisation' of Ahmedabad; Economic Weekly, March 13, 1965.

Urban-Rural Integration in Regional Development, Chicago, The University of Chicago, 1976.

Steed Gitel Notes To An Approach to A Study of Personality Formation In a Hindu Village in Gujarat, *American Anthropologist*, Vol. 57, No. 3, June 1955.

Streefkerk Hein, Too Little to Live On, Too Much to Die on: Employment in Small Scale Industries in Rural Gujarat, *Economic and Political Weekly*, Vol. 14, No 15-17, April 11,18 and 25, 1981.

Thorner Daniel, *The Agrarian Prospect in India*, Delhi, Oxford University Press, 1956,

Van der Veen Kleas W, *I give these my daughter*, Aseen Van Gorcum Comp, NV, 1972.

Yagnik Achyut, Caste Violence in Gujarat, *Economic and Political Weekly*, March 28, 1981.

Sharma Usha, Performance and Prospects of Gujarat Agriculture, *Gujarat Economy: Problems and Prospects* (ed), D.T. Lakdawala, Ahmedabad, Sardar Patel Institute of Economic and Social Research, 1983.

Sheth N.R., *The Social Framework of An Indian Factory*, Manchester, Manchester University press, 1968. Sheth NR "Industrial Relations in Gujarat" (ed) D.T. Lakdawala, *Gujarat Economy: Problems and Prospects*, Ahmedabad, Sardar Patel Institute of Economic and Social Research, 1983.

Sheth Pravin, *Patterns of Political Behaviour in Gujarat*, Ahmedabad, Sahitya Mudranalaya, 1976.

Spodek Howard, The 'Manchesterisation' of Ahmedabad, Economic Weekly, March 13, 1965.

Urban-Rural Integration in Regional Development, Chicago, The University of Chicago, 1976.

Steed Gitel Notes To An Approach to A Study of Personality Formation In a Hindu Village in Gujarat, American Anthropologist, Vol 57, No. 3, June 1955.

Streefkerk Hein, Too Little to Live On, Too Much to Die on, Employment in Small Scale Industries in Rural Gujarat, *Economic and Political Weekly*, Vol 16, No 15-17, April 11,18 and 25, 1981.

Thorner Daniel, *The Agrarian Prospect in India*, Delhi, Oxford University Press, 1956.

Van der Veen Klaas W., *I give thee my daughter*, Assen, Van Gorcum Comp. NV, 1972.

Yagnik Achyut, Caste Violence in Gujarat, *Economic and Political Weekly*, March 28, 1981.

11

Caste and Class in Maharashtra

Sharad Patil

The debate on caste and class has made the greatest advance in Maharashtra because the anti-caste *dalit* movement is strongest in Maharashtra, whereas the Left movement is comparatively weak. That is why the caste conflict on "riddles of Rama and Krishna" could develop into a debate on Indology. It was due to the inability of Marxist scholars and traditional Communist parties to give a satisfactory Marxist interpretation of Rama and Krishna that the debate remained circumscribed to the negative extremes of the Hindu fundamentalist Shiv Sena and the neo-Buddhist Ambedkarites. Y.D. Phadke, a Left historian, and Rupa Kulkarni, a militant feminist Sanskritist, merely upheld and substantiated the ethical and unhistorical evaluation of Rama and Krishna made by Ambedkar. Though the unprecedented upheavals of the *dalits* have forced the Maharashtra government to retain the appendix to Volume IV of Dr. Babasaheb Ambedkar's *Writings and Speeches*, nonetheless, the gulf between caste Hindus and *dalits* has widened further.

Though the rest of the country too is undergoing similar religious or caste-community convulsions to some extent, every cataclysm in Maharashtra is forcing the problem of caste and class to a greater forefront.

Caste in Pre-British Period

With the dissolution of guilds (*pugasreni*) in the third century in Northern India and in the sixth century in Southern India, the occupation undertaken by guilds on behalf of a cluster of castes became caste occupations. Cosmopolitan money and mercantile capital became caste capital and the craftsmen's castes became part of the *jajmani* or *balutedari* system. By Al-Beruni's time (tenth century A.D.), most of the productive castes of craftsmen had been pushed out of towns and villages and were declared as untouchables. The hardening of the caste system and the resultant decadence of the Indian feudal society based upon it, led to India's subjugation first at the hands of Arabs and then the Afghans and the Turks.[1]

The hardening of the caste system gave rise to a passive anti-caste movement led by the Mahanubhawa saint, Cakradhar, in Maharashtra who was beheaded by the last Yadav king Ramdev Rai Yadava in 1196 A.D. on the instigation of his Brahmin prime minister Hemadri.[2] He was a famous *Dharamsastri* who prescribed in his *Caturvargacintamani* that the devout should perform two thousand *vratas* in the 365 days of the year. It is said that he betrayed the fort of Devagiri to Alauddin.

The Bhakti movement which started with Janeswar (whose family was declared an out-caste by the Brahma-Sabha of Paithan) after Cakradhar who was, according to V.K. Rajwade, a Brahminic counter revolutionary against the revolutionary anti-caste religions of the Buddhists and the Jainas.[3] Saints from practically every caste in Maharashtra, even from the lowliest untouchable castes like Mahar, came forward to spread the Bhagavat Bhakti religion among the Sudra and Ati-Sudra masses. But the anti-caste discontent voiced in their poetry by all these saints remained within the Brahminical framework and did not go beyond it as did Cakradhar's.

But it should be noted that all of them, including Cakradhar, spoke out against the caste system to a lesser or greater extent and not against any class system. Had any such system existed, they would have surely spoken against it. I have proved that in the pre-British Indian society, there were no, and could not be, any classes. No ideologue or historian has been able to contradict it.

The *Ajna-patra*, written by one of Shivaji's minister Ramachandra Nilakanth, lays down that every caste should live by its hereditary occupation (*vritti*) and nobody should change his calling.[4] During the Peshva period, the rigidity of the caste system was carried to its extreme and those who changed their occupations and resorted to inter-caste marriages were punished severely.[5]

Caste and Class in the Colonial Period

Though the British imperial rule introduced the IPC which made all equal before the law, the *Dharmasastra* continued to regulate the religious and social life of the Hindus. The new educational policy of the imperial regime (1854) threw the doors of education open to all, but the non-Brahmin castes and communities continued to be denied education by the high caste teachers and bureaucrats staffing all educational institutions and the department of education.[6] Gopalrao Deshmukh alias Loka-hitavadi, a Brahmin social reformer of the last century, has directed his criticism also at this aspect of Brahminical oppression in his *Sata-patra*.[7] That is why Jotiba Phule had to declare that non-Brahmin boys would not receive education unless they are taught by teachers of their own castes.[8]

King Sahu of the Kolhapur State was the first in India to provide, in 1902, reservation in the state services for the non-Brahmins. Although he reserved only fifty per cent of the jobs for the non-Brahmins and left the rest for the high castes, yet the Brahmins in Maharashtra rose up in arms against it under the leadership of B.G. Tilak.[9]

Phule, after founding the Satyashodhak Samaj in 1873, trained and provided non-Brahmins in order to do away with the traditional customs of employing Brahmin priests. The Brahmin priests then resorted to the courts. A Brahmin priest called Vishvanath Abaji filed a suit in 1878 in the court of M.G. Ranade, the famous social reformer. Ranade gave his decision in favour of the Brahmin priest and ruled that only Brahmin priests were entitled to perform all religious rites.[10]

Thus, the highest caste stubbornly opposed any attempt to sever the inseparable unity of caste and occupation. The policy of the British rulers since the revolt of 1857 of non-interference in any Indian religion was helpful to the caste establishment.

Table 1

Caste and Offices of Power

Mamlatdars	***Deccan 1921***	***Deputy Collectors***	***Presidency***
Brahmins	58	Brahmins	33
Parsis	1	Parsis	5
Kshatriyas	1	Kayasthas	1
Christians	5	Christians	7
Muslims	3	Prabhus	5
Vidur	1	Banias	1
Marathas	2	Muslims	8
Salis	1	Lingayats	4
Unidentified	20		

Ranade had declared (in 1887) in his Essays on Indian Economics that according to the law of providence the old set of feudal ruling castes, i.e., the Brahmins and the military castes were destined to be displaced by the new set of the Brahmin and Bania castes.[11]

W.W. Hunter observed in *A Study in Indian Administration* (1885-1890) that Brahmins were the chief native administrators in Maharashtra. This fact had scarcely changed till 1920.[12] The military and the cultivating castes were far behind in the race in 1920-21, even though the non-Brahmin movement was already in ascendance.[13]

The schools which fed the bureaucracy with recruits had castewise students as follows in 1922:[14]

Table 2

Caste and Education

District	Brahmins		Marathas (and allied castes)	
	Numbers	Percentage	Numbers	Percentage
Poona	3688	60.7	695	11.4
Ahmednagar	527	33.4	127	16.1
Satara	1105	67.8	152	10.2
Sholapur	702	56.1	105	8.4
East Khandesh	451	57.9	65	8.4
Bombay	2544	19.3	880	6.8
Nasik	760	50.7	145	9.7
Kolaba	554	56.0	47	7.5
Ratnagiri	1177	57.6	288	14.2

Literacy among the cultivating castes was the lowest.[15] Ambedkar had warned in 1936 that the caste system hampers, stagnates, and distorts industrial development.[16] D.R. Gadgil notes that due to the caste system, craftsmen could not rise to the position of a general merchant or trader as in the west.[17] According to him, "the history of the rise and development of modern business becomes, to a large extent, the history of the activities of members of certain groups."[18] By groups he means religious and caste groups. That is why he is not prepared to call even the modern Indian capitalists a class, but prefers to call them a 'community'.

As a result, the religious groups in the Indian capitalist community were not forward-looking like their western counterparts, and thus being essentially revivalists they were anti-materialists. Tilak made Vedanta the official philosophy of the Indian National Congress. Gandhiji said in 1927, "Brahminism I adore. I have defended Varnashram Dharma."[19]

The enactment of the IPC, introduction of education to all and support to social reformers by the British government were seen as basically anti-caste measures and policies by the high castes as well as by the

Sudra social reformers, while the Indian National Congress was seen by the latter reformers as anti-peasant and casteist. The Samajik Parishad, led by Ranade and Gokhale, had already been driven out of the Indian National Congress by the Tilakites. Hence, the non-Brahmin movement of the Sudra peasantry and the Ambedkar-led movement of the Ati-Sudras had to search out a separate path in which they were compelled to take the support of the British government. Hence, the anti-caste movements led by Phule and Ambedkar were maligned as loyalist and communal. Nalini Pandit, though an independent Marxist, observes in her review of Gail Omvedt's book on the non-Brahmin movement in Maharashtra that all non-class struggles are communal.[20]

My book *Dasa-Sudra Slavery* (Parts I and II) shows that Indian society upto the time of Buddha was constituted by *varnas*, and with the period of Buddha it came to be constituted by *jatis*. It is the British imperial capitalist rule that brought about the new classes of capitalists and industrial workers, and it superimposed on rural castes the new classes of landlords and tenants by the enactment of permanent settlement. Even then the new class of industrial workers was recruited exclusively from the non-Brahmin castes and communities, manual work being forbidden to the upper castes by the *Dharmasastra*. N.M. Lokhande founded the first working class organisation of the Bombay mill-hands in 1884. Lokhande, a colleague of Phule, organised the workers as a part of the anti-caste non-Brahmin movement. Though the factories were British owned, their management being in the hands of the upper castes, he visualised the struggle as caste struggle. The working class movement of Bombay remained in the hands of non-Brahmins up to the end of the First World War. With the intensification of the working class struggles due to the post-war world economic crisis, the movement crossed the limits of caste struggle and went over to high caste trade unionists like S.M. Joshi and became a part of the anti-imperalist national movement. Why couldn't the trade unionists intervene in the initial period itself is a million dollar question.[21]

The first reason is that the understanding of caste and class was too confused in the initial period. The economist Ranade seems to have used the two terms interchangeably. The first attempt at a clear definition was made by S.V. Ketkar by stating in 1901 that "Classes are converted into castes by becoming endogamous."[22] Its implication was made explicit by Amebdkar in 1916 by declaring that "*a caste is an enclosed class.*"[23] These definitions meant that class is anterior to caste and caste is but a distorted form class assumed only in India. The theory of the inevitable emergence of classes in course of development of division of labour originated with Plato who said in his *Republic* that in the process of social growth the division of labour leads to the division of classes."[24] Marx's class methodology of historical materialism universalised the theory. That Ambedkar was influenced by it becomes clearly apparent in his above quoted thesis on caste.

The second reason is that the ideas of class struggle started percolating into the Indian working class movement after the Russian revolution. At a workers' meeting in Bombay in 1918 the ideal of a worker's state was held high by one and all.[25]

As pointed out above, casteism, caste riots and anti-caste struggles are invariably equated. Can temple-entry *satyagrahas* of Guruvayur in Kerala and Kala Rama in Maharashtra and the *satyagraha* for drinking the water of the Mahad tank be called casteist or communal activities? Ambedkar did not agree to the pre-condition put forward by some non-Brahmin leaders for participating in the Parvati *satyagraha* at Pune that Brahmins should be excluded from it. Ambedkar's conception of the organisational form that anti-caste struggle should take was supra-caste, rather class based. This is how Ambedkar developed Phule's teachings of caste struggle* in the twentieth century.

Caste and Class in the Post-Independence Period

With the attainment of independence, the nationalist part of the Indian democratic revolution was consummated and the democratic part remained to be fulfilled. The Left interpreted the unfulfilled task to be of accomplishing a western type of democratic revolution, i.e., land reform. According to Daniel Thorner, in the initial part of the Nehru period, seventy per cent of the land was held by the landlords who constituted ten to fifteen per cent of the rural population. The Congress government abolished statutory landlordism and enacted ceiling laws. However, insufficient they may be, it cannot be denied that landlord and tenant are no more the predominant units in relations of production in rural India. Nevertheless, according to Utsa Patnaik, fifty-three per cent of the land is still held by one-eighty of the top landholding families.[26] However, these top landholders are termed as capitalist landlords by the CPI(M) in order to prove that they are semi-feudal. The traditional Communist parties are still not prepared to concede that these top landholders are semi-feudal for the reason that they belong to the top and advanced

* Phule had declared that since the defeat of the non-Aryan Bali by the Aryan Vaman, the history of Indian has been a history of caste struggles.

landholding castes and hence are upholders of the caste system which was the basic characteristic of Indian feudalism. This unique charateristic of Indian feudalism itself is denied by B.T. Ranadive, a leader of the CPI(M), by asserting that caste belongs to the superstructure of the Indian feudal society.[27] He does not care to explain as to how this mental image arose without caste being a reflection of the outer material social reality, which violates the epistemological theory of reflection espoused by Marxist philosophy.

The Nehru government was shrewd enough to assign the task of drawing up the constitution of the Indian Republic to a *dalit*, Dr. B.R. Ambedkar, in order to conjure up the illusion that it was a bourgeois democratic constitution, having the sanction of all sections of the Indian people. In the bargain, Ambedkar made it an anti-caste one by not only making untouchability a crime, but also by incorporating the provisions of reservation for the SCs, STs and other backward communities (OBCs). The unity of these three sections of the Indian people was his strategy for abolishing the caste system. But frustration awaited him. He was compelled to withdraw the Hindu Code Bill with which he wanted to give bourgeois gender equality to Indian women, who were the the greatest victims of the caste system. With his Ati-Sudra followers he embraced the Buddhist religion in order to lead them out of the land of the ubiquitous caste system, like Moses.

It was prophesied by Marx in 1853 that "modern industry will dissolve the hereditary divisions of labour, upon which rest the Indian castes, those decisive impediments to Indian progress and Indian power."[28]

The Backward Class Commissions have gone into the task of granting reservations to the OBCs, and the second one headed by B.P. Mandal concluded in 1980 that caste disparity persists even in the Indian Administrative Services.[29]

Table 3

Government Jobs for the SCs, STs and OBCs

Category of Employees	*Total No. of Employees*	*Percentage of SC/ST*	*Percentage of OBCs*
Class I	1,74,043	5.68	4.69
Class II	9,12,786	18.18	10.63
Class II & IV	4,84,646	24.40	24.40
All Classes	15,71,475	18.71	12.55

The inequitous caste system still encompasses 74.5 per cent of the Indian people in spite of all the changes brought about in it by the forty-three years of the capitalist development of the post-independence period. Let us now see the situation in Maharashtra, industrially the most advanced state in India. The SCs and STs constitute six per cent and 5.86 per cent, respectively, of the total population of Maharashtra.[30] Literacy in Maharashtra in 1971 was 39.18 per cent, while among the SCs and STs it was 25.27 per cent and 11.74 per cent, respectively. Their reservation quota in the state employment is thirteen per cent and seven per cent, respectively. Their proportion in the state services is as follows[31] (figures for the OBC not available):

Table 4

Comparative Data Regarding Employment of SCs and STs in Government Services

Category of Employees	*SC (%)*		*ST (%)*
	1960	*1978*	*1978*
Class I	1.1	4.6	1.1
Class II	1.7	5.9	1.4
Class III	6.3	12.7	3.6
Class IV	15.2	24.7	7.0

Despite reservation, the live register of the employment exchange showed in 1977 that out of 9,22,519 people the total unemployed 1,86,893 belonged to the SC and ST communities.

The ruling bureaucracy belongs to the class I and II. Though the figures for the OBCs are not available, they cannot diverge very widely from the all-India figures. Hence, we can say that Maharashtra, like India, is administered by a high caste bureaucracy.

What about the capitalist community of India? Has it become a homogenous class during this whole period of post-independence capitalist development? From what Amalendu Guha says we can conclude that Indian capitalists are still a community.

According to a crude analysis made in 1967-68 by Ajit Ray, only thirty-three per cent of the total assets of India's seventy-five top monopoly houses, listed by the Monopoly Inquiry Commission, was accounted for by the Hindustani houses (Marwari houses 25% and non-Marwari Hindustani houses 8%). The Gujarati houses had a larger share, as much as thirty-seven per cent of the total assets, though the nationality they represent accounted for less than five per cent of India's population. Another 13.5 per cent of the assets continued to be controlled by foreign houses (all British, except one).

The Gujaratis, together with the Marwaris, are in a somewhat dominant position in the economy through the monopoly business houses they control. Dominance, economic, political and cultural, is largely exercised by higher castes and they transgress regional and national frontiers.[32]

I was tied to the class methodology of historical materialism when I wrote the paper "Dialectics of Caste and Class Conflicts"[33] in 1977, which was destined to prove a turning point in the Indian Communist movement. I had observed in it that though economic differentiation had taken place in the ruling and peasant castes in pre-colonial India, it was not able to split them into classes. In the present-day Indian society, though class formation has taken place in all castes and communities, barring the most backward tribes, it has not been able to split them up into classes. Thus, in Indian society caste and class are still in an inseparable unity of opposites.

What has happened to the "six characteristics" of caste during the whole post-independence capitalist development? The first characteristic refers to heredity, to *jati* itself meaning by birth, and it persists. "Every Indian is born and dies in his caste, he cannot change this caste." The second characteristic of endogamy also refuses to budge inter-caste marriages being comparatively far and few. The third characteristic of caste commensality, though not easily visible in urban areas, is still strong in rural areas. The fourth characteristic of hierarchy and caste localities, though weakened in urban areas, is still strong in rural areas. The SCs and STs still live, without exception, outside villages. The fifth characteristic of caste council, instead of remaining local, has become state-wide in response to the new needs of educational, social, cultural and economic reforms and political power in a semi-bourgeois democratic set-up. Castes have become vote-banks. Caste councils, in their pristine form, still exist in backward castes and tribes.[34] The sixth and the last characteristic of hereditary occupation is no longer that much ascriptive, but stays mainly because of the stagnancy of the crisis-ridden Indian society. A barber in a saloon, though a wage worker, still hails invariably from the barber caste, and his employer, may he be a petty or capitalist saloon owner also hails generally from the same caste. The forces and means of production are capitalistic, while the relations of production remain that of caste. Caste and occupation are still in an inseparable unity of opposites, though on its last legs, to which has been added another unity of opposites since the colonial period that of caste and class.

Of these two sets of the unity of opposites, the new one is pivotal.

The moribund old contradiction cannot be dissolved without the intensification of the new contradiction. Hence, caste and class struggles should be intensified in such a co-ordinated way that class will negate caste in order to negate itself. This is the dialectics of the movement of the total social transformation for the Indian society.

Notes

1. Mohammad Habib, *Politics and Society during the Early Medieval Period*, 1974, pp. 62-64.
2. V.H. Kolte, *Shri Cakradhar Caritra* (Marathi), 1952, pp. 280-318.
3. V.K, Rajwade, *Introduction* (in Marathi) *to Radha-Madhav-*, Vilas-Campuh, Saka 1894, pp. 148-156.
4. P.N. Joshi (ed), *Ajnapatra* (Marathi), 1960, pp. 28-30.
5. P.A. Gavli, Peshvekalin Guamgiri va Aspirisyata (Marathi), 1987, pp. 80-81, *Pesvekain Samaj va Jatiy Sangharsh* (Marathi), 1982, pp. 114, 118.
6. G.B.Sardar, Mahatma Phuley: *Vyaktitva ani Vicar* (Marathi), 1981, pp. 12-14.
7. Dhananjay Keer, Rajarshi Shahu Chatrapati (Marathi) 1981, pp.42-43.
8. G.B. Sardar, op. cit., pp 200-201.
9. Dhanajay Keer, op. cit., pp 122-127.
10. Ibid., p. 244.
11. M.G. Ranade, *Essays on Indian Economics*, 1898, pp. 314-315.
12. Gail Omvedt, *Cultural Revolt in a colonial society, The Non-Brahman Movement in Western India*: 1873 to 1930, 1976, p. 79.
13. Ibid.
14. Ibid., p. 78.
15. Ibid., p. 77
16. Dr. Babasaheb Ambedkar, Writings and Speeches, Vol. I, 1979, pp. 47-48.
17. D.R. Gadgil, Origins of the *Modern Indian Business Class*, 1959, p.22.
18. Ibid., p. 16
19. Sujata Patel, Construction and Reconstruction of Woman in Gandhi, *Economic and Political weekly*, 20/2/88.
20. Nalini Pandit, *Economic and Political Weekly*, 5/6/76.
21. R.P Dutt, *India Today*, 1947, pp, 330-331.
22. S.V. Ketkar, The History of Caste in India, Vol. 1, 1901, p. 28.
23. Dr. Babasaheb Ambedkar, op. cit., p. 15. Society and Culture in Northen India in the Text Century, 1973.
24. B.N.S. Yadav, p.l 76; *Plato, Republic*, Jowet's 's trans. Vol. I.
25. Dhananjay Keer, op. cit. pp. 362-366.

26. Utsa Patnaik, *Economic and Political weekly*, 3/5/86.
27. B.T. Ranadive, Caste, Class and Property Relations, *Economic and Political Weekly*, February 1977, p. 343.
28. R.P. Dutt, op. cit., p. 244.
29. Report of the Backward Classes Commission, 1980, p. 42.
30. Rakhiv Jaga Asavyat Ka?, Magova Prakaswan (Marathi), 1981, pp. 36-39.
31. Ibid., p. 41,
32. Amalendu Guha, The Indian National Question, A Conceptual Framework, *Economic and Political Weekly*, 31/7/82.
33. Sharad Patil, Dialectics of Caste and Class Conflict, *Economic and Political Weekly*, February 1979, p. 291.
34. Lakshman Mane, Upara, (Marathi autobiography).

12

Class, Caste and Ideology in Maharashtra

Rajendra Vora and Suhas Palshikar

The decade of 1980 has been marked by two sets of frequent confrontations: one between the majority Hindu community and the Muslims and the other between the upper caste Hindus (*savarnas*) and the scheduled castes and the scheduled tribes (*dalits*). In fact, this trend has set in right since the riots over renaming the Marathwada University occurred. It attracts our attention to the growing Hindu militancy and the changing character of Hindu identity in the state. The following instances testify to this fact.

Riots took place between the *savarna* Hindus and *dalits* over the issue of renaming the Marathwada University (1978). Tribals were attacked by caste Hindus in the Dhule district (1983, 1984). Not only did traditional trouble spots such as Malegaon (1983) and Bhiwandi (1984) flare up due to communal violence, communal fury was experienced by big cities like Pune (1982) and Bombay (1984) also. District towns like Nasik, Amaravati, Ratnagiri, etc. also witnessed communal disturbances (1986). Clashes between the *savarnas* and the *dalits* took place even in remote places like Satna (1983,1986), Khamgaon and Chopda (1986),Phaltan (1986),etc. Earlier, Sangli was the battle ground between Hindu and the Jain communities (1983). This list could be further extended if we were to mention stray events of atrocities against the *dalits.* This recurring caste-communal violence has thus become a remarkable feature of politics in the State. It has been accompanied by the emergence and growth of a number of caste-communal organizations.

These caste-based conflicts must be understood in terms of the class stratification in the state. Caste conflicts between the Marathas and other lower castes or between caste Hindus and *dalits* are not based on their respective caste identities and parochial consciousness alone;they reveal a more basic, materially grounded conflict of interests. In this sense, the Brahmin-Maratha alliance forms the ruling class in the state and the scheduled castes and the scheduled tribes along with other lower castes form the toiling class. Although we emphasize this Brahmin-Maratha composition of the ruling class, one should not forget the fact that the industrial bourgeoisie of Bombay shares power in the State. In fact, this class is part of the ruling class at the national level and represents that national ruling class. This industrial bourgeoisie composes of the Gujarati, Parsi and Marwari industrialists and businessmen. Another problem regarding this Brahmin-Maratha alliance is the place of Brahmins in the ruling class. In the first place,the Brahmins form part of the industrial bourgeoisie since quite a few Brahmin industrial houses have grown over a period of time. Besides, in the medium and small scale industry, the Brahmins have come to acquire visible control. Above all, the Brahmins control the cultural and educational fields, thus producing ideas for the ruling class. It is in this sense that we can speak of the ruling class consisting of the Brahmins and the Marathas. The pattern of landholdings in the state is an indication of this class stratification.

In 1976, there were 57.6 lakh landowners in the state, but twenty-six per cent among them had just less than 2.5 acres of land, while another one-fifth owned between 2.5 and 5 acres, and seven per cent landholders owned more than twenty-five acres each (Brahme and Nene, 1983: 10) Landholdings are concentrated in the hands of the top layer of the Maratha caste. The elite Marathas own larger and better chunks of land. One-fifth of the Maratha caste hold agricultural units varying between fifteen to fifty acres (Lele,1987). Just as landholdings are concentrated in the hands of a few, the ranks of agricultural labour have been swelling. In 1981, there were sixty-five lakhs agricultural labourers (27% of the total work-force in the state) against forty-five lakhs in 1960. Besides, among the scheduled castes and scheduled tribes,forty-eight per cent and thirty-eight per cent of their respective working population were agricultural labourers in 1960. This proportion of agricultural labour rose to fifty-five per cent and fifty-two per cent, respectively, in the seventies (excluding small peasant labour) (Brahme and Nene, 1983: 9-13).

This shows that the process of class formation has been under way in the state since the late sixties and the seventies. Strategic use of the state machinery and initiation of the policies of the green revolution, expansion of irrigation, provision of subsidized fertilizers, improved seeds, farm machinery, etc. helped the rich Maratha peasantry in consolidating its position. Considerable funds were pumped into the rural areas through these schemes and this helped principally the rich peasant, his cash-crop economy and his co-operative sugar factories. This is perhaps best exemplified by the case of the water resources in the state. A substantial part of the additional water resources tapped during the 1950s and 1960s was used for various cash crops. For example, almost seventy per cent of these water resources were channelized for the cultivation of sugarcane and horticultural crops (Brahme and Nene, 1983: 76-81).

The success story of the state in the field of sugarcane cultivation and sugar factories is yet another instance of the consolidation of ruling class strength. The ruling class bias in the implementation of policies is evident from the pattern of sugarcane production. As the water requirement of sugarcane is very high, its cultivation is possible only in highly irrigated areas. Two-third of the total sugarcane production in the state is concentrated in twenty-four *talukas* of Ahmednagar, Kolhapur, Nasik, Sangli, Pune and Satara districts in the western and southern parts of the state. Besides, forty-seven of the sixty-seven sugar factories in the state are also located in the same area (Brahme and Nene, 1983: 7).

These developments generated surplus further accentuating class stratification in the state. The drought of 1972 brought into sharp focus this fact of class stratification and existence of rival interests. However, massive drought relief work was undertaken. The state government also inaugurated the employment guarantee scheme and monopoly procurement of cotton. These maneouvres softened the impact of deprivation initially. In reality these schemes helped the rich more than the poor. The benefits of the employment guarantee scheme have gone to a large extent to the medium and big farmers (M.H.J., 1980: 2043-45).

Although the rich Maratha peasantry is part of the ruling class,we would not like to create an impression that this section of the ruling class can really take all the important decisions from which it can benefit. Thus, the policies as mentioned above, though beneficial to the rich Maratha peasantry, are not its own products. To understand this point, it may be mentioned that the national cake is distributed in Delhi itself. This distribution is directed and controlled by the national bourgeoisie. If the rich Maratha peasantry gets a larger share than earlier it is because that suits the national bourgeoisie. The bourgeoisie is interested in the development of agriculture because the urban market is progressively becoming saturated. It has become necessary to find out new markets in the rural areas. This could happen only when some sections of the peasants become rich enough to become consumers. Besides this, the bourgeoisie is also interested in the growth of agriculture because the agricultural sector provides raw material through production of cash crops and provides constant supply of foodgrains for the urban markets and particularly for the fair price shops. Therefore, a call for rural development and fair distribution of water resources is mainly the brainchild of the national bourgeoisie for widening the market-base for consumer articles beyond the rich peasantry. Thus, sometimes, as in case of the green revolution, policies adopted by the bourgeoisie may benefit the rich Maratha peasantry; while at other times, the rich peasantry may detect a threat to its supremacy in the policies of the national bourgeoisie. It is not at all surprising, therefore, that rural development schemes or water distribution proposals are opposed by the rich peasantry. But generally, when we speak of the rich Maratha peasantry as the ruling class, we only mean that it distributes in the rural areas those resources which it has received from Delhi. Secondly, whenever we refer to the rich Maratha peasantry as the ruling class, we think of the appropriation of agricultural surplus by this dominant rural rich.

If the foregoing discussion shows the difficulty of identifying the ruling class at the regional level, it also points out at the contradictions internal to the ruling class. Although the Marathas occupy the position of the dominant class, their interests do not always coincide with the interests of the dominant class at the national level, i. e., the industrial bourgeoisie. It is for this reason that the industrial bourgeoise has never allowed the rich peasantry to function in an autonomous manner. The industrial bourgeoisie has always adopted an interventionist strategy in regional politics. Within these limitations the Brahmin-Maratha alliance forms the ruling class at the regional level.

We now turn to discuss the strategy of this ruling class vis-a-vis the masses. We specifically concentrate on the use of the ideology of neo-Hinduism expressed in terms of unity of all castes and it was signified by the alliance between the Brahmins and Marathas.

The Maratha history has facilitated the formation of the neo-Hindu ideology. The Brahmins and Marathas have always looked upon themselves as leaders of the Hindu community. Although there are instances of Brahmin-Maratha conflicts, the traces of their alliance are deep-rooted. Adherence to "Maharashtra *dharma*" and to the caste-based social order have been the chief common bonds between the two. Just as

Shivaji is the symbol of Maratha chivalry and Kshatriyahood, for the Brahmins he is the protector of the Brahminic order. The idea of Maharashtra *dharma* has dominated the Brahmin-Maratha consciousness since the last century. During the national movement in Maharashtra, both leaders and participants were obsessed by the idea of Maharashtra *dharma* (Vora, 1987: 25). Shivaji's political revolution could come about because of the Saint Movement and religious and revivalistic integration among different castes and communities. This idea of Maharashtra *dharma* played an important role not only in the national movement but also in the Samyukta Maharashtra Movement.

The national movement in the state was popular among the Brahmins only till 1920. The reforms of 1919 (Morley-Minto Reforms) brought forward the Marathas to the political arena. The Brahminetar Party (a non-Brahmin party) was formed in 1920. This party was an attempt to organize the non-Brahmin castes vis-a-vis the Brahmins. It had the background of the non-Brahmin movement and the ideas of Jotirao Phuley. The Satyashodhak Samaj was the main vehicle of this non-Brahmin movement. A radical programme aiming at the overthrowing of Brahmnic domination was originally propounded through this Samaj by Phuley (Omvedt, 1976). But this revolutionary rigour of the Samaj soon died away. Another important influence over the Maratha community during this period was of the Arya Samaj. Shahu Maharaj (1874-1922), a proud Kshatriya and follower of Arya Samaj, encouraged the non-Brahmin movement in order to regain the spirit of Kshatriyahood. The Arya Samaj also believed in the historical role of the Kshatriyas and Brahmins.

Thus, due to the mediating factors like leadership of Shahu Maharaj and the influence of the Arya Samaj, the non-Brahmin movement did not develop into a critique of Hinduism or Brahminism but rather resulted in a temporary anti-Brahmin phase. A common perception of the historical role of the Brahmins and Kshatriyas facilitated continuation of the Brahmin-Maratha alliance. By the late 1920s, the Brahminetar Party had lost significance and a younger generation of Maratha leaders like Jedhe and Jawalkar were attracted to the Gandhian movement. Many Maratha leaders joined the national movement in the state around 1930 (Vora, 1987: 24).

After independence, the Maratha caste emerged as the most dominant caste in state politics. Later, during the Samyukta Maharashtra Movement, the Brahmins and Marathas joined forces at the regional level. In course of this movement, the Shivaji cult and the notion of Maharashtra *dharma* were revived. The slogan—"Maratha Tetuka Melvava" (all Marathi people should be unified)—brought together the Marathas and the Brahmins. This was the keynote of the Samyukta Maharashtra Movement (Bedekar, 1947: 12-15). Emphasis was laid upon the roles of Shivaji and Ramdas, symbolizing the Marathas and the Brahmins, respectively. It provided a platform for the unity of all Marathi people under the aegis of the Brahmin-Maratha leadership.

It is in this background that concerted efforts to mobilize the people as Hindus to butress a Hindu identity upon their consciousness have been taking place.

The early seventies witnessed the emergence of Dalit Panthers challenging *savarna* supremacy. This was followed by *dalit-savarna* riots in Worli, Bombay. This was the beginning of the decline of Bahujan Samaj ideology which had been successful in containing lower caste aspirations ever since independence. On the other hand, the Maratha contingent was cut to size within the Congress by giving more seats to the candidates of lower castes, scheduled castes and scheduled tribes. This process was symbolically completed when A.R. Antulay was installed as the chief minister of the state. In the meanwhile, a controversy had raged over the issue of renaming the Marathwada University after Dr. B.R. Ambedkar. The anti-*dalit* riots took place all over Marathwada and the issue of the sub-regional identity was raised (Punekar, 1981). These events led to repression and also necessitated the formation of a new ideology. It is at this juncture that concerted attempts began at redefining the Hindu social order and rediscovering Hinduism as a common platform for all castes. We call this ideology as the Neo-Hinduism.

Let us now briefly discuss the main characteristics of neo-Hinduism:

(a) ***Integration***: Unity among Hindus is the main objective of the neo-Hinduism. It premises that Hinduism itself possesses enough potential to achieve this objective. Therefore, the neo-Hindu propaganda is full of appeals to all Hindus to forge unity among themselves. No doubt, caste is the main stumbling block in this process of Hindu integration as, each caste has its own history, pride and separate identity. Therefore, the neo-Hinduism attempts at an integrationist reinterpretation of Hindu history. Caste conflict is played down and tales of caste amity are highlighted. Emotional appeals are employed to mobilize people of all castes and to bring them together. The Brahmin-Maratha alliance is the most exemplary instance of this integrationism. The Brahmins and

Marathas are seen as the main protectors of Hinduism and best representatives of the Hindu tradition. As we noted above, this alliance is deep-rooted in the history of Maharashtra. But while renewing it, the proponents of this alliance tend to ignore the immediate past full of conflicts between the two castes. It is this selective perception of history which marks the integrationist strategy of the neo-Hinduism.

Integration also implies accommodation. Thus, the advocates of the neo-Hinduism claim that the Hindu culture belongs to all and has been enriched by all castes. To signify this hypothesis the Hindu organizations now celebrate the birth anniversaries of Ambedkar and Phuley. The contributions of these leaders and their foresight etc., find praise from proponents of the neo-Hinduism. Now Phuley is not criticized for his biting attacks on Brahminsim but he is hailed as a *Mahamanav* and the writings of arch rivals like Phuley and Chiplunkar are shown as complementary and forming a common Hindu ethos (Gokhale, 1982). However, in spite of its integrationism, the neo-Hinduism has not made concerted efforts for integrating the *dalits*. On the contrary, organizations like the Patit Pawan or the Maratha Mahasangh adopt a confrontationist posture vis-a-vis the scheduled castes. Integrationist strategy has, however, been employed in a few unorganized activities of helping the *dalits* such as the Mhaisal project (Vasant Deshpande, 1983).

(b) ***Militancy***: The new Hindu offensive resorts to militancy and use of force. It turns to aggressive actions not only because it is intolerant of opposition but also because it is aware of the limitations of its integrationist appeal. The Hindu unity which it seeks to achieve is after all based on the domination of the higher castes, particularly the Brahmins and the Marathas. There are bound to be some not so willing partners in this Hindu unity. Therefore, integrationist strategy is supplemented by militancy. This militancy finds expression in words and deeds alike. Militancy in the outbursts of Bal Thackrey probably surpasses all other forms. Utter disrespect for the non-Hindus, strong words, plain threats and abusive slogans occupy the better part of the neo-Hindu writings and propaganda.

Lower castes and Muslims are the chief objects of the neo-Hindu militancy. The lower castes incur the neo-Hindu wrath on account of reservations and formation of a separate *dalit* identity. The neo-Hindus have generally opposed the reccommendations of the Mandal Commission, and have also challenged the wisdom of reservations for the scheduled castes. They fear that such reservations would separate the lower castes from the higher castes. The *dalits* are seen as already forming their own identity which has angered the neo-Hindus including ideologues such as Majgaonkar and S.H. Deshpande. Similarly, the Muslims are shown in the worst light possible, ignoring or even denying their contribution to the freedom struggle. While the Muslim religious fanaticism is constantly under criticism, the Muslims are also expected to accept the Hindu cultural framework.

The neo-Hindu militancy does not stop at verbal explosives alone. It is equally uninhibited in applying force against its enemies. Intimidation and repression are the purposes behind this use of force. While the lower castes are coerced into accepting the Hindu identity with continued domination of the upper castes, the Muslims are coerced into accepting a subordinate status in the Hindu society. Violence intimates the resolve of the upper castes to retain their advantageous position. Thus, the Hindu muscle has been used both against *dalits* and Muslims on quite a few occasions in the eighties. In cases of communal violence, use of force is glorified. It is openly preached that the Muslims should be taught a lesson. Involvement in a clash with the Muslims is seen as an act of bravery, a service to the nation. In spite of protests to the contrary, most Hindu organizations are engaged in spreading communal hatred in the state. It must be noted that this hatred benefits the neo-Hindus as such feelings rally all Hindus in one camp. Through the dissemination of such stereotypes, the Hindus come to believe that they are really one; while intimidation silences any possibility of challenge to the integrationist design.

(c) ***Nationalism***: In the neo-Hindu thinking, the Hindu society is equivalent to the Indian society and the Hindu identity means Indian national identity. Therefore, mobilizing the Hindu society and asserting its identity are considered as efforts of nation-building. It is in this context that the neo-Hindu ideological appeals attach too much importance to nationalism. Integration and nationalism are complementary features of the neo-Hinduism. The purpose of Hindu unity to strengthen the nation and nationalism implies unity in the society. For the neo-Hindus, particularly the followers of Savarkar's nationalism, aims at such ultimate value. Progress of the society is dependent upon its sense of unity. There is no room for any diversity or plurality in the ideology of nationalism adopted by the advocates of the neo-Hinduism. Therefore, only the common factors among the Hindus find favour with them. In this sense, integrationism and nationalism both work in the same direction, they invent unity, they bury internal differences in the society, and they hold the individuals as prisoners of a make-believe.

This world of make-believe identifies Hinduism as the basis of nationalism. Therefore, it becomes an intrinsic compulsion for everybody to feel as a good Hindu. Similarly, if Hinduism is the basis of nationalism, non-Hindu communities become a threat to nationalism. So, there is nothing wrong if force is used to "protect" the nation from such enemies as the Muslims. This make believe justifies intimidation. Thus, the organizations like Hindu Ekta or the Patit Pawan do not find anything wrong with violence and strong-arm methods; these are seen as service to the cause of nationalism. These and such other organizations have been successful in recent years in making such ideas acceptable to a large section of the Hindu society.

(d) *New Sergeant-at-Arms*: Traditionally, the Hindu nationalism has been the preserve of of upper castes, particularly the Brahmins. The Hindu idiom appealed only to the Brahmins. The Hindu organizations found willing supporters among the Brahmins. But the recent Hindu mobilization has broadened its constituency. Integration strategy has been used for this purpose. The main plank of the neo-Hinduism has been unity of all Hindus. This strategy has yielded fairly good results if the proliferation of Hindu organizations is any indication.

In the course of this expansion, the neo-Hinduism has engulfed many non-Brahmin castes also. The leadership as well as active following of almost all neo-Hindu organizations belong to non-Brahmin and in many cases even non-Maratha castes. These new recruits are invariably young activists ready to use their muscles. They are also remarkable for low level of their education; either they have just completed school education or they are college dropouts. Their social and educational background makes them especially vulnerable to emotional appeals and militant activities. Another remarkable feature of the neo-Hindu expansion is its penetration in the rural areas. Earlier, only the Maratha Mahasangh had rural connections. Later, the Hindu Ekta also claimed considerable support in the rural areas. In more recent years, the Shiv Sena is making headway in rural areas of almost all parts of Maharashtra. Many obscure villages today exhibit the saffron flag and experience hitherto non-existent *savarna-dalit* tensions.

Finally, the neo-Hindu following is not restricted to any particular political party. The neo-Hindu elements exist and operate in many political parties in the state. Thus, there is a considerable support for the Maratha Mahasangh among the followers of the Congress and the Shetkari Sanghathana. Many Bharatiya Janata Party followers are sympathizers of the Vishwa Hindu Parishad, the Patit Pawan or the Shiv

Sena. In other words, the neo-Hinduism permeates the political scene in the state. Ideological formulations of the neo-Hinduism too have been propounded not only by Savarkarites but by progressives, liberals and secularists as well. This broad-based composition of the neo-Hindu leadership and watchdog has given unprecedented legitimacy and acceptability to this ideology. At no time since independence had Hinduism made such impressive headway in the state. We call this neo-Hindu movement an ideological movement. It is using the powerful weapon of ideology. An ideology which communicates a distorted picture of reality and which leads to wrong and often unrelated solutions (Larrain, 1979). An ideological exercise denies the existence of contradictory forces and reformulates and projects the possibility of a coherent, homogenous society. It justifies the position of the dominant class. As the composition of the neo-Hindu organizations shows, the neo-Hinduism appeals are addressed to the lower castes as well as to the lower strata of the Marathas. Under the spell of neo-Hinduism, casteism and separatism are seen as the only enemies of the Hindu unity. It also justifies the Hindu social order by creating a false consciousness among the people as "Hindu". It negates the formation of class identity or consciousness of caste domination.

An ideological movement is never static. It changes and develops as class stratification evolves. As contradictions become progressively sharper, ideology descends to the level of mere idealizing phrases, conscious illusions and deliberate hypocrisy. Evolution of the class stratification in Maharashtra testifies to this pattern. Nationalism, regionalism, welfarism and now neo-Hinduism have been different forms of ideology. Each of these has been a set of ideas of the ruling class which in turn became the ruling ideas. These ruling ideas seek to foster unity and brotherhood among the economically differentiated members of various castes. Under their influence, people perceive themselves as forming a union in their common fight against common enemies of the entire society.

Evolution of class stratification in India does not imply erosion of the caste system. On the contrary, this evolution underlines the exploitative nature of the caste system, its divisive impact upon the society. It is precisely for this reason that the neo-Hindu movement has resorted to whitewashing of the caste differences. The success of the neo-Hindu ideology is evident from the fact that it has been able to gain adherents from non-Brahmin and non-Maratha castes. It has penetrated into various segments of the Hindu society, cutting across class loyalties.

The ruling class is so desperate to suppress the existing contradictions that it is prepared to supplement this ideological apparatus with the use of repression and intimidation against those who do not fall in line with the ideological hocus-pocus.

References

Bedekar, D.K., *Samyukta Maharashtra*, Pune, Chitrashala Press, 1947.

Brahme, Sulabha and R.P.Nene, *Maharashtratil Shetmajur*, Pune, M. Phuley Samta Pratisthan, 1983.

Deshpande, Vasant, *The Mhaisal Untouchables*, Pune, Dastane Ramchandra & Co., 1983.

Larrain, Jorge, *The Concept of Ideology*, Macmillan, 1979.

Lele, Jayant: *Class, Caste and Domination: Political Mobilization in Maharashtra* (Forthcoming), 1987.

M.H.J., 'Maharashtra: Employment Guarantee Scheme: An Evaluation, '*Economic and Political Weekly*', 6 Dec. 1980.

Punekar, S.D., *Aspects of Class and Caste in Social Tensions* (Mimeo), Centre for Social Studies, Surat, 1981.

Vora, Rajendra, '*Nationalist Movement in Maharashtra*' in A.R. Kulkarni (ed.), *History of the Deccan: Modern Period*, Forthcoming, 1987.

13

Agrarian Tensions in Rural Marathwada: A Case of the Shiv Sena

Surendra Jondhale

Limboni is a small village in the newly created Jalana district of Marathwada region in Maharashtra. It was the morning of 28th July. The *dalits* had gone for the work in their respective *gairans*. Around 10 a.m., they saw a mob of hundred people approaching them with long sticks and axes. They were shouting slogans like 'Jai Bhawani' and 'Jai Shivaji'; their foreheads were patted up with *gulal*. As they came closer, they turned violent. They did not even spare the women or children. This violence continued for hours. In this brutal attack, two *dalits* were killed on the spot and twenty-two *dalits* were badly injured. A woman was also raped. The houses of *dalits* were looted by the violent mob. This brutal attack gave such a psychological shock to Babasaheb Balaji Salwe that he lost his speech. His father was killed and the mother was hospitalised for serious injuries. A woman who was raped was unable to feed her two months old infant as she herself was ill-fed since the attack. Her father-in-law was killed. Fortunately and by-chance, her husband was out of the village on that day.

This attack on the *dalits* of the Limboni village was also an organised one like the earlier attacks in the Marathwada region. The issue was the same. The *dalits* were cultivating the *gairans* (the village pasture and grazing lands). This was not liked by the caste Hindu landlords. (For a year social tension had been mounting up between the *dalits* and the non-*dalits* of this village). An old woman, Nanibai Parade, said: "*Dalits* had refused to carry out the ritual/traditional duties. We stopped begging. Hence, the villagers took revenge. In the school our kids are not allowed to sit on the mats. They have to sit on the floor. We cannot draw water from the village well. We get water from the tap. It means that we don't get water always. Even today we are suffering social boycott. We have to walk four to five kilometres for bringing the daily household necessities and water. The number of the educated is low. In our locality only one student has studied till the twelfth standard. Because of the lack of education we have remained backward. The villagers never speak to us properly."

It is common for them to use abusive language like 'Dhed Maharda'. It is true that we never protested against this since this is where are have to line.

Kaushyabai Salve informed us: "We had taken out the Ambedkar Jayanti procession in 1968. The villagers had thrown stones at that time. Then we stopped taking out the procession on Ambedkar Jayanti. The marriage *barat* cannot move in the village. Threats always come our way. Thus, a terror-ridden atmosphere is being maintained."

In this context, it is necessary to understand the social structure of the Limboni village. Its population consists of 1,252 men and women. There are 149 Buddhists, twenty-nine Matangs, one Chamar and one Muslim. They are so poor that only twenty-five Buddhists and ten Matangs own horses. The school provides only primary education. The civic amenities are absent like any other village. There are no *pucca* roads in the village. There is about 130 acres *gairans* available in the village. Since 1968, the *dalits* have been cultivating sixty acres of the total *gairan*. Because of this 'encroachment', some of the *dalits* were even imprisoned during 1968-70. Twenty-eight *dulit* families are cultivating the *gairan*. In fact some villagers were helping by providing the plough and seeds till 1974. But since the last few years, Bhanudas, the police patil of Limboni, was compulsorily charging annually Rs. 50 per *dalit* family on the plea that there would be no danger to the standing crops of the *gairan* cultivators, and they would not suffer in the village. The minority *dalit* agricultural labourers were regularly paying this amount annually by taking loans. Last year, Sahubai, a woman agricultural labourer had no money to pay this 'tax', therefore the police patil took away a sheep from her to recover the levy.

Economy of Marathwada

In the former state of Hyderabad, Marathwada had the *raiyatwari* system. It was felt that the balance of feudal relations should be maintained in the three parts of the Hyderabad State (i.e., Telengana, Marathwada and Karnataka). Telengana had the *zamindari* system. To establish a powerful hold over the people and to check the *raiyatwari* system in

Marathwada and Karnataka, *jagirs* were created on a large scale in this region. The *zamindari* and the *jagirdari* systems imposed a rigid control over the masses of the Hyderabad State. Although the *jagirdari* was created under the Nizam's regime, it was also continued by the British. They not only preserved it, but also expanded it further.

The Marathwada region was particularly a backward region of Hyderabad State. The agricultural practices continued to be traditional, and there was an increasing problem of small holdings and landlessness because of the virtual lack of industrial development and slow pace of urbanisation. The incremental labour force had to fall back on agriculture. Consequently, the number of workers dependent on agriculture for their livelihood increased rapidly.

The problems of the tenants were acute. An agrarian reforms committee was set up to suggest ways and means to improve their lot. It's reports helped in the enactment of a comprehensive tenancy act in 1950, and it was called the Hyderabad Agricultural Lands Act. It has been extensively amended over the subsequent years.

Land Reforms

During 1955, through many enactments, the cases of *inami* lands were resolved. In 1960, the problem of *watani* lands which were reserved for the village work was settled. These *watani-inami* lands were being cultivated by the Mahar, the Matang and the Chamar castes. These *inami* land belts were not transferred to the cultivators due to the vested interest of the higher caste revenue officials working at the village and block levels.

According to the Ceiling Act, about 20,97,000 hectares of land have been declared as surplus, but in reality, about 20,36,000 hectares land has been taken into possession. In spite of this, only 10,82,000 hectares land was distributed among 30,37,000 landless labourers. The share of the scheduled castes and scheduled tribes was 43.61 per cent.

According to the Mahasashtra State Tenancy Act, 1949 and the Hyderabad Tenancy Act, 1950, a large number of tenancies were declared disputed. In Marathwada, 47,853 tenancy cases were considered till 1964. Of these, 45,446 tenancy cases have been settled. It is interesting to note that about 28, 620 cases were in the favour of the tenants, whereas 16,826 tenancy cases were in the favour of the landlords. The remaining 2,407 tenancy cases are still pending.

Later on, these cases were settled against the tenants and in favour of the landlords. At some places, the lands of the tenants were kept in the possession of the landlords. The legal loopholes and the casteis bureaucracy were the major obstacles in the proper implementation of these legislations.

After 1950, the govnment had declared certain tenants as protected tenants. They were allowed to cultivate the land under an yearly bond. While formulating these Acts, the bureaucracy had taken precautions for not giving the tenants right over the lands they cultivated.

It is sad that all these Acts have remained on paper. Thus, ineffectiveness has culminated into rural unrest. Other factors were the chronic droughts and the scarcity of water which compelled the tenants to lease-out their lands to the government. Again, from such cases the problem of the transfer of land surfaced. However, due to the pressure of movements of landless agricultural labourers the government conceded to the 'cultivation' (encroachment) of the *gairan* and forest lands.

The system of *inami* land was abolished, but the land which was in the possession of Hindu temples, mosques and other religious institutions was kept reserved. The rural landlords claimed their ownership over these lands. In spite of having their own land, the landlords have been cornering the income emanating from the temple lands. Sometimes these lands are auctioned. Only the higher castes have got a say in the auctions. The *dalits* and other backward classes obviously cannot participate in the auctions.

The scheduled castes and scheduled tribes have been given lands under different government schemes. These lands, however, are either sold or leased-out to the landlords. Some of these are given to others for *batai* cultivation or remain fallow.

When the lands were distributed to the weaker sections, requisite agricultural facilities were not provided to them. The loans or the agricultural tools were insufficient. Acute poverty and the poor quality of land compelled these people either to sell or to lease-out their lands to the rich peasants of their villages.

A committee for the evaluation of land reforms appointed by the Government of Maharashtra in 1968 found that the average landholding per family in Marathwada was 73.60 acres (taking into account the total area owned by a landlord in or outside the surveyed village). The committee found that this average was much higher compared to western Maharasthra and Vidharbha. It also found that the large landlords accounted for seventy-nine per cent of all leased lands, with the very big landlords (sixty acres) accounting for thirty-five per cent of all the leased land. Its conclusion was that leasing in Marathwada was mainly by large landowners and particularly by the very big ones.

The *jagirdari* abolition legislation could not transform the existing relations of production in Marathwada when it was a part of Hyderabad State. The simple reason was that the *jagirdari* abolition left untouched the various forms of surplus appropriation. But the tenancy act was an exception. It touched the core of the problem, namely, the relations of production.

In 1960, the Government of Maharashtra appointed a high powered committee to look into the encroachment on the *gairan* lands. This committee reccommended the regularisation of the encroachments which occurred during 1955-56 and 1959-60. But this resolution was confined to Nasik district. The government also decided to regularise the encroachments in others districts with a condition that the land under cultivation should have been possessed and cultivated at least for three years. Later on, this condition was relaxed to a minimum period of one year.

However, these resolutions have never been implemented. The forest and revenue officials are reluctant to implement these acts. The land under cultivation has never been regularised according to the government resolutions. On the contrary, in the recent years, ironically the government has issued an order for eviction of the encroachers from the *gairans*. Moreover, according to the resolution of 13th August, 1968, the government issued orders to take possession of the lands along with the standing crops. This naturally encouraged the bureaucrats to evict encroachers from the *gairans*.

The government also took a stock of these encroachments in the *gairans*. It found that the majority of the cultivators were landless labourers. It was clear that they did not have other means of livelihood. The government decided to regularise the encroachments which had taken before 15th August, 1972. This resolution was applicable to the government fallow lands, the *gairan* and the forest lands. This decision, however, was not implemented.

During Sharad Pawar's Progressive Democratic Front's rule, due to the pressure of the movements by the agricultural workers in Thane, Dhule, Chandrapur and Nasik districts, the government was compelled to declare a new policy about the encroachments. The government took the decision of regularisation of the encroachments which had occurred before 31st March, 1978. There were, however, many flaws in this resolution. The time period was arbitrary. The condition for the minimum size/area of encroachment was not acceptable to the landholders. Again, a state-wide agitation was launched by the Jabran Jot Andolan

Samiti. The government had to modify its earlier resolution. It declared that encroachments which occurred during the period 1st April, 1972 to 31st March, 1978 would be regularised. It also accepted a time-bound programme for the implementation of this resolution. It decided that all cases of encroachments would be settled before May 1980.

Role of the Revenue Administration

Although the encroached *gairan* was cultivated but the *talathi* (the village revenue officer) did not officially record this. The government, in fact, took a decision in 1965 that the *gairans*, the village ponds and the public roads would be under the control and supervision of the *gram panchayat.* It meant that for the last twenty-two years these lands have been attached to the *gram panchayat*, but till date lands have not been recorded in the possession of the *gram panchayat.* The *talathis* have not recorded the cultivation undertaken on the *gairan* lands for many years and neither have they acknowledged the fact of encroachment. There is total chaos about these lands in the village gazetteers as either a proper record has not been maintained or the record is incomplete.

Is it that *talathis* are not aware of the government orders whether the area sown in the *gairan* should be included in the cultivatable area? It is also true that since many years the *dalits, adivasis* and landless are cultivating the *gairans* but the *talathis* have not recorded this in their relevant files.

It is understandable that because of ignorance, inexperience or in the absence of proper guidance, some *talathis* have not recorded the *gairan* lands as being in the possession of the *gram panchayat.* But is this not true about all *talathis* that they have consistently been making these mistakes for so many years? And what about the higher authorities in the revenue department such as the naib tehsildar, the deputy collector and the collector? It is really unbelievable that the mistakes which have been committed for the past twenty-two years by *talathis* have remained unrectified inadvertantly by the higher authorities.

The reality is that the revenue officials have intentionally not recorded the encroached *gairans* cultivated by the *dalits, adivasis,* nomadic tribes, weaker sections and landless people for so many years because their right of ownership over the land would have been established as per the government resolution.

The Maharashtra Land Revenue Regulation Act (Vol.4) was published in 1974. It is explicitly mentioned there that the *talathis* should record the cultivation done in the encroached *gairan* in the 7/12 form. But the problem is that there are no clear directives issued to the *gram panchayat* that the encroached lands should be recorded in the encroachment list. The Government of Maharashtra, as a policy matter, has referred all *gairans* to the *gram panchayat*. Therefore, it is the responsibility of the state to see whether these encroached lands have been listed in the encroachment record or not.

The *gairan* lands, the village pond and public roads are allotted to the *gram panchayat* with specific conditions and instructions by the Government. If these lands are not accordingly utilised by the *gram panchayat*, then it is the prerogative of the revenue officials as representatives of the State to take action against the *gram panchayat*. The *talathi* must report to the tehsildar about the violation of relevant regulations.

The crux of the matter is that the *talathis* have not reported the illegal cultivation in the *gairans* as it is a violation committed by the *gram panchayat*. They have not even recorded the cultivation on *gairan*. If the *talathis* would have recorded these encroachments on the *gairan* lands, then the claims of the encroachers (the *dalits* etc.) would have been established. But due to the pressure of the higher revenue authorities and vested interests, the *talathis* have not taken a note of these encroachments in the village records.

It is pertinent to ask why was the government land cultivated by landless agricultural workers?

During the World War II, the British government launched a campaign, namely, "grow more food." It was imperative for the British to mop up as much of the foodgrain as possible for the war. It, therefore, encouraged the landless to cultivate the government fallow land including the *gairan* lands.

In post-independence India, the government has failed to provide employment or proper means of earning to the toiling masses in the countryside. Generally, the bulk of the beneficiaries of the anti-poverty programmes of the government have been from among the upper castes and classes while the poor landless labourers have been left untouched. There was no alternative for the *dalits* except to cultivate the government fallow lands.

Social reformers like Jotiba Phuley, Shahn Maharaj and Ambedkar asked *dalits* to refrain from performing the ritual duties in the villages. Ambedkar had even organised a campaign against the (the Bombay Hereditary Act, 1874. In the absence of the performance of ritual duties, the *dalits* obviously got attracted to the village common lands or the village pasture or grazing lands for cultivation.

The *dalit* landless, in large numbers, have been migrating to the urban centers for employment. In the Indian social milieu, the ownership of land is associated with social status. The capitalist system which is based on profit and competition insists on credit in the market. The *dalits, adivasis* and nomadic tribes having realised this, continue to remain attached to land, including the *gairan* lands.

Some nomadic tribes have started settling on government lands. They have also started cultivation on these lands. Since increasing industrialisation has crippled the *balutedari* system, the *balutedars* also have taken to cultivation on government lands.

Today, the Marathas in Marathwada possess special feature. Firstly, the anti-Nizam movement was led by the Brahmin intellectual elite. The allies of the local Brahmin elite were some Kshatriya families of the north and some trading Vaishya families. The rural Marathas were not mobilised by any movement similar to the one in the western region (i.e., non-Brahmin movement). The village social pattern remained undisturbed with Marathas as a dominant community. The Brahmin elite, a majority among the professional classes, lived in the towns.

Secondly, with the enforcement of the tenancy legislation, the Brahmins and trading communities lost part of their lands to the big Maratha tenants. It was noted in the survey conducted in 1969 that the owners and the cultivators of land came overwhelmingly from the Marathas and the allied castes.

Thirdly, the Deshmukhs and Patils have been at the apex of the traditional social hierarchy in the villages. They continue to wield considerable economic and political power. They have captured the panchayati raj institutions and the co-operative credit societies. They have established their hegemony as a dominant caste in the new economic and political situation. It has been observed that the upper sections of the landowning community are able to mobilise the support of the middle peasants on the basis of their positions in the co-operatives that control the supply of credit and other inputs.

In Marathwada, the landlords are exercising control over the administrative and political apparatuses in order to check the increasing awareness among the *dalits.* The landlord's capitalism, as it exists in western Maharashtra, is not present in this region. The atrocities on the *dalits* in Marathwada are due to the force or power enjoyed by the landlords in the burcaueracy and the government.

Role of the Shiv Sena

The Shiv Sena was officially started at Aurangabad in Marathwada on

8th June, 1985. Aurangabad is a divisional town of the Marathwada region. The first *morcha* led by the Shiv Sena was on 17th January, 1986 and it focused on three issues: the misbehaviour of Jordanian students in the city, the inefficient police, and the need for a common civil code. This first *morcha* itself sparked off communal riots in the city. These riots also encouraged the Shiv Sena to establish its roots in rural Marathwada. It has been said that there are four to five thousand *shakhas* of the Shiv Sena in the seven districts of Marathwada.

The entry of the Shiv Sena is a turning point in the rural politics of Marathwada. The industrial expansion in Aurangabad also paved a way for the growth of the Shiv Sena. Many industrial units have not been functioning properly, and the 'lay off' is a common phenomenon. The unskilled workers in the industrial units are from neighbouring villages who have been thrown as 'surplus' from their lands. This 'surplus' manpower includes the landless agricultural workers as well as the marginal farmers. There are numerous instances of marginal farmers and middle peasants who were forced to go to work under the employment guarantee scheme (EGS) due to chronic droughts in the region. Such a social base was conducive for the Shiv Sena to spread out its communal tentacles in the rural area with the new ideology of Hinduism. Since 1984 the Shiv Sena has been building up for itself an image of a party aggressively committed to the cause of Hindus. Its earlier 'regional' character was quite successful in the metropolitan cities and lately the Shiv Sena's new 'communal' character has been making headway in the countryside. The Shiv Sena's new support structure in the rural areas includes the members of the middle castes, the disgruntled elements of the dominant castes and semi-employed and unemployed youths.

The major reason why the Shiv Sena is getting support in the rural areas, explains Bal Thackeray, is: "There the people want an offensiveness and militancy. They have confidence that the Shiv Sena alone would speak for about the Hindus. They feel that the Shiv Sena is a defensive outfit for them and they themselves establish units before the Shiv Sena leaders reach there."

Thus, there is a notable difference in the strategy of the Shiv Sena to mobilise the rural masses. Its faith in Hinduism as the dominant culture of India, strong hard feelings against minorities—Muslims, *dalits* and Sikhs—are fuelling the communal and caste virus in rural Maharashtra. It is at its height in the Marathwada region.

The new action programme of the Shiv Sena, particularly in Marathwada, is against the *dalits*. This is done through encroaching upon and systematically destroying government lands cultivated by the landless *dalits*. The Limboni carnage is an unforgettable example. A study shows that the instances of attacks on *dalits* have occurred in about thirty-five villages of Aurangabad district. These incidents occurred during the *kharif* period, i.e., from July to October. The programme for 'social forestry' undertaken by the Maharashtra government is adversely affecting the *dalits*. The activists of Shiv Sena launched a campaign with a slogan "restore public land to public use" in rural Marathwada. Their method was very bold and open. They would call a public meeting announcing that unauthorised crops on public land would be destroyed the next day. They would use casteist language against the *dalits*. Then they would call upon the villagers with their animals for forceful cattle-grazing in the *gairans* cultivated by the *dalits*.

Conclusions

After the agitation about the renaming of Marathwada University in 1978 there was a short spell of peace in this region. This peace was again broken by the anti-reservation movement. Since then, the Left and the democratic organisations have been trying to build their credibility among the *dalits* and the nomadic tribes by organising them on different issues like minimum wages and the *gairan*. Meanwhile the communal and casteist organisations have also modified their *modus operandi*. The Limboni carnage is an evidence of the new strategy. It is considered by the casteist organisations that if a large group collectively attacks the *dalits*, then it is easy to excape identification. This new technique, namely, the social boycott individual and for cible of the *gairans* cattle grazing has been found quite effective, and are the latest examples of this new strategy of the caste Hindus. Social atrocities are more inhuman and cruel.

Casteist feelings have been so intense that the cruelties are intentionally misinterpreted and accordingly propagated. "The *dalits* of Limboni were unable to take revenge on the caste Hindus, so they killed Vithoba Parade and Balaji Salwe from among themselves and now they are blaming the caste Hindus" is a glaring example of casteist propaganda.

The role of the government is partisan and deceptive. The revenue and police officials who were involved in the atrocities were asked to investigate the very same cases.

Although there is a clear government order for the protection of the encroached *gairans*, the tehsildars have been issuing oral orders to destroy the standing crops in the cultivated *gairans*. The role of the bureaucracy has remained partisan. Whenever the revenue officials make enquiries about the social boycott in the villages, they submit false reports sitting in connivance with the *patils* and *kulkarnis* as happened in the case of Limboni.

The government is reluctant to declare the number of *gairan* cases. It has accepted that the *adivasis*' encroachment cases in the forest area are about 20,983, and are still pending with the government. Apart from this, in Marathwada, the *dalits* and the nomadic tribes have more than fifty thousand *gairan* cases.

The EGS has not provided jobs to four lakh families. Thousands of crores of rupees have been spent on this scheme. This has created the 'green islands' of the sugar factories. Agricultural workers have migrated to these 'green islands' as sugar-cane-cutting workers. Their number is around three lakhs.

It is evident that because of the pressure of the mass movements the government issued orders in 1986 and 1987 assuring protection to the standing crops on the *gairan* lands, but in reality these crops were destroyed by the caste Hindus. In some cases, the forest department has also taken the initiative in destroying such crops. Last year, the grown *jawar* crop at Hatrale was destroyed by the forest department. The standing crops in the *gairans* of Valan Pimpalgaon (Aurangabad) and Kirminavare (Osmanabad) were destroyed and the land used for social forestry. Limboni and Babra are the most glaring examples. There are also such cases in many villages of Kannad and Gangapur *talukas* where the standing crops in the *gairans* were auctioned.

Some of the *gram panchayats*, without the consultation of the *gram sabha*, have passed the resolution that the *gairan* lands should be utilised for the social forestry programme. The sheer majority of the caste Hindu members has helped to pass such a resolution. The forest officers were called upon for the implementation of this programme. When the *dalits*, who had cultivated the *gairan* lands, did not heed the warning of the caste Hindus, their crops were destroyed with jubilation. Forcibly cattle were taken to graze the crops on the *gairans*. After this whatever remained was auctioned off by the officials of the revenue and forest departments.

The forest department does not allow the *adivasis* and *dalits* to assert their 'natural' right of owning the forest land. As the landless are getting organised, the Maharashtra government has taken a decision to provide arms to the officers of the forest department for their self-defence and the protection of the forests. The targets of the armed government officials seems to be the landless who are cultivating the *gairans* and the activists of the movement.

Appendix 1

Distribution of Landowners in Marathwada by Size of Ownership (1952)

Size of landholdings (in acres)	*Percentage of landowners*	*Percentage of landowned*
Up to 5	18.20	2.59
5.1 - 15.0	37.20	17.80
15.1 - 30.0	25.67	27.22
30.1 - 50.0	11.69	22.16
50.1 and above	7.24	30.23

Source: District Census Handbooks, 1961, for five districts of Marathwada.

Appendix 2

Landownership in Marathwada (1971)

Size of landholdings (in acres)	*Ownership Holdings*		*Operational Holdings*	
	Households (percent)	*Area owned (percent)*	*Households (percent)*	*Area owned (percent)*
Landless	34.30	1.09	36.49	—
50-2.49	6.16	1.09	4.95	.89
2.5-4.99	9.57	3.59	7.66	2.84
5.0-9.99	16.98	13.13	15.75	11.94
10.0-14.99	11.40	14.58	12.25	15.24
15.0-29.99	13.75	31.05	14.92	33.29
30.0-49.99	6.39	25.06	6.46	24.77
50.0 and above	1.45	11.10	1.52	11.09

Source: National Sample Survey 26th Round, July 1971-September 1972, Tables on Landholdings, State of Maharashtra, Vol. II.

Appendix 3

Percentage of SCs, STs, Nav-Bandhas and Agricultural Labourers in 1981 (Marathwada)

District	Percentage to Total Population			Total of columns 2+3+4	Agricultural labourers
	SC	ST	Nav-Bandhas		
Aurangabad	6.18	3.11	8.15	17.44	11.78
Parbhani	5.82	4.30	11.49	21.61	17.54
Beed	11.47	0.90	2.69	15.06	12.59
Nandad	11.30	10.19	9.66	31.15	14.05
Osmanabad	15.45	2.33	4.04	21.82	14.65
Marathwada	9.93	4.08	7.21	21.22	13.39
Maharashtra	7.14	9.19	6.47	22.80	10.36

Source: Report of the fact finding Committee of Regional Balance in Maharashtra, April, 1984.

Appendix 4

Agricultural Labourers, Small Farmers and Marginal Farmers (Marathwada)

(in Lakhs)

District	Total population	Rural population	Agriculture labourers	Small farmers	Marginal farmers
Aurangabad	19.71	16.42	2.59	0.29	0.20
Parbhani	15.07	12.65	2.50	0.20	0.13
Beed	12.86	11.37	1.67	0.22	0.16
Nanded	13.98	11.70	2.01	0.25	0.20
Osmanabad	18.97	16.60	2.66	0.23	0.13

Source: Note submitted by Maharashtra Government about the scarcity situation (1980). The figures are based on 1971 Census. There is 20 per cent increase in the population during the last decade.

Quoted in H. M. Desarad, The Scarcity Problem in a Study (Marathi) Marathwada.

14

Growth, Inequities and Tensions: A Case Study of Sangli District, Maharashtra

S.P. Punalekar

India became independent in 1947 and ushered in an era of self-rule and transformation. It is wedded to the market economy, promotion of private enterprise and growth with modernisation of structures and institutions. But it also subscribes to the philosophy and principles of 'growth with justice' and the 'socialistic pattern of society'. In the process, we have a 'mixed' economy with 'mixed' policies, influencing decisively all sectors of social life and generating a variety of contradictions and tensions. The rural development scene in India, as revealed by the macro trends and tendencies, bears testimony to this. The macro trends and their analysis are vital to the understanding of the processes of social transformation in India. Their vitality and value lie in the potentiality to contribute towards shaping of class struggles and class politics as instruments of social change.

But rural development has a certain context and social and historical specificities. Policies and programmes operate in a specific milieu, which acts and reacts with its own potentialities and limitations. And for this reason, micro-level insights and experiences are valuable in building our understanding about processes of change and transformation. The present paper is thus an effort at a micro-level to comprehend the development milieu, its complexities and contradictions in Sangli district of Maharashtra. The study broadly explores two questions: (i) who are 'developing' and in which politico-economic milieu and with which supportive structures; and (ii) as a result of prevailing development processes, what tensions and contradictions have emerged in rural society?

Socio-Historical Background

Physical Characteristics

Sangli district is one of the southernmost parts of Maharashtra State. Up to 1948, the present areas of the Sangli district were partly included in the old Satara district and partly in the princely states of Aundh, Jath, Sangli, Miraj (senior and junior) and Wadi. In 1949, the district was renamed South Satara district which included four talukas of Tasgaon, Khanapur, Walwa and Shirala transferred from the old Satara district, and two new talukas, namely, Miraj and Jath were formed out of the erstwhile princely State.

In 1960, the name of South Satara district was changed to Sangli district with its headquarters at Sangli in Miraj taluka. There are two administrative sub-divisions: Walwa and Miraj. The Walwa sub-division comprises Khanapur, Shirala and Walwa talukas, while the Miraj sub-division comprises Tasgaon, Jath and Miraj talukas. In August 1964, two more talukas came into being, namely, Atpadi and Kavathe Mahankal (carved out of existing territory).[1]

Sangli district extends from the eastern slopes of the Sahyadri ranges in the east-west direction for about 205 kms. in length. The district is bounded on the north by Satara and Solapur districts, on the west by Ratnagiri district, on the south by Warna river and Kolhapur district, and on the east and south-east by common state boundaries of Maharashtra and Karnataka. The district has an area of 8565 sq.kms. and a population of 18.31 lakhs (1981 census) with seven urban and 543 rural settlements.

The population density of the district is 180 persons per sq.km. as against 164 for Maharashtra State as a whole. Walwa and Miraj talukas are thickly populated areas, while Jath taluka is sparsely populated. "This is because the land in this area is of poor quality and the area is often prone to scarcity conditions." Only about six per cent of the geographical area is covered under forests.[2]

The western zone of Sangli district comprising Miraj and Shirala talukas and parts of Tasgaon and Walwa talukas (in all four talukas) is relatively well developed. Soil in this zone is lateristic on up *ghats* and reddish-brown on hill slopes. Some parts have deep black soil which is highly moisture retentive. Barley, wheat, gram, sugarcane, chillies, etc. can be grown with little investment. The eastern part of the region comprising the area of Kavathe Mahankal, Atpadi and Jath talukas and eastern part of Khanapur, Tasgaon and Miraj talukas are agriculturally backward. They have uncertain and scanty rainfall creating conditions of drought.

The Fault Finding Committee (FFC) appointed by the Government of Maharashtra has surveyed all parts of this district and has identified and delineated the drought-prone zone.[3] According to the FFC, nearaly 62.25 per cent of the geographical area comprising Atpadi, Jath, Kawathe Mahankal and the eastern part (half) of Khanapur, Tasgaon and Miraj talukas falls in the drought-prone zone. This zone includes 275 villages (out of 543), covering a population of 6.13 lakh. In other words, over one-third of the total population lives in the officially declared drought-prone zone.

Pre-Independence Situation

Despite these disparities it cannot be denied that Sangli is one of the few developed districts in Maharashtra. That is because of accelerated growth of commercial agriculture in the western zone of the region. Though this development has taken place mostly in the post-independence era, politico-economic leadership for it was very much there even in the 1920's. It was in the hands of the upper strata of the peasantry.[4] Lineage and kinship helped this leadership to wage a united struggle against the upper crust of the rural society in Sangli district, namely, the *Shetjis and Bhatjis*. The upper crust consisted of Brahmins, Jains, Marwaris and Vaisha Vanis.[5]

It must also be noted that some leaders also moved closer to Krantiveer Nana Patil and helped him in organising raids on police stations and terrorising the pro-British elements in rural as well as urban sectors in the Satara-Sangli-Kolhapur region.[6] Late Nana Patil, a revolutionary, hailed from the village Yedemachindra of the Sangli district. But around the 1930's, the majority of the leaders joined the nationalist movement under Mahatma Gandhi. Y.B. Chavan, Vasantdada Patil, Rajarambapu Patil, V.S. Page and other literate Marathas, with a solid base in the peasantry, joined the Congress and mobilised the rural masses for the freedom movement. The Congress organisation began to take deeper roots in Sangli district.[7] In remote villages, freedom fighters emerged from the ranks of the peasantry. They organised pickets, rallies, demonstrations and village-level meetings to awaken the masses against the British *Raj* and its oppressive rule.[8]

The principal aim of those leading the movement was to gain liberation from the oppressive, anti-peasant British rule. A majority of the rank and file workers believed that the socio-economic backwardness of their region was mainly due to the regressive economic policies of the British *Raj*.[9] Deficiencies like backwardness in agriculture, poor facilities for even primary education, lack of roads, electricity and drinking water supply, inadequate health facilities were attributed to predatory British rule. Their anger and discontent was reflected through direct and indirect participation of the peasantry in the non-co-operation movement, local rallies and demonstrations, and other supportive agitational activities.[10]

The backwardness of the region was noteworthy. Some fifty years ago, the entire region was substantially under-developed subsisting mainly on moonsoon-fed agriculture. Some villages on the bank of the Krishna and the Warna rivers were relatively better off due to perennial water supply and hence at least two crops in a year were assured. At the same time, they constantly lived under the threat of loss of standing crops, flood and inundation of land during the monsoon season. The district, then, was known for the cultivation of food crops like cereals and pulses. Relatively, it enjoyed a stable agricultural season with few ups and downs. Rainfall was adequate if not plentiful. But the villages located at a distance of fifteen to twenty kilometers from the riverbeds depended entirely upon the monsoon.[11] There was very little well-irrigation. Only the better-off farmers could venture to take two crops in a year as they had private wells. There was enough sub-soil water which was tapped through wells and village ponds.

Other facilities in the villages were few.[12] High schools were located at taluka headquarters. Examination centres for the vernacular final examination were located in major towns, namely, Sangli and Miraj. Thus, opportunities for education were limited and accessible mainly to those groups or communities that could aspire for and muster enough resources to educate their younger generation. Female education was least encouraged among the farming communities. High school education among girls was merely in a symbolic form.[13] This situation began to change in the 1940's when the educational activities of Karmveer Bhaurao Patil began to spread in the Sangli region. Through the Rayat Shikshan Sanstha, he began to encourage education among the farmers' sons and daughters including those of the backward castes.[14]

In the 1920's and 1930's, agriculture was the mainstay of the district's economy. Foodgrain cultivation was the chief source of the earning for farming households. There was *ryotwari* system in the region. The landowning castes included Brahmins, Marathas, Dhangars, Malis, Vanjaris, Jains, etc. Even some backward, untouchable castes like Mahars, Holars, Mangs, Chamars, and Dhors and the artisan castes like Sonar, Lohar, Shimpi, and Tambat owned a small percentage (about 10% to 15%) of the land in each village. The landless households were also from amongst the Marathas, Dhangars, Malis, etc., and even the households of the backward castes and the untouchable castes mentioned above.

Social Differentiations and Ranking

Despite disparities in landownership lineage and caste ties were quite tenuous. These ties were nurtured through economic bonds (help in cash and kind), ritual and other social relationships. Social or psychological affinities along caste and lineage lines were quite vibrant despite visible economic differentiations within them.

The Marathas considered themselves lower to none but the Brahmins and, in some parts, to the Jains. The Lingayats too were not homogenous. They had two separate social groups with allegiance to two sectarian chiefs. The Lingayats were mainly owner-cultivators. Recently, a few of them have entered into trade and commerce.

The Dhangars have two groups: Shende and Zende Dhangars; and each asserts its individual identity as being superior to the other group.[15] Some of the Dhangars have now acquired Maratha norms and nomenclatures.[16] Similar was the case among the Chaturtha Jains (mainly the farming, landowing community) and the Pancham Jains (essentially traders and indigeneous bankers).

Even among the untouchables, there was a growing tendency to adopt ritual norms and practices of the upper caste groups to gain goodwill and recognition from them. There were Varkaris and Malkaris among the Maharas, Mangs and Chamars in the villages of Sangli district. This had been thus despite the fact that since the 1950's there have been strong supporters of Ambedkar in some villages of Tasgaon Miraj and Atpadi talukas. No doubt, some untouchables (mostly Mahars) have now become nav-Baudhs or neo-Buddhists. The Ambedkarist or neo-Buddhist movement has gained momentum in this district. But its impact is largely confined to Mahars in the urban centres like Meeraj, Tasgaon, Vita, Ashta, Sangli and Atpadi and some agriculturally developed villages within a ten kilometre radius of the district headquarters. With the emergence of the neo-Buddhist movement, intracaste distinctions among the untouchable castes have become quite weak.

The Mangs, another numerically large untouchable community, has not come significantly under the sway of Ambedkarism or neo-Buddhism.[17] During the last fifty to sixty years, there has been substantial change in the traditional functions of the Mangs.[18] Most of them were landless and worked on the farms of middle and upper castes as agricultural labourers. They are less educated than the Mahars or even the Chamars. In the last ten years some educated Mang youths in Sangli district have been trying to organise their community around issues of undesirable social customs and practices. They are also consciously trying to inculcate a sense of dignity, self-respect and self-assertion. This they are doing through the teachings of late Annabhau Sathe, a Mang by caste. He was a prolific *dalit* writer who spent his entire life in great anguish and introspective reflections. The literate Mangs are mobilising their community in rural areas around the philosophy of Annabhau Sathe, their caste leader.[19]

Thus, the Mangs are coming together, but with a separate, independent organisation. Of course, as yet, there are no visible signs of antipathy or antagonism between the Mangs and the Mahars. But, at the same time, there is no evidence of a sustained dialogue or mutual cooperation among them. The landowning castes in the Sangli villages seem to be a little condescending towards the Mangs, because the Mangs are meek, docile and dutiful. "They are obedient and hardworking. They are faithful to age-old traditions of our village. They will never act against the interest of our village", said one rich farmer from Mauje Tung village. The Mahars are more organised and militant. The landowners look upon them with suspicion and distrust.

Rural Development and Class Interests

Economic Development in the Post-Independence Era

The socio-economic situation has changed substantially over the last forty to fifty years. The post-independence developments have drastically altered the ecological and agricultural conditions in the Sangli region.

Between 1950 and 1965, three sugar factories came up in the cooperative sector. The Shetkari Sahakari Sakhar Karkhana at Madhavnagar, near Sangli, is one of the largest sugar factories in Asia. It was promoted by Vasantdada Patil in 1956. He was also known for his promotive role in setting up land development banks, Co-operative spinning mills, agricultural produce market committees, etc.

The daily sugarcane crushing capacity of the factory is 5,500 tonnes. There are two more sugar factories—one in Chikhali in Shirala taluka and another at Sakharale in Walwa taluka.

The sugar factory at Walwa came up due to the efforts of R.A. Patil, one time rival of Vasantdada Patil. R.A. Patil was a minister in the state cabinet for some time. Because of differences with Vasantdada's group, the his group could not extend its influence beyond Walwa panchayat samiti and taluka. R.A. Patil later joined the Janata Party.

The western parts of Tasgaon taluka (Tasgaon, Turchi, Kumthe, etc.) ventured successfully in growing grapes. Tasgaon Chaman grapes captured not only the internal market, but also dominated the export market. About five hunderd tonnes of grapes are exported annually to Middle East countries alone. Earlier, Nasik district was a monopoly centre of grape production. Today, some grape cultivators of Tasgaon taluka are known as Bagaitkars. They employ Karbharis, garden labourers, packers, etc. They have telephones in the grape-sorting sheds on the farms. A few of them own cars. Some of them have visited European countries to study dry-fruit processing and crop-protection techniques. All these developments have taken place since mid-1960.[20]

Geographically, the district is endowed with a rich resource, i.e., perennial water from the Krishna and Warna rivers in the region. Socially, the landowning communities, especially the Marathas, Dhangars and Chaturtha Jains, were well versed in cultivation. They were meticulous and hardworking peasants known to be patient with nature and its vicissitudes. Extreme religiosity and ritualism among them was not an accidental factor. It helped them to face adversities with sense of fortitude. Socio-political movements also exposed them to national currents and under-currents in the 1930's and 1940's. The district leaders and the freedom fighters came mostly from among the upper and middle strata of the peasantry.[21]

District-Level Leadership

The socio-political background was helpful for the leadership to advance the economic interests of the district more assertively. Association with the Congress during the freedom movement helped the district leadership after independence, in occupying prominent positions at the state and central levels. Between 1960 and 1985, Sangli's leaders were chosen as the chief minister of Maharashtra State four times. Several ministers in the state cabinet handling important portfolios of agriculture, irrigation, finance, etc. were also chosen from this district.

Vasantrao Patil (popularly known as 'Dada Patil') was one such prominent state-level leader from this district. He was known as the benefactor of Sangli district and there was enough evidence of this, especially in the western zone of the district. Incidentally, his own village Padmale is located in this part. He held many important positions. Apart from being the chief minister, he was also the president of the

Maharashtra the State Co-operative Bank, State Co-operative Sugar Factories Federation, and the State Congress Committee. He also served as the governor of Rajasthan too. He took keen interest in the developmental activities of the district.

One scholar, well acquainted with district politics, writes:

> ...Vasantrao Patil gradually increased his hold on the district politics right from the first general elections. He has been mentioned as the 'king-maker' in the Sangli district... leader of the masses. He has knocked on every door in every hut of the Sangli district...[22]

Association with the ruling party consistently for over twenty years since the formation of the separate Maharashtra State and also development of volatile and prosperous co-operative institutions in the fields of agriculture, credit, water supply, land development, dairy and other agro-based activities has ushered in accelerated growth in the district. Political linkage with the state apparatuses and development of the district are mutually dependent and reinforcing factors.[23] This has led to some expected and some intriguing consequences. We shall discuss them soon.

We must stress here that the district leadership as it evolved over the years came from particular areas of the district, essentially the western parts covering the Sangli, Miraj, Shirala and Tasgaon talukas. Thus, the district leadership was in fact sub-regional and segmental in its out-look, rather myopic, to put it crudely.

One obvious and glaring result of such myopic leadership was a lop-sided development of the district. Some parts of the district received all the attention and amenities while some parts remained in perpetual stagnation.

This lopsidedness was inherent in the leadership which mainly relied on the powerful, articulate peasantry from the western bloc of the district. The state-level political leaders bargained with these western bloc leaders, neglecting the demands and needs of the eastern bloc until the latter revolted openly under mass pressures. The farmers benefiting from the development schemes and projects seemed to be unwilling to share their gains with others, i.e., less-developed or backward parts.

The backward or under-developed villages supplied the developed ones with cheap labour in the peak seasons. This gave the inhabitants of the developed region a sense of exalted status.[24] They belonged to perennially irrigated, prosperous and politically dominant villages. They nurtured their 'pride' and also the 'vested interest' expressing this privileged status. Even the marginal farmers and landless labourers of this region acquiesced in this evaluation. Table 1 below provides data about the leadership.

Table 1

Social Profile of Panchayat Leaders in Sangli District (Village, Taluka & District Panchayats)

Parameters	*Details %*
1. *Case Composition* (N = 163)	
Advanced Caste	5.5
Intermediary	77.3
Lower	8.0
Backward	9.2
2. *Age Composition* (N = 163)	
21-30 Years	9.8
31-40 Years	35.0
41-50 Years	37.4
51 Years & above	17.8
3. *Education* (N = 163)	
Illiterate	1.8
Upto 7th Standard	42.3
8th to 12th Standard	28.8
Graduation	27.1
4. *Occupational Pattern* (N = 163)	
Agriculture	87.7
Business	3.1
Service	6.8
Profession	2.4
5. *Income* (N = 163)	
Upto Rs.10,000	46.0
Rs.10,000 - 25,000	27.0
Rs.25,000 - 50,000	14.7
Rs.50,001 and above	12.3
6. *Land Ownership* (N = 163)	
Upto 5 acres	12.8
6 - 10 acres	20.3
11 acres and above	66.9

Contd...

7. *Perceived Class* (N = 163)	
Upper	23.3
Middle	62.6
Lower	14.1
8. *Personal Possessions* (N = 163)	
Motor cars	9.2
Telephone	11.7
Scooter, Motor Cycles	38.7
Tractors	20.9
Electric Pumps	76.1
Cycles	66.9
9. *Newspaper Reading* (N = 163)	
English papers	3.7
Bombay papers	47.2
Poona papers	90.2
Local papers	93.3
10. *Political Affiliation*	
Congress (I)	74.9
Janata Party	11.7
P.W.P.	6.8
Congress (S)	5.5
Others	1.1
11. *Their Ideal Leader* (N = 163)	
Vasant Dada Patil	52.8
Mahatma Gandhi	46.6
Pandit Nehru	42.3
Y.B. Chavan	20.2
Indira Gandhi	16.0

Source: K.R. Patil, A Sociological Study of Panchayati Raj Leadership in Sangli District, Ph. D. Thesis, Shivaji University, Kolhapur, 1983.

Water Co-operatives and VIKAS Agencies: Competing Interests

Now let us talk about the developed areas in the district. Out of eight talukas, two talukas (Miraj and Shirala) in entirety and a large number of villages of Tasgaon and Walwa talukas can safely be included in this developed category. This area is situated in the western zone of Sangli district. The soil is black and alluvial. It is extremely fertile. The foundation stone of one of the biggest irrigation projects in this area, namely the Warna Project was laid in 1977.[25] The dam was constructed in Chandoli on the Warna river in the Shirala taluka. It submerged 301 sq.km.

area, and it stores 964 million cubic metres of water. Because of this dam, 49,150 hectrares of land in Sangli district and 36,275 in Kolhapur district gets irrigated. Besides this, medium irrigation projects were taken up at Yeralwadi, Sidhewadi, Morna, Doddanala and Basappawadi.

Since the 1950's, due to the influence of local leadership, a large number of water co-operative schemes have come into operation. With the assistance of state financial institutions, the entire western region is now networked with lift irrigation schemes (LIS), jackwells and tubewells. The farmers have organised themselves into village-level water co-operatives to get the benefits of uninterrupted water supply. In some villages (Kasbe Digraj, Padmale, and Sangliwadi in Miraj taluka), there are three or four water co-operatives per village. Their share capital runs into lakhs of rupees. They have built two-storeyed office buildings. They employ their own maintenance staff to ensure a regular water supply. The balance sheet of the performance of many of these water co-operatives is indeed remarkable. Most of them paid off their loans long ago. Now they enjoy a sound financial position.

In addition to these, there are multi-purpose co-operative societies known as VIKAS (Vividh Karyakari Sahakari Mandali). Each village has a VIKAS agency with its own spacious office, godown, fair price shop and many other centres and sub-centres. Like water co-operatives, the VIKAS agency enjoys financial support from the state financial bodies including the scheduled banks. The annual budget of some agencies runs into several thousands of rupees. They distribute agricultural credit, seeds, fertilisers, insecticides, etc. Through fair price shops, they distribute foodgrains, kerosene, etc. to their members. Annual turnover and profits are substantial. Hence, one witnesses a keen competition among the well-off farmers and their kinsmen to secure positions in the managing committees of these bodies. In all the villages in the developed parts of this region, electoral contests are quite lively. Even upcoming and well-off traders and money-lenders (usually the Jains) fight for the posts in these organisations.

A position in these bodies seems to provide enough opportunities and, of course, their own interests as farmers or traders are safely looked after. Besides, the posts of the president, secretary or treasurer allow them access to funds and also to meet and influence petty and not-so-petty government officials with whom they can form 'favourable' equations.

The office incumbents also wield political influence. They can get things done through subtle manipulations. The people outside the ruling 'clique' openly speak of corruption of various sorts in these bodies.[26] Those who complain (and they too belong to the well-off strata of peasantry) secretly desire to be in those very positions. They want access to power and to be able to manipulate resources in their own favour and in the favour of their close relatives, friends and sympathisers. Thus, there has been an open competition for the elective posts in these agencies. A casual visit to these villages during the VIKAS agency elections can bring home this point.

Elections, Factions and Vertical Cleavages

Elections are fought with money power and sometimes with muscle power. There are usually two panels (named as Shetkari and Sahakari) of the candidates in village level elections. But everyone in village knows who the leader of the panel is. He is often the a farmer of the village. Thus, the contest is between two farmers from the same village. Often they belong to the same caste (usually Marathas or on rare occasions, the Brahmins or the Jains). Each faction then adopts all the known tactics of electioneering: pleading, placating, browbeating, threatening, blackmailing and even physically assaulting the voters who refuse to fall in line. Communal and caste pressures are skilfully utilised to gain the support of the voter-members of these co-operative bodies.

Elections for the managing committee of Digraj village VIKAS agency in December 1985 exemplified this process.[27] There was hectic campaigning: door-to-door visits, village-square meetings and processions. The Maratha panel won the elections. All seats were captured by them with an overwhelming majority. The post-election euphoria was unbelievable. The Maratha families consisting of some sixty per cent of the total households in the villages were jubilant beyond description. Men, women and children came out on the streets, bursting crackers and shouting slogans, "Shivaji Maharaj ki Jai", "Bhavani Mata ki Jai". The crowd included Marathas and members of anti-Jain castes even from poorer strata. "It is a victory against Jain monopoly. We, the Marathas, can now show them how to run this VIKAS Agency."[28]

The defeated Jain leaders, on the other hand, were planning to dislodge the opposite panel by other means.[29] A few Jain traders and rich farmers had kept large amounts of money in fixed deposits in this agency. Some of them were thinking of withdrawing these deposits, partly to create financial difficulties for the incumbents, and partly to keep their savings at some safer place. The elderly and wiser sections of the Jain community pleaded for discretion. "After all they would need our help and guidance at some stage; we also need their favours," old Jain traders advised the younger members of their community. The rich Jain farmers and traders knew their own interests too well.

In other villages too, similar tendencies prevailed dividing them into two distinct and warring factions. Each faction carried with it members of the same or different castes and also members of different economic strata. The faction leaders were the well-off farmers supported by the members of lower castes and lower classes.

The Marathas consitituted the largest caste group in Sangli district (about 40%). Together with Malis and Lingayats, they constituted an intermediary layer. In a recent study of panchayat leadership, it was observed that this intermediary caste group (roughly about 50% of the population) captured over seventy-seven per cent positions in panchayat bodies, i.e., the village panchayat, taluqa panchayat and zila panchayat. Women members co-opted to these bodies also belonged to the rich strata of the peasantry. D'Lima Hazel[30] wrote in 1980: "The women of the upper castes, wives of big landowners and politically influential families tend to dominate the positions reserved for women in the zila panchayat and taluka panchayat." K.R. Patil confirmed this observation saying: "D'Lima's finding was found to be cent per cent true in the Sangli district since all the women respondents hailed from the rich peasantry, happened to be wives of big leaders and acted as agents of their own husbands."[31]

There was apparently a division among the rich for capturing the positions of power, money and prestige. But they also forced the lower strata to align with them in the name of caste, community, religion or any such ascriptive and operative criteria. Thus, the rural poor remained divided among themselves. Their faction solidarity seemed to be more tenacious than the class solidarity.

Uneven Development, Disparities and Social Tensions

Sugarcane Economy and Upcoming Strata

Lite irrigation scheme and canal network have brought immense prosperity to this part of the region. Already fertile land endowed with river-bed nutrients gave phenomenal yields of the traditional crops. The farmers, sensing the advantage of continuous flow of water throughout the year, changed their cropping pattern. The traditional crops were replaced by the cash crop, namely, sugarcane. Almost all farmers, irrespective of the size of land, shifted to sugarcane cultivation in right earnest.

Within a span of two to three years, the entire region in the western zone became the epicentre of the sugar economy. During the same period, the co-operative sugar factories, namely, Shetkari Sahakari Sakhar Karkhana-SSSK were set up at Madhavnagar near Sangli town and at Sakhrale. As stated earlier, the SSSK is the biggest sugar factory in Asia. It has the largest cane-crushing capacity, over eight lakh metric tonnes of sugarcane within 165 days. Recovery rate is as high as 11.33 per cent.[32]

The SSSK covers 158 villages of Walwa, Miraj, Kavathe Mahankal and Tasgaon. Besides, it covers some villages like Udgaon, Arjunwad, Jaisingpur, etc. from Kolhapur district. The SSSK has a total membership of 31,081, of which 30,979 are farmer-producers. According to Vishnupant Patial, the SSSK president, more than ninety-six per cent of the members are from the category of small farmers. More than twenty per cent belong to the backward castes or Magasvargiya.[33]

The crushing capacity of these factory units is large enough which has created a lots of problems and interesting contradictions within the ruling class of peasantry. We shall discuss them later. To run the sugar factories and to maintain their profitability, efficiency and fair returns to the cane-growers, the factory management was forced to bring in larger and larger area of agricultural land under sugarcane cultivation.

This entailed encouragement to and conscious inclusion of small and marginal farmers in production network. Even a poor farmer owning half an acre of land became a shareholder and began growing sugarcane. Thus, even the lower strata of peasantry sensed the immediate gain from cash-crop cultivation. They also got some benefits in the early years, albeit in differential terms. The larger the acreage under cultivation and greater the capacity to bear the production costs, the higher was the return or income available to the farmers through this co-operative network.

So, eventually, the middle and rich farmers of the region reaped greater advantages in this market-oriented sugar economy. The co-operative set-up helped them to enhance their socio-economic status considerably. The small and marginal farmers also gained in this process, but only in proportion to their scale of landownership, output and other attendant skills in the local polity.

The sugar factory organisation has undertaken multifarious activities. It invested lakhs of rupees on water supply, management, land levelling, drainage facility, crop protection, transport, labour supply and supervision and on many other allied matters.[34] The state government helped these ventures in liberal terms. Production of sugarcane and sugar altered the entire landscape. New economic and political opportunities were now made available, and this gave rise to competition among various sections of peasantry for enlargement of their economic and political base. K.R. Patil rightly notes: "Co-operative societies are the most powerful agencies for leaders to secure an access to power position in the political field... the co-operative societies help the leaders to secure power positions in the politics and, in turn, power positions in politics help them to secure positions in the co-operatives"...[35]

As the situation unfolds today, competition is acute among the middle and rich farmers to obtain positions in sugar factory management (SFM). There are rival groups among them bent upon defeating and dislodging one another. This rivalry apart, all of them agree on one principle, namely, "increase production, enlarge profits and control social and political institutions for the benefit of their kinsmen, friends and sympathisers."

A glimpse of the power of the rich farmers and their representatives in the SFM can be had from the recent rumblings and grumblings. D.G. Patil, a Rajya Sabha member and S.N. Deshmukh met Rajiv Gandhi, the former prime minister of India, and complained about *gunhegari* (criminalities) and *jatiya pravrutti* (casteist or communal tendencies) of the *Sakhar Samrats* (sugar barons). They conveyed that these barons have to be kept under control... because they "constitute a serious threat to the stability of the party and the government". They also referred to large-scale corruption in the sanctioning of tenders, etc. They demanded an enquiry by the Central Bureau of Investigation (CBI) into the affairs of SFMs. They also submitted to the prime minister a petition signed by about 150 farmers listing the above grievances.[36]

It is this competitive environment that has encouraged alliances within and across caste, community and class. The lower and lowest strata, i.e., poor farmers and landless agricultural labourers of this region are largely passive participants. A few among them are active agents and supporters of one or the other ruling clique led by middle and rich farmers. The leading members of these cliques hold important positions in SFM and other organisations. They have to provide and do provide help and assistance to their supporters belonging to the lower strata of their own caste group or other caste groups.[37]

The ruling group always seems to be alert and watchful in retaining a hold over their 'beneficiaries'. They are consciously on the lookout to widen this base through providing assistance in all matters—petty and not-so-petty.[38] They openly boast of 'their men' and 'their group' to remind others of their social and political clout.

Life-Style of the Rural Rich

Development gains seem to have gone more to the middle and rich farmers. This is observable through certain visible indices in all the villages along the western corridor of the district. The land values have shot up from a mere Rs. 4,000 per acre to over Rs. 50,000 per acre in the last twenty years. The upper class of farmers are now free from the day-to-day routine of agricultural operations. A rich farmer's visits to his farms are infrequent, if not rare. He now plans for weeks or months, assigning routine supervision to his *karbhari* or trusted *gadis* (permanent servants). His interests are now riveted around trade, finance and 'the politics' beyond the village frontier.[39]

In the past five years, new subjects have been added to his agenda. He talks unapprovingly of "growing interference of the state in farmers indigenous ventures", "parasitism of urban middle classes including the government bureaucrats", "too much of developmentalism and pro-poor programmes" and "restrictive sugar policy neglecting the interest of cane-growers". In the same breath, he also bemoans the lack of religiosity among the younger generation and absence of respect for the age-old customs and traditions of the village.

His life-style now exhibits significant change. Increased income is used for investment in production and improvement of land and trade. Part of the income is also used towards improvement in life-style comparable to that of upper and upper middle classes in metropolitan cities.[40]

Tensions Within the Ruling Class: Some Glimpses

The families constituting the ruling or elite groups in rural Sangli are not all without tensions or strains. Apart from the internecine factionalism which we have described earlier, there are other problems of a grave nature. Indiscriminate use of water and fertilisers has resulted in serious salinity problems in the land of hitherto well off households. Some of them have lost more than half of their erstwhile fertile lands. That is because of increased alkaline salt deposits. Technical experts called in by the SFM and the district authorities blame this on excessive use of water and over dosages of chemical fertilisers.

The rich farmers whose land is affected are now worried. Sugarcane production has gone down, so has their income. In the eyes of others, they are rich farmers, but they are 'going down-hill' (*paristhiti bighadali, kangal hot chalale*). No longer are they are looked upon as prestigious farmers. Some of them are struggling hard to maintain their life-style. "But the future is dark for us, unless our land is cured of the salinity problem."

Instances of such families in crises are plentiful in Kasbe Digraj, Tung, Audumbar, Mhaisal, etc.[41] Other farmers have now become extremely cautious. They have grown increasingly sceptical about excessive use of water, fertilisers, insecticides, etc. Not that they have stopped using these devices altogether, but they now remain watchful, and have begun to personally supervise their labourers when the latter water the crops or use fertilisers. "Once beaten, twice shy" seems to be the case with the farmers in these salinity-prone villages.

There are other problems worth noting. The rich and upcoming farmers very much desire their children, particularly sons, to get higher education. They want them to become doctors, engineers, IAS, IFS, officers and executives in private firms. They are all too willing and, of course, capable of spending as much money as required to improve the career prospects of their sons. But all of them cannot make it.

In fact, some of them do not reach even the graduation level. College life is mostly used as an outlet for pleasure, waywardness and dominance by the younger generation coming from affluent families. This has been the point of worry in some families. The parents are uncertain regarding the future of their children. One can hear the woes of the rich farmers when one moves around these developed villages.

Also related to this is the problem of leadership in future. Unequipped or ill-equipped sons cannot successfully replace their parents who achieved the position of dominance and control in their own lifetime. That does not mean that the rich farmers have completely lost their grip on the situation. They do try to secure position for their sons in sugar co-operatives, water co-operatives, and other panchayati raj bodies. But they are not too sure about the initiative, capabilities and competence of those whom they are promoting. The talk of dynastic rule, family control, kinship monopoly etc.,[42] that one hears in this region with respect to the management of co-operative institutions, is a reflection on declining leadership norms or standards within the progressive or rich strata of rural society.

The third problem concerns about a secure economic status in the future, i.e., in the coming ten to fifteen years. Salinity is one problem (which we have mentioned earlier) that has already alarmed and alerted some sections of the rich peasantry. Another problem has arisen from quite 'unexpected' quarters. Viability of the sugar factories is continuously being threatened due to altered social conditions in the region. The sugar factories were started with the assumption that they would receive an uninterrupted supply of sugarcane from the member villages. They also expected 'good quality' cane for better recovery percentage to produce quality sugar. But these calculations are going awry due to salinity of land, over-ageing of cane, etc. These are critical bottlenecks in sugarcane supply because the number of co-operative sugar factories has increased from two in the 1950's to eight in the 1980's. Even at the time of writing this essay, there was hectic lobbying for setting up one more sugar factory at Tasgaon (known as Panchwya Mailacha Karkhana). Even the backward talukas are now clamouring for a sugar factory in their region, since it gives the local leadership an opportunity for further strengthening their social, economic and political base. The ruling party conceded to their demand to influence local masses, and thereby retained electoral support.

The result of this ad hoc and short-sighted policy has been quite unhelpful (and even disastrous) to the large mass of people in the undeveloped talukas. More about this later. A point to be noted here is the cut-throat competition between the SFMs to retain control over their sugar-producing territory. Since 1984, there is a statutory regulation (zonal system) dividing the sugar-producing villages among the existing factory units. But who observes the rule? The farmers from the border-line villages supply sugarcane to both, their 'official' factory, and illegally to other factory units. They try to make hay while the sun shines.

There are watch-dog bodies of the SFM and flying squads to catch loaded trucks infringing the territory rule. The trucks are impounded, the drivers arrested and the erring farmers blacklisted.[43] But the SFMs do not always succeed in their operations. In late 1986 and early 1987 there were tensions and open conflicts between the SFM and the farmers. The police had to be called in to maintain law and order in some villages in Walwa taluka. The sugarcane cutting operation was conducted under strict police *bandobast.*[44] In some places the trucks and tankers loaded with sugarcane were diverted to 'their' sugar factory by the rival groups.

All the happenings are due to the paucity of cane against the crushing capacity of the factories. Keen competition based on rivalries persist among the sugar co-operatives and their leaders. The farmers of all ranks—rich, middle and poor—are divided in their loyalties. They constitute rival camps, each campaigning for its supremacy and for the other's downfall. In other villages, where such rivalries have not yet come on the surface, there are other points of distress felt by the small and marginal farmers. Despite their membership of the sugar factory (as shareholders), their sugarcane field is not cleared in time. The crop gets too ripe with eventually lesser weightage and income on the produce. Factory transport and labour are easily available to the better-off and well connected farmers who have influence with top layers of management.

The lower strata of peasantry growing sugarcane face a variety of other difficulties. These include lack of adequate and timely supply of water through lift irrigation scheme, delay in getting adequate credit for agricultural operation, delay in securing final payments from the factory, lack of fodder for their cattle, etc. Also, they have to buy daily necessities, including foodgrains, from the market. Sometimes they get credit from the shopkeepers, but sometimes they don't. And then they mortgage their land, house, utensils, jewellery, etc., with the moneylenders. Sugarcane cultivation has not been beneficial to the entire strata of poor peasantry. Through this cash crop, a few have managed to rise above their status, but many seem to have remained static or even have gone down economically. This aspect needs further investigation.

The Poor Labourers: Locals and Migrants

In developed villages, the condition of agricultural labourers is relatively better than those of in the backward villages in the eastern part of Sangli region. However, one must make a distinction between the local labourer and the migrant, as the two are not in the same situation.

In developed villages, the local labourers are drawn from the landless households belonging to both the 'touchables' and 'untouchables'. We have already given the details of these caste groups including their traditional occupations and obligations. Our impression is that the local labourers, irrespective of their caste, do not face the problem of unemployment to a large extent. The male members go for the field labour or factory labour, some of them have jobs in the seed farms, poultry farms, or as *gadis or karbharis* in the camp houses of the rich farmers. Caste linkages of traditional loyalties seem to help them to retain access to means of livelihood. Of course, they do not seem to have freedom to assert their rights. They cannot unduly criticise the behaviour of their patrons.[45] Most of them seem to have accepted the role of a passive participant in the politics of village development. Somewhat educated and intelligent persons from among the labourers have joined sugar factories as bill clerks, slip boys, tractor drivers or Mechanics. They earn monthly wage and enjoy a little better life than the mass of ordinary labourers.

Since 1975, the developed villages have taken advantage of a number of government sponsored pro-poor schemes. Not that all poo households have derived benefits from these schemes, but it appears tha many of them have derived some benefit (whatever may be the scal under some schemes). Some got housing sites, some constructio material free of cost. A few have obtained milch cattle and a membership in village. A few destitute families are covered under the Sanja Gandhi Niradhar Yojana. A few artisan households have reveived see capital or trade material to start their enterprises. Some barbers, tailors potters, iron-smiths, masons (*gavandis*), etc. are also beneficiaries o government programmes.

Thus, one way or the other, the local poor households are brough into contact and relationship with the officials associated with th schemes. In building this relationship, the lower strata have to take hel of the upper strata whose influence-network is wide spread and effective. Their *chiththi* (recommendatory note) or telephone message help them to secure a place in the list of 'target households'.

Thus, the government pro-poor programmes indirectly help the ric strata to retain and perhaps further consolidate their hold over the poo strata. The caste network and kinship ties get further reinforced, and no necessarily dissipated. This is what seems to be happening in the villages we visited in this region. The local poor remain obliged to the loca rich and politically well connected people. The latter's influence ove the village officials like teachers, *talathies, gram sevaks, arogya rakshaks*, PHC doctors and nurses, credit co-operatives' personnel, etc seems to be increasing and not diminishing. After all, these official have to stay in the village and build up their own carees. They know tha they can ill-afford to antagonise the better-off sections of the villag community.

The sugarcane economy in the green revolution belt has attracte migrant labourers since the 1960's. Most of these labourers come fro the drought-prone areas of Sholapur, Nipani, Chikodi, Vijaypur, Bh and Osmanabad regions. Some even come from neighbouring Karnataka. Initially, they visit these villages for seasonal work from October to May or June. Later on, many of them settle down in thes villages permanently.

In many villages in western parts of Sangli district (Sangliwad Samroli, Audumber, Digraj, Tung, Mhaisal, etc.), there are permane dwellings (huts or *kachha* structures) of these early migrants. The population is sizeable. In village Digraj, for example, one-sixth of the total households belong to these early migrants. Most of them work as farm labourers on a daily wage of Rs. 6 to 8. Their womenfolk work as maid servants or as field labourers in showing or cutting season. Interestingly, they have been smoothly accommodated (or assimilated) in the village society and its institutions.

Early migrants were given housing plots. Many of them are given residential quarters in Navi Vasahat (new colony), a village panchayat venture under the twenty-point programme. They have voting right in local panchayat elections. In some villages, they have contested and got elected in panchayat bodies. They have ration cards. They have an easy access to PHCs and other village-level service centres. Their children get admitted to village primary schools. A casual visitor to these villages might find it difficult to distinguish between the natives and these early migrants.

During their stay over the past fifteen to twenty years, these early migrants have become sufficiently rooted in the village society, polity and culture. They have learnt the rules of the game quite well. Like the local native poor, these 'early migrants' depend upon the sympathy and support of the well-off sections of the village society, be they rich farmers, traders, shopkeepers or money-lenders. They acknowledge that without the support and help from the local villagers their life would have been miserable. "We could not hope to have a roof over our heads. We got shelter, food and employment," some of them recollect.

But the condition of other migrants (outsiders) is pathetic, to say the least. These are the seasonal migrants working in the sugarcane fields as cutters, choppers, loaders, and transporters of sugarcane. Briefly, we may call them sugarcane cutters. In 1972, there was a severe drought in many parts of Maharashtra. Since then, a large number of families from the drought-prone districts of Nasik, Aurangabad, Bhir, Parbhani, Nanded, Sholapur, etc. have been migrating to Sangli and the nearby green revolution belt for seasonal employment.

According to one estimate, around 35,000 to 40,000 seasonal migrants work in the sugarcane fields between October to April every year. They are known as *Koyatas* (a pair of two male and female labourers) in *Tolis* (a group of *Koyatas*). Each *Toli* has between eight and ten *Koyatas*. These *Tolis* are under the complete control and dominance of the contractors who generally belong to the same region, village or caste as that of the sugarcane cutters. The contractors (also known as *Muccadams*) are retained by the SFMs on seasonal basis and they get the advance amount and some perquisites for recruitment and supervision of the seasonal labour.

The contractors assign the cane-cutting work to these labourers. The labourers are paid on piece-work basis mainly on the tonnage of sugarcane cut, bundled and loaded in trucks or tractors. The rate was Rs. 13 per tonne in November-December 1985. A pair could hardly get Rs. 13 to 18 for the whole day's work (about twelve to fourteen hours). Even their children had to help them to expedite the cutting operation. In peak season of cane-cutting, the trucks/tractors reach the field in the dead of night, and the labourers have to rush to the field to load the sugarcane in the vehicle. Both the farmers and the truck drivers shout at them to hurry up loading.

Thus, the migrant labourers could not always hope to have their meals or sleep without interruption. They do not get any extra wages for these additional duties. Even the *gadiwalas* (bullockcart-owners) transporting sugarcane from the field to the factory live in a hand-to-mouth fashion. Both the cane-cutters and transporters do not get their wages from the contractors in time. The latter plead helplessness saying that they have yet to be paid by the SFM. The contractors give some amount as *kharchi* (advance sum for spending) to the labourers, which is deducted from the final wage bill.

Problem of Social Distance and Distorted Perceptions

Sugarcane cutters appeared to be extremely tense and agitated about their living and working conditions. They live on the open fields or in make-shift huts like *cavemen*. They are exposed to conditions of extreme heat and cold which wears down their strength immensely. A boy of eighteen looks thirty years old after working on sugarcane fields for two seasons. Their *bastis* (place of settlement) have no roads or electricity. They have to shift their huts, goats and cattle every week or ten days on the *diktat* of the contractors.

Village people, including the local poor, do not seem to look upon them kindly, nor do they solicit participation in any of the local social events. Instead, there is an impression that these migrant labourers are outsiders. They are labelled as "cheats, lazy, immensely frugal and money-gathering persons with concealed wealth, cattle thieves, evil-eyed, shrewd and manipulating etc." It is worth listening to some natives (including the local poor) when they spont abusive epithets against the migrant cane-cutters.

How has this image or imagery has come to prevail? Who or which group spreads such feelings? These questions would need separate in-depth study. But we can make one observation here. In Maoje Tung village, about ten kilometres away from Sangli town, the local labourers have now to seek employment through the outside contractor for cane-cutting work. Two years ago they could obtain this job independently on their own through their contacts with village influentials. That situation is now changing slowly. It points towards the trend that their 'priority status' in local labour market is no longer ensured. Competition between the local and the migrant poor has been growing in the recent years.

It seems certain that there is no solidarity between the local poor and the migrant poor (i.e., sugarcane cutters). There may not be hatred or antagonism between them in all the villages. But, there is definitely no evidence of mutual appreciation of each other's conditions and problems. There is no mutual respect and understanding, let alone mutual help and support. There is an uneasy distance and separation between the two groups.

This situation is further exaggerated due to fodder shortages in the villages. Under the existing conventions, the sugarcane cutters are entitled to keep to themselves half of the *wad*, i.e., upper portions of the canes. The other half goes to the farm owner. These stems make very good green fodder for cattle. The migrant labourers use their share to feed their own cattle and sell the surplus in the village markets. By selling they get the much needed cash to buy daily necessities. The going-rate for such fodder was Rs. 12 to 14 per hundred *pulis* in 1987. The small and marginal farmers, and even the landless labourers keeping milch animals, had to buy this fodder from the sugarcane cutters. One could witness moments of tensions in the village market where such transactions of selling and buying of *wad* take place. The locals are unhappy about the fact that they have to buy the 'fodder' which they earlier used to get for free from the local farmers. Some even compel the migrant labourers to lower the price. Some poor farmers from Sangliwadi village were arguing: "These outsiders are given employment, food and shelter in our area. They have opportunities of living because we grow sugarcane. Now look at them. They are selling our own fodder to us. And that too at their prices. Look."

The poor strata in the developed villages have not come closer to the migrant labourers socially and emotionally. They still consider them "aliens, others and different". When shall this gap be bridged? We don't know.

Summary

Sangli district is one of the developed and progressive sub-regional units in Maharashtra State. Hence, experience gained here, i.e., development milieu of Sangli district, might help us to review our micro as well as macro planning perspectives, policies and programmes.

Sangli district is developed but the development is uneven, generating disparities in production, income levels and life-styles of various groups and classes. Firstly, there is disparity between the talukas. Both at concrete and abstract levels, we strongly discern two 'parts' or 'segments' in Sangli. There are two Sanglis masquerading as one. We call them Sangli I (this Sangli) and Sangli II (the other Sangli).

Sangli I has developed rather excessively own in the last thirty years. It is endowed with natural resources like good soil and sub-soil water deposits. It has a surfeit of human and technological inputs. Successful and profitable co-operatives are formed and sustained through this edifice.

Institutional support structures, like the co-operatives for water, milk poultry, paper and above all sugar factories are deep-rooted and are flourishing under the active leadership of progressive farmers of this region. The growth stategy of the state and its 'pro-farmer' policies have further helped 'this Sangli' in expanding and consolidating its gains in agriculture, trade, commerce, education, and other fields of activities.

'This Sangli' has been growing and developing by leaps abd bounds during the past thirty years. It has been helping different social strata, namely, rich, middle and poor peasants including the landless labourers. No doubt, the gains or benefits are not even. They are distributed unevenly. Their life-styles adequately reflect this disparity. But there is no distinct sign of polarisation or sharp division among them, not at least in their subjective perceptions or evaluations. This may be due to:

(a) alliance of interests nurtured through co-operative structures,
(b) caste affinities and linkages,
(c) faction solidarities along caste, community and class lines, and
(d) social and political skills of the district leadership.

It appears that this edifice is now experiencing jerks and jolts. We call them tensions or crises. These tensions are now surfacing on many fronts in 'this Sangli.' These tensions are reflected through:

(a) factionalism and rivalries among the ruling peasantry, i.e., within the ruling class;
(b) cut-throat competition between the sugar factories for control of supply;
(c) soil degeneration due to salinity and excessive use of chemical fertilisers;

(d) consequent loss of production and setback in the life-style of even the erstwhile rich;

(e) signs of discontent and militancy among the 'migrant' sugarcane (and 'regular' sugar factory workers) who have begun to express themselves against their unsatisfactory working and living conditions; and

(f) influx of persons from the 'other Sangli' (Khanapur, Atpadi, Kavathe Mahankal etc.) in the recent years as sugarcane-cutters in 'this Sangli.'

This is the first ever exposure of these persons from 'other Sangli' (of all strata, including some landowners with fifteen to twenty acres of land) to work under conditions of duress and distress. This 'other Sangli' might lead to the forces to sharpening of the existing contradictions.

Sangli II or 'other Sangli' is backward, unproductive, and devoid of any distinct development inputs. There has been drought for the second successive year here. The crops are severely damaged. The land is burnt under the scorching sun. Even drinking water is not available to many villages. Wells have dried up and the water table has gone down. Tankers, tractors and bullock-carts are pressed into service for providing drinking water to the villagers. The cattle strength is also depleting under severe strains of water and fodder shortages. A few cattle camps are set up by the sugar factories and district administration. They are trying to cope with this crisis. But the situation is too critical to be reversed by such *ad hoc* measures. The employment situation is critical despite the EGS programmes. Workers have to migrate if they want to survive (*'Jagayala Challe'*, they say).

Workers are now angry and agitated, organising protest marches and demonstrations to demand the minimum necessities of life: water, fodder and work. The situation is uneasy and tense. 'Other Sangli' is slowly realising that it has been by-passed and neglected even in the fulfilment of basic needs. This awareness gets stronger and sharper when they look upon 'this Sangli' just about fifteen to twenty kilometres away, within the same administrative zone. They now ask questions: Water for whom? Sugarcane production for what? Whose prosperity and development? These are 'new' questions. It would require a separate study to probe into this 'new' dynamics of rural development.

Notes

1. Bhoite K.R.: A Study of Democratic Decentralisation in Maharashtra with Special Reference to Satara District, Unpublished Ph.D.Thesis, University of Poona, 1970.
2. *Government of Maharashtra*: Socio-Economic Review and District Statistical Abstract of Sangli District 1977-78, 1978-79, Bombay, Directorate of Economics and Statistics, 1980.
3. *Government of Maharashtra*: Report of the Fact Finding Committee, for Survey of Scarcity Areas, pp. 160-163, 1978.
4. Satya Shodhak movement was organised around socio-economic issues in Kolhapur region. It slowly spread to the neighbouring parts like Sangli, Satara, Karhad etc. by the turn of this century. The vocal and conscious sections of Maratha peasantry took active part in spearheading the struggle against the 'Shetjis and Bhatjis', i.e. the landlords, traders and the 'rapacious' moneylenders. In this, they got the unflinching support from the lower sections of peasantry including the landless.
5. *Omvedt Gail*: Cultural Revolt in a Colonial Society: The Non-Brahmin Movement in Western India-1873 to 1930, Bombay, Scientific Socialist Education Trust, 1976.
6. They set up a 'Patri Sarkar' (parallel government) and created quite a stir in the countryside of Western Maharashtra including Sangli district.
7. *Chavan Y.B.*: Krishnakathi (an Autobiography in Marathi), Vol.I, Poona, Prestige Prakashan, 1984.
8. Many courted arrest and were jailed in the prisons at Nasik and Poona. A few went to nearby Princely State of Kolhapur, and carried out underground propoganda through leaflets and pamphlets.
9. "The farmers are crushed under the burden of land revenues. Their sons are denied even minimum opportunities of growth and self-expression. Their policies are anti-farmer i.e. anti-people. We must drive them out." This was then the conscious feeling among the majority sections of the peasantry.
10. *Desai A.R. (ed).*: Peasant Struggles in India, Bombay, Oxford Uni. Press, 1979. Also see Bagal Bhai Madhavrao (ed.), Khanderao Bagal Yanche Nivadak Lekh (Marathi), Jivan Kalyan, Kolhapur, The Kolhapur Sugar Mills Ltd.,1976.
11. *Government of Maharashtra*: District Census Handbook of Sangli, Bombay, Directorate of Government Printing and Stationary 1964, see also Sangli District Gazetteer, October, 1969.
12. Kasba villages like Sangliwadi, Digraj, Audumber, Tung, etc. boasted of Primary School upto 7th standard, Post Office, a Panchayat Office building, well-made roads, Dharamshala and a transport facility.
13. And such girl students getting higher education were mainly from the Brahmin and Jain Communities. They were from the urban areas (Sangli and Meeraj towns) and from the surrounding developed villages.

14. *MatthewAnjilvel V.*: Karmaveer Bhaurao Patil, Satara, Rayat Shikshan Sanstha, 1979.
15. These upward-looking and status-seeking tendencies seem to be closely associated with the rise in economic status which does not necessarily imply change in occupational activity.
16. *Personal Communication from* Mr. Drakshe, a research scholar, Dept. of Sociology, Shivaji University University, Kolhapur.
17. *S.P.Punalekar*: Aspects of Caste and Class in Social Tensions: A Study of Marathwada Riots, Surat, Centre for Social Studies, 1980.
18. Traditionally the Mangs performed 'unclean' duties of carrying dead cattle and also leather tanning. They also prepared bamboo products and exchanged these for food grains and spices. They acted as village watchmen, drummers and musicians during the wedding occassions of the upper caste families.
19. *Patil K.R.*: A Sociological Study of Panchayati Raj Leadership in Sangli District, Unpublished Ph.D.Thesis, Shivaji University, Kolhapur, 1983.
20. *Based on Discussions* with S.P.Patil (Village Turachi) who himself is a Progressive Bagaitkar. He passed his M.A. (Sociology) from Bombay University in 1965.
21. Patil K.R.: Op. Cit.
22. Patil K.R.: Op. Cit.
23. Sirsikar V.M.: The Rural Elite in a Developing Society, New Delhi, Orient Longman Ltd., 1970.
24. This sense or feeling was acutely felt and expressed not only by the better of sections of the developed villages, but by the lower sections including the local landless labourers from untouchable castes as well. In setting marriage alliances, the developed villages in this district occupied a priviledged rank. "We look up to them"-said some labourers from Kavathe Mahakal region.
25. Patil K.R.: Op. Cit.
26. Daily Sakal (Marathi) Pune, 28 November 1986.
27. Until then the Jains and one Brahmin family dominated the affairs of the Vikas Agency. In December 1985 elections one Maratha rich farmer contested the elections by forming a panel of Marathas. This panel included rich and middle farmers predominantly. "It is a fight of Marathas, inheritors of great Shivaji against the Jains, the traders and financiers"-the Maratha panel compaigners said. They could mobilise the support of entire Maratha caste including the poor farmers and the landless among them. "It would be a disgrace to be ruled and governed by the handful of Jains. They have dominated over us for too long"-said one landless Maratha labourer in Digraj Village.
28. *S.P.Punalekar*: Social Situation and Development Perceptions of Rural Poor in Western India, Surat, Centre for Social Studies, April, 1986.

29. One Jain middle peasant (also a college lecturer) said: "Sooner these Marathas will realise that managing a Vikas Agency is not a child's play. It requires foresight, prudence and financial skills. Only the Jains have the tradition and experience. Let us wait and see how long these Marathas handle the affairs on their own".
30. *D'Lima Hazel*: A Study of Women Members in Zilla Parishads and Panchayat Samitis of Maharashtra, Unpublished Ph.D.Thesis, Tata Institute of Social Sciences, Bombay 1980.
31. *Patil K.R.*: Op.cit. P. 79.
32. *Daily Navsandesh* (Sangli), 27 March, 1986.
33. *Daily Sakal* (Pune), 30 April, 1986.
34. It also provided subsidies and loans to the farmers for agricultural inputs, daily necessities through co-operative consumers stores, veterinary health facility and above all schooling facility to the children of the farmers within the factory complex. It also gave assistance in the form of freeships and scholarships to farmers' children. The sugar factories in the area created 'new' atmosphere surcharged with peasant power and prestige. These were 'new' vistas of opportunities for the hitherto dormant and urban-dependent villagers.
35. *Patil K.R.*, Op. cit, P. 14.
36. *Daily Sarvamat* (Srirampur), 21 March 1986.
37. This help includes: giving out-of-turn chances for clearance of sugarcane fields, for loans, subsidies and inputs, and inclusion of their names as 'target family' for a variety of government schemes, such as settling family or marital disputes, provision of employment in Sugar Factory, Seed Farm, Poultry Factory, etc., and using political pressures to keep them 'out of trouble' even in exceptional situations.
38. *S.P. Punulekur* (1986), Op.cit.
39. He talks of taluka and district level affairs, of factionalism in State-level political organs, of Sugar factory management and of Central Government towards "us, the hardworking and enterprising sugarcane growers."
40. The old houses are entirely renovated, or new houses are built with 'city-like' modern designs and decor. Some stay in the camp Houses i.e. bungalows built on the farm. New vehicles like cars, motor cycles, mopeds, etc. of the latest models are bought to exhibit their wealth and status. T.V., Video, Telephone etc. are owned by quite a few rich farmers of this area. They distinctly stand out as a separate class with considerable economic and political strength. Their word matters in the affairs of multipurpose societies, banks, sugar factory, and other politico-economic institutions in the region. They are addressed as Appasahebs, Nanasahebs, etc. by the lower gentry. The GOs or NGOs cannot afford to offend them even remotely.
41. *Daily Sakal* (Pune), 28 November 1986.

42. Daily Agradoot (Sangli), 31 March, 1986.
43. Daily Sakal (Pune), 30 April, 1986.
44. Daily Agradoot (Sangli), 2 December 86, 3 December, 1986.
45. *S.P. Punalekar* (1986): Op.cit.

15

Caste, Class and Politics in the Tanneries of Kolhapur

Gopal Guru

Caste is the most complex and hence most important specific feature of South Asian society in general and Indian society in particular. At the academic level, it seems to have proved a major stumbling block for theoretical understanding of culturally-oriented bourgeois academic interpretation, which has failed to take up categories other than caste to understand Indian society. In this category, we have all those anthropologists and sociologists from Louis Dumont to the Chicago School who interpret caste primarily in cultural and ideological terms with reference to the notions of purity and pollution and concepts of code and substance, etc.[1]

As a corollary to this approach to caste, there has been an attempt to give equal weightage to class along with caste while understanding the development of Indian society. In this category, we have Sharad Patil and Gail Omvedt who assign equal importance to caste and class and consider caste as part of the base.[2] This view of caste seems to be eclectical to those Marxists who consider caste as the part of superstructure and not the base.[3]

From the above theoretical positions one is compelled to make an observation: "It is difficult to decide the epistemic status of caste and class in the dialectical unfolding of the events in the Indian society." Therefore, in the light of this observation, the major theoretical concern of the present paper is to involve ourselves in an analysis which would help to decide the epistemic status of both caste and class.

In doing so, an attempt will be made to discover whether and how caste and class reinforce each other? An attempt will also be made to see whether the interaction between the forces concerning class and caste diffuses the class character of the community under our study? If yes, then to what extent does caste camouflage the class character under its seeming dominance which is reflected in the exploitation of the lower class tannery workers? In other words, this paper shall try to find out the need to analyse the role of caste to understand the level of class formation in the tanneries of Kolhapur.

The tanneries of Kolhapur were considered by us as being an appropriate universe object for understanding the above questions. The selection of this particular study was influenced by the fact that tanning in Kolhapur has been undergoing some radical changes in the recent years. There has been a remarkable growth in leather production effected by mechanisation in tanning industries of Kolhapur. This quick growth in leather production made us more curious about the implications of this growth for the working sections and small tannery owners in particular and the society as a whole in general. The data for the present paper were collected from July to November, 1987.

The Importance of Tanning

Tanning in India is a basic process without which no leather production can take place. Even the *Mahabharata* refers to leather sandals (footwear) and other leather articles, and later on the use of leather for book binding during the Mughal period[4] must have involved a process of tanning (the process of tanning involves curing and dressing of raw leather). Thus, India has a long tradition of some sort of tanning in the form of handicraft industry.

In contemporary India, according to a survey carried out by the Central Leather Research Institute, Madras, it has been estimated that the total availability of raw leather in the country was 144.2 million pieces in 1986.[5] The tanning of this raw leather was done by tanneries spread all over the country. The important among them are located at Madras, Calcutta, Kanpur and Kolhapur.

The tanning industry in India is also playing a very significant role in promotion of export of leather goods to various countries. The following figures bear this out:

Table 1

Export of Leather Products

(Rupees in crores)

1983-84	*1985-86*	*1986-87*
436.04	662.51	930.81

Source: *Financial Express*, August 17, 1987, and *Economic Times*, August 16, 1987.

Thus, it is clear from the above figures that the export of leather and leather products has more than doubled in just four years from Rs. 436.04 crores in 1983-84 to Rs. 930.81 crores in 1986-87. Besides this, there has been a growing emphasis on exporting finished leather from the country.

Tanneries in Kolhapur

Kolhapur has been one of the leading centres of the tanning and leather goods industry. *Kolhapuri Chappals* (footwear) are famous all over the country. In Kolhapur, before 1891, tanning was carried out chiefly as a cottage industry on a very small scale. Tanners did not have modern technical training. The tanning was done in a more conventional way and the leather was not of a superior quality. But when Kolhapur was connected with Bombay and Pune by rail, Kolhapuri leather began to be marketed at these cities particularly since 1963.[6]

Over a period of fifty to sixty years, there has been a tremendous growth in the tanning of raw hide* with a high level of sophistication. This modernisation in the tanning industry of Kolhapur was promoted obviously due to the reason that Kolhapur leather began to be sold in the national as well as the international markets (one of the tanning units in Kolhapur exports leather to Italy). Table 2 would give us the general idea regarding the development in tanning of raw hides in Kolhapur.

It is, therefore, clear that over a period of thirty-seven years the tanneries of Kolhapur have been experiencing a vast expansion in terms of influx of the raw hide and the export of finished leather. The influx of raw hide has increased from 1,200 pieces per month in 1950 to 5,600 pieces in 1987. The tannery-owners purchase raw hide mostly from Bombay (Dharavi), Malegoan (Nasik), Miraj, Jat and Surat. Kolhapur produces only five per cent of the total raw hide used in tanning.

This boost in the leather trade in Kolhapur has been possible because of the corresponding increase in the supply of finished leather to Bombay, Pune, Nagpur, Shirdi and Hyderabad. For some recent years, Kolhapuri leather is also being exported to Italy.

While there has been a tremendous growth in leather production, there has also been a steady decline in the number of small-scale tanneries with almost a stagnation in dry leather production over the past thirty-seven years. The number of small units has come down from twenty-six in 1950 to one in 1987. A contrary trend shows that the num-

---

* The word 'hide' is technically used for the skin of bullock, buffallo or cow, while the word 'skin' is used only for the skins of goats and sheep

Table 2

Showing the development of Tanneries in Kolhapur from 1960 to 1987

Year	*Raw hide Import (per month in pieces)*	*Small Unit No. of unit*	*Monthly output per unit*	*Big unit No. of unit*	*Monthly output export per unit*	*Modernised unit No. of unit*	*Monthly output per unit*
1960	2,000*	20@	20	2	200#	—	—
1970	3,400	18	20	4	200	—	—
1987	5,600	15	20	5	600	1	800

* Kolhapur Municipal Corporation, Octroi Section, 1987.

Kolhapur District Gazetteer 1960 and Officer of the Labour Commissioner, Kolhapur 1987.

\# Primary data 1987.

Note: Small unit has been identified on the basis of being that unit which produces 20 pieces of finished leather per month, a Big unit is that which produces more than 200 pieces of finished leather per month. There is no medium sized tannery which could produce dry leather between 20 to 200 pieces per month. A unit is called modernised if it produces more than 800 pieces of finished leather per month with the help of machines.

Table 3

Unitwise progress made in leather production 1960-1987

Year	*Small unit*			*Big unit*			*Grand total*	*Relative share of big units in total production %*
	No. of units	*Monthly physical output*	*Annual total output (physical)*	*No. of units*	*Monthly physical output*	*Annual total output (physical)*		
1960	20	20	4800	2	200	4800	9600	50.00
1970	18	20	4320	4	200	9600	13920	68.96
1987	15	20	3600	5	600	3600	3900	90.10

Source: This table is based on the figures outlined the Table 1.

ber of big tanneries has almost doubled from two in 1950 to five in 1987. During these years, it appears that the tanning trade has come to be monopolised by a few people from the Dhor caste in Kolhapur. As the Table 3 indicates that over ninety per cent of the total output of dry leather is produced in only five big out of twenty units. However, this kind of uneven development raises a very important point in the sense that it has introduced two major contradictions in the tannng industry of Kolhapur. Of these two contradictions one seems to be quite basic in nature. It refers to the contradiction between tannery workers and the big tannery-owners on the one hand, and between the small tannery-owners and the monopolistic tannery-owners on the other. Another contradiction, which seems to be more secondary in nature, found between the less and the more modernised units.* Now, the central focus of this article is on the analysis of these contradictions in terms of their implications on the primordial identity of the Dhor workers on the one hand and the organised growth of their corporate political consciousness on the other.

Tanning in Maharashtra in general and Kolhapur in particular is main traditional occupation of Dhors. The Dhor community is one of the major segments of the scheduled castes cluster in Maharasthra, but it is much lower in social hierarchy among the scheduled castes. Sociologically speaking, unlike Mahars or Mangs (scheduled castes in Maharasthra), this caste represents more or less a perfect homogeneity. But because of the basic contradiction based on unequal development of tanneries, this homogeneous whole has been subjected to a process leading to the formation of a microscopic class of rich people on the one hand and a class of pauperised small tannery-owners on the other. This process of class differentiation among the Dhors is represented in Table 4.

As is clear from Table 4, in the year 1960, tanning in small units was done exclusively by members of the family and not by the hired labourers. But the year 1970 marked a sharp decline in small units from twenty-six in 1950 to sixteen in 1970 with a corresponding reduction in the family labour from 236 in 1960 to 96 in 1970. It obviously means that as a result of the shutting down of ten tanneries, the family labours of the tanneries added to the hired labour to be employed by the big units which had more than doubled from two in 1960 to five in 1970. It is also clear that the family labour employed by the big units in 1960 virtually disappeared by 1970. The big tannery-owners who were themselves

* A less modern unit is one where only hirda crushing machine is used and a more modern unit is one where different machines are used for tanning.

Table 4

Showing the class differentiation in Tanneries of Kolhapur
(Figures are to the total Dhor population in the city)

Size of the units	*1960*				*1970*				*1987*			
	No. of units	*Total Dhor population*	*Family labour*	*Hired labour*	*No. of units*	*Total Dhor population*	*Family labour*	*Hired labour*	*No. of units*	*Total Dhor population*	*Family labour*	*Hired labour*
Small	20	1231	220	16	18	1561	88	8	15	2006	88	8
Big	2	1231	15	16	4	—	—	200	4	2006	—	200
Mechanised unit	—	—	—	—	—	—	—	—	1	—	—	80

Note: Regarding the small unit, it is generally found that each unit contains six workers both in all and female normally residing in a joint family.
Kolhapur Gazette 1960, P. 1982. Sample Survey data.
Kolhapur District Census, 1971 and 1981.

working in the tanneries, now only supervise the tannery and have employed about 256 hired labourers. However, the quantity of hired labour remained stagnant right through the seventies and the eighties. Now, a very important question which crops up here is that what were the reasons that pushed the Dhor people from the class of tannery-owners into the class of tannery-workers? In other words, how and why did the destruction of small units take place over a period of thirty to forty years? There could be two possible explanations.

First, the very process of tanning or curing the hide is responsible for the pauperisation of the small tannery-owner and his family who were involved in this process that lasted for one complete month. In order to understand better the gravity of the problems that the poor tannery-owner faced, it would not be out of place to outline the whole tanning process. The thirty days' process is carried out in the following manner: The hide is macerated in lime water to separate the hair, the fat and the fleshy parts from it. This process continues for the first eight days. After the hide is well soaked, the remaining hair is scraped off with a scraper and the fat and fleshy parts are removed with a knife or *rapi*. This continues over another three days. After eleven days, the hide is again washed in a running stream and soaked for nearly three days in a solution consisting of *babul* bark and *hirda* or *myrobalam* water in the ratio of three to one. To tan the hide thoroughly, soaking is carried out thrice a day which continues for two days. The soaking is done only to soften the hide. On the sixteenth day, the hide is tied up in a bag and hung up with stronger solution of *babul* bark and *hirda* water. The hanging stand is called 'Dukan' in Marathi. In the hanging position, the hide is exposed to the sun which helps to remove the scratches and wrinkles from the hide. On the twenty-seventh day of the process, the hide is removed from the stand and is torn into two even pieces and is again soaked in clean and fresh water for one day. Finally, on the twenty-ninth and thirtieth days of the process, the hide is dried. This is how finished leather is produced after a rigorous process of one month.

It is only after a month that a poor tannery-owner can market his product. During this one month's period it becomes extremely difficult for him to feed his family which is also busy in tanning the hide in their units. Thus, there is no immediate return from the investment involved in the tanning.

Even after having undergone these hardships, the small tannery-owner is not immediately paid for his leather piece by the local merchant (a shoemaker) who normally buys the dry leather on credit. This merchant very often takes fifteen to twenty days for making payments to small unit owners. It was reported to us by one of the poor tannery-owners that it has been the practice of the local shoemakers to make the payment to the tanner only after the leather products (*chappals*) are sold in the market. It means that a small tanner is compelled to wait for atleast two months to get the money.

Now the question arises: Why does he sell his product in the local market? There are two factors responsible for this. First, the wholesaler leather merchant from outside Kolhapur cannot depend upon this small tanner for a regular and sufficient supply of the leather because he is producing dry leather at a very small scale. Hence, the big merchant naturally goes to the big tannery-owners who have a more attractive price for leather.*

In this situation, a small tanner who hopes to get immediate returns for his product cannot afford to wait till the market prices are favourable to him. Many a times, these tanners are pressurised to sell their product to a local shoemaker who takes his own time in paying the tanners. In Kolhapur, the small tanner has to sell his product at the rate of Rs. 18 per kg. Thus, unlike the big tanners, the small tanner does not have protected market and hence is exploited by the local merchant. Furthermore, in recent years, the introduction of plastics, nylon and rubber materials in shoe and *chappal* industries in Kolhapur has further limited the market prospects of the small tanners.

Second, there are no leather co-operatives which could solve the financial and marketing problems of the small tannery-owners, bring fair price for their products, and liberate them from the grip of the local merchants. In Kolhapur District Gazetteer, there is a mention of the leather co-operatives in Kolhapur in 1870.[7] But there is no trace of these co-operatives today. No one in the area knows about them. There is only one co-operative operating among the tanners of Kolhapur. This co-operative consists of members from all three categories. It was formed in 1980 by the big tanners. The purpose of forming this co-operative was to acquire an abundant supply of *hirda* from the Maharashtra government at the rate of Rs. 1.25 per kg., which is twenty paise less than the market price.[8] Moreover, the government also charges only one per cent octroi on the import of *hirda* which is transported from the forests of Nasik.

---

* At present, big units in Kolhapur sell dry leather at the rate of Rs. 20 per kg. This more or less tantamount to the rate of the national market (set Leather Report, Madras, October, 1987).

However, the benefits have accrued to the big tanners who could acquire as much *hirda* as they wanted for promoting the growth of leather export.

Thus, to recapitulate our argument, the lack of a protected market, paucity of funds, cumulative poverty, introduction of plastic, rubber, and nylon materials in the shoe industry, and inability to compete with the big tanners in terms of production have led to the destruction of small tanneries pushing the poor owners from the class of tannery-owners into the class of tannery-workers.

Today, this process of pauperisation has created a class of rich people and a class of poor people within the Dhor caste of Kolhapur. Now, it is the tannery-workers who are subjected to the ruthless exploitation by the big monopolistic tanners. This exploitation is manifested in many ways.

First, in the tanneries of Kolhapur, the exploitation of the workers takes place in the form of the surplus that is appropriated by the big tanners. Table 5 would give us the idea as to how much surplus the big tanners have been able to appropriate over a period of last thirty years.

It is clear from Table 5 that the market value of the manufactured commodity increased by forty-four times over a period of thirty years, i.e., from 1960 to 1987, the percentage growth of net profit being 454.55. It is also clear that the net proft increased by little below twenty-five times in 1987. The percentage growth of net profit being 405.75. As per our data, during the last thirty years, the total profit increased nearly twenty-five times in 1980. While there is tremendous amount of growth in the total profit of big tanners, there is no corresponding increase in the wages of the workers. While the wages increased from 9.66 per cent of the cost of production in 1960 to 11.86 per cent in 1970, but in the following decade (i.e., 1970-80), there was a perceptible fall in real wages of the tannery-workers. The wages of the workers have gone down from 11.86 per cent in 1970 to 7.58 per cent in 1986. It means there has been 4.28 per cent decrease in the wages of the workers. Thus, it can be argued that the tannery-workers have not benefited from the fruits of tannery development. It is only a microscopic class which got the maximum benefits from the tanning by pumping out the surplus. The big tanners accumulated profit from the workers, but they did not offer minimum and essential facilities like better working conditions, housing, medical facilities, pension, provident fund or gratuity to the workers. Most of the workers, as we have found, live in the slums of Kolhapur and suffer from chronic skin diseases. The workers cannot fight for their rights because they are not organised. Why it is so shall be discussed later. But the fact that they do not receive governmental help in securing these facilities is a point worth considering.

The government intervention is not possible because all these big units, except the modernised ones, are not registered under the Factory Act. Is it true that these big units really have less than ten workers in their tanneries so as to avoid the implementation of the Factory Act? Are these big owners under-reporting the workers' strength? If yes, why? In our investigation, we have found that all these big tannery-owners supply incorrect information regarding the real strength of tannery-workers to the government officials. And they get away with it because the status of the workers helps them in this connection. The worker in the tannery is a piece-rate worker and not a time-rate one. Because of this, the workers in each unit work in four shifts. In each shift, only eight workers can work at a time. It means that the effective strength of each tannery is thirty-two workers. But this is generally not reported. Thus, this kind of working helps the big tannery-owners avoid legalities.

While the tannery-workers are put to a lot of hardships and inhuman conditions, in some cases we have observed that the big tannery-owners even inflict obscence abuses on the tannery-workers. Why is it that they do not fight against this exploitation by organising themselves against the big tannery-owners?

There could be possibly three reasons which seem to be responsible for weak trade union activities among the tannery-workers in Kolhapur. First, the big tannery-owners, who are Dhors by caste, use their caste workers to sabotage the trade union activities. This contention can be well substantiated by citing a couple of illustrations that were brought to our notice during the investigation.

In the year 1982, the Kolhapur unit of the Communist Party of India (CPI), tried to organise the tannery-workers in a modernised plant. The local CPI leader took up the issues of minimum wages and better working conditions for the tannery-workers in this particular unit. To press their demand, the workers went on hunger strike for two months. As a result of this strike, the functioning of the factory came to a standstill. The owner was very annoyed with the idea that his own caste people were against him. Therefore, in order to foil the strike and divide the striking workers, he used caste and kinship ties against the workers. He began to bear down on his caste people and relatives who had reccommended these striking workers to him for the purpose of employment.

Table 5

Showing the surplus appropriated by big tanners 1950-1987

Year	Composition of cost of manufacturing						Market value of processed manufactured commodity	Net Profit from manufacturing	Returns occuring from sale of wast products	Total profit
	Raw hide	Chemical costs	Workers costs	Octroi	Other* cost	Total cost				
1960	180	225	45	7.50	9.00	466.50	990	524	9/ per bag	533
	(38.63)	(48.28)	(9.66)	(1,61)	1.93)					
1970	720	260	135	11.50	12.10	1138.50	2250	1112	12/per bag	1124
	(63.24)	(22.84)	(11.86)	(1.01)	(1.05)					
1987	1080	1087	180	13.50	14.00	2374.50	4500	2126	15/per bag	2141
	(45.48)	(45.78)	(7.58)	(0.59)	(0.59)					

* Other costs include electricity cost and other miscellaneous costs.

Comparative figures of transport cost for three years years were not available hence transport cost has not been included in the table.

Figures in brackets show percentage.

Table 6

Showing the loan distributed by the Mahatma Phule Backward Class Development Corporation among the Chabhars, Mahars and Dhors 1985-87

Year	Chamar		Mahar		Mang		Dhor		Grand total	Relative share in the total amount disbursed
	No. of benefi-ciaries	Amount dis-bur-sed	No. of benefi-ciaries	Amount dis-bur-sed	No. of benefi-ciaries	Amount dis-bur-sed	No. of benefit-ciaries	Amount dis-bursed		
1985	13	50,700	14	59,700	-	-	3	10,000	1,20,620	8.29
1986	257	5,28,091	663	12,00,847	166	3,12,525	33	73,000	21,14,463	3.45
1987	72	2,00,500	367	5,89,832	-	-	7	15,000	8,05,832	1.92

Source: Office of the Mahatma Phule Backward Class Development Corporation, Kolhapur, 1987.

These middlemen responded to the call of the tannery-owner by successfully appealing to the striking workers on caste lines to give up their hunger strike. As a result of this caste-based intervention, some of the workers gave up their strike and some of the more assertive and militant were dealt with using muscle power to break this strike.[9]

Since 1982, there have been no union activities in this modern unit. To make sure that there would not be any working class organisation, the factory owner replaced all the militant and assertive workers with those who were more submissive to his command. Besides, he also brought some tannery-workers from Madras who were better trained to handle the modern machinery in his factory. These outsiders are very subservient indeed because they are conscious of being outsiders. Their sense of social insecurity makes them much more vulnerable to the pressure of the tannery-owners.

However, the CPI's unsuccessful attempt to organise the tannery-workers was followed by another unsuccessful attempt by a local medical doctor who was a Dhor by caste. In 1983, he tried to organise the tannery-workers against the exploitation of the big tannery-owners. But these monopolistic tannery-owners, who control the mechanism of socio-economic and political domination, imposed a social boycott on the doctor and his family which is not invaded in tanning.[10] As a result of this boycott, the doctor has never again tried to organise the workers. Thus, the big tannery-owners have used caste as a weapon against their own caste tannery-workers.

Besides caste, the big tannery-owners also use another very powerful weapon to keep the tannery-workers under tight control. This weapon is moneylending to the tannery-workers. The present survey shows that almost every worker takes loan from his respective employer. In fact, the worker is compelled to take a loan because the wages he gets for his work are too meagre to meet the essential requirements of his life; and secondly, for the entire rainy season he does not have employment because tanning cannot be done during this season. Hence, to feed his family, he is left with no choice except to borrow from his master who is everready to do so.

Moreover, tanning is very hard and difficult work and requires physical stamina, and preparedness to sustain the physical inconvenience caused by unhealthy working conditions lead the workers to drinking, which again make them dependent on moneylenders.

Moneylending also results in further exploition. The average tannery worker is, in this way, held in the clutches of the tannery-owners.

Of course, such moneylending requires neither legal sanction nor a paper transaction, and the terms depend on the circumstances of the borrower and lender who are bound to each other in more than one way. Though, the Workmen's Protection Act was passed as far back as in 1948, it has practically no authoritative backing and impact. However, the lender, who is a tannery-owner, provides the workers an interest-free loan with the solitary purpose that the worker shall then always be obliged to him and shall not desert his factory. Thus, indebtedness ties the workers to the tanneries.

In recent years, there have been some efforts on the part of the government to help the tannery-workers start their own tanneries. To encourage this type of independent enterprise among the tannery-workers, the Government of Maharashtra set up the Mahatma Phule Backward Class Development Corporation in 1980 to provide finance to the scheduled castes in Maharashtra. Thus, the Dhor community along with other scheduled castes, is the primary beneficiary of this plan. Table 6 shows the disbursement of the loan advanced by the Corporation.

It is amply clear from Table 6 that there is a wide disparity in the utilisation of the financial aid from the corporation. It is the Chamars and the Mahars who have got 95.45 per cent (an average for three years) of the total loan disbursed by the corporation from 1985 to 1987. In comparison, the Dhors could get only 4.55 per cent of the total loan.

Now the question arises: Why could the Dhors not avail these facilities? There could be two reasons to explain the situation. Firstly, we have found that not many Dhors came forward to take loan from the corporation as the amount sanctioned by the corporation is not sufficient to set up a viable tannery. The corporation has set a limit of Rs. 5,000 to be sanctioned to each applicant. To start a viable and stable unit, one must have at least Rs. 10,000 as the working capital. It obviously means that the loan given by the corporation is of no use to the tannery-workers to start their own tannery.

Secondly, the conditions laid down by the corporation for sanctioning the loan are so hard to meet that a Dhor applicant often feels discouraged from applying for the loan. One such condition is to own a tannery workshop and some land as a surety against the loan given by the corporation.[11] We have found that most of the tannery-workers possess neither workshop nor land. On the contrary, a Chamar can easily fulfil this condition because he can show his own house as the workshop. Therefore, this must be the reason as to why there is a large number of applicants from shoemakers (Chamars) for loan. Because of this condition, a tannery-worker is left with no option but to work as a hired worker in the big tanneries. For the big tanners, these adverse loan conditions are a "blessing in disguise".

Thus, it is clear from the above analysis that the basic contradiction is between the tannery-workers and poor tanners and the big tanners. As we have also seen above, the big tanners have always ganged up against tannery-workers and small tannery-owners. But, in recent years, tension has surfaced also between the less modernised tannery-owners and the owners of the more modernised units.

Conflict among the less modernised tannery-owners seems to be caused by a single factor, i.e., the shortage of tannery-workers. In these plants, the tanning is done exclusively by members of the Dhor caste. This being the case, and since the labour force in this industry is almost stationary, there is a fierce competition and conflict among these owners over the question of capturing the labour market. Moreover, the need to tan the raw hide urgently makes the demand for labour further acute. The competition and conflict over the labour market is reflected in the elections for co-operatives and the Kolhapur Municipal Council.

However, this kind of competition for capturing labour market does not radically improve the bargaining power of the tannery-workers because of the lack of organisation and patronage given by the owners to workers in the form of interest free-loans.

But, in more modern plants where except the primary stage of removing hair and flesh from the hide, everything is done with the help of machine, there is not much problem. The modernised nature of the unit attracts recruitment of workers from the upper castes. During the survey, we found that there are workers from Brahmins, Marathas, Christians and Muslims as well as the backward castes. These people from different castes work on the assembly line of leather production. However, it is found that these upper caste workers deal only with dry leather and do not touch the raw hide. All the same, one thing has to be accepted that the entrance of these castes in the tanneries is certainly undermining the sense of pollution that was attached to the tanning occupation in India.

The antagonism between the less machanised units and the more mechanised units is not based on the competition for capturing the labour market, but on competition for capturing the leather market. The more modernised plants produce a much superior quality and more quantity of leather compared to the rough quality of leather produced by the less mechanised plants. The well-finished leather from a more mechanised unit is used in leather garments and articles and hence has a heavy demand in not only in the national market but in the international market as well. In the past few years, the modernised unit seems to have limited the leather market for the less mechanised tanneries. Hence, out of four, two units have already started shifting emphasis from tanning to shoemaking. In this situation, if these less modernised units do not fully modernise themselves, then the dialectical logic which has caused the destruction of the small units, is bound to extend to these units too.

Thus, from the above analysis, the following conclusions emerge. First, the exploitation in the tanneries of Kolhapur is based on the materialistic interest, that is, the surplus which is appropriated by the tannery-owners from the tannery-workers. Thus, an appropriation of this surplus has created two classes, one of the rich and other of the poor within the Dhor caste of Kolhapur. Therefore, it can safely be argued that the growth of economic interests within the caste has shaken traditional caste unity. Economic considerations have certainly created a conflicting situation between the big tanners and the tannery-workers in the tanneries of Kolhapur. One has to go further and enquire to what extent are the economic considerations conflicting. The conflict between the tannery-workers and the big tanners who employ them is based on appropriation of the surplus by the latter. But the antagonistic relationship between the small tanners and the big tanners may be limited only to the extent the former is outclassed by the latter in the leather market. But, at the same time, the poor tanner who mainly employs his family labour also occasionally hires other labourers. This gives us reason to argue that the small tanners do not perceive their interests and the interests of the big tanners as being antagonistic.

Second, the conflict based on the economic differentiation in the tanneries does not clearly result into class formation because the use of caste by the big tanners diffuses the class content of the conflict. Thus, class and caste seem to be reinforcing each other. This happens at a certain stage of development of the tanneries because workers are still recruited only from the Dhor caste. Even in the most technically developed tannery caste was not undermined. However, the technical sophistication in the tanneries undermines the sense of purity and pollution.

A safe conclusion is that the exploitation of the Dhor tannery-workers is both in form and substance. This is so, because the exploiter also belongs to the Dhor caste. The common caste background certainly softens the militant attitude of the workers against the tannery-owners. In this situation, analysis of caste becomes all the more important in understanding of the class character of the tannery-workers and tannery-owners.

Notes

1. Dumont, Louis, Homo Hierarchichus (1970): *The Caste System and Its Implications*, London, Paladin, Granda Pub. Ltd., P. 217-228.
2. Patil, Sharad, Phule, Ambedkar and Marx, *Navbharat*, (Marathi Monthly), Wai, November 9th, 1980. P.6.
3. Omvedt, Gail (1978): *Class Struggle or Caste War*, Frontier, Calcutta, Vol. II, No. 8-11, September 30, pp. 30-40.
4. Gupta, Dipankar (1979): Understanding the Maharashtra Riots-A Repridiation of Eclectic Marxism, Social Scientist, Vol. 7, No. 10.
5. Bhattacharya, Amit (1982-83): Tanning and Leather Workers, in the Province of Bengal, *The Quarterly Review of Historical Studies*, Vol. XXII, No. 2.
6. *Economic Times*, August 22, 1987.
7. Kolhapur District Gazetteer, 1960; p. 376.
8. Ibid. P. 378
9. An Interview with the President Kakaiya Co-operative Society, Jawahar Nagar, 3rd Oct. 1987.
10. An interview with the CPI leader Mr. Barge, 7th Oct 1987.
11. Interview with Doctor Gaikwad, 23rd Nov. 1987.
12. An interview with the Manager, Mahatma Phule Backward Class Development Corporation; Kolhapur, 4-10-1987.

16

Caste and Land in Colonial South India

A. Nagaraja Naidu

The *dalits* did not perceive the British rulers as their enemy because the native upper caste landlords in colonial South India were their direct exploiters, and hence freedom for India had no meaning for them.[1] The immediate exploiter of the *dalits* was an upper caste man. Generally, the upper castes were landlords and the *dalits* were landless in colonial South India. The British had to accommodate the powerful groups in their revenue administration, whether it be the *ryotwari* or *zamindari* system. No doubt, the colonial state was coercive as believed by Bipan Chandra and S. Bhattacharya, but the state also had to accommodate the opposition.[2] The upper castes at first entered into the British revenue administration and later made a place for themselves in politics. "In the post-mutiny decades, the dominant idea was to seek the opinion of the natural leaders of the society, who were then identified as members of the landed aristocracy; hence the nomination of landlords and the representation of landholders' associations to the legislative council."[3] Even today the *dalits* are exploited by the upper caste people who control the State.[4]

Scope

The available evidence suggests, as we shall see below, that throughout the colonial period in South India the landless were from among the *dalits* and the landlords were upper caste people. We will now discuss the relationship between caste and land in colonial South India.

Caste and Land

As land could feed people, people grouped themselves in families and castes so as to work on land for material production. Here "the lower one goes in the economical scale, the lower the caste in the social scale."[5] Kosambi defines: "Caste is class on a primitive level of production."[6] In other words, the castes who owned the land and the castes who tilled the land were the basic factors for deciding the status of caste in India; because "the dispossessed and impoverished Aryans were also relegated to the status of the fourth *varna*."[7] Caste is generally a 'status group'. According to their status in society based on the extent of landholding, people developed their own norms and values.

Origin of Harijans

Many were of the opinion that the disintegration of the Hindu society created untouchables. Some others feel that the origin of untouchables was their low economic status. In the traditional Hindu society they were casteless. Gandhiji created Harijans as a seperate caste. Gandhiji used the term 'Harijan' (the child of Hari, i.e., God) in 1933. Only in 1935 did the British coin the term 'Scheduled Caste'. Till the 1931 census they were called the depressed castes.[8]

Hinduism and Scheduled Castes

"Mr. Gandhi also wants the untouchables to remain Hindus," observes B.R. Ambedkar.[9] The Scheduled Castes (SCs) and Scheduled Tribes (STs) are included under the rubric of Hinduism as per official categorisation. T.K. Oommen says: "It is doubtful whether both these collectivities profess Hinduism and given an opportunity they would tend to declare that they are non-Hindus."[10] He wonders that no sociologist has yet questioned the official definition of *adivasis* (aborigines) and *dalits* as Hindu. This is Hindu expansionism on the natives of India. The Hindu theory pushed these people to the lowest position in society.[11] Even the so-called welfare state has not granted them the benefits when they followed some other religion(s). Should not we call it a Hindu State?

According to Romila Thapar, Hinduism in its present form is a modern phenomenon. It never had its present meaning over the ages in India. She explains the impact of Hinduism as follows: "Hindu missionary organisations, taking their clue from Christian missionaries, are active among the *adivasis*, untouchables and economically backward communities, converting them to 'Hinduism' as defined by the upper caste movements of the last two centuries. That this 'conversion' does little or nothing to change their status as *adivasis*, untouchables and so on and that they continue to be looked down upon by upper caste 'Hindus' is of little consequence."[12] It is no wonder that our Hindu State had been creating castes as and when necessary as against the class that creates the state in the West.

Caste and Serfdom

An authority on South Indian Economic History writes: "It was peculiar to Indian society that agricultural servitude was a function of caste. Only members of certain castes could be made serfs or 'slaves'. It appears likely that at the beginning of the nineteenth century, the bulk of the agricultural labour castes was following their traditional occupations. 75.5 per cent of the Telugu Malas are SCs in Andhra Pradesh."[13] Besides Malas and Madigas, Adi Andhras are also SCs in Andhra Pradesh. In Karnataka, the SCs include Bovi, Adi Karnataka and Adi Dravida. In Kerala, they are Pulayan, Cheruman and Kuruvan. In Tamil Nadu, they include Adi Dravida, Paraiyan and Pallan. Of course there are 304 caste groups but these caste groups constitute ninety per cent of SCs in the South Indian states. According to the 1971 census, the Scheduled Caste agricultural workers consisting of cultivators and labourers are around eighty-six per cent. In Andhra Pradesh, they are 85.78 per cent, Karnataka 74.97 per cent, Kerala 85.96 per cent, and Tamil Nadu 82.17 per cent.[14] The bulk of agricultural workers are SCs in our semi-feudal economy. It is semi-feudal because these SCs are exploited by upper castes in a variety of extra-economic ways. The SCs cannot become free wage labourers in our caste-ridden society. As Malik says: "One constant factor of Hindu society has been that depressed castes and landless labour have always had to do very degrading work. By and large, they have been expected to do a fixed kind of work or occupation, and have served as a reserve force for agricultural production."[15] And even with the coming of the British in India this kind of discrimination against outcastes remained as a fact and the caste system was found useful for the industrial economy of the British.[16] Indian society is a clear reminder of the European Middle Ages. Today, Indian society is stale. If there are some kind of unreal utopian overtones in the Indian policy formulation, these are about the plight of the untouchables.[17]

According to K.N. Panikkar, in 1800 in Kerala, the landlords were Brahmins (Nambudiri) and Nairs and the landless were untouchable castes. It was caste-class correlation, as B.A. Prakash observes: "Till the end of the sixth century A.D. when ownership of land passed on to the Brahmins there was neither a caste system nor untouchability in Kerala."[18] Panikkar shows us the caste and landownership[19] in the nineteenth century as given in Table 1.

Table 1

Caste Composition of a Section of Landlords in the 19th Century

Caste	1803		1887	
	Number	%	Number	%
Nambudri	37	35.6	217	24.0
Nair	46	44.2	411	45.6
Upper Intermediary Caste	11	10.6	69	7.66
Mappila	8	7.7	92	10.22
Tiyya (SCs)	1	0.96	112	12.5
Total	103		901	

M.N. Srinivas is of the opinion that the Nambudiri and Nairs are landlords and the lower castes like Ceruman and Pulayan are landless in Kerala.[20] "Every village had a headman usually belonging to the dominant caste. The accountant was always a Brahmin in South India. The headman and accountant collected the land taxes with the aid of the Harijan village servants."[21] Until recently, in Mysore villages, there was a master-servant relationship between landowning castes and Harijans.[22]

At the end of the eighteenth century, throughout South India, a variety of titles were borne by 'superior' landholders: mirasider, caniyatchi, peddaraiyat, reddi, kapu, dora, patel, kadim, gramatumu."[23] "Such people, the elite of their villages invariably, were of high and clean caste, either Brahmins or more often, Yeoman warriors, who stood between the government and the rest of village which was composed mostly of lesser cultivators and labouring people of lower castes."[24]

"Slavery may be a thing of the past. But an important segment of our society, especially the agricultural workers belonging to the Scheduled Castes still stagger under the dead weight of the economic and social oppression of the past. Extreme poverty and squalor, indebtedness and illiteracy and even bonded labour among the Scheduled Caste communities in Kerala could be directly traced to their slave past."[25] Sardamoni observes: "Scholars today agree that a trickle of Brahmin immigration to Kerala began at least three to four centuries before Christ and became a stream in the early centuries after Christ. Between eight to twelve Centuries A.D., the Nambudiris had established their undisputed dominance over land and people in the various regions of Kerala. Perhaps these were the centuries when agrestic slavery originated and was cemented into the body politic by economic and social arrangement."[26] "By the time the English established their suzerainty in the region around 1800 A.D., these agrestic slaves were owned and treated like any other beast of burden by the masters and landlords."[27]

Class and Caste

Let us quote Dharma Kumar again: "One of the most striking and important peculiarities of the Indian form of servitude (as compared with slavery and serfdom in the western world) is its close connection with the caste system. The caste system not only confirmed the economic and social disadvantages of the agricultural labourer, but also gave him some rights—some economic and others of a social and ritual nature."[28] They were SCs. Many had no land by 1800.[29] The other backward castes, in Tamil Nadu like Nayakars and Nadars, and Nayars in Kerala, improved their hold on land, but not the SCs.

"In keeping with the dictates of the caste system, the superior land tenures were enjoyed by the superior castes, and the inferior castes were given only inferior tenures. Most of the cultivating tenants in South India were inferior tenure holders. They were also compelled to do forced (*vetti*)and bonded labour (*jeetha*) in favour of the landlords and native government and chieftains on account of the inferior caste position. Although the colonial system abolished slavery with the British India Act V of 1843, it did not bring substantial changes in the native situation of the depressed caste labourers and tenants. It could be further explained that there not only was a class difference between a landlord and tenant but also a caste difference. The difference both in caste and class made the peasant an inferior 'creature' in the society. He was not even permitted to use sophisticated language before his landlord. In British Malabar, the peasant addressed his landlord as 'Tamburam', an expression used for God as well. This feudal character of equating the landlord with the Almighty continued everywhere in South India.[30]

Alliance with Feudalism

"In most places in South India the village headmen were recruited by the British from the landowning class. They were even granted magisterial powers. Thus, landlords not only wielded economic power but also political power in collaboration with the British. Once these powers were combined in one person he acted without restraint. As members of the landed aristocracy, these local officials always supported their class interests. The authorities were conscious of preserving these officials' privileges, status, etc."[31] In Rayalaseema of Andhra Pradesh, the headmen were faction leaders. Factional politics has been the way of life of politics. The *ryotwari* system was maintained by the British with these feudal headmen. Later they turned the *ryotwari* system into a feudal agrarian economy. With the *ryotwari* system the Government (British) wanted to avoid the intermediary landlord links which had essentially, by the 1930s, turned into the usual landlord landownership system.[32]

But there are scholars who are of the opinion that "wealth and status, rather than caste alone, would serve as more realistic predictors of a group's clout in Madras Presidency."[33] This was certainly not true in the case of SCs. It was definitely true that the other backward castes competed with the Brahmins. Even Ludden also compares the Brahmins with Vellalas, the non-Scheduled Castes, in getting land rights.

Fertile Lands and the SCs Servitude

In fertile areas the restrictions on SCs were greater.[34] In these areas, the lands were given as *inams* (gifts) to Brahmins, village headmen, etc. The social and economic structure of the society was more stratified in these areas compared to the low-yield areas. The other castes were able to develop their social and economic position but not the SCs. As Dharma Kumar observed, there was a large group which was born into agricultural servitude and could rarely emerge from it. They came from the untouchable castes: the Cheruman and Pulaiyan of Kerala, the Paraiyan and Pallan of Tamil Nadu, the Holeya of Mysore and the Mala and Madhiga of Andhra. Not all the members of these castes were landless labourers. In the dry regions where the poverty of the cultivators and the risks of cultivation did not make intensive cultivation worthwhile, even the lowest castes could be tenants or small holders. They could also follow non-agricultural pursuits as leather workers. But the bulk of the depressed castes, some twelve to twenty per cent of the total population, was found in the irrigated areas and it was probable that most of them were agricultural labourers.[35]

SCs as Objects of Gifts

The agricultural labourers had a servile status. The terms used for them were equivalent to the word 'slave'. The Malayalam and Tamil terms *adima*, *adimai* are generally translated as 'slave'.[36] "They were given away as gifts to temples or to friends; or as part of a daughter's dowry. The native and British governments regarded them as their master's property. In fact the governments of Travancore and Cochin themselves owned slaves as a result of the confiscation of estates, the resumption of temple lands, and so on. There were well-established rules for assigning the wives and children of these slaves, and there are numerous quotations of the price at which men, women and children were sold."[37] Feudalism was in need of gifts to survive. Capitalism is in need of exploitation to survive.

In the second half of the nineteenth century, the position of the depressed castes improved. They began to refuse old disabilities. "Earnings from work abroad, the allocation of waste lands to depressed castes (by 1932 the government had distributed over one per cent of the total cultivated area) and the movement of landowners to the city—all helped to free some labourers."[38] But this trend is limited even today. And were not those workers Harijans who went from India? It is generally observed that the depressed castes were slave-like. "The annual average export of South Indian labour to Ceylon alone had increased from 11,531 in 1839-43 to 71,645 in 1964-65. By 1931, the total number of Tamil labourers in Ceylon was 692,540."[39]

Ryotwari System and Caste

Even the *ryotwari* system did not change the upper castes' hold on society. Caste status had a role in this system. "Along with the influence of the village leaders or headmen, caste was a traditional force with which the Company's *ryotwari* administrators had to cope."[40] The *ryotwari* system did not greatly change the social fabric, particularly during its early years from 1792-1827.[41] Frykenberg says: "In various villages different local Brahmin castes (chiefly Niyogis) tended to monopolize positions requiring clerical skill while local warrior castes, such as Rajus, Kammas, Valamas, Kapus, and Telagas dominated military occupations. Below these castes were arranged the trading, artisan and less cultivating castes. More than a score of castes were to be found at the bottom of the social order. The lowest of the low who loathed each other were the Madigas and Malas."[42] The local powerful people entered the British administration and turned it for their own sake like a white ant which enters the "stoutest wooden structure leaving it a hollow shell without necessarily destroying its outer form."[43]

Brahmins in History

During the Chola-Pallava period (9th to 12th century A.D.), the Brahmins and the Sat-sudra castes dominated.[44] A study on class and *jati* at Asthapuram and Kanthapuram villages in the Chengal Pattu district of Tamil Nadu shows that Brahmins and Mudaliars together owned nearly 600 of the 777 acres of land in the two villages although they comprised less than thirteen per cent of the households in 1916. The untouchables, namely, Pallis and Parayars, were landless people.[45] The Brahmins had been landlords in South India from the ninth century A.D. onwards.[46] "Their (Brahmins') close association with the kings of various dynasties as ritual heads and court officials got them large territories (land) free of rent. Landownership was another factor which enhanced the position of Brahmins in the South. Accumulation of wealth through substantial earning from land gave Brahmins a higher social status and greater social recognition."[47] With the advent of the British, Brahmins were the first to benefit. "While the British opposed social discrimination on the basis of caste, the conditions created under their rule widened rather than narrowed the gulf in wealth, prestige, and power, which separated the Brahmins from other communities in the south."[48] Of course, due to the introduction of the British education and western values, the non-Brahmins availed adequate opportunities to reduce the difference between the Brahmins and themselves,[49] but this was not possible for untouchables. The SCs remained where they were. The other castes competed with Brahmins. In the course of time, the Brahmins' position eroded, but they searched for new roles in the economy, and some of them became "leading industrialists, teachnocrats, directors and managers of industrial concerns and specialists in science and technology."[50]

Landholding Owned by Various Castes

The farm servants were generally from among the untouchables. In 1921, there were 21.7 million farm servants and field labourers in India.[51] For every 1,000 of the rural population the distribution of different categories in the Madras Presidency as a whole[52] is as given below:

Table 2

	1901	*1921*
Non-cultivating landowners	30	56
Non-cultivating tenants	2	32
Peasant landowners	512	398
Cultivating tenants	167	240
Debt slaves	289	97
Farm servants and field labourers	—	177

Notes: Ulyanovsky writes: "The drop in the number of debt slaves and agricultural labourers was the result of their mass deaths between 1919 and 1921 from famines and epidemics. According to official data about 12 million people died from famine and epidemics in 1921".[53]

Let us apply the same for the whole of India for every 1,000 principals of the rural populations.[54]

Table 3

	1901	1911	1921
Non-cultivating landowners	19	23	49
Non-cultivating tenants	1	4	28
Peasant land owners	484	426	381
Cultivating tenants	151	207	225
Farm servants and field labourers	345	340	317

"The number of farm servants and field labourers dropped partly as a result of mass epidemics and famine",[55] as shown in the above table. In Madras the debt slaves were called as 'Vetti', 'Padial', 'Esuid' 'Cherumi' or 'Pullia'.[56] These labels are more or less synonymous with the SCs in South India.

Conclusion

Thus, the above analysis clearly reveals that the SCs were always landless in traditional occupation. The upper castes turned to administrative services and the SCs remained in agriculture. The SCs had always been landless and the upper castes landlords in colonial South India. The untouchables had been the base of agrarian production. Hence, the mode of agrarian production cannot be understood without knowing the caste system. Since the caste factor was not taken into consideration the debate on semi-feudalism in Indian agriculture has been sterile. The forces of production are modern, but the relations of production remain feudal due to the persistence of the caste system.[57]

Notes

1. T.K Oommen, 'Sources of Deprivation and Styles of Protest: The case of the Dalits in India', *Contributions to Indian Sociology*, New Series, Vol.18, No.1. January-June, 1980, P.52.
2. Bipan Chandra, 'Colonialism, Stages of Colonialism and the Colonial State', *Journal of Contemporary Asia*, Vol.10, No.3, 1980; Sabyasachi Bhattacharya, 'Notes on the Role of the Intelligentsia in Colonial Society: India from Mid-Nineteenth Century', *Studies in History*, Vol.I, No.1, 1979, cited in Neeladri Bhattacharya, *'Colonial State and Agrarian Society, in Sabyasachi Bhattacharya and Romila Thapar*, Sarvepali Gopal (Eds.), Situating Indian History, Oxford University Press, 1986, pp.132-33.
3. Sabyasachi Bhattacharya, 'The Colonial State, Capital and Labour: Bombay 1919-1931', in *Situating Indian History*, Op. cit., p.173.

4. Number of case studies are there in this regard. For example, see A. Nagaraja Naidu, 'Harijans in Semi-feudal set-up-A Case Study of Karamchedu', *Social Science Probings*, Vol.2, No.4, 1985, pp.450-58.
5. D.D. Kosambi, '*The Culture and Civilisation of Ancient India*', p.15.
6. Ibid. p.49.
7. R.S. Sharma, *In Defence of "Ancient India"*, p.24.
8. Suguna Pathy, The Untouchables, State and Society, *Third Quarter*, 1985, p.34.
9. Dr. Ambedkar, Mr. Gandhi and the Emancipation of the Untouchables, pp.51-52.
10. T.K. Oommon, Insiders and Outsiders in India: Primoridal Collectivism and Cultural Pluralism in Nation-Building, Working Paper, XVII, All India Sociological Conference on Ethnicity and Ethnic Process in India, South Gujrat University, Surat, December; 1984, p.5.
11. Ibid. p.7.
12. Romila Thapar, 'Syndicated Moksha?' *Seminar*, 313, 1985, p.17.
13. Dharma Kumar, '*Land and Caste in South India: Agricultural Labour in Madras Presidency During the Nineteenth Century*', Cambridge University Press, 1965, p.190.
14. Census of India, 1971, Series I, Paper I, of 1975 S.C's and S.T's., New Delhi, 1975 pp.2, 98, cited in P.Hanumantha Rayappa and R. Mutharayappa, Scheduled Castes and Tribes in the Deep South, Table-VI, *State and Society*, Vol.5. No.3, 1985.
15. S.C. Malik (ed)., *Determinants of Social Status in India*, 1986, p.10.
16. Ibid. p.12.
17. I.J. Singh, "*Status Dynamics in Indian Society*", in S.C. Malik (ed)., Op.cit., p.37. [Title + Publisher + Year]
18. K.N. Panikkar, *Land Control, Ideology and Reform: A study of Changes in Family Organisation and Marriage System in Kerala*, in S.C. Malik (ed)., Op.cit., p.69; and Prakash, 'Agrarian Kerala-Down the Centuries', *State and Society*, Vol.5, No.1, 1984, p.61.
19. Panikkar, op.cit, cited data for 1803, See India Office Records, F/287/36/pp.7960-66. The data for 1887 is compiled from a petition from the landlords of Malabar to the Governor of Madras, 3rd December, 1887, (Leg. Department, G.O.No.81; 10th December, 1887-Tamilnadu Archives).
20. M.N. Srinivas, '*India: Social Structure*', Hindustan Publishing Corporation, Delhi, 1986 (Reprint) p.15.
21. Ibid. p.18.
22. Ibid. p.16.
23. Brian J. Murton, "Key People in the Countryside: Decision-Markers in Interior Tamilnadu in the late Eighteenth Century". *The Indian Economic and Social History Review*, (here after IESHR), Vol.X, No.2, June, 1973, p.166.

24. Ibid.
25. K. Saradamoni, 'Agrestic Slavery in Kerala in the Nineteenth Century', IESHR, Vol.X, No.4, December, 1973, p.371.
26. Ibid. pp.372-73.
27. Ibid. p.375.
28. Dharma Kumar, Op.cit. p.24.
29. Ibid. pp.49, 55, 61, 62.
30. K.K.N. Kurup, "Agrarian Reforms and Social Change in South India: An Analysis of Major Trends Since Independence", *India-Past and Present*, Vol.III, No.1, 1986, p.15.
31. Ibid. pp.15-16 and cited Special Commissioner to Principal Collector of Malabar, 20th May, 1824 Quoted in William Logan, Malabar, Vol.II (Madras 1951 edn.,), Document No.9 and Christopher Baker, Madras Headmen, in K.N. Chaudhuri and Clive J. Dewey (eds.,) *Economy and Society-Essays in Indian Economic and Social History*, Oxford University Press, 1979, Delhi pp.26-52.
32. Rostislav Ulyanovsky, *'Agrarian India Between the World Wars'* (A Study of Colonial Feudal Capitalist), Progress Publishers, Mascow, 1985, p.292.
33. David Ludden, 'Who Really Ruled Madras Presidency', I.E. S.H.R., Vol.XV. No.4. 1978, pp.517-19.
34. Dharma Kumar (ed)., *The Cambridge Economic History of India-II*, Orient Longman, 1984 p.209.
35. Ibid. p.212.
36. Ibid.
37. K. Saradamoni, *'Agrestic Slavery in the Kerala'*, Op.cit., p.337, cited in Ibid. p.213.
38. Dharma Kumar, Op.cit. p.240.
39. R. Jayaraman, 'Caste Continuities in Ceylon', Bombay, 1975, pp.214-215. See also S.Kodikara, 'An Unassimilated Minority-The Case of the Indian in Ceylon" in R. Dutt and P.C. Joshi (eds.,) *Studies in Asian Development*, No.1, New Delhi, 1971, pp.213-214 cited in Suaranjan Chatterjee, 'Economic History or an Apologia for colonialism', *Social Scientist*, Vol.13, No.1, 1985, p.57.
40. Nilmani Mukherjee and Robert Eric Frykenberg, *'The Ryotwari System and Social Organisation in Madras Presidency'*, in R.E. Frykenberg (ed)., *'Land Control and Social Structure in Indian History'*, Manohar, 1979, p.243.
41. Ibid. p.244.
42. R.E. Frykenberg, 'Traditional Process of Power in South India: A Historical Analysis of Local Influence', in his Book (ed), op.cit. p.220.
43. R.E. Frykenberg, 'Village Strength in South India', in his book (ed)., Op.cit., pp.265-66.

44. Burton Stein, 'Integration of Agrarian System of South India' in R.E. Frykenberg (ed)., Op.cit., p.185.
45. S.S. Sivakumar and Chitra Sivakumar, 'Class and Jati at Asthapuram and Kanthapuram some comments towards the structure of interest', *Economic and Political Weekly*, Annual Number, 1979, February, p.269.
46. E.S.A Viswanathan, '*The Emergence of Brahmins in South India with Special Reference to Tamil Nadu*', in S.N. Mukherjee and Romila Thapar (eds.,) *India: History and Thought*, Subarnarekha, Calcutta, 1984, p.288.
47. Ibid. p.319.
48. Ibid. pp.319-20.
49. Ibid. p.320.
50. Ibid.
51. Rostislav Vlyanovsky, Op.cit., p.50.
52. Ibid. p.51
53. Ibid. p.290.
54. Ibid. p.51, cited, P.P. Pillai, '*Economic Conditions in India*', George Routledge and Sons, London, 1925, p.114.
55. Vlyanovisky, Op.cit. p.52.
56. Ibid. p.174.
57. See my article, 'Harijans in Semi-feudal set-up; Op.cit., that Indian village is comparable to many American villages in regard to forces of production but the relations of production in the village are comparable to early stages of caste formation in India.

17

Caste and Class in Rural Andhra: A Historical Perspective

A. Satyanarayana

In a recent article, Rajni Kothari observed that the 1967 elections represented the "first major assertion of rural India," and "it highlighted the power of locally entrenched elite within the Congress."[1] He also maintained that it marked a "watershed in India's political development." He noted thus: "The institutionalisation of adult franchise since 1952 and the generally faithful implementation of the democratic process under Nehru (e.g., through a massive programme of rural development and introduction of 'democratic decentralisation' through panchayati raj) gave considerable power to party leadership at lower levels who could deliver the votes and who controlled local institutions, exercised leverage at higher levels and in course of time got elected to state and national bodies. All this led to a significant shift of power from the middle classes to the rural, 'vernacular', middle castes."[2]

Further, it has been pointed out that "the unfolding of the democratic process in the first fifteen years had led to a challenge to the hegemony of the educated urban middle classes from a political elite that drew its power from "control of rural institutions and the rural vote."[3] The objective of this paper is to discuss the origin and crystallization of the rural elite in Andhra over a period of time. It attempts to analyse the dynamics of the formation of 'rural elite' or what we call the rural rich[4] in the Andhra countryside during the first two decades of the post-Independence period (i.e., 1947-1967). The central focus is on the changing caste-class composition of the rural rich in Andhra over time. The formation and crystallization of the rural rich is discussed in terms of an examination of the evolution of rural political economy in Andhra. That is to say, the economic foundations of the rural rich will be discussed with special reference to the control over land, expansion of commodity production and the (agrarian) market. An attempt will also be made to relate the socio-economic position of the rural rich to its hegemony over political power at the local level. The exercise of power by the rural rich will be analysed in terms of its access to the local institutions of power and authority, viz., the panchayati raj and co-operative societies.

The paper is divided into four sections. While the first section discusses, in broad terms, the relationship between land and caste during the colonial period, the second section II examines, on the basis of micro-level data, the changing caste-class composition of the rural rich in Andhra. The articulation of political power and its various forms will be explained in the third section.

I

Land, Caste and Power: The Colonial Background

During the colonial period, the agrarian social structure in Andhra closely corresponded to the structure of landownership, power and authority. Although the British abolished the existing caste-defined position over land and other resources and imposed juridico-legal relationships of landownership (property right, private property in land, etc.), the caste hierarchies continued to exist and often overlapped with the hierarchies of economy and power. The socio-economic transformation during the colonial period (1802-1947) resulted in the formation of new classes, formally separated from the traditional caste system. Yet the categories of caste and class were, to a large extent, converged and continued to be interlinked. Broadly speaking, the fusion and convergence of caste and class in the colonial context contributed to the emergence of two distinct groups of people, namely, landlords (*zamindars*) and peasants/tenants.

The first group, consisted of the minority section of the society, though owned and controlled land and other resources but did not participate in the process of production. The second group, though heterogeneous in terms of caste, was the majority section comprising mainly of the tillers of land. In most of the cases and for a long time, the cultivators who tilled the land and harvested its yield had no rights in the land.

As a result of the British colonial policies in the nineteenth century with respect to the structure of landholding and as a consequence of the impact of new economic forces, Andhra districts (coastal Andhra and Rayalaseema) evolved a distinct system of land tenures, viz., *zamindari* and *ryotwari*.[5] "Intermediaries with control over land had been a historical phenomenon in coastal Andhra. ...colonialism for its sheer survival had propped up these rent-squeezing intermediaries and for a century and half yielded to their pressure tactics."[6] Big landlords considered the *zamindari* system as an important characteristic feature of the agrarian structure in coastal Andhra. Under the *zamindari* system, the concentration of land in some districts[7] was as follows:

Table 1

Total Cultivated Area

(in per cent)

	Ryotwari	*Zamindari and Inam*
Ganjam	55.1	44.9
Vishakhapatnam	9.4	90.6
East Godavari	59.1	40.9
West Godavari	59.7	40.3
Krishna	45.7	54.3
Guntur	70.6	9.4
Nellore	49.8	50.2

The *zamindars* in Andhra were basically the parasitic rent-receiving landholders who exercised ownership right in land and other resources without undertaking supervision and cultivation of land. But, by virtue of their 'proprietary rights' they could and did burden the tenantry with heavy taxation (rack-renting), unauthorised and illegal extractions and squeezed out as much surplus as possible.[8] Control over the means of production (land) enabled the landlords to exercise unquestioned power and authority over the peasantry. In terms of caste, the *zamindars* in Andhra were a mixed lot. The landlord class in the coastal Andhra primarily consisted of the non-Brahamin upper castes, viz., the Kshatriya, the Velama, the Kamma, and Reddy. There were few Kshatriya *zamindars*, mainly found in Vishakhapatnam district (the Maharaja of Vizianagaram and others). The important Velama *zamindars* who controlled extensive areas included the kings of Panagal, Bobbili, Venkatagiri, Pithapuram, Mirzapuram and Nuzvid; and estate holders of Challapalli, Vuyyuru, Muktyala, etc., were Kammas, while the Munagala *zamindar* belonged to the Reddy caste.

Generally speaking, landlordism was closely associated with the permanent settlement. However, in the *ryotwari* areas also, big Pattadars owned vast landed properties. The landlords of the *ryotwari* region overwhelmingly belonged to the non-Brahmin upper castes: Reddis in Rayalaseema, and Kammas, Rajus and Reddies in coastal Andhra.

In Rayalaseema especially, the village officers' families held considerable acres of land and controlled other economic resources in the countryside. Their wealth and richness enabled them to exercise power and domination over the dependent peasantry. Since they occupied village offices (Patel, Munsab, etc.) and positions, it was also possible for them to command respect and authority.

Below the landlords was found a large peasant community comprising owner-cultivators, occupancy tenants and various types of undertenants. The tenant-cultivators in the *zamindari* and *ryotwari* areas also belonged to the Sudra *varna* which included peasant castes as well as artisan castes, viz., the Reddy, Kamma, Kapu, Raju, Teleaga Balija, Saale (weaver), Chakali (washerman), Mangali (barber), Viswabrahmin (goldsmith), Goundla (toddy tapper), Yadava (shepherd), Kummara (potter) and Uppara (mason). Strictly speaking, in Andhra, landlords belonging to the Velama, Kamma and Reddy castes had a Sudra status, nevertheless they maintained their ritual distance from their dependents.

The Brahmins were the highest caste in the traditional Hindu society. During the pre-colonial days, they held landed property and monopolised learning and administrative positions. The Brahmins in Andhra primarily possessed *inam* lands, also known as *agraharams*, *shrotriyams*, etc., granted by the rulers. The British colonial government also confirmed and conferred 'proprietary rights' to the owners through the *inam* settlement (1859-61).[8] Although the *inam* land consisted of different varieties (*amaram, kattubadi, sarva, shortrium*, etc.), the biggest beneficiaries were undoubtedly the Brahmins. It has been estimated that between six and fifteen per cent of the total cultivated area in the Andhra district was under *inam* tenure.[9] By and large, in many *inams* there had been a separation between ownership and cultivation. That is to say, because of the considerations of tradition and pollution, the Brahmin landowners did not till the land themselves, but leased-out to non-Brahmin tenant-cultivators. Therefore, in Andhra, we find the widespread prevalence of absentee landlordism in *agraham* villages. The tenants of the *inam* lands had no ownership rights and were subjected to rack-renting.

The Vaisyas (Komati), third in the *varna* hierarchy, were essentially a mercantile community. Very few of them owned lands and cultivated with the help of farm servants. There were some Komati families such as the Mothey's in Ellore (West Godavari) who held vast landed properties (estates). But it was an exception. The Komatis in Andhra were actively engaged in their traditional occupation, i.e., trade, moneylending and business.

The artisan castes like Saale, Goundla, Mangali, Chakali, etc., did own some land but it was too meagre to depend upon for livelihood. Since many of these castes witnessed the destruction of their traditional occupations (de-industrialisation), they swelled the ranks of the rural poor. Consequently, they constituted a large part of agricultural labour, next only to untouchables. Many micro studies reveal that the artisan castes gradually lost their landed property in favour of other dominant castes and thus became landless.[10]

The untouchables (Harijans), who are the lowest caste, performed occupations like scavenging, leather work, etc. Under colonial conditions, they constituted the bulk of agricultural labour force and worked as farm servants and casual labourers. Very few (less than 10%) Harijan families possessed agricultural land. The main source of their livelihood was manual (menial) labour. They had no right to own land nor were they considered to be peasants or tillers of soil. The colonial land regulations never granted them the status of an occupancy tenant, though they might have cultivated lands as tenants and sharecroppers. In the case of untouchables, therefore, there was a clear correspondence/correlation between social and economic status.

After describing the position of different castes in terms of landholding, we shall now turn to the interrelationship between caste, land and power in rural Andhra during colonial period.

The evolution of the land tenure system under colonialism strengthened the position of *zamindars* as well as the big *ryotwari* landlords in terms of their control over land. It may be pointed out that for years the *zamindars* had been able to command and exercise immense power and authority in the countryside mainly because of their grip over land. The *zamindari* agrarian structure enabled the landlord class as a whole to appropriate a larger share of agrarian surplus by means of extraction of exorbitant rents. The landlords' authority was, in fact, maintained on the basis of rack-renting. The *zamindars* in Andhra held vast estates and obtained unfettered access to communal, waste, forest lands and other resources. It may be noted that they exercised rule and control over not only land and forests but also over ponds, sources of irrigation, etc. Thus, the *zamindars*' power was further reinforced since they acquired enormous wealth and affluence based on rack-renting and illegal cesses. Acquisition of wealth and control over resources enabled the landlords to maintain their higher status. It also sustained their hold and hegemony over rural society, economy and polity.

On the basis of the available evidence, it can be said that besides controlling vast areas under the permanent settlement, the *zamindars* also possessed private (*seri*) lands running into thousands of acres. It has been found out that some *zamindars* like Challapalli owned about 17,000 acres as private land. Others like the Raja of Bobbili 1,000 acres, Raja of Pithapuram 2,000 acres, Raja of Vizianagaram 1,454 acres and the Raja of Munagala owned more than 4,000 acres of land.[11] The *seri* lands were extended over time by the occupation of relinquished and evicted lands bought from the *ryots*. It has also been stated that the private lands were enlarged by illegal occupation and encroachment of communal lands.[12] The *zamindars* employed farm servants and wage labourers to cultivate their personal lands. But, in most of the estates, private lands were leased-out to middlemen and under-tenants/tenants-at-will. The possession of vast estates and private lands helped the landlords exercise control over their tenants.

As we have noted above, big landlords were not only confined to the permanently settled areas, but they were also there in the *ryotwari* system. One of the notable landlords of the *ryotwari* areas in Andhra districts was Jagarlamudi Kuppur Swamy Chaudhary who "owned 2,400 acres of agricultural land and 2,000 acres of plantation and paid Rs. 8,000 in *kist* and Rs. 480 as income tax."[13] He was one of the biggest landowner-moneylender in Guntur district. Ethirajulu Naidu was another leading landowner and tobacco merchant in Guntur. K V Reddi Naidu (Kamma) held lands worth Rs. 75,000; Dandu Naryana Raju and P. Reddi Raju (Kshatriyas) owned extensive lands in West Godavari district; Kasu Reddi of Guntur belonged to the family of village officer and held extensive lands. In the Rayalaseema region, too, many village officer families possessed vast landed property. Thomas Munroe's *ryotwari* settlement did not completely eliminate the big landed properties owned by the village officer (Patel, Munsiff, etc.) families in the ceded districts.

Thus, the landlord class in the Andhra consisted predominantly of the non-Brahmin upper class, viz., Kshatriya, Velama, Kamma and Reddy. Though it was numerically insignificant (less than one per cent of total population in 1931), yet it controlled the rural economy, society and polity during the colonial period. Most of the big *zamindars* like the Rajas of Bobbili, Venkatagiri, Pithapuram, Mirzapuram, Chellapalli, and Vuyyuru were also moneylenders. By leasing-out lands and advancing money they were able to tighten their grip over the dependent tenantry. As creditors, the landlords always commanded authority over debtors. By virtue of 'proprietorship' over land, the *zamindars* could lease-out lands to whomsoever they wanted and displace the tenants-at-will at their will and pleasure. The threat of eviction coerced the tenantry into submission. The colonial land legislation, although it granted certain rights of occupancy, on the whole failed to protect the tenants. The growth of population and land hunger further strengthened the hold of landlords over rural population. In caste terms the vast mass of the tenantry, both in the *zamindari and ryotwari* areas, consisted of the peasant and artisan castes. Particularly the lower castes among the backward communities such as Goundlas, Yadavas, and Telagas used to lease-in lands from landlords. They were the most exploited lot as they were subjected to frequent rack-renting and illegal exactions.

Control over land and acquisition of wealth and affluence helped the landlords to exercise power and authority. The growth of non-Brahmin movement and establishment of the Justice Party led to the rise of landlord power in Andhra. The opportunities provided by the colonial state in terms of local self-government and 'dyarchy' were utilised by *zamindars* to their full advantage. Their ability to extend patronage and exercise control and domination over their dependents contributed to the monopoly of power by them. As a matter of fact, the working of dyarchy (in the 1920's) witnessed the emergence of landlords as 'political bosses' in the Madras Presidency. Due to the colonial patronage, between 1921-36, out of four chief ministers three belonged to the *zamindars*' class.[14]

The legislative council and the local board elections provided opportunities for the landlords to emerge as the dominant political elite. An examination of the electoral data (of the mid-1920's) reveals the fact that landlords successfully competed with the professional elites (lawyers), in occupying positions in the Madras Legislative Council. The strength of the landlords in the council increased from twenty-eight in 1920 to thirty-eight in 1926; whereas the representation of lawyers declined from forty-eight to thirty-six during the same period.[15] Some of the *zamindars* in Andhra like the Rajas of Bobbili, Pthiapuram, Venkatagiri, Mirzapuram were active and took leading part in the Justice Party as well as in local and provincial politics. They held positions (chairmanships) in the district and taluk boards. A perceptive scholar remarked: "Landlords with local influence discovered that as presidents and members of local boards, they could wield a large amount of influence in their locality, and exercise greater power over their neighbours".[16] Being powerful men in the countryside they could and did command the votes of their creditors and dependants. Therefore, between 1920-40, many local boards were controlled by landlords belonging to *zamindari and ryotwari* areas. The landlords' control over provincial politics remained unchallenged till the late 1930's. However, it is not suggested that agrarian society below the landlords remained static and undifferentiated. What is stated here is that as a social class the landlords exercised both economic and political domination over the peasants in Andhra during colonialism.

Although the Brahmins were the highest caste and enjoyed unchallenged high ritual status, but in terms of economic status they were only next to the landlords. Of course, the Agraharamdars as well as major Inamdars who held vast landed properties could be considered as rich landholders. But, in general, the Brahmins in Andhra as a whole were not considered as a landed gentry. Initially, they were dependent on land for livelihood and the income derived from the lands was the major source of earning. However, the opportunities provided by the colonial regime enabled them to opt for new pursuits of life. More importantly, the Brahmins as a whole had occupied a very important and 'unnaturally prominent' places in the fields of education and public service. Therefore, it was rightly pointed out that "educationally the Brahmin was the leader of South India."[17] Among the college graduates of Madras University (in 1920-21), sixty-four per cent came from the Brahmin caste, though Brahmins were only around three per cent of the total population.[18] Thus, they successfully utilised the opportunities presented by the British, and many Brahmins in Andhra had taken up new occupations like law, journalism, medicine, teaching, etc. They entered the colonial administration and newly created urban professions in disproportionately large numbers. A recent study concluded that under colonialism (in South India) "urbanisation and Brahmin dominance were interrelated features of social change."[19] Besides education and public services, the Brahmins in Andhra also controlled the Congress Party and dominated public life.

As an enlightened social group, the Brahmins were also in the forefront of political organisation and the nationalist movement. During the pre-independence period, in terms of the relationship between caste rank and politics, the Brahmins dominated the political arena. The nationalist movement and the Congress Party were controlled by the Brahmins, at least till the late 1940's. Especially in Andhra, the urban professional elites like Konda Venkatappaiah, Pattabi Sitaramaiah, Tanguturi Prakasam, Kaleswar Rao (all Brahmins) had played a very significant role in politics. Therefore, it can be concluded that the advantages of landed property, education, public service and political power contributed to the emergence of Brahmins as a privileged elite group in Andhra society.

Since they had free access to the new opportunities created by the colonial state, they enjoyed a higher status even in terms of economic position and hence they could be termed as the upper class of Andhra society. Nevertheless, the source of their prestige and status was not entirely the possession of landed property. They occupied a prominent socio-economic position by virtue of their access to education and employment.

It has been pointed out earlier that the peasantry beneath the landlords predominantly belonged to the Sudra *varna.* Of course, the peasant society (both in the *zamindari and ryotwari* areas) was stratified and differentiated in terms of caste and class. There were rich, middle and poor peasants as well as upper and lower (or forward and backward) castes among the peasants in Andhra. However, compared to the lower caste peasants/tenants, the peasants/tenants (the peasantry) belonging to the upper castes (numerically preponderant Kammas and Reddys) enjoyed certain advantages. Within the constraints of colonial agrarian legislation they were able to secure occupancy rights and were protected from rack-renting and arbitrary eviction. The Kamma, Kapu and Reddi peasantry in Andhra were/are known for their hard-work and enterprising nature. The *ryotwari* land tenure, the widespread prevalence of peasant proprietorship and the development of irrigation system contributed to the rise of a stable middle level peasantry in coastal Andhra. Furthermore, expansion of commercialisation, commodity production and agrarian trade led to the emergence of a fairly prosperous peasantry. Elsewhere we have explained the process of emergence and crystallisation of 'nascent peasant-bourgeoisie' in rural Andhra towards the end of colonial rule.[20] It has also been noted that certain peasant castes such as the Gowaras in Vishakhapatnam district and Kapus, Kammas and Reddies in the delta districts of Krishna, Godavari, Guntur and Nellore were market-oriented, dynamic and acquisitive. Because of their overall dynamic nature, these communities became an assertive social class and set a new trend and direction in rural Andhra.

The emergence of a dynamic social class within the peasantry was manifested in the rise and growth of the Kisan movement in Andhra during the 1930's. The peasant proprietors in Andhra who belonged to these dominant castes provided leadership to the agrarian movements and challenged the authority of the feudal landlords.[21] They took active part in the development of the anti-*zamindari* movement and other agrarian struggles. The growth of the Left Movement (between 1934-47) which weakened the authority of landlords in Andhra also benefited the upper echelons of the peasant proprietors.

However, the lower sections of the backward castes like Yadavas, Goundlas, and Telagas as well as artisan castes continued to remain poor peasants and under-tenants. They did not benefit from the opportunities provided by the colonial situation.[22] In most of the cases they tended to lose their lands and join the ranks of the rural labour force. Micro-level village studies clearly indicate the process of the decline of the artisan castes.

II

Land, Caste and Class

By the end of the colonial rule there emerged a situation in which the hitherto dominant social groups, i.e., the landlords and Brahmins tended to lose their pre-eminent position in the realm of economy and polity in the countryside. Various factors were responsible for such a decline:

(a) The abolition of the *zamindari system and other land tenure systems.*

(b) The shift of landholding from Brahmins to non-Brahmins and migration of Brahmins from rural areas to towns and cities.

(c) The crystallisation of a dynamic agrarian entrepreneurial class which had taken advantage of the new economic opportunities of the post-1947 years and consolidation of its position as a dominant social class.

Although the landlords exercised authority over the village community for a long time, it did not remain unchallenged. Especially during the 1940's, strong anti-*zamindari* movements tended to undermine and weaken their authority and domination. The rich tenants belonging to the upper non-Brahmin castes were in the forefront of these struggles. It has been observed that the growth of left and radical peasant movements were largely responsible for the enactment of agrarian legislation which drastically curtailed the powers of landlords over time.[23] On the eve of independence, the Rent Reduction Act (1947) and the Madras Estates Communal, Forest and Private Land Act (1947) were passed as a result of the aggressive peasant struggles in Andhra. These legislations together with the anti-*zamindari* movement brought about the drastic decline of landlords power over the tenantry. The *zamindars* could no longer freely resort to rack-renting, illegal exaction and encroachment. The cumulative effects of these legislations was disastrous, since it crippled the financial resources of the landlords. Thus, the economic basis or foundation of landlords' power and authority was badly shaken by these Acts. Finally, the Estates Abolition Act of 1948 gave a death-blow to the crumbling *zamindari* institution. Although the abolition of *zamindari* did not result in the radical redistribution of land, it certainly weakened the authority of landlords to a considerable extent. The ex-tenants in the permanently settled areas could acquire occupancy rights. At least a section of the ex-*zamindari* tenants was substantially benefited by the legislation. Some of the big tenants and leasees of the *zamindars* were able to buy lands and acquire ownership rights.

Ample evidence is available with regard to the decline of Brahmins, insofar as their landed status is concerned. As we have noted earlier that they held considerable *inam* lands. But due to urbanisation and migration to cities they were forced to dispose of their lands to the non-Brahmin tenants. Various studies clearly indicate that there was a shift in the economic power from the Brahmins to the tenants. The Brahmins who were the original landowners (in the *agraharams*) sold their land to the hard-working Kammas and Kapus.[24] A study of an *agraharam* village in Krishna district highlights that there was a significant shift in landownership pattern over time, i.e., between 1930 and 1982. The Brahmins who owned seventy-seven per cent of the total land in 1930, were left with only three per cent by 1982.[25] Similarly, another study of a village in the Rayalaseema area shows that the ownership of land by Brahmins declined from thirty-six per cent in 1891 to only three per cent in 1982. It has also been observed that "the caste-wise ownership of land clearly shows that Brahmins were the single largest landowning caste in 1891, but by 1948 they had lost their supremacy."[26] Village surveys in some other districts of coastal Andhra (Vishakhapatnam, Guntur and West Godavari) also confirm that "land has been rapidly passing from the Brahmins... The *inam* lands of the Purohits and the Pujaris are being disposed of frequently."[27] The Brahmins lost lands not only to finance education of their young family members and make a living in the urban areas, but also due to their conspicuous consumption and extravagant expenditure on rituals and ceremonies. Evidence is also not lacking to suggest that many Brahmin families were ruined as a consequence of extravagance and wasteful expenditure. The decline and disintegration of absentee landlordism paved the way for the crystallisation of a dynamic rural rich in the countryside. Undoubtedly, the post-colonial economic and political developments also facilitated the emergence of the new rural rich. The implementation of zamindari Abolition Act and other tenancy legislations, though slow and halting, during the 1950's and 1960's contributed to the decline of the power of the non-cultivating landlords. The agrarian legislation thus laid the basis for the rural rich to emerge as the main landholding class. In caste terms, it consisted primarily of the Kamma, Kapu, Velama and Reddy castes. The evolution of agrarian economy during the post-1947 period also contributed to the emergence of these dominant peasant castes.28

The various village surveys conducted during the post-independence years indicate that a significant section of landholders from among the Kamma, Kapu and Reddy castes emerged as the dominant peasantry. In the districts of East and West Godavari, Krishna, Guntur and Nellore in particular, peasants have emerged as the substantial landowners. Gradually, over a period of time, peasants in these castes have increased their landholdings from purchasing land sold off by other people. It has been observed that the Kammas could maintain and improve upon their lands mainly because of their 'attachment' to land as well as 'the extraordinary care' they take in agriculture. In areas where they were numerically more they emerged as a socially and economically dominant caste. "Due to the possession of more than ninety per cent of the entire cultivable land in their hands, Kammas hold all the other castes in a position of economic subordination"[29] is reported in a village survey. A study on the pattern of land concentration in a village (in Krishna district) concludes that "fifteen families—eleven Kammas and four Brahmins—hold about sixty per cent of the land though they account for less than five per cent of the total households... But caste-wise analysis of data on landownership clearly establish the fact that 96.49 per cent land is still in the hands of Kammas and Brahmins (Kammas 84.25 per cent and Brahmins 11.80 per cent)."[30] Another study of a village in East Godavari district also shows that "2.3 per cent of families owned sixty-one per cent of land."[31] In areas where the Kapus and Balijas were numerically strong, they emerged as the dominant castes. It has been pointed out that as far as the Kapu caste was concerned, "their economic position, social standing and the numerical strength have made it the dominant caste in the village."[32] In the tobacco-rich Malkapuram village (Guntur district), "the Kammas dominated all fields, viz., social, economic, political by virtue of their riches."[33]

Similarly, where the Reddies were more in number they too emerged as an economically powerful peasant group. According to the survey of Sayana in Tamballapalle village (Chittoor district), there was "a high concentration of land commonly found in some of the *ryotwari* villages in the districts of Bellary and Nellore. Most of the land is locked up mainly with the three Reddy houses or families."[34] Also, in another village of Chittoor district, "where the Reddies constituted 5.6 per cent of the total population but held 43.4 per cent of landed property."[35] In Yelamanshipadu village (Nellore district) where the Reddy caste is predominant, "almost all the Reddy households hold lands and every year they add something to the already existing land."[36] In terms of capital formation, "of the forty-seven households surveyed, as many as twenty-six households invested money for purchase of land: if it is analysed according to community it can be seen that there are ten Reddy households which invested Rs. 10,46,000 for purchase of land."[37] Likewise, in Karada village (Vishakhapatnam district) where the Velamas were a predominant community, the larger part of the cultivable land was possessed by them.[38]

The hold of the dominant castes over the village economy can also be confirmed by the pattern of capital formation and family budgets. A village survey (in 1961) in West Godavari district concludes thus: "If one enquirès into the family budgets of different castes one is sure to come to the conclusion that family economy of the Kammas, the principal land proprietors in the village, is sound. Further among the various capital formation activities the investment on land is important both from the point of view of the number of households that invested therein. Among the different castes that invested on land, Kammas rank first. They tried to augment their land resources during the past ten years. They rank first with respect to the amount of capital invested."[39]

In a prosperous village in Guntur district, "of the total value of Rs. 1,43,365 worth of assets purchased, the share of Kammas is very large, being in order of Rs. 1,28,800 (89.8%)."[40] Similarly, in a village in Krishna district, "out of the total capital formation of land goods worth Rs. 1,98,050, as much as Rs. 1,82,200 was made by eleven households of Kammas caste only."[41] In a delta village of East Godavari district, the dominant peasant castes (Kapu and Bilija) contributed around seventy-nine per cent of the capital formation in 1961.[42] The fertility of soil and secured irrigation were the most important factors for the increasing investment in land in the 1960's.[43]

Various village studies have also brought out another significant fact, i.e., the majority of village population belonging to the backward castes and the Scheduled Castes does not own much land. A considerable majority among them was found to be landless. A noteworthy feature of the distribution of land in a village in Rayalaseema was that "majority of Harijans do not own even a small piece of land. The percentage of landless Harijans is 63.4. The backward castes are on at par with the weaker sections, 55.6 per cent of the households of backward communities are landless."[44] Similarly, in an *agraharam* village (in Krishna district), it was found that the Scheduled Castes who constituted about thirty per cent of the total population held around twelve per cent of the land. The percentage of landless among them was seventy-six.[45] Another village survey in Chittoor district has also shown that the Harijans, who constituted around twenty-three per cent of the district's population, did not own land as the sole means of their livelihood.[46] Insofar as the landholding pattern was concerned, the position of the artisan and other lower castes was also similar to that of the Scheduled Castes.

A study of the pattern of land concentration in some delta villages of the Krishna and East Godavari districts concluded that the Scheduled Castes who constituted around one-third of the village population have not been able to acquire any land.[47] This generalization is also applicable to other lower castes as a vast majority of them did not own any land. The agricultural census data (of 1980-81) also indicate that the Scheduled Castes which constituted around fifteen per cent of the total population held only seven per cent of the operated area.[48]

From the above presentation, it is clear that insofar as the backward castes and Harijans are concerned, there was no perceptible change in their position in respect of the ownership of land. In the case of Scheduled Castes, they could possess some land as a result of land redistribution. But the artisan communities and the lower backward castes owned small holdings. Their holdings were neither viable for efficient farming nor sufficient enough to meet even the subsistence needs of the peasantry. Therefore, the smaller peasantry among them had to depend on casual labour for livelihood. Many of the backward peasants possessing small holdings were forced to pledge their lands to the upper castes well-to-do families to finance cultivation. There was also a tendency on the part of the artisan castes and others to lose lands to others. It has been found that among the artisans, "the goldsmith, the carpenter and the blacksmith who constitute the bulk of artisans are losing land... The potter, it may be said, is gradually going to the wall."[49] In caste terms, land had been rapidly passing off from the Brahmins, artisans and Harijans. Broadly speaking, "the depressed classes, as a whole, like the Harijans, are being systematically robbed of the small properties of their lands."[50] A detailed survey of some villages in coastal districts reports: "The most striking feature is that the rate at which land is passing off from the groups of small economic status to those of big economic standing is almost, on the aggregate, more than twice the rate at which landownership is passing off in the opposite direction, namely, from the big to the small. Thus, the small owners are bought up by the comparatively bigger people, and this process of swallowing up is found to be a common phenomenon in many parts of the province."[51]

The reason why the upper caste's peasantry became dominant, was, besides its 'cultural ethos', 'acquisitive nature,' etc., due to the expansion of agrarian economy since 1947. Given the advantages of landownership and access to market, the rural rich were able to produce more remunerative and commercial crops. The growth of cash crops such as tobacco, sugarcane, cotton, etc., facilitated the accumulation of surplus by the rural rich, since they were not burdened by heavy taxation and indebtedness, they were benefited by the rising agricultural prices. The growth of internal trade in paddy and export trade in cash crops provided immense opportunities for the rural rich to hasten the accumulation process. Especially in the delta districts of Godavari, Krishna, Guntur and Nellore, the rich Kamma and Reddy peasantry benefited enormously by taking up commercial agriculture.

The strategies for rural development during the early decades of the post-independence period also provided ample opportunities for the rural rich to augment resource mobilisation and accumulation. In his field notes (late 1960's), Daniel Thorner observes that "there are millionaire cultivators" in coastal Andhra who "invested their gains from agriculture in trade, transport, moneylending and industry" and dominated the villages economically, socially and politically."[52] It has been noted that the development activities undertaken by the panchayati raj and other rural institutions enormously benefited them as they possessed "much land and good connections". They could take advantage of the rural co-operative credit societies to finance their enterprises. Since credit was linked to landed assets the rural rich not only cornered a larger share but also commanded control over financial institutions. Whereas, the majority of middle and poor peasantry of the lower castes were virtually excluded from the benefits of the rural credit societies. We are told that "the ordinary small and middle peasant did not benefit much from them."[53] The rural rich were also able to utilise the institutional credit to finance their agricultural enterprise as well as other business. It has been said that loans taken by the rural rich "obstensibly for agricultural purposes may not be spent on that... instead, agricultural credit is being diverted to water, transport, mica, cattle, or other business... to start or to expand their private, non-agricultural business, the bigger people form... a co-operative rural bank."[54] The evidence from other village surveys also confirms this observation.

The rural rich have not only taken advantages of the credit institutions but have also dominated the rural credit market. Since they own substantial holdings and have accumulated surplus they could diversify their economic activities into trading, business and moneylending.

In addition to institutional credit, the rural rich was also benefited by the new agricultural technology. The panchayat samitis encouraged the big cultivators to use fertilisers and improved seeds. They also supplied high yielding varieties, pesticides and other chemical fertilisers to the well-off peasants. During his tour in coastal Andhra villages, Daniel Thorner came across the 'well-to-do peasants', who obtained foreign power—cultivators, threshers, pumpsets, tractors etc., through government loan at low interest. The rural rich was thus in the forefront of agricultural modernisation. As 'progressive' and 'enlightened' cultivators they took advantage of the available new technology and adopted several of the latest methods of farming to improve agricultural yield in their farms.

The possession of landed property and accumulation of surplus by the rural rich further intensified the process of differentiation within the peasantry. Although the process of proletarianisation in agriculture of the small and poor peasantry has been a slow one, it certainly resulted in the alienation of land by the lower castes and artisans. A recent study on labour relations in Andhra has noted that "the proportion of the agricultural labourers in the total agricultural population had increased steadily and continuously from twenty-seven per cent to fifty-three per cent between 1951 and 1981.[55] It was also pointed out that marginal cultivators tended to lose their lands and thus became labourers. It has been pointed earlier that the available evidences from micro-level studies reveal that a considerable section of the lower backward castes, artisans and the Scheduled Castes do not possess land. Thus, a major section of the backward and lower castes constituted the rural poor in Andhra.

Our data also indicate that even when these groups of people possessed land, it was too meagre to become a source of livelihood for them. It may be noted that since they did not acquire any 'special skills' or 'master any craft', they had no other alternative in case they lost their land. A village survey (in 1961) has pointed out that "casual labour is the second major occupation providing employment for a majority of the poorer sections of the population. People belonging to castes like Christian, Golla, Goubdla, Madiga, Uppara, Yanadi and Yerukala usually eke out their livelihood by working as casual labourers."[56] Therefore, it is clear from the above discussion that the rural poor in the Andhra countryside was a most divided lot in caste terms. Just as the emerging rural rich cross caste lines, so do the rural poor.

III

Caste, Class and Power

The emergence of the rural rich as the dominant landowning class enabled it to exercise power and authority in the countryside. Though the ownership of land alone was not sufficient to acquire power, nevertheless it was an important means for its achievement. Various micro-level studies have pointed out that in coastal Andhra, where the Kammas were wealthy and more influential, they could wield power because of their control over land. Along with it the numerical support was also an important basis of their power. Hence, in Andhra, after 1956, the dominant castes like Reddies, Kammas, Velamas and Kshatriyas emerged as the most powerful political elite.[57] Rajni Kothari observes thus: "Representation of Reddies and Kammas in Andhra politics is higher than their proportion in the population and increases at higher levels of politics. At twenty-five per cent of the population in 1962 they occupied thirty-nine per cent of the legislative assembly seats, fifty-three per cent of the ministerial posts and the presidencies of the Congress, Communist and independent parties. The increasing pre-dominance of these castes at higher levels is also evident in panchayati raj institutions. Across the state, the Reddies held thirty-nine per cent of the samiti presidencies and fifty-five per cent of the zilla parishad chairmanships."[58]

The Congress leadership at the grass root levels was predominantly rural in nature. The rural rich became the 'backbone' of the Congress Party, especially since 1940's. Historically speaking, the rise of the rural rich as the politically dominant class meant the displacement of traditional leadership, viz., the feudal landlords and Brahmins. It should be pointed out that prior to independence the Congress Party was dominated by the educated urban professional elites who were mostly the Brahmins, whereas the *zamindars* enjoyed the privileges bestowed by the colonial state power, in terms of occupying ministerial positions under dyrchy. However, the integration of the emerging rural rich into the political field occurred towards the end of colonial rule. In fact, in order to widen the scope of the Congress Party and the nationalist movement, the Brahmin political elite secured the help and support of the rising rural rich.[59]

Nevertheless, after the formation of Andhra Pradesh and with the introduction of panchayat raj and rural co-operative societies, the rural rich could really become politically powerful. In addition to their numerical strength, their property and social status reinforced the power and authority of the dominant peasant castes in the countryside.[60] A study on Congress leadership in Andhra Pradesh noted that: "Between 1956 and 1972, three principal castes had an upper hand (Reddis, Kammas and Kshatriyas) in party politics. They constituted more than sixty per cent of the Congress Legislature Party, seventy per cent of the cabinet positions and ninety-five per cent of the zilla parishad chairmanships... The caste alignment at the lower level... reflects itself in the party organisation. This process is further promoted by the local panchayat raj functionaries who usually belong to the dominant castes and who wield powerful influence in local power politics."[61]

The available evidence from village studies reveals that a majority of the presidentships of local bodies were occupied by the members of the dominant castes. For instance, Kammas in coastal Andhra and Reddies in Rayalaseema overwhelmingly controlled the rural institutions of power. "The panchayats have not usually represented the ordinary people of the village. Rather, they have been an instrument of a majority, the most powerful group in the village,"[62] remarked a perceptive scholar. Various studies of village panchayats in Andhra have indicated that the rural rich were able to exercise power over the local bodies, because of their ability to extend patronage to lower castes. It is stated in a village survey: "Kammas, being economically dominant, enjoy social prestige much beyond the traditionally highly placed Brahmins in the society... Kammas wield power just by the grip of economic control over the rest of the people in the village as they possess about ninety-five per cent of the total village lands... Almost all the Christians and the other people are depending upon Kammas for their livelihood in one way or other."[63]

An analysis of the socio-economic background of the rural leadership also shows that it mainly comprises the dominant peasantry, viz., 'big landowners' and 'sophisticated cultivators'. The new leadership belongs to the dynamic rural rich who possess substantial landholdings and new technology. They are capable of diversifying their surplus profits into various fields—moneylending, trade, business, agro-industries, etc. Thus, it is clear that over a period of time, rural power has shifted more decisively from the traditional elite of the village into the hands of the new leaders. A study of the pattern of leadership in the co-operative societies shows that the upper caste peasantry cornered a major share of the available credit. Insofar as the positions in the co-operatives were concerned, the economically powerful castes dominated the rural credit societies. It was observed that "the formidable combination of cultivating moneylender-cum-trader dominates the co-operatives."[64] An analysis of the caste composition of co-operative societies in the countryside indicates that there is much less representation of the lower castes.

An examination of the data about village leadership also confirms the that the upper caste peasantry monopolised the positions of power in various local institutions. It is observed in a village survey: "Though all castes are represented in the panchayat, the only decision-makers are Kammas and all others just obey their verdict without any sign of protest."[65] Although the backward castes and the Scheduled Castes were in majority in the countryside, they did not have any effective participation or say in decision-making. Lack of unity among the lower castes and their economic dependence on the rural rich made it impossible for them to exercise decisive control over the panchayat raj institutions. The backward castes and Scheduled Castes could participate in these institutions simply because the rules necessitated it. Otherwise their representation might not have been there. However, in the local institutions of power, their voice carries no weight unless supported by the members of the dominant castes.

It is clear from the above analysis that political power and power structure in Andhra rural society is decidedly influenced by landownership, social status and economic dominance. In other words, the political leadership in rural Andhra predominantly emanates from the rural rich of the forward castes. The social character and composition of the political institutions reveals that they are controlled by the landed interests drawn from the dominant peasant castes. Thus, there is a convergence of political and economic power. It should be pointed out that the emerging leadership at the local level belongs to the class of owner-cultivators.

IV

Summary and Conclusions

Our analysis of the changing relationship between caste, class and power in rural Andhra during the colonial and the post-colonial periods indicates a gradual decline of the power and authority of landlords as a whole. The traditionally dominant social groups in the rural society, viz., the *zamindars* and Brahmins (insofar as they were landholders) have lost their hegemony since the post-1956 years. During the colonial period, the landlords and the Brahmins formed the dominant political elite. And the emerging rural rich from among the dominant peasant castes were subservient to them. The peasantry belonging to the non-Brahmin upper castes was not able to compete or challenge the entrenched groups during the colonial rule. The Brahmins, because of their landed property, education and employment, occupied pre-eminent position in the Congress Party and colonial bureaucracy while the *zamindars*, as they were rich and influential in the countryside, dominated (rather monopolised) the higher level of politics. Therefore, there was a clear convergence of control over land and political power. By virtue of the possession of vast estates the landlords (both in the permanently settled and *ryotwari* areas) exercised dominance and power in the countryside. The vast majority of the peasantry had to acknowledge their supremacy.

Nevertheless, during the late-colonial period and around the beginning of the post-colonial period, there emerged a rural rich peasantry. But they could consolidate their position only after the abolition of the *zamindari* system. The upper caste peasants, who were the ex-tenants of *zamindars*, purchased lands from the landlords as well as from the small lower caste peasants to enlarge their landholdings. Moreover, the post-colonial land reforms further strengthened their position by eliminating the intermediaries. The evolution of an agrarian economy during the post-independence period also provided opportunities for the rural rich to emerge as an important economic power in the countryside. Since they became substantial landholders, they could benefit from of the changing economic conditions, i.e., growth of commercial farming, internal and external trade in agricultural commodities, etc. While the peasants belonging to Kamma, Kapu, Velama and Reddy castes emerged as the dominant peasantry, the vast majority of peasants from the lower and backward castes, artisans and Scheduled Castes remained poor and subservient. In the process of economic transformation the small peasants of the lower castes were expropriated by the rural rich. A substantial section of the backward castes and Harijans today constitutes the rural poor. The upper caste peasants who replaced the feudal landlords have thus become the main exploiting class in the countryside. The contradiction between the rural rich and the rural poor has been mainfested in terms of caste conflict. It clearly demonstrates the fact that the proletarianisation of agrarian social classes cuts across caste lines.

The emergence of the rural rich as a dynamic class has brought about a change in the social basis of rural power structure. The post-independence developments such as adult franchise, panchayat raj institutions, etc., have enabled the upper caste dominant peasantry to exercise control over the rural institutions of power and authority. Thus, there is a shift of power from the landlords to the rural rich. Two factors have contributed to this change in a significant way: (a) the decline of the influence of the old feudal system, and (b) the growth of an elaborate political machinery which links the village leadership to the provincial and the national leaderships. This has made it possible for the rural rich to acquire power. The power of the rural rich is based on control over land and their preponderant numerical strength within the village. By and large, these two factors tend to reinforce each other. However, it should be pointed out that although political power has shifted from the landlords to the rich peasants, it has not gone into the hands of the backward sections of society.

Notes

1. R. Kothari, "The Rural Urban Cleavage" in *News Time*, 12 July 1987, p.2.
2. *Ibid.*
3. *Ibid.*
4. 'Rural Rich' in this paper refers to a dynamic social class which is economically, socially and politically dominant in the countryside. It is located within the production process and relations of production. It has been identified as a class which participates and/or takes active part in the agrarian production. The absentee landlords of feudal type are not included in this category.
5. The permanent settlement was introduced in the Northern Vircars (Coastal Andhra) during 1802. the *ryotwari* system had come into being during 1820-40. See M Pattabhi Ram Reddy, *Peasant and State in Modern Andhra History*, Kavali, 1986: N Mukherjee, The *ryotwari* System.

6. G N Rao, "Dimensions of Land Control in Coastal Andhra: A Historical View", *In A P Economic Association Conference Papers*, Warangal, 1984.
7. *Ibid.*, p.61
8. *Ibid.*, p.65 Also see KS S Seshan, "the problems of Inam tenures in an Andhra *zamindari-Punganur", in A P Economic Association Conference Papers, Anantapur, 1987; R E Frykenberg, "The Silent Settlement in South India, 1793-1853; An Analysis of the Role of Inams in the Rise of the Indian Imperial System: in R E Frykenberg (Ed), Land Tenure and Peasant in South Asia*, Delhi, 1977, p.39.
9. Percentage of Inam area of total area in Andhra: 1. Ganjam (11.8); 2. Vizagapatnam (12.4); 3. East Godavari (5.8); 4. West Godavari (10.1); 5. Guntur (6.2); 6. Krishna (10.1); 7. Nellore (8.3); 8. Chittoor (15.7). Source: *Statistical Atlas of the Madras Presidency*, 1931.
10. See. G Slater, Ed., *Some South Indian Villages*, Madras, 1918.
11. *Madras Legislative Assembly Debates*, Vol.VI, 1947, p.114.
12. C J Baker, *The Politics of South India*, 1920-37, Delhi, 1976, p.113.
13. For an analysis of the Non-Brahmin movement and Justice Party in South India, see. E.Irschick, *Politics and Social Conflict in South India: The Non-Brahmin Movement and Tamil Separatism, 1916-1929*, Berkeley, 1969; M R Barnett, *The Politics of Cultural Nationalism in South India*, Princeton, 1976; C J Baker, The Politics... *Op.cit.*
14. They were the Raja of Panagul 1921-26, The Zamindar of Kumaramangalam (Dr Subbrayan) 1926-30; The Raja of Bobbili 1932-36.
15. Baker, *Op.cit..*, p.155
16. M Venkatarangaiya, *Local Boards*, p.67, cited in C J Baker, *Op.cit.*, p.112
17. Y Vaikuntham, *Education and Social Change in South India: Andhra*, 1880-1920, Madras 1982, p.167.
18. Baker, *Op.cit.*, p.46-7
19. Barnet, *Op.cit.*, p.16
20. A Satyanarayana, "Agrarian Relations Under the Impact of Colonial Rule in Madras Presidency 1990-1940: A case study of Andhra districts", Unpublished Ph.D. Thesis submitted to Heidelberg University, (West Germany) 1983, Chapter V.
21. In an earlier study it has been shown that the rich peasant class belonging to the non-Brahmin upper castes was mainly responsible for the growth of Kisan Sabha Movement in Coastal Andhra. See my 'Kishan Movement in Madras Presidency, 1928-42: A study of the Anti Zamindar Agitation, Jawaharlal Nehru, University, Delhi, 1979, Ch III, IV and V.
22. The lower castes did not benefit very much by education and employment opportunities during colonialism. For the details of literacy among castes See Y Vaikuntham, *Op.cit.*, p.168.

23. A Satyanarayana, "Agrarian Legislation and the Peasantry in Andhra, 1946-48 (mimeographed).
24. Detailed survey of a village in West Godavari district over a period of 50 years is made in *Census of India*, 1961, Village Monographs (Unagatla), Hyderabad 1961, p.20. "Changes in the ownership of land which was responsible for the shift in the economic power from the Brahmins to Kammas and Kapus-Among the Brahmins, who were the original land-owners, the present position stands as a marked contrast to their past status. Only 5 households own land and the maximum size of the holding remains between 10-15 acres. This clearly indicates the gradual decline in the economic power of the community", p.19.
25. G Nancharaiah, "Land Legislation and Changing Agrarian Structure" in A P Economic Association Conference Papers, 1987, p.171.
26. D Raja Sekhar, "Land Transfers in Andhra: A Case study of a village", *Ibid.*, p.142 and 115.
27. V V Sayana, *Land Sales, Land Values and Land Transfers*, Delhi, 1952, p.21
28. During the late-colonial period the non-Brahmin upper caste peasantry had a solid land base (peasant proprietorship, occupancy rights etc.) and thus had a "head-start" over others. They also acquired a "cultural ethos" which suited the rural rich classes. Within the limits of colonial economic framework the upper caste peasantry slowly but steadily entrenched in the rural economy. They have also played an active role in the peasant economy by positively responding to the market. Since the turn of the present century commercialization of agriculture, expansion of commodity production, agrarian trade and market contributed for the transformation of agrarian relations which resulted in the emergence of a substantial section of the rich peasantry.
29. *Census of India*, Village Survey Monograph, Maredumaka Village, Krishna District, p. 96.
30. B A V Sharma (Ed). *Political Economy of India*, New Delhi, 1980, p. 507 and 510.
31. *Ibid.*, p. 506.
32. *Census of India*, 1961, Village Survey Monograph, Pasarlapudi, Lanka, (East Godavari), p. 70.
33. *Census of India*, 1961, Village Survey Monograph, p. 114.
34. *Op.cit.* p. 11.
35. Sharma,*Op.cit.*, p. 522.
36. *Census of India*, 1961, Village Survey Monographs, p.30.
37. *Ibid.*, p. 34-5.
38. *Census of India*, Village Survey Monograph, p.33
39. *Census of India*, 1961, Ungalta Village Monograph, p.37.9
40. *Census of India*, 1961, Malkapuram Village Monograph, p.95
41. *Census of India*, 1961, Maredumaka Village Monograph, p.74

42. *Census of India*, 1961, Pasarlapudi Lanka, Village Monograph, p.34
43. "Most of the people in the village are interested in investing their surplus earnings, if any only in land and livestock and other tools etc., which are helpful in agriculture. As the land are fertile and provided with regular supply of water for irrigation by canals.. the turn-out of crops is generally high. In view of these advantages everyone in the village usually thinks of improving his landed property..." *Census of India*, 1961, Maredumaka Village Monograph, p. 75.
44. Sharma, *Op.cit.*, p. 523, In a Reddy Caste Dominated Village "Most of the Malas and Madigas are not possessing any land",
45. G Nancharaiah, *Op.cit.*
46. Rajasekhar, *Op.cit.*
47. Sharma, *Op.cit.*, p. 596-8
48. *Agricultural Census*, 1980-81 (A.P.) Cited in Nancharaiah, *Op.cit.*, p. 169
49. Sayana,*Op.cit.*, p. 191
50. *Ibid.*, p. 21
51. *Ibid.*, p. 25
52. D. Thorner, *The Shaping of Modern India*, Delhi, 1980 p. 203
53. *Ibid.*, p. 74
54. *Ibid.*, p. 190
55. M Atchi Reddy, "Labour Relations in Andhra Pradesh Agriculture. 1881-1981", in *Indian Journal of Labour Economics*, Vol. XXVI, 1983, No. 3, p. 164.
56. *Census of India*, 1961, Maredumaka Village Monograph, p. 64.
57. Rajni Kothari observes thus: "The pre-eminent position of the Congress party in the Andhra Pradesh first two decades, has been due to the development of a support base, centred around the landed gentry...The medium-sized landlords and large owner-farmers are dominant in the party and Government, While the leadership of the freedom movement essentially can from the upper castes, it has now shifted to dominant agricultural castes. All the Chief Ministers in Andhra Pradesh have been from the dominant castes of Reddy, Kamma and Velama... The composition of the Cabinet has reflected the same phenomena. Upto 1971 the Reddis had the single largest representation (28 to 38 percent), together with Velamas and Kammas, the representation has varied between 45 to 58 per cent". Sharma, *Op.cit.*, p. 7.
58. Rajni Kothari, (Ed), *Caste in India Politics*, Delhi, 1964, p. 132.
59. *Ibid.*, p. 152-3
60. A village survey noted thus: "The Kammas who come to the Scheduled Caste people numerically and economically well-to-do and socially occupying a high status. Thus is an important caste which occupies a vital position in the social organisation of the village. All the other castes are so placed in the system that they subserve the best interests of this caste". *Census of India*, 1961, Marendumaka Village, Monograph, p. 111.

61. G. Ram Reddy and B.A.V. Sharma, (ed,) *State Government and Politics: Andhra Pradesh*, Delhi, 1979, p. 209
62. Thorner, *Op.cit.*, p. 164.
    "The panchayat Raj, which was introduced in 1959 has been dominated by the dominant peasant castes. In the 1970 elections to the Panchyati Raj bodies in 15 out of 21 Zilla Parishads, the Reddy community captured Chairmanship. Out of 324 Samiti Presidents nearly half of them belong to the same Reddy Caste".
    Sharma, *Op.cit.*, p. 7-8.
63. *Census of India*, 1961, Maredumaka Village Monograph, p. 19.
64. Thorner, *Op.cit.*, p. 173.
65. *Ibid.*, p. 89.

62. Thomas, Op. cit., p. 194.

Nehru, Op. cit., p. 74.

63. Census of India, 1961, Malkonnakalli, Village Monograph, p. 1[illegible].
64. Thomas, Op. cit., p. 173.
65. Ibid., p. [illegible].

18

The Formation of Caste Society in Kerala: Historical Antecedents

Rajan Gurukkal

The earliest known society of Kerala dates back to the times of ancient Tamil Anthologies generally assumed to have belonged to era 300 B.C. and A.D. 300, when the deep south as a whole remained a single culture-zone called 'Tamilakam.' It was a transitional society, a semi-tribal system combining unevenly developed forms of subsistence such as hunting and food gathering, animal husbandry, primitive cultivation, plough agriculture and primitive commodity production, fast shedding its tribal moorings to emerge as a peasant society.[1] Obviously, plough agriculture was the superior form of production in terms of technology and productivity, but it was yet to become the dominant form as evidenced by the superstructure characterised by the political authority of predatory chieftains, institutions of redistributive economy and the ethos of plunder raids which were all uncogenial for plough agriculture to expand. Though it was more or less a self-locked system, it generated, while functioning, a series of contradictions which subsequently acted as the transforming forces.

It was not a caste society by and large though Brahmins seemed to have enjoyed the highest socio-ritual status and maintained a Brahminical ritual domain of caste exclusiveness by distancing themselves from the folk as the purest. The Anthologies refer to both Brahmins and Gods *uyarndōr* or those in the high order, and naturally the folk referred to as *ilipirappālar* presupposedly constituted the low order.[2] Tolkapiam, a grammatical treatise, which the traditional Tamil scholars ascribe to period anterior to the Anthologies, describes the Tamilian counterpart of the *varna* system consisting of *antanar*, *aracar*, *vanikar* and *velalar* as the four *varnas*.[3] But modern historians and linguists alike, consider it a later work, probably of the fifth or the sixth century A.D., and moreover, *aracar*, *vanikar*, *velalar* actually do not correspond to the *kshatriya*, *vaisya* and *sudra* ranks of the *varna* system.[4] Some scholars have tried to show that there existed in Tamilakam an entirely different set of four castes, never to have anything to do with the traditional four *varnas*. This contention is based on a poem which states that there were no *kutis* excepting those of the *tudiyar*, *panar*, *paraiyar* and *kadambar* in the land.[5] The term *kuti* is often taken to denote caste which is an unwarranted translation, and actually the term denotes settlement. In the context, it denotes settlements of the clanish groups such as *tudiyar* (people with a kind of drum called *tudi* as their magico-religious symbol), *panar* (people composing and singing bardic poems), *paraiyar* (people with a kind of drum called *parai* as their magico-religious symbol) and *kadambar* (people with the *kadambu* trees as their totem). The poet does not speak of the general situation in Tamilakam and what he describes is the feature of a specific locality in the land. The question whether the ancient society of Tamilakam had caste-based stratification or not has to be better scrutinised against the background of contemporary economic processes. We understand from the Anthologies that the relatively undeveloped forms of subsistence such as hunting, animal husbandry, primitive agriculture, fishing and salt manufacturing were essentially adopted by the groups having clan ties. The Anthologies mention clannish groups like *kanavar* and *vetar* taking to hunting and primitive cultivation; *idaiyar* taking to animal husbandry; *valayar* or *minavar* taking to fishing; *paratavar* taking to salt manufacturing and *umanar* to its distribution; and *ulavar* taking to plough agriculture.[6] All the forms of production were based on kinship ties of agnatic or affinal type within which were submerged the division and specialisation even of plough agriculture. Though there were certain specialists in arts and crafts such as *taccar* (carpenters) and *kollar* (blacksmiths), there is nothing to show that they constituted themselves as groups outside the clan ties. The functional and transactional relations of the people, by and large, did not generate any rigid stratification of institutional nature leading to the break-up of kinship. The authority structure too was submerged in kinship and we do not find a ruling class totally alienated from the masses although the former had lineage identity.[7]

However, the growth of economic differentiation and the disintegration of kinship were slow but ongoing processes in contemporary society. Regular plunder raids and booty redistribution among people outside the clan ties too were causing economic differentiation. Sometimes the booty included productive lands also and their redistribution among people outside the clan was causing disintegration of kinship as the base of production.[8] This was particularly crucial when productive land was given away to Brahmins who were entitled to a share of booty as reward for performing rituals, composing eulogies to chieftains and functioning as preceptors. It gave rise to a new system of production relations transcending the framework of kinship. This would suggest that although a full blown institutional manifestation of caste was yet to surface, there existed in the society a potential nucleus anticipating the formation of castes. There was the Brahmin household that signified the new system of production relations. The novelty of the system was that it involved the relation between Brahmins and tillers who were the non-cultivating landholders and the cultivating landless, respectively. It was a relation involving two objectively antagonistic classes.

The Brahmin land as an independent unit of production required working families attached to it for ensuring permanency of labour. So naturally, several families belonging to clanish groups must have permanently resorted to for production as well as other essential functions. It is quite reasonable to presume that the beginnings of the crystallisation of functionally specific families into castes took place in the localities of Brahmin households. It is possible that those families distinguished themselves from the rest of the folk, as associated with a unit of production, supreme both ritually and economically. Also they themselves must have differentiated against one another with their tribal norms of purity and pollution. However, the germination of the concept of *jati* system must have been there in the localities of Brahmin households during the days of the Anthologies. But the number of the Brahmin households in Tamilakam was not too large for the *jati* system to characterise the society.

The social formation in the period of the Anthologies seems to have undergone a total crisis during the fourth and fifth centuries of the Christian era, which was a logical culmination of the contradictions in the formation accentuated by more extensive predatory marches, migrations and the entailing disintegration of the kinship ties in production.[9] Though the Brahmin household economy suffered a temporary set-back in the wake of the crisis, subsequently it thrived vigorously as the alternative mode of production.[10] An important feature of this development was the emergence of large Brahmin villages which meant the virtual extension of the new system of production relations to a larger society, and the emergence of the *jati* system was a concomitant development.

During the seventh, eighth and ninth centuries, the Brahmin villages, namely, *brahmadeyas* had large-scale proliferation all over the Tamilakam as a result of royal grants of land to Brahmins. Proliferation of *brahmadeyas* meant the expansion of irrigated agriculture as well of the new system of relations which was the outcome of the dissolving semi-tribal system. The process involved superimposition of Brahmin proprietorship over many a communal land tract, integration of several clanish groups and formation of new social relations. It is the formation of social relations that is particularly relevant to the present discussion. As already noted, the process of the formation of functionally specific groups with some sort of caste identity could be related to the permanent association of certain communal kinship units with the labour processes of the expansion of the Brahmin-headed agrarian economy. The evolving relations in a society headed by Brahmins were primarily based on the nature of functional association of producers, artisans and craftsmen. Their grading on a hierarchical scale depended on the nature of entitlement each group had regarding the sharing of the surplus.[11] The nature of entitlement to surplus was determined by the nature of each group's relation with the means of production, particularly land. Brahmins were the proprietors of land, but they often leased their large farms out to a group of people, which emerged as a class of intermediaries between the Brahmins and peasants. So what was crucial in the social relations of the period was the separation between the primary producers and the full-time non-producing functionaries such as administrators, warriors, etc., who were entitled to the lion's share of surplus through their managerial and protective functions. The group entitled to higher share of surplus distanced themselves from the people directly associated with the labour processes and this superior class-position formed the basis of caste hierarchy.[12] In short, broadly it was the hierarchy of entitlement to surplus that provided the real foundation of the caste structure in the Brahmin-headed agrarian society of South India.

The proliferation of *brahmadeyas* corresponded to the emergence of temples in South India and each Brahmin village became temple-centred. The temple acted as the headquarters of the village and performed a great role as the institutional agency of Brahmins in the ordering of the caste society. Through royal land grants, private land endowments, gifts of gold and other forms of resources by the devotees the temple became a fabulously rich institution.[13] Being a landed magnate by itself, it commanded a large society of people as its dependents and functionaries.[14] With Brahmins as its material and ritual custodians at the top and the various groups of people hierarchically structured on the basis of their entitlements to the temple resources in the middle and the group of primary producers at the base, the temple signified a gamut of social relations into which were introduced the principles of caste for the first time in a full-fledged form.

The period from the eighth to the twelfth century A.D., the earliest documented phase in the history of Kerala, saw the proliferation and consolidation of temple-centred agrarian villages headed by Brahmins.[15] We do not know the exact process of the Brahminical colonisation of Kerala and as a reasonable hypothesis it can be suggested that the colonisation was the result of a large-scale exodus of Brahmins from Andhra through Tamilnad and Karnataka.[16] Unlike the rest of South India, Kerala has no copper plate characters registering grants of land to Brahmins and there is nothing to show that any of the Brahmin settlements here originated as a *brahmadeva.* It seems that the Brahmin settlements in Kerala grew up on their own. Traditional sources indicate that there were originally thirty-two Brahmin settlements in Kerala and now it remains historically true in the light of temple epigraphs.[17] The establishment of these original settlements must have taken place during the seventh and eighth centuries. As evidenced by the very first epigraph of Kerala from a temple, the original settlements had started growing further into subsidiary settlements by the beginning of the ninth century. The processes of social formation since the days of the Anthologies down to the ninth century therefore can only be interpolated through a conjecture that the system of production relations evolved in the primordial Brahmin households in due course acquired a higher institutional and organisational manifestation in the huge temple-centred Brahmin villages (ss we understand from the epigraphs, by the ninth century) the thirty-two Brahmin villages became well-established in the fertile tracts best for paddy cultivation. With the agrarian activities centralised under the temple, managed by a corporation of Brahmin landlords, each village signified an elaborate agrarian order.[18] The Brahmin landlords held almost all agrarian tracts as individual holdings (*brahmasvam* and collective holdings *devasam*) and exercised proprietary control over the settlers in the village.[19] In short, a temple-centred Brahmin village was the corporation of Brahmin landlords with the people associated with them as landed intermediaries, tenants, artisans, craftsmen and tillers. Just as an ancient Brahmin household had around it the required functionaries, a temple-centred Brahmin corporation had all the required functionaries settled in the village itself. By and large, it was a self-sufficient unit with all necessary goods and services. The process of localisation often involved the bringing and settling of various functional groups on the village land. Once so settled, they all became attached and obligated to the village, i.e., to the landlords. All the functionaries enjoyed one or the other type of rights over the village land the intermediaries enjoyed the *karanmai* (tenacy), whereas artisans and craftsmen the *kutiyamai* (occupancy). The process of integration of a large number of such functionaries was evidently complex and the process of their absorption into a hierarchy of caste was all the more complex. However, we are able to draw certain inferences and insights out of the temple records of the period.

The temple-centred nature of the society and economy led to the formation of groups, classes and castes under the institutional influences and directions of the temple. The status of the temple as a landed institution and as a repository of gold and other valuables, enabled it to wield a great deal of social control. Through its control over land it harnessed landed intermediaries, lease-holders, artisans, craftsmen and tillers into a society that can very well be called the temple society. The pooling of wealth in the temple as endowments and its redistribution among the functionaries in the temple society led to the formation of power groups even among Brahmins themselves.[20] Those Brahmin landlords who were members of the village corporation (also called *Sabha*) were the most powerful in the temple society. As the custodians of the temple wealth and the proprietors of the village they had the highest economic status, and as the most learned priests they enjoyed the highest socio-ritual status too. They constituted the agamic specialists as well as Vedic priests, but there were other exceptional cases of Brahmins also who had equal land control without enjoying agamic rights and Vedic scholarship.[21] However, the rich agamic specialists gradually emerged as a separate group called *tantrikal*, as distinguished from the other Brahmins. There were *pattakal* (*bhattas*), *cattirar* (*chatras*) and *santi* (*temple priest*) among the Brahmins who received *virutti*, the land-lease as reward for their services in the temple. *Cattas* and *bhattas* had a relatively better economic status when compared to that of the temple priest, whose ritual status was higher. The interesting thing to be noticed is the formation of a sort of internal differentiation among Brahmins themselves based on the nature of land control. During the later period the differentiation became almost as sharp as that between castes and we find the major landlords among Brahmins identifying themselves as *adhya* as distinguished from others who were called *asya.* Similarly, in relation to the nature of land control or the nature of entitlement to the produce caused a hierarchical division among the non-Brahmin order also.

Potuval and *variyar* are the two most important functional categories in the non-Brahmin order.[22] *Potuval* was the common man, *madhyastha* between the custodians of the temple and the devotees for all their transactions with the temple and hence he acted as the secretary of the temple. As a functionary shouldering managerial and executive responsibility, *potuval* was relatively close to the Brahmins and received *virutti* land as reward for his service to the temple. Anyone, who was a member in any of the temple committees (*variyams*), could be called a *variyar.* But there is a specific functional group referred to in the temple inscriptions as *variyar* by profession and not by virtue of membership in any *variyam.* Members of this group were also given *virutti* land as reward for their services in the temple. These two are now names of two separate castes in Kerala. It is obvious that both *potuval* and *variyar* were two functionally specific groups attached to the temple. But their functions were hereditary since the reward was in the form of a kind of lease-holding right in the *virutti* land. Thus, they became hereditary professional groups and gradually, due to their improved economic status and association with the Brahmins in the affairs of the temple, they distanced themselves from the rest through rules of marriages and inter-dining to constitute two endogamous caste groups. In the same manner, the drummers, dancers and musicians of the temple constituted separate caste groups by themselves. The drummers of the temple are referred to in the inscriptions as *kottikal* or *uvaccakal,* and these names as such do not seem to have survived as caste names. Their modern caste name is Marar. The dancers of the temple are referred to in the epigraphs as *chakkaimar* (male dancers) and *nannnaimar* (dancing girls).[23] *Chakkiyar* is a caste name now in Kerala and *nanniyar* is the name given to the female folk of the *chakkiyar.* All these functionaries were paid in land as *virutti* which as already shown led them to become hereditary professional groups and subsequently endogamous castes. These castes are generally called the *antarala-jati,* i.e., the caste between the Brahmins and the other non-Brahmins. They are also called the temple castes suggestive of their origins.

Most of the temple lands and the individual Brahmin holdings were leased-out to *karalar* who were primarily from the non-Brahmin order. The caste which later came to be called Nairs seems to have been the foremost among them. Forming the major part of the *karalar,* this caste represented the second dominant factor in the temple-centred agrarian society. It was from this caste that the *samanta* chieftains emerged. It seems that the majority of military recruits were from among this caste. This class of intermediaries in land, with the rank and entailing privileges of nobility owing allegiance only to the Brahmin landlords, succeeded in asserting themselves in the temple society. The relations of the women of this caste with the Brahmins through a peculiar material institution called *sambandham* added to its ritual status.[24] This caste of *karalar* on the basis of the nature of land control it wielded gave rise to several divisions in it. Some of them, in course of time, eventually became part of the ruling aristocracy and differentiated themselves from the rest of the Nairs by adopting a *kshatriya* title like *'Varma.'* A few others on the basis of land control achieved through high military positions differentiated themselves as Panikkar and similarly yet another group distinguished themselves as Menon on the basis of better land control and ritual status acquired through their association with the Brahmin landlords as the latter's accountants.

In the same manner, the artisans and craftsmen also became caste groups through their attachment to the temple society. These people were settled at the fringe of the temple-centred villages and were obliged to render their services to the temple as well as to the landlords. Inscriptions refer to *taccar* (carpenters), *kollar* (blacksmiths), *kallavaniyar* (potters), *vaniyar* (oil mongers), *vannar* (washermen), etc. They were brought and settled in the temple village to ensure their services.[25] They enjoyed occupancy right over village land and this constituted the material incentive for them to be hereditary professional groups, and further, there was no other alternative for them as they were caught up in a social milieu of immobility and functional obligations. They were more or less the bondsmen of the temple village where they were settled.

At the base of the temple society were the actual tillers who constituted the most servile group and their only privilege was *atiayma* (servility). They were attached to agricultural lands and were transacted along with land as goods.[26] As a caste, they are called *pulayar*, probably a tribal name, and *cerumar*—the lowest people. All the people distanced themselves from the *pulayas* or *cerumas* and there is no need to explain the transformation of this class of primary producers into a polluting caste.

It is to be noted here that the temple society and the Brahmin villages were confined only to a small area in Kerala, i.e., the fertile wet lands. The major portion remained outside. We do not have any archival records highlighting the situation in non-Brahmin villages. However, the Brahmin-headed agrarian villages being the units of the dominant mode of production of the period, the relation evolved was characteristic to the society as whole. There are indications in certain records that in the non-Brahmin villages also agrarian relations and the land system remained the same.[27] The situation in non-agrarian tracts must have been different, and (there) the society may not have been stratified on the principle of castes. We have evidence in the ninth century Syrian Christian copper plates for the existence of certain caste groups and land tenure in the market town of Quilon.[28] The plates mention the grant of certain caste groups like *ilavar* (toddy-tappers), *taccar*, *velalar* (agricultural people) and *vannar* to the Tarsa Church. It actually registers a grant of lands required by the functionaries of the church. The above mentioned castes were the settlers of the granted land and they were to serve the church and its people according to the conditions of the grant. As the grant was made by the local ruler, the land originally must have been the *cerikkal* property (crown's land), and the alienation of the caste groups suggests that in the crown's lands also, the relations of production were in tune with the caste system. In short, just as the Brahmin villages, the *cerikkal* as well as market towns had the same land system and their functionaries were caste groups. It may be said that the Kerala society witnessed the formation of caste groups all over the agrarian region during the ninth and tenth centuries.

In conclusion, we may say that the earliest society of Kerala so far known in history was based on economics incapable of generating division and specialisation of labour leading to the bifurcation of kinship and the formation of castes. However, the germination of castes was, perhaps, in the Brahmin household economy and that involved relations cutting across kinship and required the permanent association of specific families. The actual formation of castes took place in the temple-centred Brahmin villages having extensive agrarian activities. As a landed institutional agency of the Brahmin landlords, the temple played a crucial role in the multiplication of castes and sub-castes. The peculiar land system and service-tenure were responsible for the emergence of hereditary professional groups on a large scale, and the Brahminical ideas of ritual status were instrumental in their transformation into endogamous castes. The land system and service-tenancy became widespread and therefore the caste-based social stratification, too, became all pervasive. The system of service-tenure under the king and the local rulers gave rise to hereditary offices and the entailing castes and sub-castes. Its extension into non-Brahmin villages and even to market towns is attested to by records. Caste appeared as an institutional manifestation in the hierarchically structured agrarian society in which services were paid for in the form of land rights.

Notes

1. Rajan Gurukkal, "Forms of Production and Forces of Change in Ancient Tamil Society", Proceedings of the Indian History Congress (PIHC), 1987.
2. *Purananuru* (Pn.) 221: *Patirruppattu* (Prp.) 1:35; 3:9 refer to Brahmins as *uyarndor. Ilipirappalar* is referred to in Pn. 82:3; 170:5; 287:2; 289:10; 363:14 etc.
3. *Tolkappiam*; *Porul.* 625-26; 635. It is mentioned in the text that *antanar* wore the *nul* (sacred thread), carried the *karakam* (vessel containing holy water for ceremonial ablutions), the *mukkol* (trident like staff), and the *manai* (wooden plank to serve as seat). The *aracar* had the royal paraphernalia, the *vanikar* wore a garland on their shoulder and a flower on their head, and the *velalar* carried their weapons and the totemic garland. For details see, N.Subrahmanian, *Sangam Polity* (Bombay, 1966) pp258ff. Also M.G.S.Narayanan, "The Vedic Puranic Sastraic Element in Tamil Sangam Society and Culture", in K.M.Srimali (ed.) *Essays in Indian Art, Religion and Society* (New Delhi, 1987).
4. The concept of *varna* has to be understood as the Sastraic abstraction of contemporary jati experiences of the northern India. For the dealings on the caste system in detail see C.Bougle, *Essays on the Caste System* (tr.D.Pocock, Cambridge, 1971). Also L.Dumont, *Homo Hierarchicus* (tr. London 1972). As regards the questions of origins see the scientific observations in Romila Thapar, *From Lineage to State* (New Delhi, 1984) pp18ff.
5. Pn. 335 by Mankuti kilar.
6. *Narrinai* (Nar.) 142; 303; 331; 372; 338; etc. *Ainkurunuru* (Aink.) 47; 48; 111; 195 etc. *Akananuru* (An.) 60; 65 etc. Pn. 33; 73; 82 etc. are examples. See the discussions in K.Sivathamby, "Early South Indian Society and Economy; the Tinai Concept", *Social Scientist*, No. 29 (1974) pp20-37. Also see Singaravelu, *Social Life of the Tamils: Classical Period* (Kaulalumpur, 1966) pp32ff.
7. Anthologies refer to the three major ruling lineages (*muvendar*) viz., the Cera, Cola and Pandya besides the minor ones called the Velir. But non of these seems to have completely freed themselves from the nexus of the clan ties.

8. Pn.297 describes a warrior chief discussing with his fellow warriors that he would not accept the arid gram-growing tracts as rewards for fighting, but would accept only paddy fields. This would suggest that capture of productive land was a major attraction for the warrior leaders in participating in the raids. For a substantial analysis of the question see M.G.S.Narayanan, "Warrior Settlements in the Sangam Age", PIHC. 1982.
9. The fourth century A.D. witnessed probably the climax of the crisis in the form of a large scale predatory march by a marauding tribe called the Kalabhras who swept over the region under all the three ruling lineages of Tamilakam. Brahmins were reminded of the evils of kaliyuga by the sufferings in the wake of Kalabhras aggression. The implications of Kali age in the context of northern India have been ably interpreted as transitional crisis of a social formation. See R.S.Sharma, "The Kali Age: A Period of Social Crisis", in S.N.Mukherjee (ed.) India: *History and Thought, Essays in Honour of A.L.Basham* (Calcutta, 1982) pp186-203. Also B.N.S.Yadava, "The Accounts of the Kali Age and the Social Transition from the Antiquity to the Middle Ages", *Indian Historical Review*, vol.V.Nos.1 & 2. The interpretation holds good in the context of the fourth-fifth century Tamil society too. See Rajan Gurukkal, "Agrarian System and Socio-political Organisation under the Early Pandyas", Unpublished Ph.D. dissertation, Jawaharlal Nehru University, New Delhi, 1984.pp76ff.
10. See Rajan Gurukkal, Op.cit. p.76
11. It recalls the pattern of resource sharing in the Medieval European society. See R.Rodolsky, "The distribution of the Agrarian product in Feudalism", *Journal Economic History* Vol.XI,No.3(1951)-pp247ff. Also P.Anderson, *Lineages* of Absolutist State (London, 1974) p.401.
12. See the caste and class identity question ably discussed in Claude Meillassoux, "Are there Castes in India?" *Economy and Society*, vol.2. (1973).
13. For details see Burton Stein, "The Economic Function of a Medieval South Indian Temple", *Journal of Asian Studies*, vol.27 (1960). Also *The South Indian Temple* edited by him, New Delhi, 1977. The economic position of the temple is well brought out in Karashima, "Land Donations to Hindu Temples in Medieval South India", *Journal of Asian and African Studies* (Tokyo, 1869).
14. D.N.Jha,"Temples as Landed Magnates in South India, c.A.D.700-1300", Indian Society: *Historical Probings* (New Delhi, 1974) edited by R.S.Sharma.
15. The details are given in Rajan Gurukkal, "The Socio- economic Milieu of the Kerala Temple: A Functional Analysis", *Studies in History*, Vol.II No.1 (1980).

16. The problem has been elaborately considered in M.G.S.Narayanan, "Political and Social Conditions of Kerala under the Kulasekhara Empire", Unpublished doctoral dissertation, Kerala University (1972).
17. Kesavan Velu that, *Brahmin Settlements in Kerala* (Calicut, 1976).
18. Rajan Gurukkal, *Op.cit.*
19. *Ibid.*
20. *Ibid.* The concept of redistribution is borrowed from Karl Polanyi, "The Economy as Instituted Process", Polanyi *et.al* ed. *Trade and Market in the Early Empires* (Glencoe, 1959) pp 243 ff. But the concept is used only to explain the niceties and the central perspective is that of the mode of production concept formulated by Marx. The insights of Terray and Godelier are also made use of. See Terray, *"Marxism and 'Primitive' Societies"* (New Delhi 1975) and Godelier, *Perspectives in Marxists Anthropology* (Cambridge, 1977).
21. Manur inscription of the Pandya period and the Uttaramerur inscription of the Chola period prescribe Vedic and Agamic scholarship as one of the essential qualifications for the Brahmin landlords to be a member of the Sabha. See discussions in K.A.Nilakanta Sastri, *The Cholas* (Madras, 1975) pp.495-6.
22. Rajan Gurukkal, *Op.cit.*
23. *Ibid,* Also see his "Proliferation and Çonsolidation of the Temple Centred Social Hierarchy in the Cera Period", *Journal of Kerala Studies*, vol.VI.Parts III & IV.pp.333-346.
24. *Sambandham* was a system of concubinage by the Brahmins with the Nair ladies. But it acquired the status of a loose marriage since among the Kerala Brahmins, (nambudiris) only the eldest male son was entitled to marry from the same community. Thus all the junior members of the family were forced to have *sambandham* alliance with the Nairs.
25. Rajan Gurukkul, *Op.cit.*
26. *Ibid.*
27. An inscription recently recovered from Cembra in north Malabar sheds light on the socio-economic processes in a non-Brahmin village. It is a coastal village with the tracts generally unsuitable for paddy cultivation owing to the tidal flow up of saline water into the fields. Such areas were inevitably avoided by the Brahmins. Still it appears that the relations of production were more or less the same in this village too. For details of the inscription see, Raghava Varier, "Cembra Lighitangal" (Mal.) *Vijnanakairali*, vol.16 No.2 (1985) pp.84-98.
28. See the text of the inscription given in M.G.S.Narayanan, *Cultural Symbiosis in Kerala* (Trivandrum, 1972) Appendix IV.

19

Caste-Class Situation in India

A.B.Bardhan

Among the divisive forces which afflict our national life, disrupt the bonds of unity among the Indian people, and affect social advancement and further development, casteism and caste conflict are the major factors. Those who pretend not to see them, are ignoring an important aspect of India's social reality. The frequent instances of caste confrontation, leading even to occasional outbursts of caste violence, both in urban centres and the countryside, force themselves on our attention.

The issue of reservation in services and higher educational institutions, especially its extension to other backward classes, raises a storm every now and then. Whenever during elections, the political and programmatic appeal does not become the central issue, we witness a rising tide of caste-mobilisation and caste animosities.

What is to be noted today is that this is taking place precisely in the background of sharpening of class struggles.

Forces of disruption and destabilisation are, of course, not missing the chance to fish in these troubled waters. So-called 'research scholars' from the West have suddenly developed a deep interest in studying the caste system in India, including the caste background of leaders of political parties, and so on.

Caste as a Divine Weapon

Caste has always been a powerful potential and actual weapon in keeping the people divided and weak in the face of any challenge. More than a hundred and thirty years ago, Marx, while concluding his observations on the future results of British rule in India, remarked: "How was English supremacy established in India?... A country not only divided between the Mohammedan and Hindu, but between tribe and tribe, between caste and caste; a society whose framework was based on a sort of equilibrium, resulting from a general repulsion and constitutional exclusiveness between all its members. Such a country and such a society, were they not the predestined prey of conquest?"

Indian history furnishes proof that the ideology of the caste system has been assiduously propagated and upheld by the ruling classes at all times. Imperialism harnessed it for its purpose.

Freedom Struggle and Social Reform

The national liberation movement, by mobilising the forces of the Indian people against the alien rulers, by rousing their anti-imperialist consciousness was able to relegate caste divisiveness into the background for a time, though even then a good deal of controversy was generated over the question, whether the struggle for social reform took precedence over the political struggle, or vice versa. The untouchables and the lower castes, as also the tribal people, could not be drawn into the mainstream of the national struggle in all their strength and in all parts of the country because of the failure to resolve this controversy on a correct basis. Some people went to the length of saying that those who emphasised the need for social reforms were not interested in the forward march of the freedom struggle, though it would be the greatest travesty of truth to question the ardent patriotism of men like Phule and Ambedkar.

India's freedom struggle has not only culminated in the transfer of power and India's independence, it has also created a powerful and broad-based democratic movement, with democratic consciousness influencing the minds of the masses. It is this legacy, and the powerful sentiment of national unity and integrity, that has kept the separatist, communal and other divisive forces at bay, and checked caste disturbances from crossing all bounds.

There have been constant efforts, dating from the ancient period to the present day, and ranging from assaults on the caste system as such to attempt at mitigating its harshness.

Buddhism and Jainism opposed Brahminical authority, though not the caste system as such. Their decline in the subsequent period led to a reassertion of Brahminical superiority and orthodoxy.

Reformative movements such as the Bhakti movement connected with Kabir, Chakradharswami, Tukaram and the Saint tradition; the Sanskritization movement, which was an attempt by the lower castes to rise in the social scale by adopting rituals or social norms peculiar to the higher castes; the Neo-Vedantic movement led by savants like Vivekananda, Dayanand and which Mahatma Gandhi also substantially advocated; were all attempts to mitigate the inhumanity of casteism within the Hindu framework.

The approach adopted by Mahatma Jyotiba Phule and the Satyashodhak movement, as also by the Dravida Kazgham, which asserted the intrinsic worth of a human being irrespective of caste, were basically secular, though they developed pronounced anti-Brahmin slants.

Ambedkar, frustrated at the fate of repeated attempts to 'annihilate' castes within the Hindu framework, ultimately opted for his mass conversion movement—the Dharmachakra Pravartan .

Marxist versus the Traditional RSS Approach

The problem of caste continues to plague us in several forms. It is only an objective and historical approach based on the science of historical materialism, the revolutionary ideology of Marxism that enables one to have some degree of insight into the emergence of the *varna* system and the caste system in Indian polity, and how castes and caste system have become an anachronism today, incompatible with ongoing socio-economic transformations (this, even an honest, secular democrat can realise), but also how it will eventually come to an end. This ideology (Marxism) helps one to understand that what occasionally bursts out on the surface as a resurgence of casteism, as bitter caste conflicts, or as inhuman atrocities perpetrated by the upper castes against the lower castes, are but the death-throes of a moribund system, destined to disappear in the coming days.

But this will not happen spontaneously or with ease. It will happen because of the tenacious, continuous and militant struggle waged by the revolutionary toiling masses against the present unjust social order, and against all the social forces which wish to exploit every divisive element, including the caste system, for prolonging their vested interests.

As against this, there are those who uphold the caste system as an eternal and specifically a unique Indian phenomenon. They find it relevant even in the present situation, may be, after purging it of some perversities, and restoring it to its so-called 'pristine purity'. This unhistorical and metaphysical approach is accompanied by attempts to gloss over the discriminations, inequality and inhumanity that are implicit in the system. It is not necessary to quote various religious authorities or the recent crop of 'fundamentalists' on this subject. It would be enough to quote one, whose teachings have moulded the thinking of certain sections of Hindus along aggressive communal lines represented by the Rashtriya Swayamsevak Sangha (RSS). This thought even today has an impact on our politics. The RSS front organisations like the Bhartiya Janata Party (BJP), Bhartiya Majdoor Sabha (BMS), Akhil Bharatiya Vidyarthi Parishad (ABVP), Vishva Hindu Parishad (VHP), are the self-confessed bearers of this ideology. But many others are also not immune from this. I refer to the late Guru Golwalkar, and his *Bunch of Thoughts.* Guruji asserts that "the feeling of inequality, of high and low, which has crept into the *varna* system is comparatively of recent origin. The perversion was given a further fillip by the scheming Britisher in line with his 'divide and rule' policy. But in its original form, the distinction in that social order did not imply any discrimination of big or small, high or low, among its constituents..."

That the scheming Britisher gave it a fillip, and utilised it, is of course true. But one would think, the learned Guruji had never heard of the mass of "Bramhana" literature, of the "Manusmriti" and so forth, where inequality, inhuman discrimination, high and low, were rigidly laid down, with dire punishment in case of any transgression by the lower castes. Since we know that he was well-versed in all the ancient books, it is to be presumed he was deliberately glossing it over, with a view to justifying its continuance.

We mention just a few injunctions from the scriptures, sanctified as *Dharma* the moral and religious code which must be followed, if one has to secure his position in this world and in the next. We refer only to the Manusmriti:

Scholarship, education, acquisition of knowledge except for one's own hereditary and traditional occupation, is sternly prohibited for the Shudras:

वेदः कृत्सनोडभिगन्तव्यः सरहस्यो व्दिजन्मना
न शूंद्राय मति दद्यात
न शूंद्रे जनसान्निध्यो

(Let not the Shudra be anywhere around where the Vedas and other holy books are being taught or recited. This is an absolute prohibition. If there be a Brahmin so foolish as to permit a Shudra to acquire knowledge, he is to be boycotted from religious functions).

Further, the Shudra cannot be permitted to acquire or perform jobs, as are meant only for the Brahmins and the Kshatriyas:

वैश्य शूंद्रो प्रयत्नेन स्वातिकर्माणि कारयेता
तो ही च्यूतो स्पफर्मभ्यः क्षोभयेता भियं जंगत्

(The ruler is expressly directed to see that the Vaishyas and Shudras strictly keep to their respective tasks, for if they do not, there will be chaos in the world).

The Gita repeats this behest in the following words:

स्वधर्मे निधनं श्रेयः परधर्मो भयावहः

(Even death while performing one's own *dharma* brings blessedness and taking to another's *dharma* is fraught with fearful consequences).

Here, *dharma* means binding one's caste. This exhortation had force in the context of the Gita's teaching of 'karmayoga,' of 'nishakama karma', of action without any attachment or expectation of result, and especially when Arjun was being urged to stop hesitating and fulfil his duty as a Kshatriya. But when Guruji approvingly quotes this injunction (*Bunch of Thoughts*, p. 59), without reference to time and social circumstances, wishfully hoping that this be followed in present-day society, it is anything but 'karmayog' that he implies.

In capitalist countries where we have class divisions in society, the exploited classes have had to face, and are facing all types of deprivation. Here in India, where we have the added oppression of castes by castes, in addition to the class divisions between the exploiting and the exploited classes. The deprivation suffered by the lower castes (who are also an overwhelming part of the exploited classes) is many times more severe.

Today, the attitude towards castes and the caste system, and the problems arising thereof, marks out a progressive, democratic and secular individual and/or party, from an obscurantist, hide-bound reactionary individual and party. This has undeniably become a touchstone in India's social and political life.

Rise and Consolidation of Caste Divisions in India

The uniqueness of the 'Purush Sukta' which first noted the early class-based division of society, consists in this, that it invested it with a sacred and divine origin. To quote the words of Dr. Ambedkar, "it elevated the real to the dignity of an ideal." Subsequent scriptural authorities further reinforced this stamp of divinity and also clearly defined the discrimination, inequality and exploitation inherent in it.

What started with the *varna* division, proliferated into the system of castes in the course of development of an exploitative society. The rigid framework of the 'chaturvarnya' itself inevitably led to the emergence of the 'fifth group', of those who came to be outside the pale—the *atishudras*, the untouchables.

The caste system with its barbarous inequalities, penalties and disabilities, particularly towards the Harijans, is the natural offspring of the 'varnashram dharma.' It carries all the birthmarks of the latter. The Shrutikars and thereafter the Smritikars, like Manu, have only codified them with, perhaps, additions and embellishments of their own. If despite the atrocious discrimination and degradation which is inherent in this institution it has survived through the centuries, it is not just because it gave the social structure a certain degree of stability and security, but because it more or less truthfully reflected the historical reality, legitimised and sanctified by a combination of scriptural injunction, mythology and ritual which even the tallest social reformers found difficult to challenge.

As we noted earlier, many saints and social reformers, beginning from medieval times and right up to the present, have poured their hearts out against the cruelty and inhumanity that goes along with the system, and castigated it boldly and severely. But if they have not been able to make any significant inroad, except in so far as certain new sects practising their teachings came into being, it is because preaching had not created castes and nor was preaching going to do away with it. Moreover, 'equality before God' is not the same thing as 'equality among men'.

Prolonged colonial domination and intervention in our socio-economic life thwarted and distorted our normal development, slowing down and inhibiting the class divisions and antagonisms that are related with the development in the means of production.

The factors discussed above have led to social and economic backwardness of identifiable groups getting linked up in many cases with their caste mark. In a caste-ridden society like ours, the whole system of exploitation and the resultant backwardness of major sections of the people is rationalised and justified by means of the 'myth' of 'natural superiority by birth' and the hierarchical status imposed on them. It serves to conceal the actual contradictions that are unfolding in our society.

Radical Changes in the Past Hundred Years and More

Economic and political developments from the days of the British rule, but especially after independence, have been striking at the base of the caste system, breaking up the stagnancy and status quo which it imposed on social life. New divisions and differentiations, giving rise to new antagonisms and social norms, new aims and aspirations, secular in nature and content, are taking effect.

Industrial development, beginning with the second half of the nineteenth century, but particularly during and after the Second World War, and the post-independence era, has given rise to a new social division of labour. A strong indigenous bourgeoisie, owning the means of production, has come into being. As opposed to this, a numerically large modern working class, composed of those who have to live by selling their labour power, has also come up. The social mobility which accompanied this development has broken through traditional caste barriers. It has forged a new class of the exploited, the propertyless, the proletariat, distinguished not by the earlier caste attributes of hierarchy, hereditary occupation and so on, but by a secular relation, both within its various sections, and also as opposed to the propertied class, the owners of the means of production.

In the vast rural sector too, deep-going changes in agrarian life have broken through and upset the age-old caste structure. The two factors which have played a major role in this are: (i) agrarian reforms, however, partial and incomplete; and (ii) the decentralisation of power brought about through the system of gram panchayats, mandal and panchayat samities, zilla and janpad sabhas, based on adult franchise.

The break-up of the old oppressive feudal set-up, and especially land redistribution, whether through legislative means or through mass action, has brought about changes in rural society, redistributed economic power, and given rise to new norms of social behaviour. Even the character and physiognomy of the class of landless—the rural proletariat—which exist today is different from the earlier Harijans, artisans and other non-landowning castes, even though these very castes may constitute a major section of the rural proletariat. Today, the relation is basically that of a wage-labourer on land, while earlier it was basically a *jajmani* relationship.

Elections to gram panchayats and other tiers of local government in the countryside have also enabled the lower castes to develop a consciousness of numerical strength, and wherever this has asserted itself, they have been able to secure a share in power.

Even the history of the caste system shows that no caste has been able to assert its superiority over others merely by virtue of its higher position in the hierarchical scale, unless this has been reinforced by economic power and buttressed by political power. Temporal power has had to come to the aid of spiritual power bestowed by myth and rituals to make the position of a higher caste unassailable and acceptable to the masses. That is why, mere 'Sanskritization', adoption of rituals peculiar to the higher castes or similar social norms, has never basically altered the real position of a caste, except in its own egoistic self-consciousness.

Thus, the changes in production relations, both in the industrial and agrarian sectors, arising from capitalist development, have brought about fundamental changes, realignments in social attitude and behavioural norms, within the caste system. Only the blind can fail to see the violent shake-up that the caste system has undergone, especially during the past six or seven decades.

The tribal people have also been subjected to these developments. During the British rule, political domination and the influence of market economy began to penetrate into predominantly tribal areas. Alien elements like the moneylender, the trader, the police and revenue officials and the minions of the forest department, started making their presence felt. They were responsible in up-setting the socio-cultural stability of the tribal communities. The effect was shattering in many respects, and even called forth armed resistance in several places. These were, of course, overpowered by the advance and onslaught of the upcoming economic and political forces. Tribal elements were drawn and in many cases fused into the general society, largely as a pauperised mass.

In the post-independence period, the pace of industrialisation, particularly in tribal regions, and the inexorable expansion of the capitalist market, have further speeded up the above-mentioned processes. These regions have lost their tribal exclusiveness, and a mass influx of 'outsiders' has taken place. But the benefits—social, educational and economic—have not flowed to the tribal masses. Therefore, the tribes continue to bear the stamp of social and economic backwardness, which had characterised them in earlier epochs.

Feudal and Pre-feudal Socio-economic Formations

The prevalence of feudal, semi-feudal and even pre-feudal socio-economic formations in the country, despite capitalist development, continues to nourish the caste system, and the hold of caste ideology on people's minds. Today, with the monster of communalism is rearing its head, revivalism and casteism have been given a shot in the arm. The spirit of scientific inquiry and modern rational thought is sought to be overwhelmed by a barrage of obscurantist propaganda. In the name of religious rights (*dharma suraksha*), even the barbaric incident of *sati* is glorified and claimed to be a customary right of the Rajputs. Entry to the Nathdwara temple or the one in Chattisgarh, and to so many others is denied to the Harijans even today by upper castes despite the provisions in Article 14, 15 and 17 of the Constitution contrary to any kind of discriminations based on caste and creed. Organisations like the Maratha Mahasangh and the Shiv Sena take to the streets demanding deletion of Ambedkar's writings on the *Riddles of Ram* and the *Riddles of Krishna*.

Economic Disparity within Various Castes

To sum up, capitalist development has brought about basic changes in the role and relevance of castes. It has also brought about changes in the matter of tribal ethno-cultural identity.

Capitalist development, despite the continuance of several earlier socio-economic formations, has resulted in social stratification and differentiation within the castes themselves. Over the years, the speed of such differentiation is getting accelerated. Today, a caste that is economically homogeneous is a rarity.

Among the lower castes, as also among the tribal people, a petty bourgeois has emerged. This new group has to be reckoned with in political and social life today. However, one does not yet see a significant bourgeois class, arising within the rank of the Scheduled Castes and the Scheduled Tribes. In the countryside, one may come across a few rich peasants among them. They are those who have been able to take advantage of a package of favourable circumstances. But that is about all.

Among the other backward castes, the situation is a bit different. At least within some of these castes, a strong rural bourgeoisie has emerged, and evidence is not lacking of an industrial and commercial bourgeoisie also coming up from among them.

On the contrary, these very processes have led to the pauperisation of some sections of the so-called higher castes. These sections are now compelled to rub shoulders with the mass of the lower castes in the ranks of the proletariat and the semi-proletariat. The march of time has cast some of them even among the lumpens.

Granted the existence of castes, notwithstanding the differentiations that have taken place within them, there is as yet a sub-stratum of common social bond and psychological make-up, a sentiment of 'togetherness', which enables the 'better-offs' among them, those who are educationally and economically ahead of the rest, those who are in closer proximity to the seats of political power, to rally the majority of 'their castes' behind them. The same holds good for the tribes. It follows that the 'better-offs' utilise this strength derived from their caste or tribal affiliation to further their own narrow interests in various spheres of life.

Vested Interests and Caste Division

The vested interests have a powerful weapon in the caste division that exists in Hindu society. This is being used on an increasing scale, precisely because class divisions and class struggles are becoming sharper, threatening their hegemony. The aim that is pursued by these vested interests is to manoeuvre their caste-following in such a manner as to divide the militant masses who are locked in class struggle, to keep them away from the struggles and even to engineer a split in the fighting ranks. With this in view, the caste organisations are being activated. The practice of setting up caste organisations is pretty old. Some of them engaged themselves with social reform work within their castes, and also undertook educational and other activities generally for members of their own castes. But their reactivisation in the present context has a different significance.

In some places, caste-based private armies have been organised. These are used to terrorise the lower castes, and to perpetrate atrocities on them. This is especially so in a state like Bihar where feudal and semi-feudal relations still persist and are strong. But so-called advanced states like Kerala or Maharashtra are also not free from this disease, though here, the methods pursued by casteist organisations are more sophisticated.

Castes and Elections

In elections to all types of representative bodies, one's 'own' caste and community, or perhaps a 'group of allied castes' (KHAM, AJGAR and so forth), provides an easily accessible vote bank and a power base. Therefore, the tendency, born out of the opportunism of bourgeois and petty bourgeois parties and groups, is to rely on this, appeal to ethnocentrism. Cynical calculations are made while putting up candidates and conducting election propaganda. This applies equally to the upper, the middle and the lower castes. Against the casteism of the upper castes, a sort of 'inverted casteism' of the lower castes is set in motion. But here, there is also a bit of contradiction. The democratic election appeal itself, as also the pressing need to gather additional votes, requires a multi-caste approach. Thus, the two contradictory processes—one operating above the ground and the other below—go together. Such are the facts of life in a bourgeois democratic system operating in a caste milieu like ours.

The Congress, in particular, has developed a sort of expertise in these matters over a period of four or five decades. Other bourgeois parties have learnt to follow suit. The left parties are generally free from this, though sometimes parliamentary cretinism and the lure of votes make a few individuals fall prey to this disease.

Actually, it is only where the left parties have patiently built up a truly democratic and secular base and infused class consciousness among a majority of the toiling masses, where the social reform movement has gone deep into the grassroots of society transforming the social psyche, that we do not find such a revolting and disruptive casteist and communal atmosphere vitiating the elections. Instead, politics and programmes are in the forefront. At other places too, whenever national, political and programmatic issues are to the fore, the influence of the caste factor recedes temporarily.

The point that has to be noted is that the exploiting classes are relatively more homogeneous, in as much as they generally coincide with the upper castes. But the exploited masses are far more heterogeneous in their caste composition. This enables the exploiting classes to utilise the caste factor to divide the toiling masses and protect their own class interests. If anything, this underlines the duty of the working class movement to fight back casteism in the interest of its own class unity.

Caste and Class

What we have in the specific Indian situation today is a mixing up of two social differentiations. One, based on caste, is a legacy of the past but has been carried over into the present. The other is class differentiation, based on the development of productive forces and the commensurating production relations. Inevitably, the second one is growing more powerful each day, and is breaking up the rigid framework imposed by the caste system. Objective developments are strengthening class divisions and antagonisms, and the struggle between classes is becoming sharper. It is necessary to state here that when the constitution speaks of 'socially and educationally backward classes', and the courts discuss it in their judgements, what they mean by 'class' is, "a homogenous social section of the people with common traits and identifiable by some common attributes, and not class in the sense of a social group distinguished by its relation to the means of production."

Some persons, who desire to take advantage by playing up casteism, equate caste with class and even caste war to a form of class war in Indian conditions. This is totally a wrong and disruptive concept. It ignores reality and the march of time. While class consciousness and class struggle unite all sections of the exploited masses against their exploiters, caste consciousness and caste struggle divide the exploited masses according to their castes while claiming to fight the exploiters. The caste ideology of the dominant castes cannot be fought by building a caste ideology of the lower or backward castes.

In this connection, the emergence of the Bahujan Samaj Party (BSP) and the 'DS4' in certain parts of the country, especially in the Hindi heartland, has to be regarded with great concern. The war cry of this party "*Thakur-Baman-Baniya Chor, Baki-Sab-Hai DS 4*" is a call for a caste war. This is no laughing matter. Similarly, the move to set up caste-based unions, by harping on real or imaginary grievances and preaching caste exclusiveness should be considered a dangerous move. Workers with a backward tribal consciousness and sometimes even other minorities are also sought to be dragged into such unions or cultural associations.

"Man does not live by bread alone. Self-respect and human dignity is no less important." Utilising this dictum, the BSP and the DS4 seek to rouse passions and sentiments which are divisive and disrupt workers' unity. Other than this, they have no political or economic programme. Their main weapon is thus directed against those who advocate and work for class unity, the unity of all the working people. The leadership of the BSP invokes the name of Ambedkar. But let it be remembered that Ambedkar, who all the time thought about the emancipation of the *Dalits*, had this to say in 1935: "How can there be a revolution if the proletariat cannot present a united front?"

Caste not to be Underestimated

Some sociologists have underestimated the part played by the caste system in the stratification of Indian society and in perpetuating exploitation, making it a hundred times more oppressive and degrading. Some have tended to ignore the specific social and ideological struggle against castes and the caste system and its fall-outs while concentrating on the economic and political struggle. This is a mistake. To think that the industrial revolution is itself giving death blows to the caste system and that the economic and political struggle being waged by the workers against the capitalists and against the feudal elements will finally seal the fate of the caste system and bury it, is to vulgarise Marxism. Writing in his *A Contribution to a Critique of Political Economy*, Marx had observed: "Man is a social animal... not only social, but an animal that can be individualised only within society."

For a majority of Indians, a man is born as a 'social animal' not only in the wider sense of general society, but also in the narrower sense of being an individual within his special *samaj*, an euphemism for his caste or community. He may work shoulder to shoulder with other men on the same machine in the same work place for eight hours a day and even fight common class battles, but thereafter he is dissolved, engulfed and 'individualised' within his 'special society' which still regulates important aspects of his life and social existence. This is why the struggle for overcoming caste consciousness and for elimination of the caste system demands special attention. Even assuming it as a 'super-structure,' it does not follow that it will disappear when the 'base' has been demolished. The superstructure influences the caste, and in this case gives it a toughness and tenacity, which makes the demolition many times more difficult. Engels had indicated the same in one of his writings: "According to the materalist view of history, what is in the last instance decisive in history is the production and re-production of actual life. More than this, neither Marx nor I have ever asserted. But when anyone distorts this so as to read that the economic factor is the sole element, he converts the statement into a meaningless, abstract, absurd phrase. The economic condition is the basis, but the various elements of their results, the constitution—the legal forms, and also all the reflexes of these actual contests in the brains of the participants, the political, legal, philosophical theories, the religious views—all these exert an influence on the development of the historical struggles, and in many instances determine their forms."

Issue of Reservation

Marxists base their stand on reservation on this understanding. The Scheduled Castes and the Scheduled Tribes have suffered due to age-old discrimination and social oppression. The practice of untouchability debased large masses into something less than human beings. It debarred them from entry to administration and educational institutions, which can qualify them for decision-making positions in social and political life. Facts and figures show that what actually exists is an undeclared 'reservation' so far, operating to the advantage of the upper castes, a 'reservation' so tenacious, that even the 'constitutional' measures for enforcing reservations for the SCs and STs find it difficult to undo it. Stratification among them has led to the emergence of a petty bourgeois class, but not of a bourgeoisie worth the name. In their case, therefore, the constitutional provisions have to be fully implemented and all the ruses, pleas and sleight-of-hand by which an upper caste dominated administration has continued to deny them their share. This must be totally condemned.

In the case of other backward castes, the so-called 'socially and educationally backward classes' which the Mandal Commission (1978-80) has gone into at great length, note has to be taken that the stratification is much deeper and greater. Among them there are powerful sections of the rural bourgeoisie and even elements of a rising industrial and commercial bourgeoisie. Therefore, in their case, reservation has to be subject to an income limit, reasonably agreed upon and specified. The question also arises for extending reservation to those sections (irrespective of caste in their case), who are below the poverty-line and have therefore no access to jobs or education.

To oppose reservation on the ground of providing 'equal opportunities' to all, and enforcing 'absolute equality' is actually to perpetuate inequality. To talk of 'formal equality' when there is 'actual inequality'-moreover an inequality which carries the brand of centuries of oppression and discrimination by the upper castes, is not only to perpetuate this inequality, but actually to demand the right of the oppressors to lord over the oppressed.

Reservation is a temporary measure. That is how we should look at it. It is one of the several measures needed to create the conditions for bringing about social equality. Therefore, as this inequality is reduced, reservation has to be tapered off. As and when a group (whether defined on caste basis or not), becomes socially and educationally advanced, it has to be taken off the list. Likewise, where there is no income limit today, such a limit may be imposed tomorrow, and then further raised the day after tomorrow, depending on the steady advance registered. How long will this take? It is difficult to say today. However, one thing is clear: the more honestly and earnestly this is implemented, the sooner will that stage be reached, when we can do away with reservation based on caste as the criterion.

20

Caste, Class and Social Consciousness: Reflections on Contemporary Indian Situation

Javeed Alam

I

This paper aims at providing an analysis of how the mass consciousness in present-day India gets constituted and to work out the modes of its political expressions. Concern with the political articulation of mass consciousness in India has become important in view of the significance of two closely interrelated and easily observable features of Indian politics. First, there have been, in recent years, relatively rapid shifts in the political involvement of people from socio-economic struggles of a democratic nature to caste and religion-based communal and sectarian fights. Why do the same people agitate one day for democratic fights or economic well-being leaving aside considerations of caste and community, and yet on other occasions they take to struggles, leading very often to communal-sectarian violence, as Muslims and Hindus, as Sikhs and Hindus, as Harijans and Swarans, and as forwards and backwards. This tendency, although widespread, is more pronounced amongst the unorganised masses. It is not totally absent even among the more organised sections. People organised through the trade unions, especially of the non-communist parties even fight for democratic demands, but outside the framework of trade unions have indulged in communal vandalism. These tendencies are not something new to the mobilisations in the present-day Indian politics. Right through the freedom struggle such a pattern has repeated itself. What however is significant today is their increasing virulence and the sheer rapidity and mobility with which these tendencies manifest themselves.

Secondly, there has been a long-term trend since 1960s in Indian politics towards mobilisations of a communal and sectarian mode of political activity. Tendencies made up of various types of communal consciousness based on caste or creed or chauvinistic regionalism have come to the fore posing an increasing threat to the unity of the country and to its secular and democratic institutions.

To understand this development, two points need to be emphasized. The growth of revivalist forces and communal politics has been accompanied with the strengthening of the left-democratic and secular forces in a general way, especially in certain regions of the country. Yet the communal forces have grown sharply and much more menancingly posing a serious danger to the integrity of the nation. Moreover, while the mobilisations of the type mentioned above are based on caste and communal entities, their causes lie elsewhere; they have much more to do with the growing strength of class conflicts under the impact of the worsening of conditions of social existence. What is important however to note is the ease with which class conflicts are being deflected into caste and communal conflagrations. Deflections of this type do not allow class conflicts to develop into class struggles and secular oppositional movements as the dominant political trends; rather class conflicts in such conditions assume the most reactionary forms. How can one explain these phenomena? Let us look at the patterns a little more closely before attempting an explanation.

II

The decade 1980s in Indian politics has so far been one of the violent sectarian upheavals which have put, relatively speaking, the growth of democratic forces into the background. Never after 1947 have so many people died or allowed to be killed in the name of religion, caste and community. The inherited "social identities" of our society have been the source of passions and frenzy that have gripped the minds of our people. The very definition of what constitutes a danger to national unity has got tied up with these identities. What is most worrying is the rapid communalisation of social perceptions and political understanding of the people. This creeping communalisation is no less dangerous than the various overt forms of communalism. In fact, it has provided the more widespread ground for justification of sectarian and nascent fascist forces. The communalisation of political understanding is also creating hierarchies of treason that people are beginning to associate with different communities living in India.

In so far as this goes, 1980's till now stand in sharp contrast to the 1970's. And 1970's too were years mostly of struggles, turbulences and crises; however great the hopes of renewal with which they started. But the struggles and crises were of a different nature. Whether in Gujarat, Bihar or the J.P. movement, they were essentially secular and wholly social in nature. The "agitators" were all the same men and women, ready to kill each other now, who were showing their discontent and exasperation with the performance of our economy, management of the polity, and the corroding influence of corruption in society. Although the class-outlook of the leadership of the movements and the contents of the demands that were raised were basically oppositional, those movements were essentially democratic and anti-authoritarian in character. In spite of the bourgeois formations providing the leadership, the movements had an all-people's character. There is evidence to assert that in the mobilisation of people the inherited structures or ideologies, whether of caste or religious community, did not divide the people. In fact, there did take place a great deal of self- mobilisation by people across such social divisions.

The mass movements and agitations of 1970's were built upon and were a continuation of those of 1960's but with one difference. The most important mass movements of 1960's were more clearly class-based around the interests and demands of the exploited classes and toiling masses. They were led, unlike in 1970's, by the left opposition political parties and groups. We find during this period either the communist or socialist political parties leading the extra-parliamentary agitations and popular struggles, the right wing opposition generally shunned the path of extra-parliamentary struggles. The repeated let-down of popular hopes and the aggravation of old miseries due to the deepening impact of the crisis of capitalist development created during the course of this decade a widespread predisposition among people to take to agitations. None of the organised political forces could have survived this situation without channelising the growing discontent.

Whatever the differential perceptions of the crisis by different ruling parties and also of the debates about the varying tactical approaches to the crisis, they could not evade any longer the necessity of building popular movements under their leadership. It is perhaps possible now to suggest with hindsight that it was also a reflex action on the part of the ruling class opposition to preempt the left-opposition from becoming the leading force in mobilising the popular exasperation and its search for a popular alternative. The absorption of the entire bourgeois opposition in such agitations and the maneouvering to outwit the left-opposition also explain the radicalist posturing and conservative back-stepping. Such an agitational mode of politics by these parties and groups without any change in their class preferences and social bases of support compels them to take to the easy option of mobilising people by playing upon traditional social identities and thus forcing people to look at their interests in terms of given traditions based on pre-capitalist ideologies. It is also as a manipulative device useful to divert popular energies into dissipation and thus disrupt the democratic struggles. This gets further aggravated by intra-ruling class conflicts becoming more and more intensified. Developments of this kind have, as it seems to me, far-reaching long-term implications in bringing about changes in the forms of political activity and articulation of popular political preferences. It is, therefore, important to go into questions that have a bearing for the understanding of factors as determinations and constraints in the politics of the country.

Given the adoption by people of contradictory postures in struggles and mobilisation, it has often been the case that scholars belonging to different intellectual persuasions have counterposed class versus caste in seeking to look for determination. The question that they ask can be put down as: Is it class or caste and community which is the main determinant in the shaping of mass consciousness and behaviour? Such a question straightway calls for an equally rhetorical alternative question: Is it possible to determine the relative salience of such factors? No detailed empirical investigations are needed to know that there is the relative ascendance or descendance of class and allied social forces in the political domain vis-a-vis caste and community-oriented factors. In other words, increasing or decreasing salience of different forms of social identities or "structures" becomes a focal point in Indian polity. From such shifts, can we logically infer changes in the structure of social consciousness or the ideological moorings of people belonging to different classes and communities? Or, can there be the same consciousness or the ideological moorings the people belonging to different classes or communities? Or, can the same consciousness be a source of varied forms of social and political activities despite being contradictory in nature? Thus, we are looking for caste or class, or for caste and class. It seems that behind the rhetoric of such a question lies the problem of determination of the consciousness and behaviour of the people more than any other factor. It is, therefore, important to know how this consciousness is constituted of.

If these questions have some validity, how does one then look for determination and identify the causality shaping the events. Analytically speaking, one way to find out the location of a determination is to understand the nature of intersection of class and caste. If we extend the logic of this question, then it is also necessary to ask: What is the epistemic status of factors like caste and class in the dialectical unfolding of events under conditions of retarded capitalism?[1] The significance of this question becomes clear if we contrast it with the ascendant capitalism which destroyed the pre-capitalist formation and created the modern classes as the main social categories. If the material foundations of society—the mode of production and the class formation there from—are the main determinants of social forms, then it should also be obvious that the character of the contemporary Third World capitalism as one of stunted growth and of a retarded nature will condition the strength of social forces in its own peculiar ways. These determinants cannot be of the same nature as in the epoch of rising capitalism. One o the essential features of ascendant capitalism was to bring about all round, independent industrialisation which is no longer so with the retarded capitalism in the Third World countries. How and in what ways capitalism in the Third World countries differ and will continue to differ from those of the period of ascendant capitalism with its revolutionary transformative capacities can only be a matter of concrete investigation. And its consequent implications will vary from society to society, there cannot therefore be any *apriori* understanding.

Marxist theory has been more than adequate in accounting for economic crisis and the stunted growth patterns of imperialist economic development. But it seems that it has not paid sufficient attention to similar phenomena in the non-economic spheres of social reality. Retarded capitalism leaves none of the spheres of social life free of its distorting determinations. Such a capitalism has a tendency to give rise to social and political deformations. These deformations are in no way comparable with the imperfections which monopoly imperialist capitalism has been creating in advanced capitalist societies. These deformed social forms develop their own inner force and growth patterns. Under this kind of retarded capitalism, controlled by imperialism in varying degrees, modern class outlooks cannot develop to such an extent as it did happen under ascendant capitalism so as to displace the pre-capitalist forces. Therefore, the question whether class or caste and community is the main determinant in the shaping of mass consciousness and behaviour is a misplaced one. This, however, does not reduce the importance of developing capitalist economy in understanding societies like ours. But what is crucial for us to understand here are the casual chains generated by the specific nature of capitalist retardation and the determination implied by them. After all in a materialistic dialectical way of looking at social reality, it is the social being that determines consciousness, and consciousness based on classes or castes is not like antimonies but a part of social being. Retarded capitalism as the basis of the developing mode of production is the main structured material complex, and this totality has an ontological priority over any of its elements. Looking at the problem this way will permit us to establish the correct relationship between ontology and epistemology in dialectical understanding, which is one of the primacies of ontology over epistemology. We have to know how the mass consciousness in societies like ours is constituted and how the capitalist and pre-capitalist forces combine to give it a specific articulated form.

III

It is a striking feature of the bulk of mainstream social science analyses that they have picked out the caste and communal mobilisations from out of a wide range of the struggles people have engaged in to demonstrate the importance of religious sensibilities and caste consciousness in the Indian psyche. They have used these mobilisations to establish the determining influence of "primordial" factors, and the cultural influences emanating from them, on Indian polity. This shadow-boxing with Marxist thinking has its roots in the intellectual urge to demolish the relevance of class as a social category of importance and therefore the usefulness of class approach for understanding social reality. The terms of debate set by the mainstream social sciences have become, in an important way, a trap for the Marxists. It is a debate conducted in terms of a wrong notion of determinsm; to quote as an example out of many such debates, the one between Dipesh Chakravarty and Ranajit Dasgupta is most revealing.[2] In this debate, the community consciousness and class consciousness are, as it seems to me, erroneously counterposed.

Regarding this thorny question, the underlying assumption is that modernisation does not quieten the primordial feelings but rather it quickens them.[3] The corollary that follows is that since independence the pace of modernisation has been much more rapid, it is natural that there should be more of caste and communal mobilisations, and their organisational forms in politics should multiply. Rudolphs,[4] Kothari,[5] Weiner[6] and many others, in varying forms, have been the main spokesmen of such a theoretical argument. They have also differently argued that such developments are also an essential element in the "democratisation" of the inherited social structures which are part and parcel of democratic politics. They seem to be saying that for the non-coercive incorporation of people into modern forms of political activity, as against the alleged coercive models of socialist states, such a pattern of communally-oriented entry into politics is a necessary though a transitory phase. It is, therefore, natural for them to concentrate on the period after independence. They have in general failed to pay attention to the fact that caste and communal differentiations and the separatist understanding based on these were built into the nationalist ideology itself and were not just accommodation of a pragmatic nature with the forces released by modernisation. The nationalist ideology never did away with them. It tried to build coalitions of mass support upon them; not in every case successfully as for example the anti-Brahmin movements in Madras[7] and Maharashtra,[8] the Namasudra movement in Bengal,[9] etc., apart from the general thrust of constitutional Muslim politics since 1920's.[10] How the dominant national leadership in India has appropriated the two parallel crises, of the pre- capitalist structures and of the capitalist economy and polity, to confound popular consciousness has not been carefully studied so for.

This point has serious implications. Because if one can use caste and community as "democratic" fora mobilising or inducting people in politics, one can as well use them to counter or disrupt oppositional mobilisation which may pose a threat to the ruling groups. The consequences of these two uses however cannot be of the same order of significance. In the second use, the thrust invariably is to push back and disrupt movements around secular and economic issues by the force of backward ideologies and not simply to induct people in for democratic bargaining as these theorists tend to see onesidely. Communalisation of the political process then has to be a natural consequence of such a maneouvre. The more the challenge to the dominant bourgeois political leadership and to the landlord classes greater has been the resort to such primordial tactics. All theorising about the democratic potential of castes and communities has failed, may be advertantly, to grasp this inbuilt, hidden potential of this type of politics. By excluding these tendencies, the kind of logic these frameworks use, has stagnated. Thus, there are genetic defects of serious proportions in all the explanations based on such frameworks of analysis.[11]

The leaders of the Indian National Congress, the nationalist historiographers and the mainstream social scientists have therefore never been able to account for the paradox that the great mass upsurges and the united popular uprisings within the national movement as well as later on after independence degenerated into bloody communal and caste riotings. Modernisation theorist may explain one facet of democratic franchise and political mobilisation based on the "politicisation" of caste-community affiliations, but his parameters are totally inadequate to account for such degenerating phenomena.

In the context of modern world, it is not "modernisation" or "democracy" simply as formal structural conditions or institutional set-ups that have to be looked at, but the analytical focus has to be on the historical limitations of the social and political implications of contemporary capitalist transformation under conditions of the present-day world. Without reference and close attention to the content of socio-economic transformation, modernisation becomes an empty concept. One has therefore to look at, when examining India, the determining of several casual chains emanating from a stunted and retarded capitalist expansion in terms of social forms and the ways of their expression in the sphere of politics. It is only by explicating these implications that one can begin to grasp the *relational essence* of different "structural" features in Indian society and may look for the grounds of their *altered existence.*

Generally, it is agreed that today in the situation of the post-colonial imperialist domination of the Third World, as in the colonial phase earlier, capitalism is no longer capable of effectively destroying the political salience of the "pre-capitalist" or "pre-modern" social forms and belief systems. It is, therefore, also incapable of creating new social unities on its own terms. Incapable of relentlessly breaking down all barriers to its unhindered conquest of all spheres of productive activity and social life, it is also not capable of amalgamating people into new outlooks and social identities and of unifying life-experiences in the form of a modern language and thinking. What has been observed in history is the global tendency of capitalism to sweep away all collective solidarities of a traditional type replacing them by modern ideologies, even if non-rational ones, like nationalism, have a weak objective basis in our society. Retarded capitalism fails to simplify the multiplicity of social relations by polarising them into dialectical opposites as was the case with ascendant capitalism. Instead as it continued to grow and expand erratically and undermine the pre-modern social forms and pre-capitalist ideologies, it is also forced to compromise for its political survival with forces that it cannot conquer. An infirm capitalism needs crutches and therefore pretty awkwardly it sits upon and feeds on the pre-capitalist forces in the society in a parasitic relationship. Under such conditions, the more the capitalist forces spread across in society the more the pre-capitalist, feudal factors come into play in politics. Under retarded capitalism, we thus find that pre-capitalist forces, like caste and community, themselves are modes of control for capitalism uses culture and tradition as incompatible even with its own presuppositions to keep people down and props up its own domination.

In view of this, the argument which often advances about the resilience of the traditional Indian social structures or the strength of communal consciousness of people seems to be a misplaced one in a specific sense. In any society where the old system provides material sustenance, it continues to give meaning to the inherited structures and ideologies and hence it is bound to resist strongly the new system which is not powerful to dissolve and replace the old one. There is logically no way to try to determine the nature or extent of resilience. To try to do so would require, methodologically speaking, empirical scales or logical criteria to measure and assess both the resilience of the old and the strength of the new (capitalism); we are unlikely to succeed in this. What seems to be more likely, as a conjuncture on the basis of global trends, is that the so-called resilience is more a result, as already noted, of the infirmities of the superseding historical forçe—the Third World capitalism as the main instrument of contemporary transformations. On another level, the revolutionary forces are also not strong enough to put a brake on their articulation.

The stunted and disjointed growth of modern economy under capitalism and the deepening stranglehold of the imperialist economies over the economic processes in the Third World countries land to the internationalisation of national economies of these countries. Under retarded capitalism, all this results not only in the premature growth of monopolies but also leads to a distortion of the organic composition of capital. This forestalls the widespread development of capitalist enterprises across the society which is a necessary condition for the real subsumption of labour process as against the mere formal subsumption. Formal subsumption can come about through the expansion of generalised commodity production and by the invasions of capitalism through the sphere of accumulation, that is, simply by the expansion of market. So long as the real subsumption does not take place more or less evenly throughout the society, the pre-capitalist ideologies and the pre-modern outlook can continue to have the ground for their survival and can drag into their hold every section of society including the proletariat and the intelligentsia. Let us look at this process a little more closely.

In the period of ascendant capitalism in the countries which are now successful capitalist societies, more or less a levelling up of the technological structure of capital exists in the economy as a whole. Due to the initial evening out, advances in the technological level ever since then proceed relatively evenly across the economy. In contrast to this, the capital in the modern industrial sector in the Third World countries remains at various levels of technological development. What further aggravates the effects of this technological unevenness in modern manufacturing is the continued prevalence of numerically very large and diverse pre- capitalist economic units. Under retarded capitalism, which is incapable of conquering these productive sectors and under which economic modernisation proceeds in a highly selective fashion, employment generation increases much slower than the rate of growth in the economy, especially of the most modern sectors.

In these conditions, relatively more people continue to depend upon the pre-capitalist economy. Significantly, therefore, of the available labour force in the society, a very large part continues to remain in agriculture, especially of the subsistence type, and declining associated crafts along with lower forms of industry, petty retail trade, unorganised sectors and so on. Some of these forms of production or economic activity are not clearly separated one from the other and yet may also represent various stages or routes to the modern world. In societies like ours, these forms point to the numerous mini-structural patterns important in themselves for conditioning the life-processes of people; in some ways these become something like the life-saving drugs for the larger pre-capitalist tendency is the dominant force in the economy, a substantial part of society's labour power works outside the capitalist productive sectors, and therefore real subsumption remains far from being complete. Not only this but the relative income of labour in these backward sectors as compared to those highly skilled in the modern sectors of economy continues to decline. By reduction of wages more and more below the cost of reproducing labour power, the relative competitive nature of pre-capitalist or lower forms of capitalist production units is assured and hence their survival as viable economic units.[13]

The strengths and weaknesses of these units are relative, they look weak, but in relation to totality they have a certain strength. Moreover, these conditions in addition result in pauperisation on the one hand, and create lumpen proletariat on the other. Situation like these objectively increase the pull of pre-capitalist or pre-modern structures which provide sustenance to people; increasingly, in the process, their dependence on kith and kin and thus the psychological attachment of the people to the ideologies embodied in these structures. It is thus that in the material being of people the social roots of caste and community maintain a powerful presence. Consciousness centered around them therefore has a multi-dimensional influence under retarded capitalism.

Internationalisation of economy discussed above strengthens all these tendencies in the economy and society. It goes straight to give strength to more than anything else the technologically most sophisticated sectors of economy. International finance capital in production, as against that in trade where it may encourage "sweat labour" in unorganised sectors, cannot but collaborate only with this sector through transfers of technologies and capital leading to income through transfers of technologies, and capital leading to income concentration within certain ruling class groups becomes stronger in the economy and hence their clout in political decision-making. Monopolisation under these conditions of stunted growth cannot but have grave social implications as pointed to above and thus an essential aspect of retardation. Anti-imperialism has therefore to be integral to any effort to politically weaken and fight the hold of caste and communal ideologies. But this is a question of strategies to which this argument does not explicitly address itself.

It is suffice to point out here that in understanding the dynamics of these forces the interrelated nature of the socio-economic content of modernisation in the contemporary Third World countries and its repercussions for the social existence of man in these societies cannot be ignored. If social being has primacy, then the consciousness of people cannot be free of their existence. The socio-economic content determining so much else in society is itself derived from packages developed by bourgeois social science and marketed more and more through the coercive negotiating tactics of the World Bank and International Monetary Fund. The motives, impulses, patterns of resource deployment, etc., are therefore alien to the needs and requirements of people in the local societies. All the same the links between the most modern sectors of the economy, imperialism and backward ideologies and consciousness continue to remain strong. Given this objective situation, when the ruling classes represent a combination of the bourgeois and landlord interests, the landlords can play a role in politics out of all proportion to their economic standing or numerical strength.

Nevertheless such a capitalism goes on undermining the traditional (pre-capitalist) bases of society and economy. It enters into all spheres of productive activity through the sphere of accumulation or the circulation process in general. In the intermingling of capitalist and pre-capitalist forms of exploitation, a superficial capitalist form is given to all production relations. In this mode of accumulation (of money-capital), the traditional exploiting strata develop capitalist aspirations through their enduring links with capitalist classes. This goes to make their relations with the labour force under them move of a predatory nature by knocking off whatever there is of social life. In this category of traditional exploiting strata with bourgeois aspirations, the landlords of all hues come to occupy a place of extraordinary structural importance. Most of the other traditional exploiting strata classes exist either merged or in tacit connivance with the landlords. Landlords employing pre-capitalist exploitative practices not only provide the grounds for the sustenance of the pre-capitalist structures and ideologies and pre-modern outlooks but also politically control the reservoir of conservative forces in society. They are therefore also the potential constant divisive forces in society and as allies of the bourgeoisie can unleash pre-modern sentiments whether of caste or religious communities whenever their interests so require. If the bourgeoisie enjoys a socially privileged position whenever the capitalist tendency becomes the dominant one in economy, their alliance with landlords helps them to convert the privilege into a political licence. With landlords an important alliance partner of the bourgeoisie, the ruling class combine is itself divided in its social composition by caste, religious, ethnic and such other features and the bourgeois aspirations of landlords are built upon such social foundations. The actual nature of the spread of these is the compatibility of these diverse currents in the secularised realm of politics as a dominant trend. This makes possible the intellectual discourse among people across the political spectrum. In any case, this provides a schematised contrast with the situation in the Third World countries. Even as a schematised contrast this difference needs to be taken only as a most general global trend because even some developed bourgeois societies have experienced fascism or powerful fascist movements or other forms of jingoism on a mass level.

On the contrary, the Third World countries, the disarray in the thinking and cognitive processes and the conceptual currency of people is crucial in understanding the case with which the social and political behaviour of people can change gears. In the situation of incomplete transition what we have is a world without a definable outlook. Alternative world outlooks co-exists but not as unified totalities. It is a situation in which people are, to put it figuratively, always falling between the stools. They are not allowed time to settle down on a stable basis of hope in future.

IV

Elements of the original, unified communal ideologies and though frameworks get broken off from their foundations and become, to use a spatial term, scattered and float around in the social atmosphere as fragments of the original, often outside their temporal frames. These scattered bits from the original wholes may remain emotionally charged and are available when needed. They can be useful for different forces in societies depending on the situation. The ruling classes use them to disrupt alternative mobilisations, especially when they are of a radical nature or to the imperialist forces to weaken national resolve. In rare case people fall back on them for self- mobilisation or in self-defence when they are beaten back or forced to retreat. These residual remains or what may be called remnants in whatever form they may continue to exist are rampant in the social situations people encounter but with their material roots withering away, however slowly.

These rampant, floating bits are not simply in the nature of surviving, residual consciousness without material basis. Their strength lies precisely in the underlying hold of pre-capitalist relations of production, stronger in some areas or with sections of population than in other areas or spheres. What nevertheless is important in understanding their significance is the extent to which pre-capitalist ideas, sentiments, perception-patterns and so on which survive for outstrip the survival of pre-capitalist relations in the sphere of production. Therefore, if caste consciousness persists, then it cannot be simply equated with surviving material relations. In addition to their extent of influence over and above the surviving elements of material relations, they have an added significance; they impede the crystallisation of consciousness based on new and emerging relations of production through the development of capitalism. It may happen that modern consciousness lags behind the level of development objectively achieved by capitalist forces of production through the development of capitalism. It may happen that modern consciousness lags behind the level of development objectively achieved by capitalist forces of production and in such a situation the emerging class consciousness may be made to retreat by the active intervention of ruling classes from above to protect their class combine or to divert the growing class conflicts into sectarian type of conflicts. Now to understand the character of caste and caste-based consciousness, it is important to guard against two possible and sometimes common fallacies. First, one must ground against assigning abstract position and thus attach philosophical status to terms and categories associated with caste *a la* Louis Dumont.[14] Secondly, it is equally important to guard against reducing or equating them to material relations and their reflections as quite some analyses within the dialectical tradition tend to do.

A curiously interesting pattern of the traditional wholes getting broken up into bits and then getting recombined in unusual ways in disruptive modes of activity can be taken from the Hindu social system.[15] In the Hindu *dharmic* world-view, occupational activity or work in this world has two important components. One, the right kind of work gets prescribed by the innate personality traits with which an individual is born- *karma*, and this work gets defined in the *varna-jati* order to which all are equally subjected instrinsically as unequals, this is the initial basis of the path of *moksha*, but it has its extensions in life-activity according to life- stages. Thus, secondly, to earn a living, create and look after family, fulfil household duties as incumbent and in so doing one satisfies one's spiritual and sensuous being. This provides the initial basis of social recognition and social recognition is a necessary ground for self-esteem and personal legitmation. Now the point is: in their world-view if one cannot do this, then he goes down in self-esteem.

With the cracking up of the feudal social order, the philosophical nexus of *karma-varna* work conception is getting badly undermined but to earn living for fulfilling what life enjoins is getting pronounced and becoming increasingly important as employment opportunities contract in the stagnant capitalist economy. The simplest instance of the breaking down of the philosphical nexus of work is that it does not any longer matter whether you as a Brahmin get work in a shoe factory examining the quality of leather for making shoes or say a Ksatriya becoming a sanitary inspector. Yet the reverse of it is the ascendance of the need to get an adequate living which has a certain degree of recognition with those who matter for in life; one got to have some kind of livelihood however far removed from the *jati-dharma* so that one can fulfil the duties as a householder.

The retarded capitalism which has kept caste alive as a factor in life also fails to give you job. The YOU on a social plane is also a very large collectivity and increasing in size all the time and thus forces people back upon traditional modes of survival all the time.

But this situation can have an interesting inner logic for the individual's subjectivity. Failure leads to depression and disaffection. When this is materially rooted on a large scale in society, then there is a diffusion of this subjectivity *inter alia* it becomes inter-subjectivity. Now when YOU, as well as the social collectively which is a heap of those who have "failed", agitate outwards from this emotional position, then you partly fill up the sense of loss by the warmth of companionship of activity-struggle together. When you are at the stage of *Charchistie*, it is your right to ask for and agitate for your due that is being denied; that is, disaffection also compels one to act upon the world even in a passive tradition.

This is where the peculiar intermixing of subjectivity and objective circumstances creates now grounds for caste activity and agitations in society. Caste here is handy. It is a ground of pre-existing solidarities—a sense of belongingness—and therefore an easily available channel for transmission and diffusion of similar disaffection and as a basis to seek wherever most easily available. It acts both as a boundary and gate because when you are down you turn to those who you think belong to you.

In the situation of incomplete transition both material and social prevailing in India, in agitating on caste basis the togetherness formed acts as a psychological bulwork against being looked down upon. Moreover, the sense of self-esteem is partially insulated from being terminally damaged because all others acting with you are in a similar condition. As a psychological prop, it creates a new, however unstable, comraderie of those who are not succeeding when the expectation (of others) and the urge (of self) is that you should; people here re-achieve primary relationship which are in another sense getting lost in the transformations of the external world.

In this mode of activity of people living in a mixture of two worlds, there is both an enemy—the other—to fight against, the schedule caste or the "backward" who you can declare is taking away what belongs to you as a right. It is also a situation in which economic aspirations combine with caste concerns centered around bits of *jati-dharma*. So "caste conflicts", including minigenocides, have here a materially grounded basis which informs people's subjectivity. Such activities also lead to a displacement of concrete loss by a psychic sense of liberation, a kind of mini-*moksha*.

It seems to me that when people are agitating as a modern workforce on socio-economic issues in a democratic way, then too in their subjective understanding it is not something that is necessarily counter to the caste struggles (e.g., on the reservation issue) but simply for the same goals on different grounds. New under conditions created by the stunted economic growth where job opportunities, to take one instance, contract greatly relative to growing needs and claims, such a consciousness can take roots due to peculiarity of the Indian cultural milieu.

In the tradition inherited by most of the people in Indian society, integrated and critically active personality is not a common demand upon the individuals, as it may be in some other traditions influenced by Hellenic philosophy. Rationalised passivity among individuals which is so much encouraged and prevalent permits situations of contradictory mobilisations. This type of rational passivity in face of contradictory postures reduces the introspective responsibilities or burdens on the individuals when they act in some kind of a primordial collectivity.

In specifying the concrete working out of possibilities what seems reasonably clear is the absence of unidirectional responses among the people. Rather what emerges is the existence of a social canvas on which a large number of incompatible responses are spontaneously possible from within the social collectivity, but equally significantly, it also seems clear that given the vast manipulative capacities of the ruling classes and other dominant groups, different responses can also be alternated at will on this social canvas far beyond the range available within spontaneity. One purpose of the argument is to explicate the extent to which mass response can vary without any drastic or radical alteration of the existing structures and the consciousness they entail. If so then it also implies the importance of political education and ideological propaganda in combating these tendencies.

Dispersal of elements of tradition creates social configurations in which mobility of action based on contradictory or incompatible grounds not only becomes possible but also permissible. Thus, the disintegrated bits broken off from the whole come and go in peculiar combinations within the individual psyche because each disintegrated bit has a material basis for its existence in the survival elements of pre-capitalist relations whereas the whole has been becoming *undermined* under the impact of capitalist economic transformations.

And this process of undermining is the key to the understanding of social and political implications of the capitalist political transformations. The process has a distinct logic of its own; it consists essentially of partial erosions and not of dissolutions. Dissolution has been a pattern, without necessarily having a law-like regularity, of successful capitalism, whereas situations of incomplete transition do not allow for the complete superseding of the old forms. These old forms get shaken and disintegrated no doubt but they persist in many ways with consequences for the social being. Therefore, change in the context of social consciousness requires analysis of material conditions, the changing basis of the relations of man and the conditions of this social existence.

This then is the framework in which the pre-capitalist past enters polities. Even while some of it gets irretrievably lost and the rest inevitably shrinks, whatever remains acquires a new frame of reference and a tenacious shape. This past which people still cherish in many ways gets back in the realm of thought what it is losing in the material world of living reproduction. Though categories do not die off or can be cast away as easily as the material forces that initially give rise to them.

Retarded capitalism not only disintegrates the unified belief systems and modes of cognition but it also creates a whole range of new ideas and ways of perception and understanding along with diverse new interests—some material and some non-material. The new features too are also not as yet fully or firmly rooted in society. Here we get various expressions of the contradictions of the infirm development of capitalism in the sphere of social consciousness. One of the more important repurcussions for the people of the invasion without conquering the old world by modern developments in economy, education and culture is to give rise to increasing incompatibilities between the pre-existing, pre-capitalist ideologies and the merging new ideas and interests and is the source of contrary pulls within the intellectual equipment of people. All of these continue to remain as meaningful thought categories and provide grounds for political activity. As noted earlier, it is important to grasp how these collide and combine in understanding the subjectivity of the people as well as to differentiate their ideological positions from their consciousness. It is in this sense that the same social consciousness, as suggested in the beginning, can be the source of contradictory and incompatibly varied forms of political activity. Unlike the dialectical opposites loading to unity, we have seen absolute opposites which combine in unforeseen ways without any possibility of their unification in the thinking processes. When faced with complex external phenomena and bombarded with contradictory messages people's judgement collapses. Such situations tear their subjective equanimity apart, leaving them victims to malicious ruling class manipulations.

People as part of communities and classes left to their own devices have no way of unifying all their experiences into a totality of choosing one set of ideas as against another as a consistent choice. There is no objective basis for the resolution of these contrary pulls or a logical ground of reconciliation as far as the ordinary people are concerned. They become prone to contradictory appeals of diverse elements in their subjective world. Radical sensibilities born of dissatisfaction with the conditions of their social existence may become the source of many private dissents co-existing with formal assent and conservative compliance with existing social arrangements. Yearning for change and the absence of clarity about the meaning of new is something that has become widespread in society. The immediate present can therefore impose quite intolerable claims on the consciousness of people. This is so because the data of immediate experience is (generally) available to people separated from its relational context and therefore is also cut off from the wider meaning system. It can be made sense off only by inserting in into the context. For such a theoretical leap into objective meaning people are not at all equipped and will need effective, independent organisations to help them out of the situation of potential confusions. In fact, social formulations in transition do impose added burdens on the people. Their choice of judgements can be tempered with by the dominant modes of thinking which dichotomise the wholes and present them as alternative choices for the people. Relations of the individuals to the surrounding world are mediated by the prisms of the social groups and classes through which they appropriate social reality. The urge for economic betterment may be countered by the demands of kinsmen in a situation of limited opportunities. A stray item of local or community well-being may claim precedence over concrete material relief for the poor. The postulated glory of the country may make people agree to give it priority over their hunger and poverty.

The (political) consciousness people come to have is therefore one of stress and unease and a confusing sense of possibilities. And this makes possible alternative types of mobilisations based on both class and community with their varied combinations. The unease and tensions towards the contradictory elements remains the crucial aspect of the mobilised groups in any type of mobilisation; whether it is directed against another community or against exploiters who may include some who belong to one's own community. In other words, both class and communal mobilizations are potentially equally fragile as the experience of the Kisan Sabhas and trade unions amply demonstrates or as sections of ruling classes have learnt from the sectarian-chauvinistic movements which they so often mount.

All this however is not something that happens in an *ad hoc* way. Struggle for democratic rights or caste privileges is not a random choice.

There seems to be a logic to it. Class conflict in society is there in a generalised diffused form. With the growing self-awareness of the people together with the intervention and work of left forces this, class conflict has a tendency to move to take the form of class struggle. To barricade their class-combine it is in the interest of ruling classes to deflect class conflict into ethnic struggles and communal strifes. The ruling classes use all the instrumentalities in their hand even including state power to confuse people's thinking, to disrupt their unity and to dissipate their energies.

In a situation of dislocation and awakening, people are caught up in a confusing network of possibilities, obstacles and opportunities which generate a range of dispositions to be responsive in alternative ways. Their life's meanings are derived as much from their urge for "progress"—living standards, social justice, effective power—as much as from their sense of belonging, where they come from—caste, religion, region and so on—and both are integrally tied up together in living experiences and changing receptivity to problems of society. The explicit shapes that varied alternative mobilization can assume are largely determined by the issues at stake. What will be the issues that come to the forefront is not always entirely in the hands of the people. Those are induced as much by the postures and politics of other political groups and formations contending in the situation. The shifting ideological stances of the common people vis-a-vis the various on-going mobilizations are based on a constantly shifting configuration of disparate elements taking recourse to by the contending political forces within and across classes and communities.

This in a way is a "super-structural" reflection of the contradictions and indeterminacies specific to incomplete transition affected by the capitalist mode of production in societies of the Third World. Power in societies undergoing bourgeois transformations under a retarded capitalism is, in a way, absolutely malleable. It becomes difficult to encapsulate the endless variety of its manifestation. The sum of all this is more than the identifiable structures in society. It is, therefore, important to be conscious of the relationship between the form—given as the different structures and institutions in society—and the content—contradictory and shifting amalgams that enter in infinite ways within the same structures. What enters as content is not moulded by the existing structures, as water in the pot, but the articulation of the structures is conditioned by the content. It is one area which points to the reductionist nature of much of contemporary mainstream sociological and political analysis. In the context of this argument, it is reductionist in the sense that it cannot account for the continuous temporary transformations in the structured whole. It cannot also account for the sheer mobility with which the same phenomena change the mode of their expression. Instead, it engages itself with the importance of the uniqueness of India's primordial features.

A retarded capitalism, however rapid the growth of bourgeoisie in it or of productive forces in some sectors of economy or of differentiations within the peasantry, keeps alive in disoriented forms the communal ideologies and pre-modern identities. It cannot generate conditions for a radical break with the past. The casual chains emanating from it are radically different from those of ascendant capitalism for social and political change.

In the absence of stable and powerful organisations of the oppressed and exploited people under radical parties, the unbridled manipulations of the bourgeois-landlord politics and the unpredictable vacillations of the leadership of ruling classes makes it possible for remnants of tradition and pre-capitalist ideologies to combine and recombine in unexpected ways with elements of new ideologies, ideas and interest; all of this in rapid progressive or retrogressive succession. Social conditions like these on the one hand obstruct the stabilisation of the new emergent outlooks and political patterns and on the other create the objective grounds both for reactionary manipulation and slide back into conservative self-mobilisation.

V

While concluding it may be useful to refer to a few methodological questions concerning the arguments contained in this paper. First of all, there is a certain tension underlying much of the reasoning which may need a brief clarification. One thrust of the reasoning implies that with the development of capitalism and the expansion of its sinews, caste and caste-like structures and the consequent processes are becoming *secondary* even if not extinct, and yet they remain politically potent. They are secondary in the sense that they are no more indispensable, in any objective sense, to the social existence of man in the emerging society. This is quite unlike the modern classes which are continuously in the process of formation and development creating international equivalences of varying degrees on a global scale and thus represent a primary process.

The question therefore arises: Why then pay so much attention to caste and caste-like phenomena in understanding consciousness and political behaviour in society. It seems to me that through an analytical exhaustion of their role—limits and possibilities—in the contemporary historical process, we can first of all theoretically establish, by abstracting these elements from the situation, the consciousness compatible with modern social classes emerging in the society, and secondly, by the same analytical process, clarify for practice the maximum and minimum possibilities and the possible routes of their realisation for forces that stand for radical transformation and social emancipation of the masses; this process of knowing and acting can only be possible by leaning on universal values and criteria of judgement.[16]

Secondly, methodologically or rather from an epistemic point of view, this follows from treating class and caste and social consciousness as component aspects of a significant totality, that is, the social being[17] as something changing within society which itself is undergoing constant transformations via retarded capitalism. This proves fruitful in isolating and identifying these categories as useful objects of study both synchronically and diachronically. Approaching reality this way may help better in grasping objective meaning of the empirical data. Splitting the reality of social being into opposite categories or antinomies like caste and class and then inserting data into such slots can lead to distorting influences of terminological determinism, as happens in so much of existing analysis.

Thirdly, in conceiving and making use of social being as a category representing a significant totality and understanding the mode of its evolution, or, in other words, in grasping the transformation potentiality of its different constituent elements, two aspects must be constantly interrelated in analysis as they are ontological. They are: (i) the processes of undermining and dissolution, even if partial, of the old structures based on pre-capitalistic forces and located in old social formations, and (ii) the processes of emergence and development of the new social formation based on capitalism and the corresponding class structure and the struggle and the potentiality entailed by tnem. The futuristic significance of various social forces cannot be made sense of without looking at this process as a part of global developments. The global development can further or impede the development of capitalism or class formation or emancipatory struggles in different societies in specific ways but cannot resurrect the old structures to old historical significance. Their essence in contemporary politics is mainly of a negative nature—to disrupt, divide, dissipate and so on but under no circumstance can the old structures play a rejuvenating transformative role. This what the non-Marxist critiques should keep in view while trying to get the better of Marxian social understanding in the domain of thought. They must ask: What is or can be the optimal level of functioning of caste or caste-like forces? Do they have transformative potentialities? In the day-to-day working, how do they effect the on-going transformations? What can be their epochal significance within India which cannot be conceived cut off from world-wide changes. Minus these questions talking of the influence or analytical role of caste can lead to impermissible social position and within the domain of thought to empty determinism. The genetic defects in the mainstream analyses referred to earlier are largely due to their inability to address to such question in the course of analysis.

Notes

1. I find the use of the term 'retarded capitalism' more appropriate than any other because it captures all the essential features of capitalist transformation in the Third World countries, much better than any other. The stunted growth and stagnation, the infirmities, the under-development along with high technological sophistication in few industries much have a faster growth rate than overall economic development are implied within it. In such a pattern of development, the dependence of more and more people on pre-capitalist sectors for social existence increases resulting in giving a few significance to pre- capitalist ideologies. Equally important, the social and political repercussions of such a capitalist transformation are not revolutionary but may be to arrest and and impede social evolution. It cannot bring about a bourgeois democratic revolution. On the contrary, it thwarts the realisation of potential of society and its capacity to seek solutions autonomously. I first used this term as an extension of the organic analogy, as in a living body. See my "Dialectives of Capitalist Transformation and National Crystallisation: The Past and Present of National Question in India," in *Economic & Political Weekly* (Political Economy Supplement), 29 January 1983. See also, Amiya Kumar Bagchi, *Political Economy of Underdevelopment* (Orient Longman, 1984).
2. For a quick look, one can see the debate summed up in Dipesh Chakravarti and Ranjit Dasgupta, "Some Aspects of Labour History in Bengal in Nineteenth Century: Two Views," *Occasional Paper No. 40*, Centre for Study in Social Sciences, Calcutta, See also Dipesh Chakravarty, "Communal Riots and Labour: Bengal's Jute Mill Hand's in 1890's," Occasional Paper No. 11, and Ranajit Das Gupta, "Material Conditions and Behavioural Aspects of Calcutta Working Class," Occasional Paper

No. 22, both from CSSSC.

3. Clifford Geertz, "Primordial Sentiments and Civil Politics in the New States" in his *Ed.*, *Old Societies and New States* (Amerind, New Delhi, 1963), pp. 105- 57.
4. Rudolphs, Lloyd & Susanne, *The Modernity of Tradition:Political Development in India* (Chicago: 1967); see also their's "The Political Role of Indian's Caste Association", *Pacific Affairs*, XXXIII, March 1960.
5. Kothari, Rajni, *Politics in India* (Delhi: Orient Longman), Chapters VI & VII and his edited volume, *Caste in Indian Politics* (Orient Longman, Delhi, 1970).
6. Weiner, Myron. Among his numerous writings see in particular "India: Two Political Cultures" in Lucian Pye & Sidney Verba *eds.*, *Political Culture and Political Development* (Princeton, University Press 1965), pp. 199-244.
7. M Rossfarnett, *The Politics of Cultural Nationalism in South Asia*; and N. Ram, "Pre-History and History of the DMK," *Social Scientist*, December, 1977.
8. Gail Omvedt, *Cultural Revolt in a Colonial Society:The Non-Brahmin Movement in Western India* (Bombay:1977); and B T Ranadive, *Caste, Class and Property Relations* (Calcutta: 1982).
9. Shekhar Bandopadhyay, *Caste and Politics in Eastern Bengal:The Namasudras and the Anti-Partition Agitation, 1905-11* (Calcutta: Flurionty, Mimeographed).
10. E.M.S. Namboodripad, *A History of Freedom Struggle* (Trivandrum, 1986), and Sumit Sarkar, *Modern India 1985-1947* (Delhi:1983).
11. This is the point that has completely escaped the recent incisive critiques of Kothari in his numerous writings on the recent phase of the working of Indian democracy.
12. Alexi Leokovsby, *The Developing Countries:Social Structure* (Progress:Moscow, 1987).
13. Ibid.
14. Now is this so about caste and caste consciousness what then about the virulence of religious consciousness in India or the Third World countries as such. How can one analytically grasp it? This question is important because religion *per se* unlike caste has no simple or straight-forward basis in one type of material relations of people. Hinduism or Islam, with their changing mode of expression, though these changes are very important and are materially induced, have strong and lasting elements of continuity as a complex whole; this is so unlike caste. It seems to me that the problem about understanding religious consciousness lies to a great extent in the way that it is posed for analysis. For the concerns of politics and cooperative social endeavour, if the religious sphere is distinguished between religion as spirituality and spiritual-ideological

differentiation of people between different religions and religions as the cause of political conflicts, antagonism and social confrontations, then it is easier to understand the problem. The problem changes its connotations. It is the second aspect that concerns us as it stands, as a barrier on human cooperation for democratic advance and emancipation. In its latter aspect political consciousness based on religious differences communalism is not different from the communalism of a caste. Social existence in which the downtrodden condition of masses, their hopelessness and helplessness in the face of developing situation, feeling of being confronted by blind external forces provide the material ground for the backward, chauvinistic pull of religion and for its manipulation. Minus manipulation these provide the immediate useful basis for waging a struggle; the easily available mode of activity becomes or looks to people when unassisted by powerful, independent organisations (alternative) the natural or normal mode of activity as well as a useful tool society; a political viewpoint for the tycoons.

15. In writing the following ten paragraphs, I have benefited greatly from the brilliant analyses of Sudhir Kakkar, especially his *The Inner World:A Psycho-Analytical Study of Childhood and Society in India* (Revised Ed., Delhi: 1981).
16. The point here is based on an extension of the argument developed by Lucian Goldman concerning the relationship between the "effective consciousness" and "maximum consciousness" where the maximum is the crucial conceptual instrument for understanding the emerging social relaity. See his *Philosophy & Social Science*, p. 65.
17. Lukas, *Ontology:Marx, and Goldman, Literature and Sociology.*